COWBOYS AND GANGSTERS

COWBOYS AND GANGSTERS

Stories of an Untamed Southwest

SAMUEL K. DOLAN

TWODOT®

GUILFORD, CONNECTICUT
HELENA, MONTANA

A · T W O D O T® · B O O K

An imprint and registered trademark of Rowman & Littlefield

Distributed by NATIONAL BOOK NETWORK

British Library Cataloguing-in-Publication Information Available

Library of Congress Cataloging-in-Publication Data Available

ISBN 978-1-4422-4669-0 (paperback)
ISBN 978-1-4422-4670-6 (e-book)

∞™ The paper used in this publication meets the minimum requirements of American National Standard for Information Sciences—Permanence of Paper for Printed Library Materials, ANSI/NISO Z39.48-1992.

In loving memory of

Representative John F. Dolan

Ipswich, Massachusetts

1922–2013

And for Jack and Suzie

Most of these men have passed on. In the hills and vales of Arizona they sleep the sleep eternal. Yet sometimes when my night campfire burns low on the moonlit desert or in the forested solitude of the mountains, methinks my eyes see passing by shadowlike, a phantom rider with wide-brimmed hat, belted six-shooter and carbine, and that my ears hear the faint tinkle of spur chains on rowels. But 'tis only the form of the night hawk sweeping low on his evening flight and the night wind rustling the leaves of the trees.

—*Jem McKem,* Mohave County Miner and
Our Mineral Wealth, *May 12, 1922*

CONTENTS

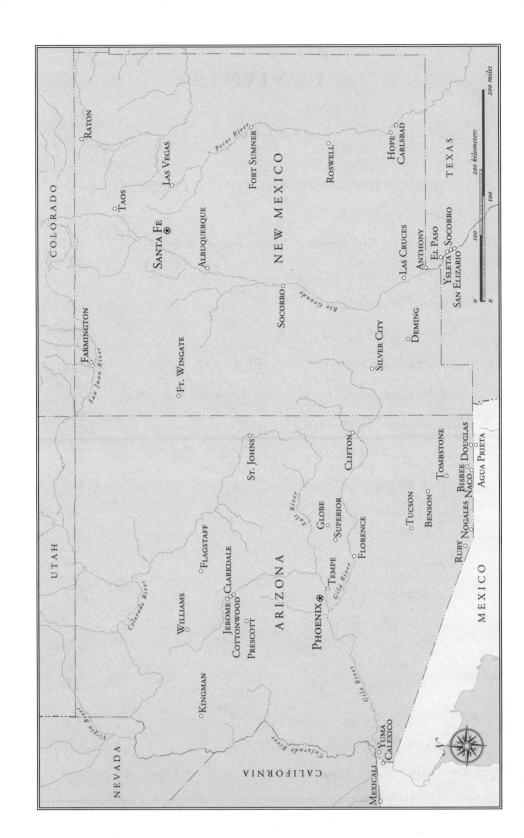

SIX-GUNS AND AUTOMOBILES

They live—and succeed—though the instrumentality of the
mechanical successor of the cow pony of their earlier days,
and of their big .45 calibre pistols, which nothing has yet
succeeded.

—*Major Grover Sexton, "The Arizona Sheriff"*

On the morning of June 21, 1928, sixty-nine-year-old Yavapai County
Deputy Sheriff James Franklin Roberts prepared to leave his house in
Clarkdale, Arizona. Stuffing his .45 caliber Colt single-action revolver in his
pocket, Roberts, who was known locally as "Uncle Jim," bid his wife Jennie
farewell and walked into town. By that summer morning, Roberts could look
back on a law enforcement career that stretched back nearly forty years. The
Missouri native had been raising horses in the Arizona Territory's Tonto Basin
when the Pleasant Valley Feud erupted in the late 1880s. As an ally of the
faction headed up by brothers James, John, and Edwin Tewksbury, Roberts
would participate in a number of bloody gun battles in what would become
the deadliest range war in Arizona's history. During one particularly violent
incident in August of 1887, Roberts is alleged to have shot a gunman for the
rival faction through the head with his big .45-90 caliber Winchester.[1]

By the early 1890s, Roberts had left the Tonto Basin and had accepted a
deputy's commission under Yavapai County Sheriff William "Buckey" O'Neill,
in the mining camp of Congress. "Jim Roberts works in the mine nights and by
day keeps peace in the village, he being deputy sheriff," the *Arizona Republican*
reported in the summer of 1891. It was also while living in Congress that same
year that Roberts married Amelia "Jennie" Kirkland. In January of 1893, Roberts was assigned to the mining town of Jerome by O'Neill's successor, Sheriff
James Lowry.[2]

Roberts established himself as "one of the most efficient and fearless officers in Arizona," and after serving as a deputy sheriff and precinct constable, was elected as Jerome's city marshal. Following several very active years spent policing the mining town, Roberts and his wife relocated to Cochise County in southern Arizona, where Roberts would work as a special officer at a smelter owned by the Copper Queen Mine, and later, as a constable in the town of Douglas, which sat along the US-Mexican border directly opposite the town of Agua Prieta, Sonora.[3]

Returning to Yavapai County with his wife in the 1920s, Roberts, who was then in his sixties, accepted a position as a special officer for the United Verde Copper Company in the smelter town of Clarkdale, a job that came with a Yavapai County deputy sheriff's commission. Many changes had taken place in the Verde Valley since Roberts had last worn a badge in Yavapai County. Statewide Prohibition had come to Arizona at the beginning of 1915, and as the Eighteenth Amendment to the United States Constitution became law across the nation in 1920, the valley—which included the communities of Verde (later Clemenceau), Cottonwood, and Camp Verde—became a haven for moonshiners, who produced "white mule" in stills made from the very same copper mined from the hills around Jerome. Raids by Prohibition agents and members of the Yavapai County sheriff's office were common throughout the 1920s, and gunplay was not exactly unheard of.[4]

The job of a deputy sheriff assigned to one of United Verde's mining operations was not without its risks. During World War I, labor disputes in the mining towns of the Verde Valley had resulted in several deadly collisions between area peace officers and members of the local workforce. On the afternoon of Tuesday, July 16, 1918, sixty-three-year-old James Lowry, a former Yavapai County sheriff, was working as a deputy at the United Verde Extension Mine in the community of Verde when he was shot and killed by a man named Porfidio Hernandez during a labor dispute. Hernandez was killed three days later in a shoot-out with Coconino County Deputy Sheriff Frank Dickinson.[5]

Thus, when Jim Roberts left home on the morning of June 21, 1928, it was not merely out of habit that he packed his Colt .45. Just before eleven a.m., while Roberts made his rounds, two armed men, later identified as Willard Forrester and Earl Nelson, walked into the Clarkdale branch of the Bank of Arizona, pulled out their guns, and within a few short minutes had stuffed $40,000 in cash in a burlap sack. The bandits then herded manager David O. Saunders and his staff into the vault, and would have sealed them inside if not for Saunders's pleas. "You have robbery on your hands now," Saunders told them. "[T]o lock these people in that vault will mean murder. No man can live in there five minutes."

Forrester and Nelson finally relented and only shut the auxiliary door before rushing outside with their bag full of stolen cash. Out on the street, Forrester and Nelson jumped into a 1927 four-door Chrysler Model 60 touring sedan with a convertible roof. Forrester threw the car into gear, stepped on the gas, and the outlaws were soon headed north on Main Street. That's when the shooting started.[6]

Before the bank's front door slammed shut, Saunders managed to unlatch the auxiliary door, then grabbed a .45 caliber automatic pistol and ran out onto the sidewalk. As the Chrysler reached the corner of the T. F. Miller store, Saunders fired off two rapid shots. Both rounds went wild. One of the plucky banker's lead slugs flew down the street, passed through Clarkdale's Santa Fe Railroad station house, and ricocheted off of telegrapher Lee Snyder's pocket watch and then slapped against the chest of Mr. Omar Twitty. Neither man was seriously injured.[7]

As soon as Jim Roberts saw Saunders with a gun in his hand, yelling something about the bank being robbed, he sprang into action. Roberts would later recall that Nelson spotted him right away, and banged off five quick shots in his direction. If the twenty-one-year-old bandit thought he'd put a scare into the old man, he was dead wrong. Roberts didn't flinch. Instead, he calmly pulled out his well-worn Colt single-action revolver, thumbed back the hammer, and took aim.[8]

Roberts would tell a coroner's jury what happened next: "I pulled down on the fellow at the wheel and fired three shots. The car had about reached the rear of Miller's store when it swerved to the left, struck a guy-wire on a telephone pole, and brought up at the corner of the new high school building." Forrester's Chrysler could move pretty fast, but not fast enough to outrun a two-hundred-grain lead slug from Roberts's six-gun. One of the lawman's three .45 caliber balls tore through Forrester's head, lodged in his brain, and killed him instantly. After the sedan slammed into the local high school, Nelson, who was splattered with his partner's blood, attempted to make a run for it. Moments later, he was apprehended by a pair of citizens who turned the bank robber over to "Uncle Jim."

The following day, the *Verde Copper News* would report the results of the coroner's inquest in the killing of Willard Forrester by Clarkdale's aging peace officer, finding "that the shooting was justified and it was done in the discharge of duty." Nelson and Forrester had planned their heist for several weeks, stockpiling an arsenal of firearms, including a rifle, two shotguns, and several pistols, along with roofing nails which they intended to spread on the roads to slow down any pursuers. Forrester, who had been arrested in Yavapai County on a number of other occasions, and had served time for automobile theft in Nebraska, had even dyed his hair red. In October of 1928, Nelson was sentenced to serve thirty to forty years in the Arizona State Penitentiary. "The court is very generous with my time," Nelson declared when he learned his fate.[9]

According to some accounts, when Roberts returned home for lunch that afternoon, he said nothing to his wife Jennie about having shot and killed a bank robber that morning. "There was a little trouble downtown" was all that Roberts allegedly told her. In the years that followed, Roberts continued to serve as a special officer for the United Verde Copper Company. The Yavapai County deputy sheriff was still on duty the night of January 8, 1934, when he suffered a fatal heart attack. "Even in the end," the *Prescott Evening Courier* reported, "he upheld tradition by 'dying with his boots on.' "[10]

In November of 1925, less than three years before Jim Roberts took on a pair of motorized bank robbers on the streets of Clarkdale, copies of a fifty-two-page illustrated booklet entitled "The Arizona Sheriff" began circulating throughout the United States. Published by the Studebaker Corporation of America, the slender paperback volume was written by "The Deputy from Yavapai," a forty-year-old native of North Port, Wisconsin, named Grover F. Sexton. According to the pamphlet's introduction, when executives at Studebaker learned that the sheriffs of twelve of Arizona's fourteen counties drove their automobile, the company sent Sexton—a former major in the Illinois National Guard, with a background as a newspaper editor—to visit those twelve sheriffs, "and see just what service Studebaker cars were rendering to the people of Arizona."

While traveling throughout the state that year, Sexton spent time with numerous county sheriffs and other lawmen, recording anecdotal stories of raids on hooch-makers and dangerous encounters with other lawbreakers, especially when they featured the Studebaker. "From murder to moonshiners, from accidents to arson, the life of the Arizona Sheriff is spent mostly in Studebaker automobiles these days," Sexton wrote. "They live—and succeed—through the instrumentality of the mechanical successor of the cow pony of their earlier days, and of their big .45 calibre pistols, which nothing has yet succeeded."

In Coconino County, Sexton met with Sheriff John Parsons, later recounting a story that found Parsons and a deputy tracking horse thieves in the sheriff's Studebaker. During a visit to Tucson, Major Sexton encountered Sheriff Walter Bailey, and later reported that not long before, Bailey had relied on his own Studebaker to trail a murder suspect through the mountains for five days and nights. Bailey also noted that during his travels, he had seen "abandoned wrecks of half a dozen other makes of cars," allegedly broken down and left to travelers scavenging for spare parts.[11]

To the average visiting tourist from the East, whose preconceived notions of the "typical Western sheriff" were based on silent films starring silver-screen cowboys Tom Mix, Hoot Gibson, and William S. Hart, Sheriff Bailey might have been a disappointment. Indeed, when Sexton encountered Bailey in person in Tucson, the soft-voiced elected official hardly lived up to the popular Hollywood image. Dressed in a wide Panama hat, blue jacket, white flannel trousers, white socks, and white, rubber-soled shoes, to Sexton, Bailey more resembled a wealthy Eastern tycoon than the man who had once patrolled the border on horseback as a "Line Rider" for the US Customs Service.

But when the discussion turned to shooting irons, Bailey didn't disappoint. According to Sexton, the lawman reached under his country club attire and produced a massive Colt .45 single-action revolver. "No movie gun that Bill Hart ever carried was a more desperate-looking weapon than this horn-handled, silver-mounted, junior field piece," Sexton recalled. "He drew it out slowly, but there are those in Arizona and Mexico—and others not living now—who could tell that this self-same weapon can come from his hip holster so fast that lightning seems to be going backward."[12]

Plagued by poor health and distraught over the shooting death of Undersheriff Ed Bowers in 1921, Yavapai County Sheriff Warren G. Davis suffered a fatal heart attack in September of 1922. *Courtesy of the Yavapai County Sheriff's Office*

Though Sexton traveled throughout Arizona putting together material for his booklet, he appears to have spent a considerable amount of time in Yavapai County, where for a brief time he was commissioned as a deputy by Sheriff Edwin G. Weil. On one occasion Sexton joined Weil in arresting a bootlegger suspected of having murdered a fellow moonshiner. "The Arizona Sheriff" also includes a colorful depiction of a raid by Weil and his men at a pool hall in the town of Cottonwood. "He lined 45 men and 22 women in the place up against the wall," Sexton recalled, "sent his deputies through the place to gather up two truckloads of evidence, drove the whole crowd out into the street, nailed up the dive, and went on back home." According to Sexton, the tough, "wide open, vicious Cottonwood dives are wide open no more. A little white mule corn liquor is smuggled in there, of course, as everywhere, but just try to buy a drink after word has come that Ed Weil's big Studebaker car is on that side of the mountains!"[13]

Reading like a collection of pulp magazine articles, Sexton's action-packed accounts of manhunts, liquor raids, and arrests made by "low-voiced but quick-shooting" lawmen presented Studebaker with an excellent opportunity to showcase the company's Big Six Phaeton. Although at first glance "The Arizona Sheriff" is little more than a fifty-two-page promotional device, Sexton's booklet offers a unique window into the state of Southwestern law enforcement during the 1920s, illustrating the collision of nineteenth-century images with twentieth-century technology.

Six-guns and automobiles, cowboys and gangsters, crusty frontiersmen versus motorized bank robbers. For many of us living in the twenty-first century, showdowns like the one that pitted Jim Roberts against the Clarkdale bank robbers, or the stories told by Sexton in "The Arizona Sheriff," would appear to be rare instances of connection between two disparate historical eras, both of them shrouded in a fair amount of mythology and romance. Thanks in large part to Hollywood, we see the "Wild West" as a story set sometime before 1910, featuring larger-than-life characters like Wyatt Earp, Billy the Kid, and Jesse James that suddenly vanishes with the coming of the automobile, telephones, radio, and the motion picture. At the same time, the 1920s and early '30s are equally mythological in their own right, a story of jazz, speakeasies, flappers with bobbed hair, and gangsters like Al Capone, Arnold Rothstein, and Charles "Lucky" Luciano, set in a mostly urban environment in the East.

George C. Ruffner would serve as the sheriff of Yavapai County during two vastly different periods in the history of Arizona. Having first held the office in the late 1890s, Ruffner was again elected as sheriff in 1922 following the death of Warren G. Davis, and served for another two years. In January of 1927, Ruffner succeeded Edwin G. Weil and once again assumed the duties as Yavapai County's chief law enforcement officer. Seen here with his staff in 1930, Ruffner stands in the front row in shirtsleeves. The older man with a mustache seen standing in the third row wearing a bow tie is "Uncle Jim" Roberts, who shot and killed bank robber Willard Forrester in Clarkdale in 1928. *Courtesy of the Yavapai County Sheriff's Office*

However, in truth, clashes between frontier characters like Jim Roberts and more modern-day hoodlums like Willard Forrester and Earl Nelson were not that unusual. Nor was Roberts himself such a uniquely aged relic of the past. His boss at the time of the shoot-out in Clarkdale, Yavapai County Sheriff George C. Ruffner, was only a few years younger than Roberts, then serving his third stint as sheriff. He first held the office in the 1890s, before serving for a second time following the untimely death of Sheriff Warren G. Davis in 1922, and then succeeding Edwin G. Weil in 1927. And though civilization had indeed come to the Wild West by the early years of the twentieth century, the land that men like Ruffner and Roberts inhabited, particularly those vast stretches of desert that lay along the US-Mexican border, was not completely tame. As Grover Sexton would himself learn while traveling throughout Arizona in 1925, horse theft, cattle rustling, and murder were still fairly common.[14]

At least some of the violence that occurred in the Southwest after 1910 can be attributed to the Mexican Revolution, a period of political upheaval, bloodshed, and civil war that raged throughout Mexico during the second decade of the twentieth century. It occasionally spilled across the border through bandit raids, political intrigue, threats of invasion, and violent insurrection.

The most infamous foray across the boundary line by revolutionary forces would occur in March of 1916, when José Doroteo Arango Arámbula, better known as General Francisco "Pancho" Villa, led his Division del Norte on an assault against the town of Columbus, New Mexico. Villa's attack on the United States and the American military campaign into Mexico that followed had come at a time when there was already a considerable degree of panic in the borderlands, much of it caused by the publication of the notorious *Plan de San Diego* in 1915. Originally conceived in the town of San Diego, Texas, the *Plan de San Diego* was a call to arms for a violent uprising by Mexican Americans and Mexican nationals living in the United States that would, among other things, lead to the independence of Texas, New Mexico, Arizona, Colorado, and California. It would also carve out a separate republic for African Americans, restore Native lands within the Southwest to the Apache and other tribes, and, most sensationally, summarily execute all Anglo males over the age of sixteen.[15]

While the social unrest caused by the Mexican Revolution, tension between Anglos and Hispanics, and labor disputes would all contribute to the violence that took place in the Southwest during the 1910s and 1920s, Prohibition and the smuggling of illicit alcohol and narcotics would prove to be the chief cause behind the vast majority of deadly encounters between federal and local lawmen and outlaws in Arizona, New Mexico, and Texas.

Although the official birthdate of the Prohibition era in popular memory is January 16, 1920—the day when legislated sobriety took effect across the United States—Prohibition was actually introduced in the Southwest years earlier. In November of 1914, just two years after Arizona had been admitted to the Union and had become one of the first states to grant women the right to vote, 25,887 of its citizens voted in favor of a statewide Prohibition law.

As of January 1, 1915, the sale and manufacture of alcohol became illegal within the boundaries of the state. According to the amendment: "Ardent spirits, ale, beer, wine, or intoxicating liquor or liquors of whatever kind shall not be manufactured in, or introduced into, the State of Arizona under any pretense. Every person who sells, exchanges, gives, barters, or disposes of any ardent spirits, ale beer, wine, or intoxicating liquor of any kind, to any person in the State of Arizona, or who manufactures, or introduces into, or attempts to introduce into the State of Arizona any ardent spirits, ale beer, wine or intoxicating liquor of any kind, shall be guilty of a misdemeanor, and upon conviction shall be imprisoned for not less than ten days nor more than two years, and fined not less than twenty-five dollars and costs no more than three hundred dollars and costs for each offense; provided that nothing in this amendment contained shall apply to the manufacture or sale of denatured alcohol."[16]

The law, which didn't explicitly prohibit the consumption or "personal use" of liquor, also made exceptions for medicinal alcohol and wine used for sacramental purposes. Aside from these loopholes, Arizona was virtually dry, and her sister state, New Mexico, would soon follow. "If we abolish the saloon, banish graft from our politics, purchase from our elections, enforce the laws and go to work," Governor Washington Lindsey declared in 1917, "our salvation is as inevitable and will be as glorious as our mountain sunrise."[17]

America's entry into World War I in April of 1917 transformed the liquor question from a moral debate into a patriotic crusade. When the US government placed a wartime ban on the production of grain alcohol that year, Governor Lindsey's wife gave a speech in which she appealed to voters to take up the Prohibition cause, explaining that "Aside from the long list of awful tragedies following in the wake of the liquor traffic, the economic waste is too great to be tolerated at this time. With so many people of the allied nations near to the door of starvation, it would be criminal ingratitude for us to continue the manufacture of whiskey."

Progressive newspapers also took up the cause, with the *Santa Fe New Mexican* telling its readers, "If we are to win this war, we cannot do it if we stay pickled." Apparently 40,000 residents were convinced, and in November of 1917 a Prohibition amendment passed by a margin of 16,000 votes. Statewide Prohibition took effect in New Mexico on October 1, 1918.[18]

"The liquor traffic is a permanent menace to the nation," Senator Morris Sheppard of Texas declared in an editorial published in the *El Paso Herald* in January of 1917. "It is the distribution for profit of a habit-producing drug in liquid form, a seductive poison that breaks down the vital processes of the body, destroys the capacity to resist disease, undermines intelligence, strength, and health, impairs the moral sense, composes the chief source of poverty, insanity, feeblemindedness, sickness, [and] crime, and transmits a hereditary taint that seriously handicaps posterity." Sheppard went on to add that "the preservation of the republic" was dependent on the end of liquor traffic. The forty-one-year old first-term senator was already one of the most vocal advocates of temperance in the nation, and would ultimately serve as one of the architects of the Eighteenth Amendment in 1918.[19]

Just as with Arizona and New Mexico, progressive politics, evangelical Protestant clergy, and temperance organizations joined forces to wage the battle for Prohibition in Texas. The issue had come up during the Democratic primary in 1908, when Texas voters just barely approved the request for an amendment, 145,130 to 141,441, and again in 1910, after the legislature hadn't acted on the 1908 initiative. But, once it was placed before the general electorate, the bill was defeated, and no further measures would be actively pursued in Texas for another eight years. Then, after the Texas legislature ratified the Eighteenth Amendment in March of 1918, the "dry forces" in the state renewed their efforts, with the result being a Prohibition law that in some ways would exceed the coming national policy.[20]

Known as the Dean Law, after its author State Senator W. Luther Dean of Huntsville, the new statute went into effect in October of 1919, the same month that the US Congress would pass the Volstead Act.[21] Thus, by the end of 1919, the states of Texas, Arizona, and New Mexico were all completely "bone dry"—at least as far as the law was concerned. As of January 16, 1920, the entire country would follow, signaling the beginning of an era steeped in romance, brutal violence, and not a little mythology.

While the Volstead Act would place the ultimate responsibility for enforcement of National Prohibition on the commissioner of Internal Revenue—leading to the creation of an all-new federal law enforcement agency—in the far Southwest, where law and order had been slow to take shape in the early years of the twentieth century, frontier lawmen would continue to

Deputy Sheriff Carroll E. Gilmer (center, wearing glasses) and fellow Pinal County lawmen, circa 1920s. Several officers still sport Colt single-action revolvers. Gilmer carries a Colt M1911 automatic in his waistband. The deputy on the far right carries a German Luger.   *David Flam*

enforce their own state's dry laws, while also combating the regional issues of livestock theft, train robberies, and murder, along with periodic outbursts of bloodshed stemming from instability in Mexico.[22]

A photograph of Pinal County Deputy Sheriff Carroll E. Gilmer and his colleagues taken in the 1920s serves as an almost-perfect illustration of the brand of Western lawman called upon to keep the peace and maintain law and order in the Southwest during the Prohibition era. Lacking anything in the way of uniforms or formal police training, officers patrolling the borderlands and mining towns of Arizona, New Mexico, and Texas had one foot in each century, adapting to the technology of automobiles and telephones while still climbing into the saddle when pursuing fugitives into those areas where a car was next to useless. Gilmer and two other men are seen packing M1911 Colt .45 automatics, and one man even carries a German Luger, while others still cling to the Colt single-action "Peacemaker" of the past—an arsenal that in and of itself is symbolic of the era and the juxtaposition of frontier tradition with modern technology.

This collection of stories is meant to highlight the careers and adventures of men like those seen posing with Deputy Gilmer and those encountered by

Grover Sexton on his journey to Arizona, whose job it was to keep the peace in the American Southwest between 1915 and 1935, the latter being the year Texas became the last state in the region to repeal its own liquor ban.

Written during a time when our nation struggles with the issues of border security, immigration reform, and the ongoing debate regarding the use of deadly force by members of our police agencies, many of these accounts may bear increased relevance to the contemporary reader. If I have accomplished nothing else by writing this narrative, I hope that at the very least I have helped to preserve the memory of a nearly forgotten generation of Western peace officers who frequently put their lives on the line, and all too often made the ultimate sacrifice. It is for those men that this book has been written.[23]

CHAPTER ONE
THE WAIL OF
THE BOOTLEGGER

> It is axiomatic that men cannot be made to change their habits by command. Men will not stop drinking just because the law says they must.
>
> —Bisbee Daily Review, *March 3, 1914*

The moon was high and bright when Sheriff Harry Wheeler and Constable Lafe Gibson pulled their Overland touring car off to the side of a dirt road near Kelton, Arizona, in the predawn hours of March 7, 1917. The Chiricahua Mountains, once a refuge for Apache warriors and American outlaws alike, loomed ominous against the night sky, standing watch over a desert carpeted with mesquite and cactus. Forty-one-year-old Harry Wheeler had been sworn in as sheriff of Cochise County on February 14, 1912, the very day that Arizona had become a state. His election on the Democratic ticket had followed a decade of hard duty as a peace officer in the borderlands—first, as a member of the Arizona Rangers, where he had risen from the rank of private to captain; and after the Rangers had been abolished in 1909, as a deputy sheriff, US Mounted Customs Inspector, and Deputy US Marshal. During that long career, Harry Wheeler had trailed his fair share of murderers, cattle thieves, and other bandits, both on horseback and behind the wheel of an automobile. But on this particular night Wheeler and Gibson were out for other prey: They were hunting bootleggers.[1]

The two lawmen had set out the day before, scouting along the New Mexico state line for the smugglers that frequently drove liquor in from towns like Rodeo, which sat just east of the state boundary, or brought it up on the backs of burros from Sonora. After a long night on patrol along the desert highways and rougher back roads, Wheeler and Gibson decided to catch a few hours of sleep before heading back to the county seat at Tombstone.[2]

Constable Gibson and Harry Wheeler had made a number of arrests together during the early years of statewide Prohibition in Arizona. In January of 1917, the two lawmen had confiscated two hundred gallons of whiskey that had been shipped to Gleeson on a freight car. Only weeks later, on February 7, Wheeler and Gibson were staking out the highway between San Simon and Stein's Pass on the New Mexico border. "A big car approached, and when the headlights fell on the two men," the *Bisbee Daily Review* reported, "the machine was stopped and the driver fled into the brush. As Wheeler and Gibson ran toward the car, Mr. Bootlegger fired six shots at them and then started breaking all records in a dash back to New Mexico." The culprit left behind a Mitchell sedan loaded with 1,800 half-pint bottles of whiskey, which Sheriff Wheeler later destroyed in Tombstone.

The following month, Wheeler and Gibson captured four carloads of whiskey and arrested six smugglers along the state highway near Silver Creek. "The booze was destroyed at Silver Creek, and the prisoners who were from Bisbee and Tucson were taken to Tombstone," the Tombstone *Weekly Epitaph* reported.[3]

As Wheeler and Gibson bedded down for a few hours of rest that night outside of Kelton, the two lawmen no doubt kept their weapons close, and probably slept light. Sure enough, not long after they'd rolled themselves into their blankets, a gunshot suddenly boomed in the night, and a bullet shattered the windshield of the sheriff's Overland. Both officers immediately jumped to their feet and armed themselves, Gibson grabbing his revolver, and Wheeler, his Winchester rifle and a belt of extra cartridges. Then they hurried up a railroad embankment from where they could see several figures moving in the darkness, some two hundred yards away.[4]

"Both opened fire in the darkness," the *Weekly Epitaph* declared, "which was answered by a fusillade of rifle shots from four directions." Realizing that they were silhouetted by the moonlight, which made them easy targets, Wheeler and Gibson dropped to a prone position and continued to fire, aiming at the moving shadows and the muzzle blasts that flashed in the night. Their assailants would later be identified as four Mexicans, "who during the fire yelled challenges to the officers to 'come and take them' or 'we'll fix you gringoes,' followed by a storm of vile oaths."

Within a matter of minutes, nearly one hundred rounds were fired between the opposing forces. "Several times during the shooting bullets struck close to the officers," the *Weekly Epitaph* reported, "one striking at their feet throwing up sand in their faces." After one of the gunmen "came within an ace of hitting the Sheriff," Wheeler sent six rapid-fire rounds into the brush where the man's shots had come from. "Following this, groans could be heard, with the result that further shots came from that quarter, and it is presumed that he must have been badly wounded, for the daylight disclosed a large pool of blood and knee and elbow prints in the sand."[5]

Sheriff Wheeler and Constable Gibson stayed on their bellies for at least an hour and waited for the moon to go down before they rushed forward into the bandits' camp. By then, the gunmen had already vanished, taking their wounded cohort with them, but leaving behind four burros loaded with ten cases of whiskey. Two of the burros had been hit during the exchange of gunfire, and both animals would have to be killed.

Daylight revealed horse tracks leading into the Chiricahuas, but with their ammunition low, and not wanting to abandon the large cache of liquor, Wheeler and Gibson decided to head for the town of Courtland, where they telephoned for backup. Help arrived in the form of Chief Deputy Guy Welch and Deputy Sheriff Harry Rafferty, who assisted Wheeler in taking the booze back to Tombstone to be destroyed.

The following day, Wheeler and Gibson followed the bootleggers' trail into the mountains, and arrested two of the men in Apache Pass, seizing yet another burro loaded with hooch. Newspaper accounts of the time provide little detail as to the fate of the man Wheeler shot and very possibly killed, or his accomplices, most of whom probably escaped into Sonora. However, several weeks after the shoot-out, a man identified as Santiago Garcia, known along the border as "The Fire Eater," was taken into custody in connection with the incident and housed in the Douglas jail.

"Garcia, if that is his real name," the *Weekly Epitaph* declared, "according to [a] local officer, is one of the most desperate men that has ever been placed in the Douglas jail. He is a former Sonora outlaw, and since taking up his residence on this side of the line about a year ago, when things got pretty warm for him in Sonora, he has continued his lawlessness." Garcia claimed "not to [have fired] a shot," and that he had even tried to get his comrades to cease fire once he realized it was the sheriff that they were shooting at. It appears that nobody believed his story, however, and as the *Weekly Epitaph* stated, the fact that "the murder of the officers had been planned is clearly evident, and it was only due to the poor marksmanship of the Mexicans that they did not succeed, having every advantage over the officers. [The] officers [are] due much credit for their bravery in frustrating the attempt to murder, as well as capturing the consignment of contraband, while it is a certainty that one of their members was wounded by the officers' fire."

Garcia was later charged with introducing intoxicating liquors into the State of Arizona, sentenced to four months in the Cochise County Jail, and fined $25.00.[6]

By the time Sheriff Harry Wheeler and Constable Lafe Gibson shot it out with the Mexican bootleggers at Kelton in the winter of 1917, Arizona had been a dry state for a little over two years. Though the law was generally intended to curb the manufacture and importation of liquor for commercial purposes, there remained some confusion over the "personal use" of intoxicating spirits, which was not clearly defined in the Arizona amendment. Months would pass before the Arizona Supreme Court ruled that alcohol could in fact be imported into the state by individuals for their own consumption.

During the early years of statewide temperance, many Arizonans who fell out of compliance with the law often elicited a certain degree of sympathy. Such was the case when German immigrant Heinrich Schuerman was arrested in the summer of 1917. Schuerman, an early pioneer of the Red Rock Country of Sedona, had been raising grapes and making wine for many years. Prior to the law taking effect in 1915, Schuerman made several barrels of wine, which he then stored on his ranch and either consumed or sold to thirsty locals. In August of 1917 he arranged to sell the last two barrels to a man from nearby Clarkdale.

"An auto was sent for the liquor and while the machine was en route back to Clarkdale it was held up by an officer. Two young men who were in the car were given thirty days apiece, but Schuerman got six months and a fine of $300," the *Coconino Sun* later reported. However, thanks in large part to the efforts of his many friends in the community and his standing as a longtime resident, Schuerman eventually received a pardon from Governor Thomas Campbell. "I'm through. Never more will I transgress the law, even technically. Governor Campbell will have no reason to regret issuing me this pardon," Schuerman declared. The old pioneer appears to have made good on that promise, and in 1918 voters in the Red Rock Country largely supported Campbell's reelection, "partly because of the earnest work of his friend, Henry Schuerman."[7]

In late 1915, Tucson journalist Thomas K. Marshall published a study on the effects of liquor law entitled *The First Six Months of Prohibition in Arizona and its Effect upon Industry, Savings, and Municipal Government*. In it, Marshall included a detailed report on the dramatic decrease in crime throughout the state, showing a dramatic drop in counties where saloons had prevailed in 1914 by 37.3 percent, and a 50 percent decline in Arizona's largest cities. In the meantime, arrests for drunkenness and public intoxication had all dropped by a stunning 85 percent.

But, while there was certainly a steep decline in arrests for misdemeanor drunkenness and other more serious crimes across the state in the first six months of 1915, during that same period there were no fewer than 199 liquor violations throughout Arizona, with the largest number of violations, fifty-one, occurring in Santa Cruz County, where the border town of Nogales straddled the international boundary with Mexico. "While the sheriff may exert his best efforts to prevent traffic in liquor," Marshall announced, "the task is a heavy one owing to the city's location on the international border line, with the settlement on each side of the border divided by but a street's width. With saloons running wide open on the Mexico side of the street and people going and coming as usual, there is not only the chance for smuggling liquor, but there is nothing to prevent anyone from crossing the border and filling up on booze."

Only weeks after Arizona went dry, the *Bisbee Daily Review* announced that saloons in the Mexican city were doing a "flourishing trade," and that one of the most unusual operations, known as "The Stope," had been set up in an abandoned mine drift, "where enlarged space has provided rooms, booths, a bar, and a den of the most characteristic and novel type."[8]

Bootleggers weren't exactly unheard of in Arizona prior to the state's Prohibition amendment. For years, newspapers throughout the territory had carried the reports of those arrested for selling liquor to Native Americans, or violating various local option restrictions. However, with the arrival of

Arizona's new liquor policy, the state experienced a steady increase in arrests for illicit bootlegging. "The 'dry' era is upon us in earnest," the *Copper Era and Morenci Leader* declared on January 8, 1915, "but the 'boot-legger' may be expected to soon make his appearance in our midst, and when he does, we hope to see our peace officers hunt him into his hole and give him the full penalty of the law. To exchange the licensed, regulated saloon for the irresponsible, criminal boot-legger, would be jumping from the frying pan into the fire."[9]

That very day, officers with the Phoenix Police Department made one of the first arrests for bootlegging, when they apprehended J. T. Sanders and Jay Foy for selling a pint bottle of whiskey to an informant at the corner of First Street and Adams. "Armed with a dollar and a half of marked money the informant of the officers met Sanders and Foy at First and Adams streets and negotiated a purchase of the pint bottle of the 'Old Jordan.' The prospective purchaser was told to remain at the corner for a moment while the 'bootleggers' disappeared up a nearby alley, returning shortly with the whiskey. The bottle was not sealed and gave indication of having been tampered with," the *Arizona Republican* reported.

When facing a city magistrate later that week, Sanders attempted to pass it all off as a joke. He told the court that he had disposed of the whiskey and that the police informant had bought nothing more than a bottle of water. But, when the pint was introduced as evidence, "the general opinion was that it was fairly good whiskey." Sanders was found guilty of violating the liquor law and was given the choice between a $100.00 fine or 100 days in jail. Foy, who had apparently only played a minor role in the illegal transaction, was given a $10.00 fine or 10 days behind bars. As neither man had enough money to pay their fines, they both went to jail.[10]

Less than a week after Sanders and Foy were arrested in Phoenix, authorities in Yuma, a town along the US-Mexican border that sits just across the Colorado River from California, took two suspected bootleggers into custody. On January 16, 1915, Cochise County Deputy Sheriff Billy Brakefield arrested bar owner Mike Schmalzel, who was caught in the act of selling bottles of whiskey through a hole cut in the back wall of the Bank Saloon in the mining town of Lowell. "From almost every county comes the news of arrests being made under the prohibition law. Swat the 'boot-legger' wherever you find him and give him the limit," the *Copper Era and Morenci Leader* announced on January 22.

A few weeks later in the northwest corner of the state, a Mohave County deputy sheriff apprehended a bootlegger crossing the Colorado River from California with five gallons of liquor. "The man was bringing the booze over to this side to peddle it to the thirsty ones when caught. No action has yet been taken against the man," the *Mohave County Miner* reported.[11]

On the night of February 28, a joint operation by Maricopa County Sheriff Jefferson Davis Adams and the Phoenix Police Department resulted in the arrest of seven suspected bootleggers. The roundup by city and county lawmen took place after what many residents had considered a lag in activity in enforcing the law. "In conversation with Chief Brawner and Sheriff Adams, a *Republican* reporter learned that the officers have been working under a great deal of criticism, it is said especially from the churches, because booze joints had not been hauled on the carpet," the *Arizona Republican* explained. "While we have been quietly working up these cases," Phoenix police chief Walter Brawner told the *Republican,* "we have been rather aided than hindered by the cold talk of our critics. We are now in a position to begin gleaning some of the offenders, and from now on, things will begin to drop."

Armed with twenty-three warrants, Adams, Brawner, and a team of city and county officers started out after their prey that afternoon. Henry Rosenstein was taken into custody at his store on East Washington Street by Constable Roy Morell. "There is surely some mistake," Rosenstein told the officer. "I never have had any whiskey." This statement was immediately disproved when Morrell discovered a half-empty pint bottle on a table in Rosenstein's living quarters, along with fifty other empty bottles stashed around the premises.

Denny Fraught was found operating out of a poolroom above a clothing store, where he conducted his business "in a quiet, unostentatious way, slipping the bottles to his purchasers from the toilet in the rear of the room. His price varied from $1.50 to $2.00 per pint, and from $2.50 to $5.00 per quart. Some difficulty was had in obtaining a confession from him, but finally seeing the uselessness of denying the charges he came through with a complete confession."

In addition to Rosenstein and Fraught, five other suspects were also arrested, including Henry Hernandez, George "Brownie" Holmes, and D. K.

Black, who sold an undercover member of the sheriff's department a case of pint-size bottles of whiskey at $2.50 per bottle. Also taken into custody were John Lee and his wife Mary, an African-American couple who had been detected selling their wares in the neighborhood known as "China Alley." "I hope that the judge gives each of them the stiffest fine possible," Sheriff Adams told reporters, "and with this staring them in the face, prospective bootleggers will not be so eager to take chances. We are certainly going to stamp out this traffic."

The following day, Adams's deputies and other local authorities arrested four more suspects in their campaign to discourage bootleggers in Phoenix, and, according to the *Republican*, triggered an exodus of sorts among the city's other violators, with rumrunners dashing off to the Southern Pacific and Santa Fe railroad stations in a hurry to get on the next trains to California. "A reign of terror among dispensers of bad booze followed the announcement in yesterday's *Republican* that the fight was on. So quiet have been the operations of the officers," the *Republican* reported, "[that] not even those underground news agencies, employed by the crooks and their ilk, had learned much about the campaign. That secrecy which caused talk about official disregard of open bootlegging also prevented the suspects from getting 'hep.' The result was a bombshell in their midst, and their scattering had all the effect of an explosion."[12]

Cochise County Sheriff Harry Wheeler proved to be one of the state's toughest enforcers of the Prohibition law. On November 21, 1914, just weeks after Cochise County reelected him (albeit at the same time widely rejecting the Prohibition amendment), the *Tombstone Prospector* published a public letter from Wheeler in which the sheriff told his constituents, "I will enforce this law with whatever power, intelligence, and ability I may possess, and I call upon every good citizen to aid me in all ways possible, regardless of how any of us felt before election."

The following year, Thomas K. Marshall reported on Wheeler's progress. "The total commitments to the county jail from January 1 to August 30 for 1914 was 173, and for the same period of 1915, the total was 148. Of the latter, thirty-three were for violation of the Prohibition amendment. Sheriff Harry Wheeler is enforcing the law vigorously throughout the county. He has the most difficult place of any sheriff in the state," Marshall declared, "owing to the great size of the county and its long border line."[13]

Aside from his own professional stance on liquor violators, Wheeler's firm enforcement of statewide Prohibition may have also been motivated by reasons that were very personal. In March of 1915, his sixteen-year-old son Allyn was fatally injured in a drunk-driving accident that occurred only two months after the law took effect. However, even before this terrible tragedy occurred, Wheeler had demonstrated a tough enforcement policy on liquor. He had firmly opposed the manufacture and sale of "two per cent" beer, which had appeared to some, at least, to be exempt from Arizona's Prohibition law. Wheeler made his position on the matter clear in the January 10, 1915, edition of the Tombstone *Weekly Epitaph* when he stated, "I shall proceed as I have announced previously, arrest any one whom I find either making or selling 'two per cent' in Cochise county. It will be then up to the courts to decide whether or not it is illegal to make and sell it."[14]

A former captain of the Arizona Rangers, Harry Wheeler served three terms as sheriff of Cochise County, Arizona.   *Bisbee Mining and Historical Museum*

On March 1, 1915, Wheeler's deputies, working alongside the officers under the command of Police Chief W. S. Kirby, staged a roundup in the border town of Douglas, in which they arrested thirteen offenders of the liquor law. Of those taken into custody, twelve were residents of the so-called "restricted district," and most were African-American. "Of the twelve residents of Sixth St. arrested," the *Bisbee Daily Review* reported, "one was white and one in doubt. Bonds were placed at $500 each. Earl (Speck) Williams has two charges against him for selling whiskey on different dates, as has Eva Will and 'Kid' Lee. D. J. Genardini is charged with selling a bottle of wine, while

Mary Gary of 332 Eighth Street is said to have disposed of a half pint of the stuff. The others under arrest are Alex Cungle, Dora Foster, Maude Baker, Bessie Leroy, and Eva Hurley."

Apparently, the raids in Douglas caused an exodus from that city similar to the one triggered by the sweep conducted in Phoenix that same week. Reflecting the unfortunate attitudes toward race at the time, it was reported that the "sudden increase in Tucson's colored population is due to the arrival of a number of negroes from Douglas, from which they came to escape arrest as bootleggers. The sheriff and the police have been active in the Smelter City for several days, and as a result a number of colored men and women and one white man have been arrested for violating the anti-booze law. John Doe warrants for a number of other colored lawbreakers were issued, and hearing of this step on the part of the officers, the bootleggers who had not been arrested left for other parts, mostly for Tucson."[15]

Two weeks later, Wheeler's name made the papers again when he arrested alleged bootlegger Percy Rodgers and made "one of the biggest hauls of liquor in violation of the Prohibition law." In mid-March, the sheriff received information that Rodgers had left Cochise County in a car, bound for El Paso, Texas, with the intention of returning with a heavy load of booze. On March 15, Wheeler, along with Deputy Charley Cross and Constable Sam Hayhurst, a former Arizona Ranger, intercepted Rodgers on his return from El Paso and discovered sixty gallons of whiskey in his vehicle. "Rodgers admits that this was not the first trip he has made with whiskey from El Paso to Tucson," the *Bisbee Daily Review* reported.[16]

Among the deputies who carried out Sheriff Wheeler's campaign against bootlegging in Cochise County, Percy Bowden would emerge as one of the most aggressive. Driving a fast-moving automobile known locally as "The Yellow Peril," Bowden prowled the desert highways throughout the early years of Prohibition in Arizona, nabbing countless smugglers who introduced "wet goods" into the state. In one particular case in the spring of 1916, Bowden used his six-gun to shoot out a tire on a fleeing bootlegger's automobile. Such was Bowden's reputation that in February of 1918, the lawman became the subject of a poem that appeared in the *Bisbee Daily Review:*

THE WAIL OF THE BOOTLEGGER
By Ned White of Bisbee

We started for Rodeo
Along about two-thirty
One Frosty winter morning;
With a load of booze we started,
With a load of good red liquor
For the thirsty ones in Bisbee,
For the thirsty population
In the canyons of Mule Mountains.

As we sped along the highway
We watched for Percy Bowden—
A terror to bootleggers!
Is that the Bowden person
In his car the Yellow Devil?
Oftentimes bootleggers meet him
On the highways and the byways.
Oftentimes the crafty Percy
Lies in wait in lonesome places.

As we sped along that morning
Feeling lucky and elated,
(We had passed the danger point
And our fears had most abated;)
When bang! We ran right into something,
And the flivver groaned and halted.
There he stood beside the roadway,
Happy as a goat in clover,
For he knew the goods were on us,
And we knew the game was over.

With a grin he up and told us
How our little game was blasted
By the putty-faced stool-pigeon
Who gave us our bum steer;
(For he said the road was open
To the line of Arizona.
And from there on down to Douglas
Everything was clear.)

So beware of Percy Bowden!
All you hop-heads and bootleggers;
Soon or late he's going to get you—
His plans are well laid;
There will be a trip to Tombstone,
A little hard-luck story,
And a little six-month sentence
To work out on the grade.[17]

Wheeler's task remained a gargantuan and often very thankless one. A January 1916 newspaper interview with the sheriff highlighted the frustrations and many of the challenges that Wheeler and his subordinates faced in enforcing the law: "The reason why we, the law enforcement officers of Cochise County, succeed in keeping down robbery, murder, arson, and other felonies is because the people believe such offenses to be crimes. From ninety-five to ninety-eight percent, or even a larger proportion of the population, are against such crimes. When a business man, a professional man, or a laboring man knows of a crime having been committed, or about to be committed, he will notify the officers. He will not be afraid to go on the witness stand and tell all he knows. He wants to see the law upheld," Wheeler stated.

But, as the lawman pointed out, this was clearly not the case when his department pursued violators of Arizona's liquor laws, explaining, "During the twelve months, comprising the year of 1915, the Sheriff's office did not have the testimony of a single non-official citizen of the county in the prosecution of any of its bootlegging cases." Clearly, Harry Wheeler and his fellow peace officers were facing considerable risks in order to enforce a state law that many Arizonans had never supported in the first place.[18]

Another issue that frustrated authorities charged with enforcing the liquor law was the number of cases that resulted either in dismissal or modest fines. Guilty parties could be sentenced to hard labor on a "Bootleggers' Boulevard," so named for the road gangs who worked on the roads in Yavapai and Cochise Counties, though this hardly discouraged most of the smugglers. "Officers have [a] hard enough time [capturing] bootleggers without having them released or given small fines after they are captured," Wheeler told a reporter the *Bisbee Daily Review* days after several of the violators that he had arrested in Douglas that winter had their charges dismissed.[19]

In addition to those bootleggers caught smuggling liquor across state lines or over the international boundary from Sonora, Mexico, Arizona lawmen also had to contend with the moonshiners who brewed their own product to supply local tastes. In August of 1915, officers in Pinal County arrested Maria Encinas in the mining camp of Ray for manufacturing and selling "tiswin." An intoxicating beverage made from fermented corn, tiswin had long been popular among the Apache of Arizona, and had contributed to a number of violent incidents in the Southwest during the Indian Wars of the 1800s.

For quite a while, local authorities had been puzzled as to the numerous "drunks" observed in Ray, and while Encinas had been suspected of distributing liquor for some time, it wasn't until a young girl named Conchita Gonzales came forward that they were able to make an arrest. "She stated that her two younger brothers had come home intoxicated several times," the *Arizona Republican* reported, "and she had wheedled the fact out of them, that they had secured the booze from the Encinas woman, and that it was the celebrated 'tiz-vin [*sic*],' manufactured by the Apaches long before they ever heard of a white man." Officers raided Encinas's home, where they took the woman into custody and seized a barrel of the homemade intoxicant.[20]

On the evening of November 5, 1915, Maricopa County Deputy Seriff Jim Murphy discovered an impressive winery operated by a Sicilian immigrant named Louis Fausone. As soon as Murphy had taken Fausone into custody, he summoned Sheriff Adams and together the two officers returned to the Sicilian's winery with a truck, where they loaded up a barrel of perfectly good wine, and a second cask still in the process of fermenting. "The scene was one over which a movie man would have had fits. Little low-ceiling palm-thatched hut, cluttered with boxes of carrots and other evidences of the marketer's trade, and in every conceivable corner, the tools for turning out 'vino.' Bottles and jugs of liquor, funnels, strainers, wine presses, and, as aforesaid, casks of the product, equipped with handy faucets, and with plenty of drinking cups, were added to the supply of evidence," the *Republican* declared. Charged with manufacturing "Dago red" in violation of the state liquor law, Fausone was later sentenced to serve ten days in the county jail and ordered to pay a fine of $150.00.[21]

Of course, it did not take long for gunplay and the possibility of violent death to begin figuring into the exchanges between Arizona lawmen and outlaw bootleggers. Walter Brooks—a thirty-eight-year-old watchman for the Copper Queen Mine in Bisbee, and a former police officer—was murdered by a pair of alleged bootleggers he encountered during the early-morning hours of June 27, 1915.[22]

A few weeks later, on the night of July 17, Cochise County Deputy Sheriffs John Newell and William J. Graham shot and killed a liquor runner named Martin Olivas just outside the bordertown of Naco.[23]

Violent episodes and shooting scrapes between Arizona lawmen and bootleggers would occur throughout the next several years. In March of 1917, just a few weeks after Sheriff Harry Wheeler and Constable Lafe Gibson traded shots with Mexican bootleggers at Kelton, Arizona, Cochise County Deputy Sheriff Frank Homan encountered two men with a wagon loaded with several cases of whiskey. Homan had just placed both men under arrest when one of them made a run for it. "The officer says he chased the Mexican about 100 yards, frequently commanding the fugitive to halt. When he refused, Homan opened fire on him at a distance of about fifty yards, shooting four times at the man's feet," the *Bisbee Daily Review* reported. Homan then fired a fifth round and shot the outlaw dead with a bullet through the back that struck the man's heart and exited out through his chest. "A coroner's jury brought in the following verdict this evening: 'Death due to gunshot wound fired by F. A. Homan, a deputy sheriff, in his official capacity, trying to recapture an escaped prisoner,'" the *Daily Review* stated.

A similar incident just a few weeks before had resulted in the wounding of an innocent bystander in Morenci. Greenlee County Deputy Sheriff George Hill had just arrested a suspected bootlegger when the man knocked him over a concrete wall and attempted to flee. Hill quickly regained his feet and cut loose with a shotgun, striking a baker named Leo Bailard in the leg with several lead pellets. That September, Constable Bob Roe was badly wounded when he came upon a gang of bootleggers attempting to dispose of a load of alcohol near the mining camp of Chloride in Mohave County. As Roe confronted the men, "one of the gang named Romula Lazo pulled a revolver and deliberately fired. The bullet entered the constable's right side and passed down and out of the thigh." Lazo and his companions were later arrested.[24]

The following year, in April of 1918, Constable William Hazelton "Haze" Burch put a bullet through the head of a suspected bootlegger during a gunfight on the corner of Henshaw Road and Sixth Street in Phoenix. Two months later, Wilcox police officer Harry Weese engaged noted bootlegger William Krupp in a high-speed pursuit in Cochise County. Krupp was transporting a load of booze from Lordsburg, New Mexico, when Weese and Constable Jess Moore attempted to intercept him on a road some twenty-five miles west of Wilcox.

"Krupp realized that the officers were after him and began to ditch his load. The officers came up close to Krupp and he opened fire on them with a .45 automatic, the bullets hitting the car in which the officers were riding," the *Bisbee Daily Review* reported on June 12, 1918. While Moore kept his foot on the gas pedal, Weese leaned out on the car's running board with a .30-30 Winchester and shot Krupp through the heart, killing him instantly. According to Cochise County Sheriff Guy Welch (who had taken over for Harry Wheeler when the lawman joined the army to fight in World War I), the shooting was completely justified, and a coroner's jury certainly agreed. William Krupp had shipped his last load of bootleg whiskey.

Seven months later, on the night of January 6, 1919, Yavapai County Deputy Sheriff John Munds got word that two automobiles loaded with bootleg whiskey were headed toward the Verde Valley from California, and set out intercept the shipment. Munds, who was fifty years old and had once served as the county sheriff, was "accompanied in his expedition only by a sawed-off shotgun and by a boy whose principal duty was holding a flashlight for Munds while his prisoners and their cars were being searched." The officer stopped the first car on the road to Camp Verde, Arizona, and ordered the driver, Fred Clemens, to halt and get out of the vehicle. But when Clemens climbed out of his Dodge with a gun in his hand, Munds was already one step ahead of him, and "cut loose with his shotgun and blew the bootlegger's gun hand to small bits. The revolver was scattered around with the hand by the roadside." When Clemens's fellow bootleggers drove up in the second car, none of them felt like taking on the shotgun-wielding lawman, and all "surrendered without resistance."[25]

CHAPTER TWO
COLD IN DEATH

As the result of the affair many of the soldiers who were absolutely innocent of any connection with the affair were roughly handled and it is possible that two or three of them were seriously injured. This was due largely to the activity of Deputy Sheriff Joe Hardwick, who has the reputation of being a gun-man and who on this occasion almost completely lost his head as was demonstrated by the readiness with which he fired upon any negroes who did not give themselves up immediately.

—Agent Otto L. Tinklepaugh,
Bureau of Investigation, July 1919[1]

During the early morning hours of May 11, 1918, word reached the headquarters of the Bisbee (Arizona) Police Department that a twenty-two-year-old African-American teamster named Joel Smith was terrorizing Upper Brewery Gulch, once home to gambling houses, pool halls, and brothels. According to the *Bisbee Daily Review*, Smith, who was armed with a revolver, "had shot some Mexicans, had kicked in the door of the No. 9 Colored club, and beaten up and robbed a sick man asleep upstairs in that place." Responding to Smith's one-man rampage in Brewery Gulch were Bisbee police officers Ed "Tex" Barton and Joseph B. Hardwick, the latter "rated as one of the best shots on the local force."

Known to the people of Bisbee as "Montana Joe," by that spring morning, the thirty-seven-year-old Hardwick had already lived an eventful life on both sides of the law. Though there's no evidence that he ever actually resided in Montana, Hardwick had called various parts of the American West home, and had killed at least two men, one in Oklahoma and another in Arizona, and along the way had lost a finger on his left hand. A member of the Bisbee Police Department for a little less than a year, Hardwick had tangled with his fair share of bootleggers and other assorted hard cases.[2]

When Smith spotted Hardwick and Barton headed in his direction, he immediately barricaded himself in an adobe house, where he traded his revolver for much heavier firepower. As the two lawmen approached the adobe, "Hardwick went to the front door and opened this to find himself gazing down the barrel of a 12-gauge shotgun. The officer ducked just as the negro shot, and was almost knocked off the porch by the concussion of the shot." The blast of lead pellets narrowly missed Hardwick's head and peppered a house across the street, where they came within inches of striking a baby sleeping on a cot. "The buckshot went through the door of the room where the child was asleep on the cot and tore the end of the cot and went into the baseboard and into the carpet at the foot of the cot. The officers found seven of the buckshot out of the ten that went through the door. Had Smith stood about a foot further to the left or fired a foot further to the left," the Bisbee Daily Review explained, "the little one would have been riddled with buckshot."

Partially blinded by the flash from Smith's shotgun, Hardwick retreated, firing his pistol over his shoulder as he ran for cover. Minutes later, Hardwick spotted Smith in a window, took aim with his Colt .45, and fired. Hardwick's bullet plowed into Smith's hand, mangling his fingers and knocking the shotgun out of his grasp. Then, before Smith could get a firm grip on the weapon to fire his second barrel, Hardwick charged into the room and grabbed the shotgun from the wounded outlaw. Smith, who lost at least one of his fingers to the slug from Hardwick's six-gun, was later sentenced to a three- to five-year term at the state prison in Florence.[3]

Joseph Burney Hardwick's near-death encounter with Joel Smith's twelve-gauge in Bisbee was only one of the many misadventures of a law enforcement career that spanned the better part of two decades and three different states. Born in Oklahoma on February 14, 1881, and a registered member of the Chickasaw Nation, Hardwick was nineteen years old when he married seventeen-year-old Alma Bell Lindsey. The two would produce six children, five of whom would survive into adulthood.[4]

In the early twentieth century, the Hardwicks moved on to Hoquaim, Washington, where Joe Hardwick would eventually find employment as a mill worker, and later, as an officer with the local police force. In May 1911, their eldest son, eight-year-old Herman Hardwick, disappeared when he slipped and fell into the Hoquaim River while jumping back and forth between a pair

After nearly blasting Joe Hardwick with a shotgun, Joel Smith was sentenced to serve three to five years in the Arizona State Penitentiary at Florence.

Arizona State Library and Archives

of scows moored alongside the Grays Harbor Construction Company dock. Six weeks later when two young boys discovered Herman's body, Joe Hardwick had already turned in his badge and taken his family back home to Oklahoma.[5]

A little over a year later, Joe Hardwick was arrested by the sheriff of Marshall County, Oklahoma, for the murder of J. M. Peoples. In November of 1912, Hardwick was found guilty of first-degree manslaughter and was sentenced to five years of hard labor at the state penitentiary in McAlister, Oklahoma. However, in mid-April of 1913, Hardwick escaped from custody and traveled all the way to New Orleans before writing prison officials to inform them that he would return to custody. On Thursday, April 24, he telephoned McAlister to let the authorities know that he was once again back in Oklahoma, and the next day he turned himself in. According to several newspaper accounts, Hardwick "became ashamed of the way he had acted after he had been made a trusty, would pay any expense incurred in trying to find him, and would serve his time."[6]

In February 1914, after only a year in prison, Hardwick became one of four inmates doing time for manslaughter to receive early paroles from the governor of Oklahoma. The Hardwicks left Oklahoma, for good this time, and settled on a ranch near the small town of Bowie in Cochise County, Arizona. There, Hardwick would also once again find himself serving as a lawman, when in September of 1916 he was hired as a special officer for the Tucson division of the Southern Pacific Railroad.[7]

While ranching in Bowie, Hardwick would have his first known shooting scrape since the killing of J. M. Peoples in Oklahoma in 1912. In late February of 1917, newspapers reported that while Hardwick was away working on a neighboring ranch, a laborer named Francisco Caniaz allegedly assaulted Joe and Alma's nine-year-old daughter Lillian. "The little girl escaped," the *Arizona Republican* explained, "and, with her mother, went to a nearby ranch and notified her father." On hearing what had happened, Hardwick immediately returned home, armed himself with a Winchester rifle, located Caniaz, and shot him dead. After turning himself in at Bowie, Hardwick was held under bond pending a hearing, but was ultimately cleared of any wrongdoing.[8]

Within a few short months of the shooting death of Francisco Caniaz, and following the birth of the Hardwicks' youngest child in June of 1917, City Marshal James Allison hired the thirty-six-year-old Oklahoman as an officer with the Bisbee Police Department. Originally founded in 1880, by the summer of 1917, Bisbee was one of the largest communities in Arizona, and one of the most important mining centers in the American Southwest. Bisbee lay thirty miles south of the Cochise County seat in Tombstone, and just eight miles from the Mexican border. Having begun its life as collection of crude miners' cabins known as Rea's Camp some forty years earlier, the community that Joe Hardwick patrolled as a policeman had long since evolved into a modern city of streetcars and electricity. It was also a company town, where the mineral industry was largely dominated by the Copper Queen Mine, owned by Phelps, Dodge and Company, Inc. Altogether, Bisbee's three major corporations would ultimately produce close to eight billion pounds of copper, as well as hundreds of millions of pounds of silver, zinc, gold, and lead.[9]

Bisbee's town marshal kept an office in Bisbee's City-Fire Hall, which overlooked the entrance of the Copper Queen Mine and the depot for the Southwestern and El Paso Railroad. The two-story structure also housed the mayor's office, the fire department, and the city jail. To the west stood the headquarters of the Copper Queen and Phelps-Dodge, and behind it, the Copper Queen Hotel, completed in 1902, and "equipped throughout with modern hotel conveniences." From there Main Street, Bisbee's principal business district, ran along the bottom of Mule Pass Gulch and wound its way past Castle Rock, a tall outcropping in the canyon where soldiers and civilian packers had first discovered traces of some of the area's mineral wealth in the 1870s. Intersecting with Mule Pass Gulch and not far from the police station and offices of Phelps-Dodge was Brewery Gulch, a winding thoroughfare that ran north along the bottom of another canyon, formerly home to many of Bisbee's pre-liquor-law saloons, gaming establishments, and bordellos.[10]

Hardwick's arrival in Bisbee came during a troubling period in the city's history. Unlike some of Arizona's other mining towns, which regularly employed Mexican miners, Bisbee had long been known as "a white man's camp," where Mexicans were barred from the better-paying underground labor and Chinese immigrants were forbidden from living there, and were generally not allowed out on the streets after sundown. Thus, the more profitable employment opportunities were dominated by Anglo-American miners, and relative newcomers from Europe, including Serbs, Welshmen, and Finns, as well as Italians and Slavs. Despite the fact that its population was fairly diverse,

Bisbee embraced its white man's camp identity. In 1916, when the *Washington Times* reported that American soldiers had claimed that half of Bisbee's population was "composed of Mexicans" and crowded with "begging Indians," an indignant former resident felt the need to defend the town's reputation in a letter to the editor. "There are no Indians in Bisbee," he wrote, "nor is there a beggar of any kind. There are few Mexicans. It is a white man's camp."[11]

In June of 1917, with the nation at war in Europe and copper prices on the rise, the city's racial dynamic, ongoing concerns over the Mexican Revolution, and fears of German intrigue would all play contributing roles in one of the most infamous events in the history of Arizona. Demanding better working conditions for both underground miners and the Mexican surface laborers who worked in Bisbee, the Industrial Workers of the World, or IWW, called for a strike.[12]

Fifteen-year-old Miriam Tefft was a firsthand witness to the drama that enveloped the mining town that summer. "You could almost smell fear. Men didn't look at each other in the face. Everyone was under suspicion. Loyalties were divided. One could sense an undercurrent of outrage seething. Our fathers were often from home. They were closed-mouthed when asked questions, so one did not ask too many questions. Something was brewing in this atmosphere of wild emotions," she recalled. Regional newspapers, including the *Bisbee Daily Review*, owned by Phelps-Dodge, were quick to denounce the IWW and its members, who were derisively referred to as "wobblies." "Wobbly tactics can be traced for several years, throughout the country," one article read, "but particularly in the west. The I.W.W.'s marched into communities, their banners of promise flying at their head, promising Utopian reforms. They have left these same communities with a trail of bloodshed, horror, and strife behind them."[13]

While the Wobblies held meetings throughout the district, so too did Bisbee's Workman's Loyalty League and the Citizens' Protective League, both of which were formed by non-striking miners and other concerned citizens, some of whom were no doubt motivated by fear that the strikers included enemy agents who planned acts of sabotage. On July 11, 1917, two weeks after the strike began, Cochise County Sheriff Harry Wheeler penned the following statement to be published in the next morning's *Bisbee Daily Herald*:

I have formed a Sheriff's posse of 1,200 men in Bisbee, and 1,000 in Douglas, all loyal Americans, for the purpose of arresting, on charges of vagrancy, treason, and of being disturbers of the peace of Cochise County, all those strange men who have congregated here from other parts and sections for the purpose of harassing and intimidating all men who desire to pursue their daily toll. I am continually told of threats and insults heaped upon the working men of this district by so-called strikers, who are strange to these parts, yet who presume to dictate the manner of life of the people of this district.

Appeals to patriotism do not move them, nor do appeals to reason. At a time when our country needs her every resource, these strangers persist in keeping from her the precious metal production of this entire district.

Today I heard threats to the effect that homes would be destroyed because the heads of families insisted upon their rights as Americans to work for themselves, their families and their country.

Other threats have and are being daily made. Men [have] been assaulted and brutally beaten, and only today I heard the Mayor of Bisbee threatened and his requests ignored.

We cannot longer stand or tolerate such conditions! This is no labor trouble—we are sure of that—but a direct attempt to embarrass and injure the government of the United States.

Sheriff Wheeler then called upon all loyal Americans to assist him in peaceably arresting "these disturbers of our national and local peace." Wheeler also stated that those arrested would be handled humanely, and insisted that he desired no bloodshed. "However," Wheeler added, "I am determined if resistance is made, it shall be quickly and effectively overcome." By the time many of Bisbee's residents had read Wheeler's statement on July 12, 1917, the roundup of suspected Wobblies by the sheriff and his civilian posse had already begun.[14]

Hundreds of miners are marched away from Bisbee toward Warren, Arizona, during the Bisbee Deportation of 1917.   *Bisbee Mining and Historical Museum*

Armed with an assortment of firearms and identified by strips of white cloth tied around their sleeves, Wheeler's army of deputized miners and local merchants swept through the town and arrested hundreds of striking Wobblies, as well as lawyers, businessmen, and others who had demonstrated open sympathy for the IWW. The roundup turned violent when IWW member James Brew opened fire on a party of special deputies at a rooming house and killed Orson McRae, an employee of the Copper Queen Mine and a member of the local Loyalty League. "Brew then ran through the house and out the back door and round the premises," the *Daily Review* reported. "As he turned around the side of the dwelling, one of the deputies shot him through the breast."

At 7:30 a.m., the so-called "trouble makers" were marched two miles away to a baseball field in Warren. "We began to see that deputies and armed citizens were keeping the strikers in line as they were herded into the ballpark behind the high board fence. The men had evidently been taken completely by surprise; some were still in their nightshirts," Miriam Tefft later recalled, "many in long underwear; some apparently hadn't been given time to put on their shoes." A few of those arrested were immediately released from custody, once they had either expressed a willingness to return to work, or were cleared of any actual allegiance to the IWW. Then, a little after 11:00 a.m., the rest of the strikers—some 1,250 men, most of whom were Mexicans—were loaded onto the manure-infested freight cars of the El Paso & Southwestern Railroad and hauled out of the state to New Mexico. "It was an anti-climax when President Wilson, breathing fire and brimstone, sent a commission to investigate. No law could be found against kidnapping people en masse and dumping them into another state," Miriam Tefft remembered.[15]

Special Deputy Orson P. McRae was one of two men killed during the Bisbee Deportation. He is buried in Evergreen Cemetery in Lowell, Arizona. *Mike Testin*

As the leader of what would be forever remembered as the "Bisbee Deportation," Harry Wheeler would eventually face both a federal indictment and the efforts of the IWW to block his ability to accept an army commission to fight in World War I. Charges against the well-known lawman were eventually dropped, but Wheeler would be compelled to later defend his actions during the kidnapping trial of one of his posse-men. In 1920, the former sheriff would tell a Tombstone courtroom that among the Wobblies were former members of Pancho Villa's army who had hidden a cache of arms and ammunition in the Ajo Mountains, which they intended to use in Bisbee. Wheeler also explained to a federal commission that some of the strikers may have been motivated by the *Plan de San Diego*, and that agitators "had gone among the Mexicans and told them that it would be in the interest of Mexico and Mexicans for Germany to win the war, and he believed, he said, it was the purpose of the strike at Bisbee to tie up the copper industry and hamper the United States war efforts."

On July 12, 1917, 1,250 strikers were loaded onto freight cars during the Bisbee Deportation. *Bisbee Mining and Historical Museum*

When all was said and done, neither Wheeler nor any of his deputies would ever face any long-term legal consequences or see the inside of a prison cell for their participation in the Bisbee Deportation. However, the mass expulsion of striking miners to the deserts of New Mexico would play a direct role in the lead-up to a violent episode on the streets of Bisbee almost exactly two years later, one that would find "Montana Joe" Hardwick in the middle of a wild night of gunplay between local peace officers and the US Army.[16]

In 1917, Hardwick had left his wife and children at their ranch in Bowie and had gone to Bisbee to assume his duties as a member of the city's police department. Throughout the months that followed, Hardwick would have plenty of opportunities to demonstrate his nerve, his skill with firearms, and his no-nonsense attitude toward criminals. On one chilly evening in January of 1918, Hardwick was on patrol when he encountered two Mexican men loitering in a lumberyard. As Hardwick approached them, he noticed a bulge in one of the men's pockets, which he was certain came from a concealed pistol. When the officer demanded that the man with the gun throw up his hands, the suspect refused. At the same time, his accomplice started to reach for something stashed in his own coat pocket. Sure enough, Hardwick discovered that the bulge in the first man's pocket came from a very businesslike .45 caliber automatic pistol, with a loaded magazine and a round in the chamber, while the second man had been wrapping his fingers around the handle of a six-inch stiletto knife. Hardwick quickly covered them with his six-gun and relieved both men of their weaponry, and a bottle of wine, and then hauled them off to the city jail.[17]

The following month, Joe Hardwick was involved in an incident that could be viewed as a sign of the changing times and the Western peace officer's gradual transition from horses to automobiles. On February 11, 1918, Hardwick and two other officers raced out of Bisbee in an automobile, intending to join the manhunt for brothers Tom and John Powers, who along with an accomplice, were wanted for the murder of Graham County Sheriff Robert McBride and deputies Martin Kempton and Kane Wooten. McBride and his posse had gone to the Powers ranch the day before to arrest the men for evading the wartime draft when a bloody shoot-out erupted that claimed the lives of the three lawmen and Tom and John Powers's father. Now, with Hardwick behind the wheel, the Bisbee officers planned to "head off the slayers," who were believed to be on their way to Mexico.

But, somewhere on the highway east of Bisbee, Hardwick hit a patch of soft mud and overturned the car. Deputy Sheriff Red Gannon was pinned underneath the vehicle for several minutes before Hardwick and the other deputy managed to pull him out from under the wreckage. The badly injured men were taken back to Bisbee, where Hardwick's and Gannon's wounds were treated in the Phelps-Dodge dispensary at the Copper Queen Mine. Hardwick and Gannon must have made a rapid recovery, however, as both lawmen were back on duty by early March.[18]

On the night of March 29, Hardwick and Sergeant James Kempton, whose brother had been one of the lawmen killed at the Powers cabin, raided a distillery in Upper Brewery Gulch, where they discovered a large quantity of raisins, prunes, grape juice, and grain, seized forty gallons of homemade wine, and arrested the Mexican woman in charge of the operation. Apparently, the woman was under the heavy influence of her own brew; she was very indignant when the officers destroyed her source of profit, "and offered to show fight, but she soon decided it was no use when Kempton caught a hold of her."[19]

Bisbee's Brewery Gulch as seen in November of 1917, when Charlie Chaplin's *The Adventurer* played at Bisbee's Orpheum Theater.   *Border Heritage Center, El Paso Public Library*

In June of 1918, Sergeant Kempton succeeded James Allison as chief of police, and within a few days Hardwick had tendered his resignation with the police department. However, Hardwick's hiatus from law enforcement would prove to be a brief one, and according to his selective service registration card filed that September, Hardwick was working as a deputy sheriff for Gila County. In November of that same year, former Deputy US Marshal James F. McDonald won election as the new sheriff of Cochise County, and within days of being sworn into office in January of 1919, he appointed Joe Hardwick as a deputy to replace Percy Bowden, who had taken a job as an officer with the Douglas Police Department. Hardwick's early days as Bowden's successor in Douglas were active ones. Before his first month as a deputy was over, he had joined Sheriff McDonald, Deputy Arthur E. Parmer, and federal agents on a liquor raid at a ranch belonging to George Medigovitch on the Bisbee Road, just west of Douglas. The lawmen managed to seize a total of 2,500 pints of whiskey, three barrels of wine, and several cases of beer, all of it with a total estimated value of $15,000.00.[20]

A few weeks later, on February 15, 1919, Hardwick and Parmer fell in with Douglas police sergeant H. M. Rose and Constable George Newman on a gambling raid in a Douglas pool hall. As the officers came through the door, they found twelve men, all Mexicans, in the middle of a card game. "When Police Sergeant Rose arrested the men, one of them, Francisco Gomez, reached in his pocket," the Tombstone *Weekly Epitaph* declared, "and before he knew it was shot in the arm by the police officer, resulting in his arm being broken. Later an ugly looking knife was found near the place where the injured man had been standing."[21]

Joe Hardwick would be near the scene of another shooting the following month. On the night of March 19, Hardwick rode out to a ranch owned by Matt Keaton, some forty miles north of Douglas, with Sheriff McDonald and a party of officers that included Deputy US Marshal Jay F. Wilmouth, as well as Frank P. Moore and George Kelly with the Arizona Livestock Sanitary Board, who were "in search of hides from stolen cattle." When the officers arrived at the ranch, they found three men, Keaton, James Alvord, and thirty-six-year-old Ralph A. Williams. They also discovered a large distillery operation along with several barrels of moonshine. McDonald ordered the men to return with the officers to Douglas, and soon a "team of horses was hitched up and the eight men started on their trip to the smelter city."

Before the group had gotten very far from the ranch, however, the team of horses somehow became excited, and in the confusion, Williams managed to jump out of the wagon and quickly disappear into the darkness. Assuming that he would simply return to the ranch, Frank Moore volunteered to go back alone to wait for him while the other officers continued on to Douglas. Sure enough, at about 2:00 a.m., as Moore lingered in the dark with a rifle, Williams approached on foot. When he spotted the lawman, Williams rushed him and tried to wrestle the officer's gun away. As they fought over the weapon, Moore jerked the trigger and shot Williams through the heart. The livestock inspector remained by the body until the other officers returned to the scene later that morning. Williams's remains were later taken to Douglas, where a coroner's jury exonerated Moore of any wrongdoing. Keaton and Alvord were both charged with transporting and manufacturing liquor without a license. As Sheriff McDonald informed the *Weekly Epitaph*, "[T]he distillery found on the Keaton ranch was capable of making 20 gallons a day."[22]

Throughout the first six months that Hardwick served as a Cochise County deputy sheriff, he made frequent trips back to Bisbee, and local newspapers often reported his passing through the city on official business, or the social calls he made on friends from his days as a member of the police department. On July 3, 1919, Joe Hardwick was once again back in Bisbee, where the African-American troopers of the Tenth US Cavalry Regiment were scheduled to ride in the next day's annual Independence Day Parade.[23]

By the summer of 1919, many of Bisbee's citizens were on familiar terms with the "Buffalo Soldiers" of the Tenth Cavalry. The regiment, which had been formed in 1866, was one of four segregated combat units in the US Army, serving throughout the frontier during the Indian Wars, from the Great Plains to the deserts of the Arizona Territory. They had later seen action in Cuba during the Spanish-American War in 1898 and the Philippine-American War, and had also helped hunt Pancho Villa in Mexico following the 1916 attack on Columbus, New Mexico.[24]

The Tenth Cavalry spent World War I guarding the Mexican border, with Arizona's Fort Huachuca as the regiment's principal headquarters, but with squadrons variously garrisoning the towns of Nogales, Lochiel, and Arivaca, and with one company, Troop L, stationed at Fort Apache. Late on the afternoon of August 27, 1918, a squadron from the Tenth, along with several companies of American infantry, engaged Constitutionalist soldiers in a heavy firefight in the streets of Nogales, Sonora. The battle, which had begun as a shoot-out between Mexican customs officers and members of an army detail guarding the port of entry, resulted in the death of the mayor of Nogales, Felix B. Peñaloza, and featured a full-frontal assault by the men of the Tenth on the hills overlooking the twin Mexican and American towns, during which Captain Joseph D. Hungerford was killed. "The arrival of the Machine Gun Troop and several other troops of the Tenth Cavalry, and some artillery from El Paso on the following day, settled all disturbances for the time being," an official history of the regiment later explained.[25]

The Tenth Cavalry's time along the border also placed the black troopers in close proximity to Bisbee. Bisbee may have been "a white man's camp," but that didn't stop the crowds from gathering on summer afternoons to watch members of the regiment's baseball team play one of the local clubs at the Warren ballpark. "The Tenth Cavalry during its long stay on the border, and in Mexico chasing Villa, has developed one of the strongest ball teams in the United States Army," the *Daily Review* reported on May 8, 1919, "and their appearance here on Sunday will give the locals a chance to prove their mettle." Indeed, the seasonal matches between Bisbee's players and the "black boys" frequently drew large and boisterous crowds. Doubleheaders with the "dusky batsmen" typically included a performance by the regiment's forty-eight-piece band, "knocking off 'The Darktown Strutters' Ball' and a few other selections" in the lead-up to the festivities. It was apparently at one of these fairly routine ball games, however, that the seeds of the "Bisbee Riot" were sown in June of 1919.[26]

Two years after the IWW strike and the deportation, and more than six months after the end of World War I, Bisbee and the surrounding communities of Warren and Lowell remained under the surveillance of agents from the Bureau of Investigation, the Justice Department's precursor to the modern FBI. As a result, the US government had a number of special agents and confidential informants monitoring subversive activity in Bisbee, when violence suddenly erupted on the evening of Thursday, July 3, 1919. According to a report later filed by Special Agent John Foster, a former Arizona Ranger and Deputy US Marshal, the incident "of the night of July third had its incipiency a week or two ago at one of the Sunday baseball games, between the local team and that of the negro soldiers from Ft. Huachuca. Several friendly disputes arose during the game and some criticism followed. The game was finished but seemingly an uncanny feeling has existed since. It appears that a number of spectators were enthusiastic in their cheering for the negroes, which naturally caused dissention."[27]

Foster's account also suggested that members of the IWW, still nursing resentment over the 1917 deportation, were quick to take advantage of a situation that played on both the racial dynamic within the community at the time, and the notion that the army represented the might of Arizona's copper industry. As Foster reported, "This first rupture was enlarged and exaggerated by a few of the I.W.W. leaders, along the Gulch. Several negro soldiers have been coached from time to time during the past two weeks, just how they would be treated here on the fourth. They were told that they would not be permitted to enter the restaurants or soft drink stands, were merely being invited to Bisbee to protect different interests, and urged to start trouble at the least provocation."[28]

Concerned that the incidents at the Warren ballpark were a sign that Bisbee might become the scene of the type of unrest that would erupt throughout the nation during the so-called "Red Summer of 1919," both Sheriff McDonald and I. C. E. Adams, chairman of the County Board of Supervisors, voiced their concerns to the committee planning the Independence Day events, "expressing themselves as fearing race riots in the event that colored soldiers did come."[29]

Nevertheless, the troopers left their post at Fort Huachuca right on schedule, departing on July 2, and arrived in Bisbee the following day. The Tenth Cavalry pitched their tents in Warren, and while many of their officers attended a dance at the Warren Country Club, hundreds of soldiers were permitted to venture into the city, many of them armed with their .45 caliber pistols. "In the afternoon it was noticed that practically all of the colored soldiers coming up town bore Army automatics concealed on their persons," Chief Kempton later reported, "most of them carrying them inside their blouses or in other places where they were not visible. I immediately started taking the guns from these men, advising them to leave them at the Police Station and that they would be returned to them on their way returning to camp."

According to Kempton, he and Officer William Sherrill were in the process of disarming several soldiers when they were approached by a lieutenant and a captain from the regiment, who informed the chief that they didn't object to the soldiers carrying guns if Kempton didn't. "I replied that I did. At that time Officer Millruff called five of the soldiers whom we had disarmed over to us. The captain told them to tell the soldiers to go back to camp and put their guns up and then return if they wanted to, and added at that time that he had given orders for no men to leave camp armed," Kempton recalled.[30]

Later that evening, IWW members John Newton and Billy Cornow headed for the "Old 33," a club located in Upper Brewery Gulch, where a large group of soldiers had gathered. Newton, who had allegedly been behind the efforts to stir up trouble among the troopers during the previous weeks, mounted the steps, telling a group of soldiers that the Copper Queen Mine had brought the soldiers into Bisbee "to show off, and that the Queen would make them eat out of the garbage cans like yellow curs before leaving. He explained how the gun men had treated men, women and children during the deportation, and that the negroes would be treated the same." By this time, many of the troopers had apparently imbibed in the bootleg whiskey and moonshine booze that was available in the Gulch, and despite the fact that Chief Kempton and his men had already disarmed dozens of the cavalrymen, some three hundred soldiers were now roaming the streets of Bisbee, many still packing their government-issued .45s.[31]

Sometime later, two white military policemen from the Nineteenth Infantry Regiment, Private George Sullivan and a Private Ridgeley, made their way through the Gulch with orders to disarm any soldier they caught with a weapon. Outside the "Silver Leaf Club," one of Bisbee's segregated night spots, the two men took a .45 from one of the troopers. Minutes later, a corporal from the Tenth and four other soldiers demanded that Sullivan return the pistol. Instead, both MPs decided to run for it, each going in a different direction. Ridgeley tried to make his escape through a restaurant, but was unable to exit through the rear door. Heading back out through the front of the building, he encountered the five troopers, who then "drew their guns on me and took my gun away from me and struck me in the face." The soldiers then asked Ridgeley if he "wasn't acting smart," to which the military policeman told them that he was only doing as he was ordered. Witnesses immediately telephoned the police station and informed Chief Kempton that a riot had broken out "between the white and colored soldiers."[32]

Kempton started for the scene with Joe Hardwick, whose presence that night in Bisbee might have had something to do with Sheriff McDonald's belief that trouble was brewing. The two lawmen were followed by several other police officers who trailed them in an automobile. Along the way, they encountered Otto Tinklepaugh, a twenty-six-year-old agent with the Bureau of Investigation, and another man later identified as C. J. Mueller. Kempton informed them that a "riot" had been reported among the troopers in Brewery Gulch. Then, according to Tinklepaugh, the officers "headed up the gulch and were met on either side by crowds of civilians who stated that the colored soldiers had continued up the Gulch with their guns in their hands." Kempton recalled that as they rounded a bend in the gulch, "we, Hardwick and I, saw two negro soldiers ahead of us, one about forty yards distant, and he started running, at the same time shooting at Hardwick and me. Others of the colored soldiers came out of the club a short distance beyond and there followed a regular pitched battle between us, the other police officers joining us before it was over." During the initial exchange of gunfire, Hardwick was grazed in the arm, while other .45 caliber bullets slapped off the wall behind the officers, clouding their eyes with brick dust. According to the *Bisbee Daily Review*, Officer Sherill managed to hit one of the troopers in the neck, before he and the men retreated back to the station for more firepower.[33]

While Hardwick and the city policemen replenished their ammunition and grabbed rifles and riot guns, Tinklepaugh and Mueller rushed to the Copper Queen Hotel, where they found Lieutenant Ryder, one of the Tenth's officers, who immediately set out to investigate the unfolding drama in Upper Brewery Gulch. Then, both Tinklepaugh and Michael Cassidy, a claims agent with the Copper Queen Mine and one of the organizers of the Independence Day events, each placed telephone calls to the Warren Country Club, where the regiment's commanding officer, Colonel George Philip White, was still attending a dance. When they failed to get White on the phone, Tinklepaugh asked Cassidy to drive to the country club and inform White of the incident in person.

In the meantime, Kempton, Hardwick, and the other lawmen had ventured back out into the street, joined by "special officers" that Kempton had deputized for the Fourth of July, "and a general demonstration took place in the center of Bisbee, when they began apprehending all of the negro soldiers who appeared on the streets, disarming them and placing them in jail." As the officers moved through the town, they opened fire on any soldiers "who took to their heels" and at automobiles loaded with troopers who attempted to get past Hardwick and the city policemen.[34]

Amid the sporadic gunfire, an innocent bystander, Teresa Leyvas, was hit by a stray round while she stood at the railroad depot waiting for a train. The bullet struck Leyvas on the right side of her head, but miraculously didn't kill her. Neither newspaper accounts or the army's narrative on the "riot" identify who exactly shot Leyvas, but the government's report would heavily criticize the actions of the local officers, particularly Joe Hardwick, "who has the reputation of being a gun-man and who on this occasion almost completely lost his head, as was demonstrated by the readiness with which he fired upon any negros [*sic*] who did not give themselves up immediately."[35]

While the shoot-out between civil officers and "Buffalo Soldiers" continued, Tinklepaugh made his way to the Warren Country Club, where Cassidy told him that Colonel White had dispatched Lieutenant Ryder and seven men to the scene in order to disarm the troopers. Tinklepaugh entered the club and informed White "that the situation was such that it did not justify his remaining at a dance when there was a pitched battle going on in which over 100 shots had [already] been exchanged, and probably some of his soldiers had been killed or wounded and to which there was no certainty as to what the outcome might be." According to Tinklepaugh, White appeared somewhat indignant at having had his social engagement interrupted, and nearly a half-hour passed before the colonel left the party to take command of his regiment.[36]

While Tinklepaugh had been urging White to take direct action to prevent a "veritable race war," Lieutenant Ryder had in fact taken steps to bring some sense of order to the scene in Bisbee. Ryder headed up Brewery Gulch with Chief Kempton and B. P. Guild, the editor of the *Bisbee Daily Review*. Guild had been inside the Copper Queen Hotel when the fighting broke out, and witnessed firsthand Ryder's bold attempts to defuse the situation. As they entered one of the segregated clubs they found some forty or fifty men inside the building. Guild also noticed a large number of empty bottles scattered around the club, "and that the smell of liquor was strongly in evidence there."[37]

Ryder addressed the troopers, "requesting them to bring their guns and lay them on the counter. None of them responded." Ryder then ordered them to turn over their automatic pistols, "the only response being when one of the sergeants informed him that they did not intend to disarm to be beaten up by the white folks." However, once Kempton had promised that he and his officers would provide them with protection, the soldiers agreed to line up outside and march out of the city in an orderly formation, provided that they could keep their weapons.[38]

Once they were out on the narrow street, the troopers marched down Brewery Gulch toward the main part of downtown Bisbee, with Ryder in the lead, the police officers following behind in a pair of automobiles. But, as the column made its way through the Gulch, a small group of four or five soldiers began to lag behind, and, according to Kempton, "one of them who had been acting mean throughout the affair continued to drop behind and curse." Kempton ordered the soldier to move it along. "Fuck you," the trooper replied. "I am a United States soldier and I don't have to." Kempton immediately pistol-whipped the man over the head and threw him into one of the

Contemporary view of Brewery Gulch, where members of the Tenth Cavalry were escorted out of the city on July 3, 1919. To the far right is the entrance to City Park, where Deputy Sheriff Joe Hardwick shot the last soldier wounded in the "Bisbee Riot." *Jeff Dolan*

police cars. When Guild noticed another soldier taking cover behind a telephone pole with his automatic pistol drawn, the newspaper editor climbed onto a pile of lumber and called out a warning to the officers, "whereupon the Negro withdrew, yelling to me, 'I will get you for this, you white son of a bitch.' "

Minutes later, Guild saw the same man take a position behind another post at the entrance to the city park. This time Joe Hardwick was ready, and as soon as the soldier raised his weapon, Hardwick shot him through one of his lungs. The other stragglers were then disarmed and forced into the officers' automobiles. "They resisted," Guild later told investigators, "two of them attempting to take the guns from the Chief of Police, at which time both of them were struck by the officers. In picking up the man who had been shot by Deputy Sheriff Hardwick, liquor was very noticeable on his breath." With the final round fired from Hardwick's six-gun, the Bisbee Riot of 1919 was over.[39]

As Colonel White and the unit's other officers finally assumed some level of command, the troopers of the Tenth Cavalry were marched back to their camp near Warren. The next day, the regiment participated in the annual

Fourth of July parade as if nothing had happened. The Buffalo Soldiers rode in an impressive column that included Sheriff McDonald, local fire companies, the Boy Scouts, nurses from the Red Cross, veterans of the Spanish-American War and the more recent fighting in Europe, as well as aging survivors of the Union and Confederate armies. That same day, the *Bisbee Daily Review* published an account of the riot that applauded the efforts of Chief Kempton and the other lawmen in suppressing the violence of the previous evening, claiming that "the occurrence was deeply deplored by practically the entire regiment as of a nature not at all typical of the relations existing between the cavalrymen of Fort Huachuca," and that the episode had been caused by those who had fallen under "irresponsible influences."[40] The US Army's official report was particularly critical of Bisbee's city "Bulls" under the command of James Kempton and Deputy Sheriff Joe Hardwick. "Other reports indicate that he was the only civil officer who shot a soldier," an army intelligence officer declared. "In view of the fact that it is estimated that there were between twelve and twenty civil officers in Bisbee at the time of the trouble," the officer continued, "in the opinion of the District Intelligence Officer it is significant that he is probably the man who shot every man who was injured by firing."[41]

With the parades and festivities over, Hardwick returned to his station in Douglas, but the fallout from the Bisbee Riot must have rankled him. On the night of July 8, 1919, just five days after the shoot-out with the Tenth Cavalry, Hardwick got into an argument with the Douglas chief of police and Lieutenant Thomas E. Pratt, who commanded the army's provost guard in the "smelter city." During the altercation, Hardwick allegedly drew his pistol and threatened to kill both men. Mayor Charles Overlock demanded that Hardwick be removed from the city and prosecuted for his offense. Sheriff McDonald transferred Hardwick from Douglas to Tombstone, and on Tuesday, July 15, Hardwick appeared in court, where he pled guilty to charges of assault and paid a $25.00 fine.[42]

On September 10, 1919, the *Bisbee Daily Review* announced that Hardwick had tendered his resignation in order to accept a deputy's job from Sheriff Henry Hall in neighboring Pinal County. Hardwick was evidently "incensed over a false report circulated in Bisbee that he had been 'canned,' stating that this was an absolute untruth," and that he had simply turned in his badge in order to take on a better-paying position with Hall's department. On

September 16, Hardwick left Tombstone for the mining town of Ray, where he took on his new assignment as a Pinal County deputy sheriff. However, by the time the Hardwicks relocated to Pinal County that fall, Alma Hardwick had been suffering from tuberculosis for nearly a year, and on January 28, 1920, she died at the age of thirty-six.[43]

Six weeks after Alma's death, on the evening of March 5, 1920, Joe Hardwick and a fellow deputy, forty-four-year-old Patrick Gorham, were called upon to serve an arrest warrant on Jose Sierra in Superior. Sierra, a Spanish-born miner, had allegedly threatened to take the lives of both himself and his wife. As Hardwick and Gorham approached the Sierra home, they found Mrs. Sierra "running and crying, with Sierra in pursuit with a gun." Then, as Sierra spotted the two deputies, he turned his weapon on Hardwick's partner. "I know you, Gorham," an enraged Sierra uttered, and "was in the act of pulling the trigger on his forty-five" when Hardwick jerked his own revolver from its well-worn holster, thumbed back the hammer, and blasted Sierra off his feet. The wounded man was loaded into an automobile and driven to Magma Hospital, but "was cold in death by the time he reached the sanitarium." A coroner's inquest was held the following day, during which the killing was ruled justified.[44]

Hardwick would serve as a deputy for the remainder of Sheriff Hall's term in office. Between September of 1921 and the spring of 1922, Hardwick variously worked as a watchman with the Southern Pacific Railroad and as a police officer in the town of Yuma, in the far southwestern corner of Arizona.[45] Then, in April of 1922, he was hired as a deputy by T. J. Worthington, the newly sworn-in chief of police in Calexico. When Worthington stepped down from his position six months later, Hardwick took over as the California border town's principal law enforcement officer. Altogether, Hardwick would hold down his job as chief of police for the better part of five years, during which time he survived both an attempt by a disgruntled subordinate to have him dismissed, partially on the grounds that he was a convicted felon, and yet another attempt on his life by a dangerous criminal.

On the night of January 4, 1925, Hardwick and two private detectives were searching for a man identified as Otto Best when they encountered R. D. Feathers, an African-American fugitive wanted in connection with a string of crimes in Idaho, Ohio, and California. As Hardwick entered the shack where Feathers was hiding, the outlaw opened fired with a revolver, the bullet striking a lucky Mexican coin that Hardwick carried as a watch ornament. Hardwick answered this assault by pumping five rounds into Feathers, killing him instantly.[46]

Hardwick's luck finally ran out two years later in February of 1927, when he shot a Los Angeles produce buyer named William A. Taylor, whom Hardwick allegedly discovered in a parked car in a compromising situation with a woman. After a brief struggle, Taylor made a move that Hardwick interpreted as threatening, and, thinking that Taylor was about to draw a weapon, the officer hauled out his trusty .45 and shot the unarmed Taylor in the chest, but didn't kill him. Hardwick was later charged with assault with a deadly weapon and went on trial that April. Once on the witness stand, Hardwick was questioned about his manslaughter conviction in Oklahoma fifteen years earlier. However, his lawyers were not permitted to bring up the veteran peace officer's official pardon. On May 6, 1927, Joseph B. Hardwick, referred to as the "Czar of Calexico," was found guilty and later sentenced to serve a maximum term of ten years in the California State Penitentiary at Folsom. During a sentencing hearing that May, Hardwick explained that he had been a lawman for many years. "But I'm through now," he told the court. "I've had enough."[47]

As it would turn out, Hardwick never spent a day behind the prison's walls. Pending an appeal, he was released on a $25,000 bond, and six months later, in November of 1927, Hardwick's conviction was reversed by the appellate court. The court's decision was based largely on the fact that Hardwick's attorneys had been unable to introduce testimony during his trial to show that he had been pardoned for his earlier manslaughter conviction in Oklahoma. His legal troubles behind him, the man who had worn badges in three different states and had shot and killed at least four men and wounded multiple others in shoot-outs with lawbreakers, settled into the mundane life of an auto mechanic. In January of 1931, a little over three years after his conviction was overturned, Hardwick's appendix burst, and he died on February 3, 1931.[48]

CHAPTER THREE

THE TOUGHEST TOWN ON THE SANTA FE

In his testimony Torres stated that he could have killed Town Marshal Shafer, Sheriff Harrington, and a number of other people had he seen fit to do so. He rather sneeringly remarked that shooting at the people who had surrounded him where he hid in the house from which he was taken captive, would have been like "shooting blackbirds for a pie."
—Williams News, *July 18, 1919*

To look at Victor H. Melick, or to talk with him, you would hardly suspect that he is a candidate for any office," the *Williams News* reported on September 6, 1918, "but he is. His candidacy may be attributed to the urgings of his friends more than to the aspirations of Mr. Melick, but there is no doubt of his ability to efficiently fill the office of constable of Williams precinct if the voters see fit to place him there."

Born in Vernon County, Missouri, on June 18, 1867, Victor Hugo Melick had first arrived in Williams, Arizona, in March of 1905, when he was thirty-seven years old, arriving just a few years after his younger brother, Dr. Prince Albert "Doc" Melick, had opened a medical practice there in the 1890s.

Located forty-four miles from the Coconino County seat in Flagstaff and sitting at an elevation of 6,748 feet, Williams had officially come into existence in 1881, when a post office was established there in anticipation of the arrival of the Atlantic and Pacific Railroad. Pioneer cattleman Charles Thomas Rogers was appointed as the settlement's first postmaster. According to Prince Albert's son, Durmont, the first Melicks had moved to Williams from Missouri during a time when Williams was still a "God awful frontier town," with more than its share of saloons, gambling houses, brothels, and Chinese "hop joints," as the town's opium dens were called.[1]

While mining towns like Jerome and Bisbee owed their growth to copper, gold, and other precious metals, Williams was built on sheep and cattle ranching, the logging industry, and the railroad. Eventually, with help from the Atlantic and Pacific (and later, the Atchison, Topeka and the Santa Fe), Williams served as a principal gateway to the Grand Canyon for tourists, and home to a fairly diverse community that included Anglo-Americans, Greeks, Swedes, Bulgarians, Mexicans, and Chinese, many of whom worked for the area's lumber companies.[2]

Like many boomtowns that sprang up throughout the Southwest in the 1870s and 1880s, Williams had gained a reputation for violence and ribaldry that would later inspire one writer to call it "the toughest town on the Santa Fe." Before the Atlantic and Pacific had even finished laying tracks through the settlement, Williams and the surrounding countryside had been the setting of a number of violent episodes that had ended in bloodshed.

One of the area's first shooting scrapes occurred in June of 1881, when a man named John Burton opened fire on one James Douglass at McCullum's Station near the base of Bill Williams Mountain. According to the *Arizona Weekly Miner*, the trouble began after Douglass had made some joking remarks to Burton about the stock that Burton was driving, "which so exasperated him that he retired to the stable, procured a shotgun loaded with buckshot, and returned firing at Douglass; one shot entered through his mouth, tearing out teeth and passing out behind the jawbone." Despite his injuries, Douglass managed to retrieve his own weapon and shoot Burton through the head, killing him instantly. Because Williams and its surroundings were then a part of Yavapai County, the painfully wounded Douglass had no choice but to mount up and ride more than fifty miles to the distant county seat at Prescott, where he was later examined and acquitted.[3]

Even after the turn of the century, as the Melick family and others settled in the community and civilization gradually began to take hold, Williams retained at least some of its raw frontier edge. "Williams is a unique town. It contains a population of about 1,500," a visiting Canadian journalist remarked in early 1902, "whose principal occupation seems to be gambling. There are numerous fine saloons in Williams, in which gambling games of all kinds, including roulette, faro, crap shooting, etc., are running constantly, and more particularly on Sunday, which happened to be one of the days the wandering scribe struck the place. There are said to be more shooting scrapes in Williams than any other town of its size in America. We found the saloonkeepers very nice, agreeable gentlemen, and when we left they presented us with several specimens of a familiar product known as 'Canadian Club,' and also some boxes of splendid Mexican cigars."[4]

The *Williams News* was quick to condemn the Canadian visitor and his entourage, who had apparently ventured no farther into town than the saloons and bordellos of Williams's "tenderloin district." "Williams, no doubt considering that she is a typical western town, has more decency and less lawlessness than is found in many a large eastern city," the *Williams News* explained, "and many were the exclamations of surprise and disgust at the free-and-easy manner in which some lady members of the party 'hung around' the so-called gambling dens."[5]

For years, primary responsibility for policing the region had fallen on the shoulders of the sheriff of Yavapai County. However, even after the county seat was connected to the Atlantic and Pacific Railroad by the Prescott and Arizona Central, keeping the peace and enforcing the law in this vast swath of northern Arizona proved to be a challenge for even the most capable of Western lawmen. In 1891 Coconino County had been formed by carving out huge portions of northern and eastern Yavapai County, and with it, a new sheriff's office under Ralph H. Cameron, headquartered in the county seat at Flagstaff. That same year, a new jail was established in Williams, and for the next ten years the town was policed by Coconino County deputy sheriffs and various precinct constables.[6]

Unlike a deputy sheriff or police officer, hired directly by the county sheriff, municipal chief of police, or city marshal, constables were elected officials whose primary function was to serve the needs of the district justice court. In the absence of a full-fledged local police force, county constables often played a more central role in keeping the peace in rural Western communities. And while they often worked closely with the county sheriff, and sometimes even held dual commissions as deputies, constables only earned a modest salary; in fact, many continued to pursue civilian careers while working as lawmen.[7]

During Williams's early years, the town was policed by a series of colorful lawmen who served as constables. One of them, a former deputy sheriff named Frank Morrell, earned the reputation as "the man taker of Williams." As a Deputy US Marshal, Morrell alternately chased outlaws throughout northern Arizona while also holding down the positions of constable and sanitary officer. In December of 1898, just a few weeks after winning reelection, Constable Morrell shot it out early one morning with fellow Williams constable Ed Hardesty in the Palace Saloon, and died with one bullet through his chest and a second round through his head. Hardesty immediately turned himself over to a Coconino County deputy sheriff and was acquitted of any wrongdoing by a coroner's jury. "Prior to the unfortunate affair both men were friends," the *Coconino Sun* explained, "and both were members of the same lodge of red men, and no one regrets the affair more than Constable Hardesty."[8]

In July of 1901, just a few days after thirty-six businesses, two hotels, and ten residences were consumed by a fire that swept through the town, the people of Williams petitioned the Coconino County board of supervisors to incorporate their community, in part to organize a more effective firefighting department. On July 9, Williams was officially incorporated, and within a week the town council took the first steps in creating their own police force by electing James Kennedy as their first town marshal. In the spring of 1908, Kennedy was succeeded by Charles S. Patterson, who brought to the job invaluable experience as a Coconino County deputy sheriff and special officer for the Santa Fe Railroad.[9]

The people of Williams didn't have to wait long to see what their new marshal was made of. On Friday, July 17, 1908, Coconino County Deputy Sheriff Esquipula Dominguez and James Duncan, an African-American bartender and veteran of the Philippine-American War, fought a wild gunfight at the Cabinet Saloon. "It seems that on the evening of the shooting Duncan had had some trouble with a 'soiled dove' of his own color, and had abused her," the *Williams News* explained, "whereupon the woman told her troubles to Deputy Dominguez, who went on a search for Duncan." Gunfire erupted almost as soon as Dominguez stepped inside the saloon. Duncan fired off five rapid shots, two of which hit Dominguez in the chest and in the throat. Dominguez managed to get off three rounds, with one bullet cutting Duncan's clothes and the others wounding bystanders Frank Shea and Jesus Sacramento. As soon as the mortally wounded deputy hit the floor, Duncan struck Dominguez over the head with his pistol.

Dominguez was quite popular with the Mexican community in Williams, and his violent death caused quite a commotion among his friends. According to Duncan's later statement, as Patterson escorted him toward the railroad depot, "there was a large crowd of Mexicans following us, and I am sure they would have killed me if I hadn't gotten away as soon as I did." As the angry mob closed in on the rail yards, Patterson loaded his prisoner onto the caboose of an eastbound freight train and waited for it to pull out of town. "The mob approached the caboose," the *Williams News* explained, "evidently on violence bent, when Patterson stepped outside and at the point of his gun persuaded the leaders to consider the situation thoroughly." Patterson's demonstration of grit had the desired effect, and the mob of would-be vigilantes kept a respectable distance from the caboose until the train pulled out for Flagstaff. Duncan was indicted for murder that September, though his case was later dismissed.[10]

In June of 1915, Robert Burns, the town's very capable night marshal, took over as marshal following the resignation of Charlie Wade. Throughout his tenure, Burns proved to be a "sleuth" when it came to solving crimes, and also earned a reputation for fearlessness in dealing with the various rough necks, bootleggers, and "hop fiends" that passed through Williams. Burns's time in office would also be marked by the passing of Arizona's Prohibition laws. According to Thomas K. Marshall, there were very few arrests in Williams for drunkenness during the first six months of Prohibition, "for Williams is now regarded as one of the cities in the State where it is impossible to get liquor, and Marshal Bobbie Burns has his eye on the only suspicious joint in the town. Those who knew Williams in the early days can scarcely recognize it now without its saloons and drunken men lounging about the streets. The lumber mills and logging camps find much greater efficiency, and the sheepmen have commented favorably upon the effect in lessening their trouble with sheepherders to practically nothing."[11]

However, just as in other parts of Arizona, bootleggers did not wait long to begin catering to the needs of area residents, and, in fact, Williams, "formerly known far and wide as the toughest town on the Santa Fe" was the scene of one of the first arrests for liquor violations just weeks after the state's Prohibition law went into effect in January of 1915. There was also the occasional encounter with a "hop jointist." On July 9, 1915, just a few weeks after he took over for Charlie Wade, Burns apprehended a man named "Shorty" Dunbar, "a hop fiend, who seems to have entertained hopes of opening up a hop joint in Williams. He was caught with the goods—pipe and pills, dope gun and supplies." And while Williams might not have been as tough as it was during its rough and rowdy boom years, frontier-style gunfights were not exactly unheard of during this period.

In July of 1916, Burns arrested Louis Montoya and Albinicio Rel after the two men "cut loose with their sixshooters at a bunch of other Mexicans." The suspects, who had come close to killing two men on the city streets, were later sentenced to terms in the Florence state prison.[12] Two months later, Burns tangled with a heavily intoxicated sheepherder named Augustine Balderamos. According to the *Williams News*, Burns "met Balderamos on Railroad Ave. between Taber and Park streets. The Mexican was drunk and in a fighting mood. He had a small automatic in his hand. Marshal Burns appropriated the gun, but not without much resistance from Balderamos, who clawed the marshal's face and tore his eyeglasses loose." Then, while Burns was in the process of recovering his spectacles, Balderamos made a run for it. Burns immediately drew his revolver and fired two shots at the fleeing man. One bullet lodged in Balderamos's foot, and he was apprehended by a local merchant a few minutes later.[13]

Despite his exemplary record as a keeper of the peace, Burns landed in hot water with the town fathers in the fall of 1918, after he publicly criticized the restrictions that had been put in place in Williams during the influenza epidemic that swept the nation at the end of World War I. During a town council session in January of 1919, Burns was removed from office and was replaced by sixty-two-year-old Peter Shafer, a native of Virginia with no particular experience as a peace officer. Despite his age and inexperience, the town fathers and the local newspaper placed enormous faith in their aging marshal. "He is a capable man," the *Williams News* reported, "and will do credit to the town in the capacity as Town Marshal. His friends—which is almost the same as saying all of the people in Williams—expect to see him make it unsafe for all lawbreakers, and especially the local bootleggers."[14]

Just a few weeks before Peter Shafer pinned on his marshal's badge, Victor H. Melick was sworn in as the new constable for the Williams precinct. Exactly why Melick decided to enter into law enforcement for the first time at the age of fifty is uncertain. Like his younger brother, Prince Albert, from the time that Melick had first arrived in Williams, he had sought to establish himself in the community and put down roots. Prior to announcing his candidacy for constable in 1918, Melick had once served as the manager of the Grand

Canyon Electric Light and Power Company, and by the time he took office as constable, he was still acting as the president of the Overland Telephone Company.

Throughout his years in Williams, Melick had also been an active member of the town's social scene, and though he was known as "a rather quiet sort of fellow," he had appeared in a number of amateur stage plays performed for local audiences. In March of 1911, Melick married twenty-four-year-old Saffronbelle Campbell, a "charming young society lady" who originally hailed from Kentucky.[15]

Despite his outward appearance of modesty and apparent lack of arrogance, it's possible that like so many other Western lawmen before him, Victor Melick saw the position of constable as a springboard to higher political office: justice of the peace, sheriff, or even a seat in the legislature. "He is an old resident of Williams," the *Williams News* noted in September of 1918, ". . . and during that time he has pursued his trade as an electrician and general mechanic. Thru his industry he has won a home for himself and family, and he is always reckoned as one of the permanent and substantial citizens of the town. He will not sour the town if he loses, and he will perform his duties . . . conscientiously if elected. He disclaims being a politician, and refuses to get out and campaign after the usual manner of candidates, but he has a large number of friends who are working hard for him, because they believe he is the man for the office."[16]

Third Street in Williams, Arizona, circa 1920s.   *Williams Public Library*

That November, Victor Melick beat his democratic opponent, Constable George "Scotty" McDougal, by forty-seven votes, and in early January of 1919 he assumed his responsibilities as a duly sworn constable in Williams, Arizona. Just like Peter Shafer, Melick replaced a peace officer with years' worth of experience as both a constable and a Coconino County deputy sheriff. Now, two novice lawmen were policing a community that, much like the mining towns along the border and the numerous rough-and-tumble settlements scattered throughout the high country of Arizona, still clung to a bit of a wild streak from its frontier past. And as it would turn out, Shafer and Melick would soon inherit from their predecessors a particularly troubling challenge in the form of a young repeat offender named Simplicio Torres.[17]

On a spring day in late April of 1919, just three months after Pete Shafer and Victor Melick had assumed their duties as peace officers, Simplicio Torres returned to Williams after serving a one-year hitch in the Arizona State Prison at Florence for burglary. The twenty-four-year-old was greeted with the familiar whine of steel saw blades from the lumber mills, mixed with the smells of fresh-cut logs and cool mountain air—a welcome reminder of life before the steel bars of Florence and endless hours spent in the prison's "dark cell." Having grown up in the high-altitude town along the Santa Fe railroad, Simplicio Torres was well known among the people of Williams, albeit mostly for a string of arrests and run-ins with the law, and a tendency toward erratic behavior.[18]

In September of 1916, Torres had been arrested on a charge of disorderly conduct, fined $25.00, and sentenced to ten days in the county jail. "Torrez [sic] is a bad Mexican who has been seeking a sentence of this kind for some time," the *Williams News* reported. However, Judge F. O. Twitty apparently had a change of heart, and soon had Torres released from custody, an act of kindness that quickly proved to have been wasted. "It seems that Judge Twitty reconsidered his decision in the matter and suspended [his] sentence and let the Mexican go," the *Williams News* explained on October 5, 1916, "and he did go, sure enough. He appropriated a horse and rode it nearly to death; he assaulted a cowpuncher and emerged from the fracas in a badly battered condition; he was again arrested and bailed, and he was finally tried last Tuesday and found guilty by a jury of six. Judge Twitty sentenced him Wednesday morning to pay a fine of $50 and serve 60 days in the county jail. Probably this will stick."[19]

Two months later, Deputy Sheriff Charlie Wade, former marshal of Williams, arrested Torres for breaking into a barn owned by the Pitman Valley Land and Cattle Company and stealing several bales of hay. Placed under a $500.00 bond, Torres was lodged in the city jail, where he continued to misbehave, and "during the night tore up the furniture and succeeded in getting hold of the hatchet used by the jailer in building fires." Apparently nobody noticed the missing hatchet until after Torres had appeared in court with it. "He claimed his intention was to break out of jail with the aid of the hatchet," the *Williams News* reported, "but it is suspected that he meant to make other use of it, since he had threatened the life of the judge."[20]

In February of 1917, Marshal Robert Burns escorted Torres to Flagstaff, where he was adjudged insane by the Superior Court of Coconino County and committed to the Arizona State Insane Asylum in Phoenix. Simplicio Torres's hospitalization was relatively brief, and within six or eight weeks he was once again back in Williams.[21]

In January of 1918, Torres was again arrested by Deputy Charlie Wade for burglary. According to court records, Torres ransacked the home of Oswald Miller and made off with a shotgun, a Winchester rifle, a pair of spurs, some boots, and number of other items. The following day, Miller tracked Torres to his camp, where he found the stolen weapons and other articles, which Torres freely admitted to having taken. Miller also discovered a fresh beef carcass about a mile from Torres's camp, and suspected that Torres had killed and butchered it. "He has been convicted here in the past two years of cruelty to animals and carrying concealed weapons," a judge's statement read, "and might have been convicted many times for the same offense. He seems to have a mania for stealing everything he can get his hands on."[22]

After pleading guilty to the crime of burglary, Simplicio Torres was sentenced to a one- to five-year term at Florence, and arrived at the state prison on February 5, 1918. According to his prison records, Torres almost immediately had trouble adjusting to prison life. On February 11, he was confined to the "dark cell" for four days for insubordination, and spent another sixteen days in solitary that March. In June, Torres was again placed in solitary for refusing

234

Name of Convict *Simplicio Torres* ; Alias ; Registered No. 5115

Property found on Convict

Expiration of Sentence with Credits *S* *8-24-1920*

STATE PRISON AT FLORENCE, ARIZONA

DESCRIPTION OF CONVICT

Crime *Burglary* ; Sentence *1 to 5 years* from *1-26-18* ; No. of Commitment

Received *2-5-18*

From *Prescott* County: *Yavapai* Race *Mexican* : Nativity *Arizona* ; Religion *Catholic*

Age *17* yrs. *6* mos.: Height *6* ft. *4½* inches; Weight *147* lbs.; Complexion *Dark* ; Expression *Pleasant*

Size of Head *7¼* inches; Forehead *Medium* Color of Hair *Black* ; Color of Eyes *Brown*; Size of Foot *6½*

Physical Peculiarities *—* Carriage *Erect* ; Condition of Teeth *Complete*

Scars and Deformities *Scar on knuckle of first finger of L hand.*
Scar on L temple V shaped Sc. on R side fore head Sc. on top of
of head Sc. on back of head

India Ink Marks *No*

Legitimate Occupation *Cow Boy.* : Knowledge of Other Trades *No*

Temperate *No* : Tobacco *Yes* ; Opium *No* ; Beard Worn When Received *No*

Married *No* ; Wife Living ; Has Children ; How Many ; Has Parents *Both*

Name and Address of Nearest Relation *Margarita Torres Box 113 Williams Ariz.*

Can Read *Yes*; Write *Yes*; Where Educated *Ariz* ; What System *Public*

Had Former Imprisonment *No*; in What Prison *Former inmate of State Insane Asylum*

When and How Discharged

PRISON RECORD

2-4-18. Insubordination. 4 Days Dark cell
3-11-18 " 16 . Condemned Cell
Wister Pear Camp 7-24-18
Locked in con. cell refusing to work
7-24-18. Released 7-6-18.
4-2-19 Ret'd to Prison
4-18-19 Paroled

By 1919, Simplicio Torres had experienced numerous run-ins with the law, and had spent time in both the Arizona State Insane Asylum and the Arizona State Penitentiary. *Arizona State Library and Archives* to work. His third visit to the solitary unit must have made an impression on the young outlaw, and Torres appears to have finished out his sentence without any other notable incidents. Torres would ultimately spend another ten months in prison, before receiving parole in the spring of 1919.

During the early-morning hours of April 20, 1919, just two days after her brother had been paroled from Florence, Torres's twenty-year-old sister Clarita committed suicide. "When her husband, who is employed by the Santa Fe, returned from his night's work," the *Williams News* reported, "she asked him for his revolver. He asked her what she wanted it for. She replied, 'I'll show you.' She then placed the revolver to her right temple and fired, dying instantly." It's possible the violent, self-destructive behavior that Torres would display on the streets of Williams in little more than a month was in some way triggered by Clarita's sudden death.[23]

Whatever his motivations might have actually been, however, sometime during the afternoon of May 31, 1919, Torres slipped into a stable located on Grant Avenue, between Third and Fourth Streets in Williams, and made off with a horse belonging to Ambrose Means, a prominent trapper and hunting guide, who had "piloted hunting parties of America's most prominent citizens, including Theodore Roosevelt." Accounts vary, but according to one of his granddaughters, Means may have actually given Torres permission to borrow the animal before leaving town on another hunting expedition. If this is true, then it would appear that Means had failed to inform his wife Mary. Sure enough, later that same day, Mary Means found Torres watering the horse just half a block away from her house, and noticed that the animal now wore Torres's saddle. She also saw "that someone, presumably Torez [*sic*], had tried to in some measure disguise the animal, having bobbed its mane and tail."[24]

Mary Means immediately confronted the former convict and demanded to know what he was doing with her horse. She also asked who had bobbed its mane and tail, and then insisted that he surrender the animal. Torres handed her the reins and headed home on foot.

Mary Means was not yet satisfied, however. Convinced that Torres had stolen the horse from the family stable, she sought out State Cattle Inspector Ed Hamilton and reported the supposed theft. Hamilton, along with Coconino County Deputy Sheriff John Paddock and fellow lawman Tom White, went to Torres's home to question the young man. When the officers arrived, Torres's mother claimed that her son wasn't at home, and the trio of lawmen left. A few minutes later, Hamilton returned and located Torres just as he was getting out of the bathtub. He called for the young outlaw to come out and "settle this thing up." Torres replied that he would come along just as soon as he was dressed.

"When he came out of the house," the *Coconino Sun* reported, "Hamilton took him by the arm and said: 'Come on, we'll go over to Means' and straighten this thing up. Torez [*sic*] replied that he did not want to go, and a few words were followed by a slight scuffle between the two men, in which Hamilton got a good hold on Torez's wrist and thought he could manage him that way." Then, Torres jerked a .32 caliber Colt semiautomatic pistol out of his pocket and said, "Drop 'er, Ed, right where you are, or I'll kill you." Hamilton let his own weapon drop to the ground, and with the lawman as his prisoner, Torres escorted Hamilton off in the direction of the Means home. Moments later, the two men were joined by Deputy Paddock, who drove up in an automobile on his way back to the Torres house to check on Hamilton. "Want a ride?" Paddock asked. "No. We'll walk on over," Hamilton replied.

"As they got in front of the White Garage," the *Coconino Sun* continued, "Hamilton suggested he go inside and telephone the man whom Torez [*sic*] said had given him permission to pick a horse out of a certain bunch, his claim being that that was the manner in which he got hold of Mrs. Means' horse. But the gun held ready in Torez's pocket prevented." Still unaware that Torres had the drop on his fellow officer, but perhaps suspecting that something was up, Paddock climbed out of his car and fell in with them as they continued up the street. As the trio passed a storefront, Hamilton whispered to Paddock, "This fellow has me disarmed; drop behind." The deputy then slipped away and went to retrieve his rifle.

Moments later, Hamilton himself "managed to get a little behind Torez [*sic*], saying, 'You go on up to Mrs. Means,' turned and dodged around the corner of Duffy's store, continuing on home to get another gun. The first thing he found was an automatic shotgun, which he discarded in favor of a .30-30 rifle." Just how Torres managed to lose both of his captives so easily is uncertain. It's likely that he was simply making it up as he went along, and that once he had Hamilton and Paddock covered with his automatic pistol, he didn't actually know what to do with them. In any case, Torres continued on to the

Williams, Arizona, as it would have looked just a few years before Constable Victor H. Melick's encounter with Simplicio Torres. This photo was taken a short distance from where Torres took a horse from the stable belonging to Ambrose Means.
Williams Public Library

Means home, his .32 tucked away in his pocket but still within easy reach. As he approached the house, Torres could see that Mary Means and Constable Victor Melick were both waiting for him, and Marshal Peter Shafer was not far away.[25]

"You are under arrest," Melick told Torres as the young man stepped toward them. "What for? I haven't done anything," Torres replied. The constable then began to question Torres about the stolen horse, and as the discussion went on, Torres started to turn away from Melick. "I want to go eat my supper," Torres told him. "I haven't had my supper yet, and you can wait as well as I can," Melick replied. Then, before the fifty-one-year-old lawman could react, Torres whipped out his .32 Colt and fired off three rapid shots at a distance of no more than ten feet. The first bullet hit Melick in the chest and perforated his heart. The second passed through his right lung. Both bullets tore through Melick's body and exited out his back, about three inches from his spinal column. As Torres took off running, Melick, who never fired a shot in anger in his entire life, "proved that the West still breeds men who die without a whimper, and, facing death, think only of the job [at] hand. Without a cry or moan of any kind, still standing, and without saying a word, he drew his gun, fired three times at the dodging figure before him, and slowly sank to the ground. He was dead within about five minutes."

As Victor Melick collapsed and died in front of Mary Means and a handful of other bystanders, Peter Shafer fumbled. "Marshal Shafer did not fire," the *Williams News* reported, "or offer assistance to his brother officer, as his revolver proved useless, and failed to go off. Torres ordered Shafer to remain where he was, or he 'would get him too.' " Shafer later defended himself to the city council and explained that he was sick at the time, and was only in town to mail some letters when the shooting took place.

While Shafer stood on the sidewalk with a jammed revolver in his hand, Torres briefly took cover behind an automobile belonging to Dr. George Rounseville, and then sprinted toward the Saginaw Manistee Lumber Yard, before turning east and heading for the Frank Adams house on the edge of town. In the meantime, while Marshal Shafer helped load Melick's body into Rounseville's car, the citizens of Williams took matters into their own hands. The death of one of their peace officers, the well-liked and highly regarded brother of one of the town's respected physicians, wasn't something that they were about to tolerate. "Every known weapon in all kinds of hands were soon seen everywhere. Not just one or two," the *Coconino Sun* reported, "but a number of women and youngsters who were really children, were on the streets with guns. The hunt for the murderer was on."[26]

While the people of Williams armed themselves and formed a posse, Deputy Charlie Wade, the former town marshal who had arrested Torres in 1916 and 1918, trailed Melick's killer to the Adams house. "Charlie Wade was close after him," the *Williams News* explained, "and asked the people occupying the Adams house if they had seen a Mexican running that way. The lady of the house replied that she had, and giving Wade a description, he felt sure of his man. At this moment she cried to Wade: '[T]here he goes now.' " As Torres raced toward what had once been the town's red-light district, Wade followed close behind and watched as the outlaw ducked into a house at the corner of Railroad Avenue and First Street. "Feeling sure of his game," the *Williams News* reported, "Wade quickly summoned a portion of the posse and surrounded the block."[27]

Meanwhile, as Wade and the enraged civilian posse cornered Torres in the vacant house and began to pepper the building with gunfire, someone had the presence of mind to telephone Coconino County Sheriff John Harrington in Flagstaff. Having won his badge in the same November election as Melick, Harrington, a fifty-six-year-old cattle rancher, commandeered a brand-new car from the Red Star auto line and set out for Williams with Undersheriff Bill Hicklin, County Attorney F. M. Gold, and Assistant County Attorney George Harbin. Hoping to reach Williams before the town's residents carried out some form of vigilante justice, the sheriff's party bombed down the country highway, "going faster than fifty miles an hour over some road that normally holds you down to twenty."

When Harrington arrived on the scene at 8:30 p.m., "things were moving fast toward a swift ending of the murderer's life." Taking charge of the situation, Harrington ordered Torres to "come out or be killed." Torres didn't respond to Harrington's demand, but was seen through an open window. "He threw himself flat upon the floor. Sheriff Harrington ordered the posse to fire," the *Williams News* reported, "and a volley rang out, that spelled death. The posse evidently fired high. A second and third volley was discharged through the walls of the frame building. Probably fifty shots were fired altogether, to none of which Torres responded." According to the *Coconino Sun*, the gunfire continued for about five minutes, "when Bill Hicklin caught sight of Torez [*sic*], just a glimpse of a shoulder and arm, and rushed into the house, through one vacant room and into the next room, where he found Torez on his knees, hands in [the] air, crying repeatedly, 'For God's sake, don't shoot me, help me!' "[28]

While Hicklin and Harrington pulled a slightly wounded Torres off the floor, the local vigilantes swarmed in on them. As Torres himself would recall two months later, "they no sooner got me to the door [when] the people rushed in and kicked me to a pulp. I was spitting up blood for over two weeks." Once he had Torres in custody, Harrington realized that the suspect would probably not survive the night if he remained in the Williams jail. Rather than risk the possibility that the killer would be lynched or beaten to death by the outraged citizenry, Harrington decided to try to sneak the wounded outlaw out of town and transport him to Flagstaff, where he could be secured in the more formidable county jail.[29]

Four days later, on the afternoon of Tuesday, June 3, 1919, Constable Victor Melick's funeral was held in the home of his younger brother, Dr. Prince Albert Melick, and "was one of the largest ever seen in Williams. Immense quantities of beautiful flowers marked the great esteem in which the deceased was held. Interment was made at the Odd Fellows cemetery, and the service of the Methodist church was performed by Rev. D. L. Reid, pastor."

The following day, while a bruised and battered Simplicio Torres lay in the county lockup under the care of his mother, Sheriff Harrington swore out an official criminal complaint against his prisoner, stating that Torres "did, then and there, willfully, unlawfully, feloniously, premeditatedly, and of his malice aforethought, kill and murder Victor H. Melick, a human being." On June 10, Torres was arraigned for felony murder.[30]

Torres's murder trial began on July 15, 1919, and lasted for a total of three days. Mary Means and other eyewitnesses described the theft of the horse and the details of the shooting death of Constable Melick, while Melick's brother, Dr. Prince Albert Melick, and two other doctors detailed the officer's fatal injuries. Mercer Hemperley, one of Torres's attorneys, "promised that no attempt would be made to deny that his client committed the murder, but that he would prove by the witnesses that the murderer was insane." Adding to the

Victor H. Melick's gravesite in Williams, Arizona.   *Jeff Dolan*

fact that Torres's sister had committed suicide that April, and that both Torres and an uncle had been admitted to the State Insane Asylum, Hemperley suggested that his client "was afflicted with homicidal mania," and that his criminal troubles had all begun when a "disreputable woman" had taught him how to drink liquor and smoke marijuana and had helped Torres "run through his savings of $600 in one month." On July 17, Torres himself testified that Melick had fired the first shot, and that he had only killed the officer in self-defense.

"In his testimony Torres stated that he could have killed Town Marshal Shafer, Sheriff Harrington, and a number of other people had he seen fit to do so. He rather sneeringly remarked that shooting at the people who had surrounded him where he hid in the house from which he was taken captive would have been like 'shooting blackbirds for a pie,' " the *Williams News* reported. That same afternoon, Torres's mother (in testimony translated by an interpreter) insisted that her son had "been good until he was twenty years old and bad after that," and was in fact insane and needed medical care. But, according to the *Coconino Sun*, "Orville Brown, cowboy, of Marshall Lake, formerly of Williams, was then called. Instead "of giving an opinion that Torez [*sic*] is insane, he said he thought he was simply a bad Mexican."[31]

Apparently, the jury agreed with Orville Brown's assessment, and on July 18, 1919, Simplicio Torres was found guilty. "The verdict was no surprise," the *Coconino Sun* declared, "and it was highly satisfactory to practically all of our people, even the Mexicans, apparently, among whom there is little sympathy wasted on the condemned man." Within days, Torres's lawyers had filed an appeal and gathered statements to support their position that Torres was mentally ill. Despite Hemperley's attempts to obtain a new trial, on August 4, 1919, Simplicio Torres was sentenced to death for the murder of Victor Melick, with the execution to be carried out on October 24 at the Arizona State Penitentiary at Florence. "After the sentence was pronounced," the *Coconino Sun* reported, "Torez said: 'Thank you very much, Judge; I hope when you get there, you'll get justice too.' "[32]

Appeals filed by Torres's lawyers, and the efforts of many passionate supporters to have his mental condition reevaluated, delayed Torres's execution until the following spring. Finally, on April 16, 1920, almost exactly a year after the suicide death of his sister, Simplicio Torres became the first convicted murderer to be hanged since the state had reinstituted the death penalty in 1918 after a brief two-year abolition of capital punishment.[33]

Heavily criticized for failing to stop Torres after he had killed Victor Melick, Town Marshal Peter Shafer was removed from office and replaced with his predecessor, Robert Burns. Likewise, former Constable George "Scotty" McDougal was appointed to assume Melick's post in June of 1919.[34]

Though Victor H. Melick may not have been the type of seasoned gun-fighting lawman who had helped to settle the West in its early days, and while he exhibited little of the heavy-handed nature of contemporaries like Joe Hardwick, Melick had nonetheless died "game" in the parlance of the fading frontier. Today, Victor Melick's grave lies just a few yards from the asphalt of Route 66, resting under a canopy of tall pines on a hillside overlooking the modern community of Williams, the toughest town on the Santa Fe.

CHAPTER FOUR
THE PURITY SQUAD

Smugglers in this district are getting desperate. They are well organized and they have openly made their boasts that they intend to kill any officer who tries to interfere with their operations.[1]

—*Jesse C. Stansel,*
El Paso County Deputy Sheriff, December 19, 1919

It was after midnight on Saturday, January 3, 1920, when Captain Claude T. Smith and Detectives Antonio Varela and Elmer Reynolds arrived at the end of Raynor Street in El Paso. Smith was a former Texas Ranger and a career lawman who had only recently been promoted to captain. Varela and Reynolds were also seasoned officers, tough men who were familiar with the nightlife in the border city. Just five months earlier, a knife-wielding burglar had slashed Varela when the detective tried to arrest him for breaking into a house. Despite his injury, Varela shot the man in the leg when he tried to escape and took him into custody. Reynolds, who had been with the El Paso Police Department since 1915, was known as an officer who was willing to walk "where angels fear to tread." That fall he and Varela had both taken part in the department's campaign against the "snowbirds," "cokies," and "hopheads," drug addicts who flocked to El Paso, Texas, in search of the narcotics that were readily available just across the Rio Grande in Ciudad Juarez.

The trio of officers was after a shipment of bootleg whiskey that was supposed to be coming across the border. Guiding them on this mission was Henry Renfro, a thirty-year-old African American and native of Malakoff, Texas, who had lived in El Paso for eighteen years. Renfro had told the detectives that he knew when the booze would be coming up from Chihuahua, and had agreed to show Smith and his men the spot where the *contrabandistas* would enter the United States with their illicit cargo. Renfro had a checkered history; less than three months earlier, he had been arrested and charged with federal liquor violations after he'd tried to sell several gallons of bootleg whiskey. The officers were probably just a little bit wary, keeping their hands close to their guns as they moved through the dark street. Legal enforcement of the Eighteenth Amendment, National Prohibition, was still two weeks away. However, by the time Claude Smith and his men stepped into the night's shadows with Henry Renfro, lawmen in El Paso had already been dealing with bootleggers for nearly three years. And just as smuggling had increased in the months following the end of World War I, so had the number of violent encounters between rumrunners and city police officers.[2]

Adding to any apprehension that the three detectives may have had during their nighttime journey was the news spreading through the ranks of local law enforcement that a colleague had just died in an area hospital. Two days earlier, Constable Sam Stepp, a thirty-three-year-old lawman who helped to police the Smelter District, and Special Officer W. H. Cain, had attempted to arrest two soldiers from the Nineteenth Infantry Regiment for the holdup of a railroad switchman. When Stepp and Cain caught up with the suspects, one of them took off on foot, while the other opened fire on Stepp, shooting him through the abdomen and right wrist. Another bullet knocked the grips from Stepp's revolver. Somehow, though, the badly wounded constable had still managed to shoot the soldier dead with a bullet to the heart.

"When the constable reached the hospital, he was still conscious," the El Paso *Herald* reported the next day. " 'I am just shot all to pieces,' the officer told the nurse who answered the door. He walked to the operating table, called for his wife, and told her he was going to get well." Sam Stepp held on until 6:30 p.m. on January 2, when he died with his wife by his side at Providence Hospital.[3]

Six hours later, Claude Smith and his fellow detectives followed Henry Renfro into a neighborhood that would prove to be one of the deadliest battlegrounds in Prohibition-era El Paso. As the lawmen and their informant passed Cypress Avenue and reached the end of Raynor Street, they came to Cordova Island and the International Boundary. Known to locals simply as "the Island," Cordova was the result of an engineering effort to redirect the main flow of the flood-prone Rio Grande twenty years earlier that left a 382-acre zone of dry land north of the river that remained the sovereign territory of Mexico. Sticking into Texas like a thumb, and surrounded on three sides by the City of El Paso, "the Island" would prove to be a popular haunt for bootleggers moving their contraband across the border.[4]

Just as they reached the Island, Renfro whipped out a pistol and opened fire on Smith and Detectives Reynolds and Varela. As if on cue, with Renfro's gunshots still echoing in the lawmen's ears, "a squad of men" began shooting from the darkness on the Mexican side of the line. It was an ambush. Caught off guard and facing a sudden assault by Renfro and an unknown number of gunmen, the three officers drew their own weapons, turned them on their double-crossing informant, and let him have it. Renfro was hit by five bullets that penetrated his head, chest, and leg, and was dead by the time he hit the ground. When the smoke cleared, an estimated forty to fifty rounds had been fired between the lawmen and the smugglers, with Renfro the only known fatality. In less than seventy-two hours, three men—Constable Sam Stepp, Henry Renfro, and a US soldier—had all died violent deaths in El Paso. The year 1920 was barely three days old, and already the legendary Texas city had seen its first casualties for the bloody decade later remembered as "the Roaring Twenties."[5]

In this circa 1918 photograph, El Paso Police Chief Charles E. Pollock poses with members of his senior staff. From left to right: Dr. J. A. Hardy, police surgeon; Sgt. J. D. Thompson, Capt. S. H. Veater, Capt. William A. Simpson, Pollock, Inspector James Walter Reese, Capt. Harry Phoenix, Sgt. J. F. Caplinger, and Sgt. Claude T. Smith. *Border Heritage Center, El Paso Public Library*

Charles E. Pollock had only been the chief of the El Paso Police Department for a little over two months when he was called to attend a mass meeting inside the chambers of the El Paso City Council on Wednesday, December 26, 1917. The past few days had included raids by his officers that had shut down some 160 illegal clubs throughout the city, and somehow the chief had still found the time to dress up as Santa Claus for the children at the local Rescue Home. America was at war, and for six months, El Paso had been in the process of reshaping its wild frontier image. It had been hoped that, given the city's long relationship with the US Army, El Paso would host one of the sixteen divisional cantonments that the War Department was establishing to prepare the National Guard for the battlegrounds of the Western Front. "Because of its strategic location," the *El Paso Herald* reported in May, "its climate and railroad facilities, El Paso will probably be selected as the location of a division cantonment of the new national army, according to Brig. Gen. Harry A. Greene, president of a board of army officers in session here." However, El Paso's notoriety for vice and gambling that had once earned the city its dubious reputation as "the Monte Carlo of the United States" had worked against it. "Evils exist and have for thousands of years, and if there is any way by which we can rectify them we are willing to do so," Mayor Davis had told the *Herald* on June 2.[6]

While much of the gambling and prostitution that made up El Paso's nightlife had relocated across the river to Ciudad Juarez in the early years of the twentieth century, as recently as the spring of 1917, a red-light district, or "neutral zone," had continued to operate within South El Paso's mostly Hispanic *Chihuahuita* ("Little Chihuahua"). "Prostitution was an accepted thing in the early days," newspaperman Chester Chope recalled. "When I came here, police were moving nightlife women from downtown houses and hotels to a newly established zone of tolerance, as they called it . . ." And if a cowboy, railroad worker, or curious visitor couldn't find what he was looking for in El Paso's zone of tolerance, he could just as easily take his chances across the river in Ciudad Juarez, which had already developed its own notoriety as a tourist destination where vice was rampant.[7]

Throughout its early history, El Paso had been one of the Wild West's wildest towns, where some of the frontier's most legendary gunfighters and lawmen had made their mark, or found a permanent residence in one of the town's two principal cemeteries. While the death of El Paso's last semi-famous gunman, Mannie Clements, in 1908, marked the end of an era, there remained a bit of a dangerous wild streak left over from El Paso's storied past. "In those days, El Paso was a wide open town," Chester Chope later remembered. "The prisoners were primarily dope addicts, drunks, etc. Marijuana was common in those days, and narcotics addicts came to El Paso because it was easy to get drugs. The drugs were manufactured across the border. There were frequent fights and killings; every Saturday night we expected to have a shooting before the first edition."[8]

Having taken office just days after the American declaration of war against Germany, on April 6, 1917, and with patriotic fervor at an all-time high, Mayor Charles Davis was determined that El Paso would fulfill her obligation to the nation. Where Protestant clergy and other progressive reformers had come up short in their previous efforts to clean up El Paso, the battle against Germany would now succeed. Besides, not only was the city's honor at stake, but El Paso's economy had also enjoyed a financial boost during the buildup of forces during the campaign against Pancho Villa in 1916. The sudden influx of tens of thousands of American troops mustering in El Paso was sure to have an even greater impact on the local economy. "Each cantonment will have a population of close to 30,000 men and 7,000 animals," the *Herald* had reported in May, "and in addition to substantial quarters for the troops, there must be lighting, sewerage, and water facilities, roads and railway connections."[9]

Not ready to squander an opportunity that would both boost El Paso's economy and demonstrate its support of the war effort, on Wednesday, June 6, 1917, the El Paso City Council ordered Chief of Police B. J. Zabriskie to shut down "the segregated district in Chihuahuita and all other houses of immoral character, regardless of location in the city." Brothel owners were then warned that they had until Saturday night, June 9, to shut down, or risk being raided by Zabriskie's officers.

Regardless of these efforts, Davis's cleanup campaign wasn't enough to convince the federal government that El Paso should host one of the cantonments. Adding to the concerns over vice and "social disease" that soldiers might be exposed to, a series of dust storms in late June convinced the army to locate their cantonment elsewhere. As Rotary Club President Robert Krakauer explained to a group of Red Cross Workers, "God had given El

Paso a sandstorm one day and thereby this city lost an army cantonment, but despite this El Paso is willing to do its share for the government during the war."[10]

While Chief Zabriskie and his officers had begun shutting down El Paso's brothel industry, the US government had taken steps to eliminate another popular pastime. The country's entry into World War I had provided ample fodder for American prohibitionists to push their dry agenda and institute policies that would ultimately affect the entire nation well after the conflict had ended. Enacted on May 18, 1917, the Selective Service Act authorized the raising of a national army to fight in Europe by establishing the first wartime draft since 1865, and outlawed both prostitution and the sale of intoxicating liquors to soldiers within a zone of five miles from any military garrison. Naturally, with Fort Bliss just outside the city limits, this had included El Paso. "What's a poor El Paso saloon man to do?" the *Herald* asked. "The Government tells him he will be fined $1,000.00 if he sells liquor to a soldier in uniform. The city of El Paso has an ordinance making it a fine of $200 for any person in the city to discriminate in a business way against a man in uniform."[11]

Almost as soon as the law was in place, El Paso had had some of its first trouble with bootleggers. On June 12, 1917, the *Herald* reported the arrest of Frank McDougall, who was taken into custody by police on a charge of selling liquor to soldiers in South El Paso. "Many schemes are resorted to by the soldiers to get their 'drams,' " one article explained, "and equally as many are resorted to by civilian bootleggers to get the drinks to the soldiers." Apparently, one of the favored methods involved groups of soldiers checking into cheap hotel rooms and sending out one of their comrades in a set of civilian clothes to buy a suitcase of booze for his partners. "In other words," the *Herald* described, "instead of going to the saloon and drinking, these small groups form private clubs, buy their booze wholesale, and thus thwart the law and acquire a jag with impunity."[12]

While El Paso had missed its initial opportunity to welcome the divisional cantonment that summer, by the early winter of 1917, there was renewed hope that the War Department would reconsider El Paso as a site for one of the training camps. In December, Mayor Davis had traveled to Washington, DC, with Senator Claude Hudspeth in order to meet with federal officials and plead their case. Returning to El Paso just before the Christmas holiday, Davis told the *Herald* on the morning of December 26, "[W]e are going to do what the government asks, no matter what the costs nor what methods have to be adopted." Then, Davis summoned Charles E. Pollock and a large gathering of county and city officials to meet with him that afternoon at 3:00 p.m.

Known for his "unqualified popularity," forty-seven-year-old Charles Pollock did not much look like the typical Western lawman. He was a big, round-faced "roly-poly man," a far cry from the gunfighters who had once worn the badge of El Paso city marshal. Born on a farm in Lincoln, Illinois, Pollock had gone west with his family at the age of seventeen. After a few short years punching cattle in New Mexico, Pollock turned his back on the cowboy life and took a job as a railroader in the Pecos Valley. Later, he moved to El Paso, where he worked on "the old White Oaks line," marrying Miss Cora Phillips in August of 1900. Having moved up the ladder over the years, from brakeman to engineer and, finally, conductor, Pollock was working for the Mexican Central when the Revolution broke out in 1910. Returning to El Paso, Pollock's career in public service had begun with a stint as the inspector of city parks under Mayor Tom Lea, followed by an appointment as desk sergeant of the police department. In the spring of 1917, Pollock had been elected as judge of the El Paso Corporation Court, where he presided over a courtroom located on the second floor of the Central Police and Fire Station.

Throughout his tenure, the likable Judge Pollock developed a reputation for the colorful rulings, or "Pollockisms," that he made from the bench, many of which were reprinted in the El Paso *Times*. In one such case, Pollock was faced with a ten-year-old boy who had thrown a rock at a young girl. " 'Have you ever been arrested before?' [the judge asked.] Tears came to the boy's eyes as he explained that it was his first offense. 'That being the case,' continued the court, 'I am going to send you home; but next time you are before me, I may keep you all summer long. Do you understand?' The lad only nodded an affirmative. A big lump in his throat kept him from talking. He turned and fled from the courtroom as fast as his bare feet would carry him."

That October, Pollock was appointed as chief of police to fill the vacancy caused by the resignation of B. J. Zabriskie. "He has not won his popularity

A former railroad engineer and conductor, Charles E. Pollock served as judge of the El Paso Corporation Court prior to his appointment as chief of police in 1917.
Border Heritage Center, El Paso Public Library

by long and brilliant speeches," the department's 1918 yearbook would read, "nor by impressing one with his importance; he has done it with his presence. When you look at him you like him, when you hear him speak four words you are his friend. He is the biggest evidence in the world that the old adage '[N]obody loves a fat man' is all wrong."[13]

Thanks in large part to the arrival of the railroads in the early 1880s, the city that Pollock safeguarded as chief of police had come a long way from its origins as a dusty adobe village in a remote corner of the Southwest. For decades, the small American community of El Paso, Texas, had stood in the shadow of its older sister across the Rio Grande, *Paso del Norte*, as Ciudad Juarez was known prior to 1888. The El Paso of 1917 was a modern metropolis of streetcars, telephones, paved boulevards, brick buildings, and automobiles that some of its earliest pioneers might not have easily recognized. A $1 million cement factory had been built in 1909, and the massive smelter owned by the American Smelting and Refining Company (ASARCO) employed hundreds of workers and processed ores from mines throughout northern

Mexico and the American Southwest. That May, the Wigwam Theater, once a saloon where gunman John Wesley Hardin had owned an interest, had shown Cecil B. DeMille's *Romance of the Red Woods*, a Mary Pickford western set during the California Gold Rush. A few weeks later, Hollywood cowboy William S. Hart appeared in *Wolf Lowry* at El Paso's Grecian Theater, playing a "tyrannical cattleman suddenly changed into a bashful suitor." According to a special census conducted the year before, El Paso's population had once again swelled, from 39,239 in 1910, to 61,898 in 1916, an increase of over 20,000 residents, many of them refugees who had fled the revolutionary violence that had ravaged Mexico for six years. By 1920, El Paso's population would reach 77,560 souls, more than 40,000 of whom were foreign-born.[14]

However, just as in other parts of Texas, the turmoil of the Mexican Revolution had exposed some of the racial tensions that existed between Anglo Texans and Hispanics in the city. El Paso was the only major American city to witness firsthand some of the most critical fighting of the war. Given its location at the terminus of the Mexican Central Railroad, and its proximity to the supplies and weaponry available in El Paso, Ciudad Juarez was considered one of the most critically important objectives in northern Mexico. Between 1911 and 1919, a series of battles would be fought for control of the border town, each one drawing crowds of spectators to the banks of the Rio Grande and to El Paso's rooftops. Between the various engagements, El Paso acted as a base of operations for exiled politicians, soldiers of fortune, and arms smugglers, and a destination for Mormon refugees and thousands of Mexicans who fled the chaos.[15]

Though El Paso had yet to witness one last revolutionary battle for its sister Ciudad Juarez in 1919, the ongoing troubles in Mexico were now of little concern to the men who answered Mayor Davis's call for a meeting on December 26, 1917. In addition to the Falstaffian chief of police, the gathering included County Sheriff Seth B. Orndorff, US Customs Collector Zach Lamar Cobb, Chairman A. P. Coles of the Chamber of Commerce Military Affairs Committee, the entire city council, Davis's two predecessors in the mayor's office, Charles E. Kelly and Tom Lea, as well as Senator Hudspeth. Once the session had been called to order, Davis informed the officials of the details of the meetings that he and Hudspeth had taken with Secretary of War Newton D. Baker and Raymond Fosdick, chairman of the Commission on

Training Camp Activities. "Secretary Baker doesn't feel unkindly towards El Paso," Davis told them, "but demands that we secure a clean bill of health from Mr. Fosdick before he locates a cantonment here."

"When I discussed the matter with the secretary," Hudspeth added, "he referred me to Mr. Fosdick, who told me he would recommend the placing of a cantonment here if we did certain things." Hudspeth then explained that he had been shown several government reports on El Paso that claimed, "Prostitution widespread; no police suppression," and "Bootlegging universal, mainly by jitne [sic] drivers and Mexicans." "Between prostitutes and bootleggers and soldiers," Davis told them, "we prefer soldiers." "While the secretary was friendly to El Paso as a whole," Customs Collector Zach Cobb added, "he was just as unfriendly to those things that have crept into our city that are as much a detriment to us as to soldiers . . . We cannot get a cantonment unless we in good faith eliminate those evils. We are confronted with the fact that things exist here that cannot exist side by side with a cantonment. We have to put the illegal dives out of business."

"If you give me the men I want and keep the taxpayers off my back, I'll clean up the city." Chief Pollock told them. For his part, Pollock had already carried on with the work begun by B. J. Zabriskie that spring, and that had included the raids he and Sheriff Orndorff had ordered earlier in the week. "Chief Pollock has struck the keynote of the situation. From Saturday to Tuesday he has done wonders by way of cleaning out clubs. There were 161 in the city and practically none remain. But a fight of that kind has to be kept up and extra police officers are needed," County Attorney W. H. Fryer told them.

Before the meeting had been brought to a close, "every citizen present raised his hand in pledge to support mayor Charles Davis and the city officials and sheriff Seth B. Orndorff and the county officials in the work of eradicating the evils complained of by the government. The eradication is to take place at once, according to declaration of the mayor." The council also voted to adopt a new city ordinance, to take effect immediately, that would impose a $200.00 fine on anyone caught selling liquor to soldiers, adding their own local penalties to the federal law that had taken effect that spring. That same day, Davis instructed Chief Pollock to establish two separate four-man squads of police officers, "which will be on duty day and night" with specific orders to shut down vice in El Paso.

Before the month was over, these two units of city detectives would become known as "purity squads," and they would include some of El Paso's toughest and most seasoned lawmen. If there was any doubt about how serious Davis may have been about wiping out what remained of El Paso's nightlife, it was certainly cleared up in early January when he addressed a special committee created to help oversee the reforms. "I have appointed you to clean up the city," Davis told them, "and go as far as you like."[16]

Of all of the lawmen in El Paso who would serve as one of Pollock's front-line soldiers in the city's campaign to rid itself of vice, few would have as much of a role to play as Detective Claude T. Smith. Born in Williamson County, Texas, in April of 1878, Smith had followed his older brother Ed into law enforcement, first serving as a deputy constable in their hometown of Taylor, and later as a member of the Houston Police Department. Then, in July of 1909, just three months after his thirty-first birthday, Smith enlisted as a private in Company B of the Texas Rangers under the command of Captain Tom Ross.[17]

Smith's early days with the Rangers had provided him with one of his first opportunities to enforce local liquor policies. On August 10, 1909, less than two weeks after Smith joined the company, Ross's men conducted a raid in the "dry" city of Amarillo, in which they seized some two thousand bottles of beer, wine, and whiskey, and then destroyed the contraband alcohol. "At present the Rangers are acting under the provisions of the recently enacted search and seizure statute. They searched many places and discovered intoxicants in different quantities. The raid last night was the first in which the wholesale destruction of wet goods was practiced," the *Brownsville Herald* reported. Three months after the Amarillo raid, Company B was transferred to the town of Ysleta, in order to trade places with the Rangers of Company D, under the command of the legendary Captain John R. Hughes.[18]

While based in Ysleta, Claude Smith worked out of the El Paso County sheriff's office with fellow Ranger James Walter Reese, and in a preview of things to come, Smith again found himself dealing with violators of liquor ordinances. "C. T. Smith of the Ranger force has warned all saloonkeepers here and on the road to El Paso that the saloons must be kept closed on

J. F. Caplinger
Traffic Seg't.

John Wood
Seg't of Police

J. D. Thompson
Seg't of Police

C. T. Smith
Seg't of Dectives

Prior to joining the El Paso Police Department for the first time in 1911, Claude T. Smith (far right) had worn a number of badges as a Texas peace officer, and had served in Company B of the Texas Rangers under the command of Captain Tom Ross.   *Border Heritage Center, El Paso Public Library*

Sunday according to law. The Rangers will see that this law is not violated," the El Paso *Herald* reported on March 22, 1910.[19]

The following year, Smith resigned from the Texas Rangers and signed on as an officer with the El Paso City Police Department. He would spend two years with the force, during which time Smith quickly moved up the ranks, from patrolman to detective. Then, in 1913, he left the city police in order to take a job as a railroad policeman, a position he held for the next two years. Returning to the El Paso PD in 1915, Smith once again served as a "city sleuth" under the command of Chief of Detectives Jesse C. Stansel, a veteran El Paso lawman and investigator.

Smith's second term with the police department was a short one, however, and on May 6, 1915, he was relieved of duty by Mayor Tom Lea. It would appear that his dismissal came as a result of collecting fees from local prostitutes, a long-standing system of enforcement and vice control that Mayor Lea had shut down that very day. After losing his job in El Paso, Smith went to

While many rural departments in the Southwest lacked anything in the way of uniforms, by the time of the World War I–era cleanup campaign, the El Paso Police Department had long since adopted uniforms for its force of patrolmen. *Border Heritage Center, El Paso Public Library*

work as an officer for the Chino Copper Company in New Mexico, where he remained employed throughout 1916. Then, in August of 1917, while El Paso was in the midst of its wartime cleanup efforts, the thirty-nine-year-old lawman was again reinstated as a city detective. Regardless of what may have led to his being dismissed two years earlier, Smith was still a highly qualified lawman, known for his "energy, intelligence, acumen, observance, and ability."[20]

Compared to the rural law enforcement agencies scattered across the Southwest at the time, the El Paso Police Department was a professional organization that included a uniformed patrol division, a team of mounted officers who alternately rode horses or drove automobiles, a motorcycle unit, and a traffic squad. There was also a four-man unit of patrol drivers, a trio of jailers, and a female police matron. Having finished out his term as sheriff the year before, Peyton Edwards now acted as police court attorney, while Ben F. Jenkins had taken Charles Pollock's position as police court judge. Commanding El Paso's force of rank-and-file uniformed officers and plainclothes city detectives was a trio of well-liked captains, including Captain S. H. Veater, a Utah native, and the popular Harry Phoenix, a native of New York, who, like Claude

CAPT. P. H. PHOENIX
Police Department

CAPT. W. A. SIMPSON
Detective Department

CAPT. S. H. VEATER
Police Department

A native of New York, Harry Phoenix (left) was a well-liked captain in the El Paso Police Department who would meet a violent end in 1921. Captain William A. Simpson (center) had a reputation as being both hard and bighearted. A native of Utah, Captain S. H. Veater (right) had once patrolled South El Paso on horseback, and in 1915 had shot and killed a man who opened fire on him during an altercation at a dance.   *Border Heritage Center, El Paso Public Library*

Smith, had first joined the department during the early years of the Mexican Revolution. Taking over the detectives' bureau that autumn was Captain William Simpson, who had once been in charge of the city's chain gang, and was known as "the hardest-hearted man in El Paso, and at the same time, the biggest-hearted."[21]

Serving as an El Paso detective for the third time in five years, Claude Smith was reunited with his old Ranger comrade James Walter Reese, and a colorful team of plainclothes detectives who would find themselves on the front lines of Mayor Davis's campaign against vice as members of the purity squads. Among those Smith now served with were Detectives Ed Mebus, Tom York, Anthony Varela, Elmer Reynolds, and Juan Franco, a Hispanic officer who had originally come to El Paso in the 1880s and was then the oldest man on the department's roster. An additional member of the detectives' bureau was another old-timer, the Australia-born Charles E. Matthews, a former

John Redmon   W.J.Stewart   Ed Mebus   (Billy Smith) Chas. Matthews

P.M.Jacobs   T.M.York   Juan Franco   Elmer Reynolds

El Paso's team of "city sleuths" included Charles Matthews (upper right), a former prizefighter known as "The Australian Billy Smith," and Juan Franco (bottom, second from right), both of whom had served as peace officers in and around El Paso since the 1890s. Elmer Reynolds (lower right) was working with Claude T. Smith and Antonio Varela the night they faced an ambush by Henry Renfro.

Border Heritage Center, El Paso Public Library

Rough Rider and retired prizefighter who was known as "The Australian Billy Smith." In time, they would be joined by Smith's older brother Ed, who would work as an El Paso city detective on and off until 1923. "Every officer is and necessarily must be a distinctive type," the department's 1918 yearbook would read. "He carries his life in his hands every minute of the day and night. He must be keen of eye, quick in action, and cannot know the use of fear. It is traditional the members of this department have met every emergency in a manner which spells the gallantry of the best of the [S]outhwest . . . They are men of whom the city and the country are justly proud."[22]

Working closely with their counterparts in the sheriff's department, and backed up by uniformed army soldiers from Fort Bliss, El Paso's purity squads got to work almost as soon as they were assembled by Chief Pollock on December 27, 1917. The purity squad idea was not an altogether original concept. In Utah, the Salt Lake City Police Department had a similar organization to enforce Prohibition, as did police departments in Denver, San Francisco, Tulsa, and a number of other large American cities. El Paso's squads got off to a bit of a rocky start, however. During one of their first operations on the night of December 28, just two days after the city had adopted its ban on the sale of liquor to military personnel, one of the squads engaged in a gun battle that nearly cost an innocent man his life.

Believing that a house located at 3921 Madison Avenue was the scene of a bootlegging operation, a team of detectives that included James Walter Reese, Captain Simpson, Ed Mebus, and a party of soldiers traded shots with the home's owners, who turned out to be US Army Captain Wylie White and his startled wife. Only minutes before, White had been awakened by the sound of burglars breaking into the residence and had run them off at gunpoint. " 'The purity squad' hunting for a reported bootlegging place and not knowing they were near Capt. White's home, came up as the three burglars were running off," the *Herald* reported the next day. When the officers began knocking on his doors, White mistook them for the hoodlums, and opened fire from his bathroom window. Firing a salvo of pistol shots, Captain White managed to hit an army lieutenant in the hand and hip, and grazed Mebus with a round to the shoulder. The detectives and their military backup then returned fire with their own weapons, striking White in the chest with a bullet that penetrated a lung, but didn't kill him. "The shooting will be investigated in the court of Justice J. M. Deaver," the *Herald* explained, "technical charges of assault having been lodged against the members of the 'purity squad.' "[23]

Despite the shoot-out at the White residence and the resulting legal complications that followed, El Paso's purity squads continued with their sweeps across the city, raiding clubs and residences without warrants, targeting prostitutes and bootleggers dealing in illegal liquor within the five-mile zone. At the same time, Sheriff Seth Orndorff initiated his own cleanup crusade outside of the city limits. On Sunday, January 13, Deputy Charles Litchfield arrested an entire family in the Smelter District, "from a 65-year-old-grandmother to a 10-year-old grandson," on bootlegging charges. Then, just a few days later, Orndorff and a squad of deputies raided a bawdy house right across the street from the county hospital, where they arrested its madam, Pearl Rogers, and discovered a fourteen-year-old girl working as a prostitute. Rogers was indicted on state charges of assault, as well as federal charges for operating a brothel within five miles of a military reservation and violations of the Mann Act., a law that made it a crime to transport women across state lines for "immoral purposes."[24]

Regardless of any progress that Orndorff's department might have made during the winter of 1918, the sheriff encountered numerous obstacles that prevented a more effective campaign from taking place. During a mass meeting held at the El Paso Chamber of Commerce on March 3, 1918, Orndorff explained why the cleanup had so far come up short. Orndorff even admitted that two of his men were on intimate terms with prostitutes, "but we knew this when we employed them. They were employed for the purpose of getting information that we could get in no other way." Orndorff explained that the vice crusade had been forced to let up because of a lack of funds with which to hire additional men. "At the present time," Orndorff told those gathered in the chamber, "we have but two deputies engaged in vice work. We need at least a half a dozen. There are more women in the county jail today than there ever have been in the history of El Paso. We cleaned up a notorious dive across from the county hospital. But it is hard to find deputies who will not protect prostitutes."

Five days after the chamber of commerce meeting, on the night of March 8, 1918, James Walter Reese and six other detectives were deputized for a raid on the Franklin Inn, eight miles east of El Paso on the road to Ysleta, where they took thirty people into custody. At the same time, Captain Simpson and another team of deputized city officers also raided the Venice Road House, another club on the outskirts of the city. Rounding out an active night of combating vice, Claude Smith and three other detectives arrested a trio of women on charges of "vagrancy," while two others were apprehended by a uniformed patrolman. The following week Claude Smith and his "purity squad" broke up an illegal card game at the Hollenbeck Hotel.[25]

While the purity squads under Sheriff Orndorff and Chief Pollock tackled prostitution and the sale of liquor to American soldiers, the "dry forces" in El Paso, and in the Texas Legislature, continued their crusade to outlaw alcohol across the state. That winter, El Paso's anti-saloon faction circulated a petition that called for a special "local option" election to take place on January 30, 1918. "Whiskey killings cost the taxpayers of the city and county thousands of dollars," Judge Dan M. Jackson told the men's club of the First Presbyterian Church just before the election. "El Paso can't afford to have saloons, simply as a business proposition. They must be throttled as nonproducers and public waste, in this time of conservation." Despite the passionate arguments that the "drys" made in favor of Prohibition, the people of El Paso voted against the local option, 2,421 to 2,207.

A simultaneous effort on the county level also came to a similar conclusion. While many El Pasoans might have supported the closing of the red-light district and a ban on the sale of intoxicants to Uncle Sam's troops, the city's older residents—who still held on to El Paso's frontier heritage—and many of its Hispanic (Catholic) voters were simply unwilling to take reform any further.[26]

Though the "drys" may have been dismayed by the local election returns in January, a statewide effort to control alcohol was still under way. On March 11, 1918, just one week after Texas ratified the Eighteenth Amendment, the legislature passed a law that banned the sale of liquor within a ten-mile zone of any training camp in the state, effectively turning El Paso into a dry town, whether its voters liked it or not. That same month, Texas passed its own Prohibition law, similar to the dry policy that had been adopted in Arizona three years before, which would take effect on June 26, 1918. Already faced with the immediate impact of the ten-mile-zone policy, on April 15, 1918, every saloon in El Paso shut its doors in order to comply with the new legislation. "A wild night is the report made by the majority of the city policemen who were on duty Monday night. The last moments of king booze's sway were celebrated in every beer garden and saloon in El Paso in a manner which indicated the belief of the celebrants that whiskey would never come back," the *El Paso Herald* reported the next day. While another two months would pass before the entire state went dry, as far as El Paso was concerned, it was clearly the end of one era, and the beginning of another.[27]

By the time Texas had gone dry, Claude Smith had been promoted to sergeant of detectives. Smith, who was forty years old and as yet unmarried, had long since abandoned the range clothes, wide cartridge belt, and Winchester rifle that he had used while serving in the Rangers ten years earlier, and instead now sported dark suits, bow ties, and a Smith & Wesson .38 caliber service revolver. A photograph taken around this time showed a man whose thick dark hair had started to turn to gray, and a pair of eyes that seemed to have grown weary after nearly twenty years in law enforcement.

That July, Smith told the El Paso *Herald*, "Immoral women practically have deserted the city of El Paso," and that things had gotten to a point where "a man can walk the streets till the small hours of the morning, and never see a woman of questionable character. This does not mean that they have left the district, because they have not, but they are out of the jurisdiction of the police department." Indeed, on July 6, newspapers had reported that only four women were then serving time in the city lockup. "This marks about the lowest ebb in the history of the new city jail," the *Herald* reported, "as contrasted with three months ago, when the female prisoners numbered around 40 and 50." Clearly the purity squads, while operating in a legal gray area, had made something of an impact on at least one aspect of local vice.[28]

Although the squads had done much to clean out prostitution in El Paso and arrest those caught selling alcohol to soldiers stationed at Fort Bliss, World War I would end that November without El Paso ever receiving the training cantonment, which had inspired the cleanup in the first place. In the meantime, wartime liquor laws and statewide Prohibition had helped to trigger an epidemic of bootlegging in El Paso that would not end for another fifteen years. On August 12, 1918, Captain Veater and a uniformed sergeant arrested a man identified as C. N. Gibson, who had been selling whiskey out of a "well-equipped 'joint'" for six dollars a pint. Two weeks later, Veater and Captain Phoenix arrested forty-year-old E. M. Fairhurst after they caught him making a $3.00 liquor sale. The officers then discovered an additional two hundred half-pints stored in a building that Fairhurst used as a garage. Within days of Fairhurst's arrest, Sheriff Orndorff intercepted an automobile coming from New Mexico that was loaded with an estimated $2,000.00 worth of alcohol. The following month, Captain Veater caught a pair of bootleggers selling seventeen pints and twenty-one quarts of so-called "Chinese whiskey" (or "tew loo") to some women in a basement on Oregon Street. "It is said to contain much more alcohol than the average American whiskey," the *El Paso Herald* stated.[29]

In addition to the increased level of bootlegging throughout the region, Claude Smith and his fellow "purity men" would also continue to wage a battle against the so-called "dope fiends" and narcotics traffickers who kept El Paso's addicts supplied with ample amounts of opium, morphine, cocaine, and heroin. Though rarely associated with America's frontier experience, narcotics had actually been a common feature of El Paso's nightlife throughout the late 1800s.

Known as "hop joints," opium dens had first arrived in El Paso with the Southern Pacific's Chinese construction crews. By 1882, the city had taken steps to restrict opium use through a series of ordinances that ultimately did little to keep the "pipe hitters" out of the dens. However, while opium smuggling along the border would continue long after the Opium Exclusion Act of 1909, by the 1910s, local authorities had become particularly concerned about the rampant use of marijuana in El Paso. "Marihuana [sic]," the El Paso Herald had reported in a sensational article on January 2, 1913, "that native Mexican herb which causes the smoker to crave murder, is held accountable for two deaths and a bloody affray on the streets of Juarez Wednesday afternoon. Crazed by continual use of the drug, an unidentified Mexican killed a policeman, wounded another, stabbed two horses, and pursued an El Paso woman and her escort, brandishing a huge knife in the air. The man finally was shot and pounded into insensibility. He died early Thursday morning."[30]

During the years of the Mexican Revolution, when marijuana use was common among the soldiers in Pancho Villa's Division del Norte, local newspaper articles helped stoke the irrational fears of "reefer madness" that many Americans felt at the time. In reporting the arrest of a sixteen-year-old boy, caught while allegedly smuggling marijuana across the border in May of 1913, the Herald explained, "Marihuana is credited with being the drug when taken that incites the user to atrocious crimes. The bloodiest murders committed in Mexico have been attributed to the users." That summer, the El Paso Morning Times devoted an entire column to "Mexican Opium," comparing the drug's effects to those of opium, while incorrectly suggesting that "a devotee of the weed will commit arson to satiate his desire. Eventually he descends lower and lower in the scale of manhood until his willpower is destroyed and he is nothing more nor less than a ghoul, prowling around on earth to satisfy a passion over which he has not the slightest control."

In May of 1915, El Paso Chief Deputy Sheriff Stanley Good Sr. had told the *Herald* that "Much of the crime in this city is committed by men under the influence of marijuana. The drug is especially dangerous in view of the fact that it makes the coward brave." Thanks in large part to the efforts of Chief Deputy Good, the El Paso city council adopted an ordinance that June that outlawed the sale and possession of marijuana and imposed a $200.00 fine on violators, declaring "The dangerous properties of marihuana [*sic*] and the increasing sale, with resulting injury to public health and public morals, are given as the reason for inserting the emergency clause, making the ordinance effective immediately following its publication."

In the years that followed the city's prohibition on marijuana, "India hemp" continued to figure prominently in reports on violent crimes committed in and around the city. When Officer Octaviano Perea and Deputy Tax Collector Juan Garcia were killed during the violent rampage of Felipe Alvarez in February of 1918, marijuana was cited as one of the most likely causes behind the incident. Four months later, newspapers reported that marijuana was believed to have been behind the killing of former district clerk and Mexican-American political figure Ike Alderete on June 22, 1918. According to the *Herald,* Aniceto Vargas, "crazed" by marijuana, had just come out of the Rex Movie Theater when he approached a group of US soldiers on the sidewalk and opened fire on them with a .38 caliber pistol. Vargas shot two of the soldiers through the chest, then turned his weapon on Provost Guard P. D. Scott. Vargas fired two rounds at the trooper while Scott crouched in the middle of the street, trying to get his own double-action revolver out of its army-issue holster. Alderete, who was standing in the doorway of the nearby Fraternal Union Club, was hit by a stray round from Vargas's weapon that slammed into his forehead and killed him instantly. Scott finally managed to get his pistol clear and shot Vargas through the intestinal tract, mortally wounding him.[31]

Like marijuana, opium had continued to thrive in El Paso long after city ordinances imposed heavy fines on anyone involved in its sale, possession, and use. Throughout the early twentieth century, authorities in El Paso and Juarez attempted to crack down on hop joints and the dealers who pushed other hard drugs on both sides of the border. "But, despite this, despite every effort that is made by officials to check and control the use of opiates, 'dope fiends' get the drugs," C. A. Brann explained in a detailed editorial in 1911. "Some of them get them in El Paso, and some of them get them in Juarez, where it is easier to obtain them."

Even after the implementation of the 1914 Harrison Narcotics Act, which levied a tax on anyone who produced, distributed, or imported opium, coca leaves, and their "salts, derivatives, or preparations," opium, morphine, and heroin were common in El Paso. "Of course, importation of morphine, of a narcotic, was a serious offense," Dr. E. W. Rheinheimer would recall in 1974, "unless they brought it over for their own use. What they would do is go over to Juarez and get maybe two or three grains of morphine, and come over here and sell half of it for what they had had to pay for the whole thing in Juarez, and that would be their money for the next day. They had all kinds of ways of getting it over."[32]

"With whiskey and drugs banned in the United States as an official of the federal government pointed out today," the *Herald* reported in February of 1919, "dope fiends and whiskey hounds are going to look at the map and see that El Paso, the neighbor of Juarez, is the closest place to what they want. They are going to flock here, he said, and, if some law is not enacted to stop their free passage between El Paso and Juarez, El Paso will become the center of the greatest gang of criminals in the country."

On Monday, May 5, 1919, Claude Smith and Detective Varela arrested Jose Orozco for selling narcotics and transported him to the El Paso County Jail, where Orozco was held for federal authorities for violation of the Harrison Narcotics Act. According to newspaper accounts, Orozco had allegedly partnered with Chinese merchant Mar Ben, in a scheme to sell three hundred grains of morphine sulfate to drug addicts in South El Paso.

Testifying for the prosecution in Orozco's trial that October, Spanish-American War veteran John P. Force described his own twenty-one-year addiction to morphine. "I have seen the time when I would give my last cent and would be willing to pawn even [my] clothes for one grain of dope," he told the court. "The sufferings I have undergone in a frantic effort to break loose from the iron chains of the dope habit are beyond description." According to Force, dope peddlers lined the canal banks of the Rio Grande in South El Paso. The drugs were always in small packages, and missing the revenue stamp required by the Harrison Narcotics Act. Another witness, "Sonny" Hooks, explained that addicts experienced little difficulty in securing their "snow" in El Paso, and that "peddlers were easily found, and that 'dope to one's liking' could be secured in [cases where] the addict furnished the money." Orozco was later sentenced to a three-year prison term at Fort Leavenworth.[33]

While both drug smuggling and bootlegging along the Rio Grande increased in the months that followed the end of World War I, so did violent encounters between area lawmen, American soldiers, and outlaws. On Sunday morning, April 13, 1919, Immigration Inspector Clarence Childress and his partner encountered seven Mexican smugglers attempting to cross the border with five sacks of liquor at the end of Copia Street. As the two federal officers approached, the outlaws opened fire on them and shot Childress in the stomach. Then, they turned and ran for the other side of Rio Grande, leaving behind 175 pints of tequila. Childress, who had walked several blocks to call for help, was taken to the Hotel Dieu Hospital, where three days later, the forty-two-year-old husband and father died from his injuries. Childress's killers were never identified.

Ten days later, on the night of April 26, 1919, Corporal F. J. Wagenbrenner, a soldier in Company C of the Nineteenth Infantry Regiment, was patrolling the border near the Santa Fe Bridge when he spotted an "unidentified Mexican" attempting to wade across the Rio Grande with a load of tequila. When the stranger ignored Wagenbrenner's repeated orders to halt, the soldier raised his Springfield rifle and shot him through the heart.[34]

On November 1, 1919, Deputy Sheriff Jesse C. Stansel, the former chief of detectives who had served with Claude Smith in 1915, and Deputy Juan Parra were in East El Paso when they spotted a suspicious-looking vehicle crossing the border. Just as the two lawmen approached the car, a group of eight bootleggers tumbled out of the vehicle and opened fire on them with rifles. Parra quickly took cover behind a tree and got off fifteen rounds, while Stansel hid behind an adobe house and returned the smuggler's fire with his six-gun. After nearly a quarter of an hour, during which both sides fired a total of fifty rounds, the bootleggers made their escape. Of the eight gunmen involved in the attack on the deputies, auto mechanic Mike Salazar was the only suspect taken into custody. Though initially charged with assault to commit murder, Salazar was later acquitted of all charges.

The following month, on the evening of December 10, 1919, Lieutenant W. H. Little and four soldiers from the Eighth US Cavalry were guarding

Among those engaged in the wartime cleanup of El Paso and the early battles against smugglers were US Army soldiers stationed at nearby Fort Bliss. *Border Heritage Center, El Paso Public Library*

the border not far from the spot where Inspector Childress had been fatally wounded in April, when twelve bootleggers attempted to cross the dry riverbed from Cordova Island with a wagon. The soldiers had just ordered the men to halt when the smugglers opened fire. For the next thirty minutes, a battle raged between the troopers and the Mexican smugglers along the riverbank. The firing was so heavy at one point that some residents living along Alameda Boulevard apparently thought that El Paso was being attacked by Mexican revolutionaries. Finally, the bootleggers broke off their assault, leaving behind a jug of wine as well as thirty pints and thirty quarts of bonded whiskey.[35]

A little over a week later, at 4:00 a.m. on December 18, 1919, Juan Parra and fellow deputies T. G. Giron and H. B. Garcia were riding back into town from a trip down the Rio Grande Valley in a car driven by a civilian chauffeur, when a Ford pulled off of Hammett Boulevard and raced past them on Alameda Avenue. "It speeded past us in the same direction we were going and Giron said: 'Let's follow that car.' The Ford speeded up and Giron urged our driver to speed up," Parra later explained during a coroner's inquiry. "We followed a distance and then Giron blew a whistle as a signal to the Ford to stop."

No sooner had Giron blown his whistle, however, that two men climbed out of the Ford, braced themselves on the car's running boards, and opened fire while the vehicle sped west on Alameda. As bullets bounced off their vehicle, Giron reached for a .30-30 Winchester on the floor by his feet, levered a round into the chamber, and opened fire on the fast-moving Ford. At the same time Garcia drew his revolver and fired at the Ford from the backseat. With the lawmen's rounds cracking the air over their heads, the two shooters ducked back into the car as it raced toward Piedras Street, a road that would take them to the border.

Then, as the Ford turned left onto Piedras and headed south in the direction of Cordova Island, the deputies watched as two bodies were thrown from the vehicle and rolled out onto the street. The lawmen paused just long enough to look at the men, later identified as twenty-one-year-old Jose Lopez and nineteen-year-old Eliodoro Esquivel, both of whom had apparently been shot at close range. The deputies jumped back into their vehicle and continued their pursuit. They caught up with the Ford just as it made another turn onto Raynor Street. But, as Giron later explained to the *Herald*, "As they neared a small canal bridge we could have caught them had we not run into some mud, which caused us to skid. They made it across the bridge and escaped across the border." Lopez was still alive when the deputies returned to Piedras Street to check on the two men thrown from the Ford. According to Parra, Lopez begged to be taken to the hospital, but died before the officers could call for help.

Jesse Stansel soon arrived on the scene to begin an investigation, and quickly identified Esquivel as one of his informants. According to Stansel, Esquivel had been feeding the sheriff's office information on smuggling operations. "My theory is that when the battle occurred, the men in the car, who were undoubtedly bootleggers, thought Giron and his party knew that, and believed Esquivel had informed. I think he was shot by one of the men in the car, and that before he died, he shot Lopez," Stansel explained.

Evidence gathered during their autopsies certainly supported Stansel's theory. There were powder burns on Esquivel's clothing, suggesting he had been killed at close range, and the .32 caliber bullet extracted from Lopez's body was much too small to have been fired from either Giron's .30-30 or Garcia's revolver. According to Stansel, Lopez and Esquivel had both been members of a gang of smugglers that had recently made threats against members of the sheriff's office. "We have received word," Stansel told the *Herald*, "that an organized band of bootleggers is operating on the border near the scene of this shooting, and that they will kill any officer, sheriffs, or state rangers who attempt to interfere with their doings. This shooting is the second, staged between us and bootleggers recently, and they are trying to make good their boast to kill any officers who interfere with their operations."[36]

The following night, on December 19, six troopers from the Eighth Cavalry, including three of the men who had been involved in the shoot-out on December 10, Corporal Michael Engledinger and Privates Fleer Embler and George Raquepaw, were ambushed just as they arrived on the border for guard duty. Embler was immediately struck by a soft-nosed bullet that slammed into his chest and mushroomed in his left lung. While Engledinger and the other troopers returned fire with their Springfields, one of their comrades ran to summon reinforcements. As the two sides exchanged gunfire, Engledinger spotted muzzle flashes in a clump of tall grass where one of the gunmen had taken cover, "and at once a volley of shots was poured in his direction." When the firefight was over, the soldiers would discover the smuggler's bullet-riddled body in the brush. A female police matron later identified him as a man named "Ramirez."

After nearly an hour of intermittent shooting between the provost guards, police officers, and Mexican bootleggers, the smugglers withdrew and left behind a cache of six sacks of liquor. In the meantime, an ambulance sent to the battleground from Fort Bliss ran out of gas and nearly an hour had passed before Embler reached the hospital. Though valiant efforts were made to save the soldier's life, an artery had been severed in Embler's lungs, and the trooper died from a loss of blood at 7:30 p.m. In a little more than thirty-six hours, four men had been killed in the liquor war in El Paso. "Previously the smugglers were wary and would run rather than fight," Jesse Stansel told the *Herald* the day Embler was killed, "but that day is gone. When we mix with a bunch of smugglers now, we expect to fight, and fight hard. Several officers that I know have had narrow escapes when they were fired upon by these outlaws." To any of the lawmen working the border at night, it was becoming clear that bootleggers were becoming more brazen in their efforts to slip booze across the Rio Grande, and more willing to draw blood in their brushes with the law. As the *Herald* reported on December 20, 1919, "One squad of officers report that they were standing on the American side of the border as a band of smugglers was tying sacks that contained liquor. One smuggler laughed and called out, 'Better keep away tonight.' "[37]

"Has El Paso that notorious gang they call [a] purity squad yet?" an outsider asked the *Herald* on May 20, 1919, to which the editor replied that as far as anyone knew, the special squads of detectives had in fact been disbanded. Indeed, by the spring of 1919, the purity squads organized by Chief Pollock and Mayor Davis had ceased their late-night raids on illegal clubs and suspected bawdy houses, although the vigilance committees organized during the winter of 1918 remained in place to supervise El Paso's ongoing cleanup efforts. While James Walter Reese and his fellow purity squad members had avoided prosecution for the shooting of Captain Wylie White in December of 1917, White pursued a $10,000.00 claim against the city of El Paso for damages. The city council rejected White's claim in April of 1919, with Mayor Davis stating that while Reese and several other city detectives had certainly participated in the raid on his home, the squad had actually been led by the army officer that White himself had shot and badly wounded.

By that time, Charles E. Pollock had resigned as chief of police in order to once again run for office as police court judge. Though his tenure as El Paso's principal lawman had been relatively brief, Pollock had helped to oversee a massive cleanup that had done much to reshape the city's image. While World War I had served as the catalyst for the campaign against vice and alcohol, the effort would continue long after the final shots had been fired in France. As Mayor Charles Davis told reporters that March, "The city of El Paso will never again be an open town. It is not settled yet who is to be the new chief, but I, as mayor, will see to it that no wide open town will be allowed as some of our citizens seem to fear."

That June, thirty-nine-year-old Major John Montgomery, a newspaperman and a veteran of the Spanish-American War, the Philippine-American War, and the recent fighting in Europe took over as chief. "The police rules and regulations are printed in a book called the police manual. My policy will be to see that these rules and regulations are strictly observed by every member of this department," Montgomery told the *Herald*. While former members of the purity squads, like Claude Smith, Juan Franco, and Elmer Reynolds, would continue to prowl the streets in search of bootleggers and other underworld characters, the late-night raids without legal warrants were over. As city attorney Victor Moore explained at the end of the year, "Purity squad wholesale raids and wholesale raids without warrants are not within the law. When a person is believed to be guilty, the way to do it is to get a warrant and make the arrest lawfully. This is the way to get results."[38]

That November, James Walter Reese, Claude Smith's old comrade from the Texas Rangers, was badly injured in a car accident. Reese, who had been made captain of detectives in July, suffered a fractured skull and lingered for more than a month before dying on December 12, 1919. Having stood in for Reese while he was in the hospital, Claude Smith's promotion to captain of detectives was made permanent on December 23. Ten days later, Smith would follow bootlegger Henry Renfro into the shadows at the end of Raynor Street.[39]

On January 12, 1920, nine days after Claude Smith and Detectives Elmer Reynolds and Antonio Varela shot him to death, Henry Renfro was laid to rest in Concordia Cemetery, the same burial ground as John Wesley Hardin, and many of the city's other legendary shootists. While Renfro's actual connection to the bootleggers that ambushed Smith and his men on the night of January 3 was never clearly established, it's possible that the gunmen that opened fire from Cordova Island were the same gang of "desperate" smugglers that Jesse Stansel had warned newspapers about the month before. With the exception of the shooting death of the unidentified bootlegger by Corporal Wagenbrenner, nearly all of these shootings took place in the same South El Paso neighborhood, within just a few blocks of each other.

Five days after Henry Renfro's funeral, on January 17, 1920, the Volstead Act became the law of the land throughout the nation. The stage was now set for one of the longest and most deadly battles with outlaws in the history of the American West.[40]

CHAPTER FIVE

MANHUNT

They were a tireless bunch of real men and deserve the commendation of the people of the state. I feel sure that Sheriff
Harry Saxon, known to all as the unrelenting sleuth, joins
me in this message. Not one man in the various posses complained of hunger, thirst, or fatigue, and they were happy
when on the trail.

—*Captain Thomas H. Rynning,*
Bisbee Daily Review, *July 19, 1922*

On Friday, August 26, 1921, Josefa de Ortiz stood on a small hill in front
of her house and watched as seven horsemen slowly rode past her home
and headed toward the small town of Ruby, Arizona. It was just about 11:00
a.m., and until that very moment, it had been a typically quiet late-summer
morning in this remote settlement located in the heart of the Oro Blanco Mining District in Santa Cruz County, just a few short miles north of the Mexican
border.

As the riders passed within ten feet of her front door, the nineteen-year-
old wife of miner Jose Ortiz recognized three of the men immediately. One
was a twenty-one-year-old native of the Oro Blanco who Josefa had known
all of her life, named Placidio Silvas. The second man was a friend of her husband's, a bootlegger named Manuel Martinez, who the young woman had met
for the first time just the month before. The third man she recognized was
Samaniego, "a cripple" and an alleged horse thief whose real name was Juan
Valencia. The other four riders were all strangers. From her position overlooking the village, Josefa watched as the men reined in their horses in front of
the Ruby Mercantile and Post Office. Then, while their companions waited
outside, she saw three of the riders dismount and enter the store.[1]

Inside the mercantile, US postmaster Joseph Frank Pearson, who was
known as Frank to his friends and family, and his seventeen-year-old sister
Irene were both working behind the post office counter. Frank's thirty-year-
old wife Myrtle and their four-year-old daughter Margaret were in the living

quarters behind the store with Myrtle's twenty-four-year-old sister, Elizabeth Purcell. While most of the Pearsons' customers might have come in to mail a letter or to survey the canned goods, clothing, and other merchandise that lined the walls and filled the glass showcases, the three men that now stood before Irene Pearson were more interested in the safe that stood inside the post office.

"Tobacco," one of them said.

Irene came around the service counter that separated the post office from the store and was just about to fill the man's order when one of the three *vaqueros* suddenly jerked out a pistol and opened fire. Frank Pearson was instantly knocked off his feet by a round through the stomach, though according to the *Arizona Republican*, he somehow managed to grab his own gun and "fired five shots at the bandits as he lay on the floor." His assailant then fired a second round that slammed into his head and killed Frank Pearson instantly. As the gunfire echoed in her ears, Irene bolted from the store and ran toward the living quarters, two of the bandits right on her heels.

"My mother and I were in the kitchen," Margaret Pearson would remember seven decades later, "and I was up on a kitchen chair getting a drink of water, and we heard shots down in the store. She just left me and ran. 'Frank, Frank!' [she called], and ran down the stairs. I jumped down off the chair, and I ran and I looked, and I still don't know what I saw. It's a black curtain."

Though accounts vary as to the actual order of the events that followed, while the outlaws chased Irene out of the mercantile and into the living quarters, they encountered Elizabeth Purcell, or "Gigie," as Margaret called her. The girl had armed herself as soon as she had heard the gunfire in the store, and tried to take a shot at her attackers, but her weapon either jammed or misfired. Then, one of the bandits pointed his own pistol directly at Elizabeth's head and at close range, pulled the trigger. But, at the very moment the gun went off, the girl raised an arm to cover her eyes and the bullet smacked into her hand instead. It's probably the only thing that saved her life. "Blood gushed . . . she fainted," Margaret recalled, "I guess from fear, and he thought he'd killed her, so he left her."

According to a statement Irene later provided to Mexican Consul Joaquin Terrazas, as soon as the bandits were satisfied that Elizabeth was dead, they grabbed her sister-in-law Myrtle Pearson "and took her to the store." While her four-year-old daughter looked on in horror, the woman was dragged into the mercantile and shot to death. Area residents would later find Myrtle lying some twenty-five feet from the front door, shot once through the hip and a second time through the head. Not content to simply murder the woman in front of her child, one of the bandits allegedly bashed Myrtle's mouth and jaws open with the butt end of his gun, crushing a part of her skull in the process, all of it in a barbaric effort to extract the gold fillings from her teeth.

"Everything else I remember with detail, but my mind has *never* let me accept what I saw," Margaret Pearson would recall in 1994. "I turned and ran and one of the men came up out of the store and started chasing me," she remembered. "We had a screen porch along the side of the house, and I was running down that porch, which was an outside entrance . . . I fell spread-eagled. I can still remember his spurs, his chaps, his boots, as he was chasing me. For some reason when I fell, he turned around and went back, I don't know where."

Moments later, Irene appeared, picked up her niece, and then ran from the building. "I took the baby out to the bunkhouse, 25 steps from the house, thinking I could find some guns out there," Irene later explained in court. However, the young woman found neither guns nor the men who had been staying in the Pearsons' bunkhouse, brothers Frank and Ed Ott, who had left Ruby early that morning to check their traps. "Irene is a good shot," her father would tell the *Nogales Herald* a few days later, "and I am sure that if she could have gotten hold of a gun last Friday, there would have been some dead Mexicans." A few minutes later, the two girls were joined by Elizabeth Purcell, who had regained consciousness and slipped away from the mercantile when no one was looking. Together, the young women fled into the hills, hoping they might find the Ott brothers on their way back from their morning hunt.[2]

Though most accounts at the time suggested that the girls were unable to find anyone who could help them, Margaret would clearly recall finally meeting up with the Otts on the road outside of Ruby. "We did," Margaret remembered. "They were on horseback, and they were coming in. I remember what they said: 'Oh, God damn, God damn.' I still remember Gigie had a blue-and-white-checked dress, and it was stained with blood."[3]

Back inside the mercantile, the outlaws used tools they found in the store to hack their way into the Pearsons' safe. They also smashed several of the glass showcases and seized whatever cash they could find, as well as a stack of postal money orders and Frank Pearson's personal firearms. The bandits gathered up most of the mail and dozens of shoes, shirts, Stetson hats, and other dry goods, and ripped the telephone off the wall. Then, the gang tied the stolen goods onto their horses, climbed into their saddles, and headed for the desert. From her position on the hill, Josefa de Ortiz had heard the gunfire that had erupted from inside the store. Now, just as she had seen them ride into the little town a few minutes earlier, Josefa watched as the killers rode away from Ruby in the direction of the Mexican border, with Manuel Martinez in the lead. She noticed the bundles of new hats, trousers, and shoes strapped to their mounts with fresh-looking ropes.

Later that afternoon, four-year-old Margaret and her aunts Irene Pearson and Elizabeth Purcell returned to the Ruby Mercantile, where a small crowd would gather around the scene of the brutal double murder and robbery. "My wife dressed Miss Purcell's hand that had been grazed by a bullet she got in return for one she pluckily shot at one of the gang," mining engineer George Camphius explained in a letter several days later. "Altogether too maddening a mess to write about calmly without swearing." One of the onlookers, Bert Worthington, picked Margaret up and carried her away from the mercantile, "and I remember his walking back and forth by the woodpile. Somehow I knew that they were in there in that store. I don't know what my concept was of 'dead,' but I knew something terrible had happened."

When word of the slayings finally reached Nogales that evening, Santa Cruz County Sheriff George White climbed into an automobile with Deputy Sheriffs William Oliver Parmer, Charlie Jones, "one of the Clark boys," and Parmer's bloodhound, and set out for Ruby, driving through a heavy summer thunderstorm. When they arrived the following morning, the officers found the store in complete disarray. According to Parmer, they found Frank Pearson's body where it had fallen behind the post office counter, while Myrtle was found lying on the floor in the mercantile.[4]

While the savagery on display inside the Ruby Mercantile that summer morning in 1921 may have been especially blood-chilling, William Oliver Parmer was no stranger to the hardships of life on the border. By age nineteen, Parmer was living in Pecos County, Texas. "That's when I voted for Dud Barker, the Sheriff," Parmer told the *Tucson Daily Citizen* in 1960. "He killed

This photo of William Oliver Parmer was taken just a few years after the Ruby Mercantile murders. Prior to serving as a Santa Cruz County deputy sheriff, Parmer's career in law enforcement had included stints with the El Paso Police Department and the famed Arizona Rangers.   *Credit: Barbara Jordan*

seven outlaws in one day and served 32 years without being killed—which is a wonder." Parmer's own career in law enforcement began a short time later, in El Paso, Texas, where Parmer would serve stints as a mounted patrolman with the El Paso Police Department, and briefly held a deputy's commission under Sheriff Florence J. Hall. This shift from ranching to peacekeeping appears to have been something of a Parmer family tradition. In addition to his brother, James M. Parmer, who joined the ranks of the El Paso PD in 1907, his father John Parmer would later serve as a lawman in Arizona, as would younger brother Arthur E. Parmer, who eventually pinned on a deputy's badge in Cochise County, where he worked side by side with Joe Hardwick.[5]

In late 1907, Parmer tendered his resignation with the city police, and together with wife Clodie and their two daughters, left El Paso bound for Arizona Territory, where they would join the rest of the Parmer clan in the smelter town of Douglas. "The trip took 30 days," William Oliver told the Tucson *Daily Citizen* more than fifty years later. "We just dawdled along and camped where it pleased us."[6]

In July of 1908, Parmer enlisted as a private in the Arizona Rangers, then under the command of Captain Harry Wheeler. As a member of the territorial force, Parmer was paid a salary of $100.00 per month and was expected to provide his own horse, saddle, .30-40 caliber Model 1895 Winchester rifle, and a .45 caliber Colt single-action army revolver. The Territory of Arizona would provide the ammunition for his weapons and the forage for his mount. Like their counterparts in Texas, early Arizona Rangers had worn no badges when the company was first organized in 1901. However, along with instituting marksmanship training and the proper methods for disarming a suspect, Wheeler's predecessor, Captain Thomas H. Rynning, had adopted a large, five-point star for his men with "Arizona Ranger" boldly engraved on its face, along with a number. Throughout his service as a Ranger, Parmer would wear badge number 12.[7]

Four months after he signed on with the Rangers, on Sunday, November 15, 1908, Parmer rode out to the Harmon Ranch, just two short miles from the town of Benson, in search of William Van Vaeler, a twenty-two-year-old hoodlum, who was wanted for a series of robberies and escapes from custody. "He started out early in the evening alone to capture his man," the *Arizona Silver Belt* reported, "and when a short distance from the Harmon house he was accosted by Van Vaeler. Before the Ranger got within revolver range, he called to him to throw up his hands." Van Vaeler responded to Parmer's order by drawing a six-shooter and firing off a wild shot at the Ranger. Parmer then leveled his 1895 Winchester and pumped out two .30-40 slugs at his assailant. One bullet hit Van Vaeler's wrist and knocked the gun out of his hand, while the other struck his ankle. "It was growing dark by this time, and the ranger again called upon Van Vaeler to surrender," the *Arizona Silver Belt* explained. "The latter then turned and disappeared into the mesquite bushes."

Parmer attempted to track Van Vaeler through the mesquite, "being guided by bloodstains along the trail," though he abandoned his search as darkness settled over the desert. Parmer and other officers eventually tracked Van Vaeler to his family's homestead; by that time, however, the young outlaw had jumped on a freight train and once again made his escape. While Parmer was able to recover numerous stolen items from the Van Vaeler residence, the youthful bandit remained at large. As far as Captain Wheeler was concerned, the young man's incessant reading of dime-novel adventures had no doubt inspired Van Vaeler's criminal escapades. As Wheeler explained to a reporter in Tucson, "two copies of cheap Jesse James stories were found in the cabin which Van Vaeler occupied. They were thumb worn and there was every indication that they had been read many times by the owner of the hut."[8]

Three months after his run-in with Van Vaeler, Parmer was mustered out of the territorial service when the Arizona Rangers were disbanded on February 15, 1909. Though the territory had abolished its Ranger company, that same month the legislature passed a bill that authorized county sheriffs to appoint as many as four so-called Ranger deputies, "especially charged with the duty of enforcing the law and preserving the peace in remote and outlying sections of their respective counties."[9]

While several of his comrades continued on as Ranger deputies, deputy sheriffs, or even as federal officers, William Oliver Parmer appears to have used the demise of the territorial force as an opportunity to go back to ranching. Though he made one attempt to join the Douglas Police Department, and briefly held a deputy's commission in Cochise County, Parmer would spend most of the following decade working as a cowboy, managing ranches, and entering rodeos.[10]

Then, in 1919, the same year that his younger brother Arthur wore a deputy's badge in Cochise County, Parmer once again pinned one on of his own, this time as a member of the Tucson Police Department. In March of 1920, the former Arizona Ranger arrested a pair of soldiers who had gone AWOL from the First United States Cavalry. "Officer Parmer has acquired a reputation for picking up deserters as well as civil prisoners wanted in other parts of the country," the Tombstone *Weekly Epitaph* reported, and added that the same day Parmer had apprehended the two troopers, "he took into custody Dennis F. Devon, alleged to have deserted from Camp McIntosh at Laredo, Texas, with $200 in government money." It was while working as a mounted patrolman in Tucson that winter that Parmer would have heard the news of a brutal double homicide down along the border in the mining camp of Ruby, Arizona.[11]

Located just a few miles north of the international boundary, Ruby, Arizona, first came to life as a rough-and-tumble settlement called "Montana Camp," so named for the nearby Montana Mine located by miners James M. Kirkpatrick and Isaac Flood in 1877. Later development of the Montana Mine was financed by prominent German-born merchant Louis Zeckendorf, and supervised by Philadelphia native George Cheyney, who established the camp's first mercantile in the 1880s. In 1895, Cheyney turned the mercantile operation over to John B. "Pie" Allen, a former treasurer of the Territory of Arizona, who within a few short months allowed the business to fall into debt. However, Ohio native Julius Andrews arrived in Montana Camp later that year, took over management of the store on Allen's behalf, and quickly turned around its fortunes. Andrews eventually purchased the business from Louis Zeckendorf in 1897 for $900.00. When Arizona gained statehood fifteen years later in 1912, a US post office was established at Andrews's store, with Julius Andrews as the camp's first postmaster. Montana Camp and its post office were then renamed "Ruby," in honor of the maiden name of Andrews's wife, Lille B. Ruby.[12]

On May 6, 1913, Andrews sold his business to an Irish immigrant named Phil Clarke and his wife Gypsy, who bought the entire operation for $3,700.00. "We had to sell our chickens to add the money to what we had saved to make the purchase," Clarke later recalled. In addition to running the store, Clarke also took over as postmaster. In 1915, Clarke expanded his operation and established a new store; a 62x32-foot adobe structure that included living quarters for the Clarke family complete with running water, a rare commodity in this remote corner of Santa Cruz County.[13]

But, while the Clarkes' business might have prospered, Ruby's mines were in the midst of a period of inactivity, and the settlement remained little more than a lonely frontier outpost compared to larger mining towns like Bisbee, Globe, and Jerome. Adding to the sense of desolation for the Clarke family were the perils associated with life along the border during the later years of the Mexican Revolution. On January 14, 1917, a pair of cowboys from the nearby Arivaca Land and Cattle Company crossed the border in pursuit of a party of twenty Mexicans who had made off with ninety head of cattle. "They followed the Mexicans across the border and started to herd the cattle back," the El Paso Herald reported. "The Mexicans opened fire, and the cowboys, from behind boulders, killed six of the Mexicans and took home their cattle."

Fighting near Ruby broke out again less than two weeks later, when, on January 26, American cowboys and troopers from the Utah National Guard (one of the numerous National Guard units sent from other parts of the country to patrol the border during this period) engaged another force of Mexican raiders at "the Stone House" a few short miles from the Clarkes' store. "Everyone along the border was afraid and nervous during this period," Clarke remembered. "My wife and our first two children and I were the only people at Ruby. There were two Mexican men living down the canyon. We slept with guns under our pillows and guns in every corner of the house."[14]

By the end of 1919, after more than six years in Ruby, the Clarkes were ready to move on. Having amassed a sizable herd of cattle, a large portion of which had been taken in trade, Phil Clarke began looking for someone to lease the Ruby Mercantile so that he and Gypsy could go into the ranching business full-time. "I made good money there in [19]16, '17, and '18, and I also collected a large herd of cattle," Clarke remembered, "so, I went into the cattle business, moved to Oro Blanco, and leased the store."

On February 16, 1920, brothers John and Alexander Fraser signed an agreement with Phil Clarke to take over the Ruby Mercantile and Post Office. The mercantile represented a new start for the Frasers, particularly for John, whose wife Ines was now expecting a fourth child at their family home in San Diego, California. Feeling optimistic over their new venture, John felt that they'd have no trouble at all making their first payment of $765.00 by April 1, 1920. However, just in case, John wrote a letter to Ines letting her know that she might need to draw on their savings account for a while.[15]

On February 27, 1920, eleven days after they had closed the deal with Phil Clarke, two armed men rode up to the store, dismounted, and entered the mercantile. Once inside, the bandits opened fire on fifty-eight-year-old Alexander Fraser. "John, who was in the back washing the breakfast dishes, heard the door of the store open and close," Clarke recalled, "then a shot that was almost immediately followed by the ring of the cash register. Although I had cautioned them repeatedly and thoroughly about keeping guns in every room, and they had taken my advice and placed a shotgun or rifle in several corners, John rushed into the store without a gun."[16]

As he entered the mercantile, John encountered Ezequiel Lara, a laborer he had once worked with in the Oro Blanco Mines, standing over his brother's body with a smoking gun in his hand. Lara's accomplice was later identified as

Between 1920 and 1921, the Ruby Mercantile and Post Office, built by Phil Clarke in 1915, was the scene of two sensational double homicides. Today, little remains of the store except for a few adobe walls.   *Mike Testin*

Manuel Garcia, who was wanted in connection with a violent 1916 bank robbery in Buckeye, Arizona. "Lara, he says, grasped him by the throat and forced him to open the store safe and surrender all the valuables it contained," the *Nogales Herald* reported. "Then, in cold blood, he says, Lara deliberately shot him, the bullet passing through his right eye and out the back of his head." As Clarke later remembered, "The Mexicans took what else they could carry and started off for the border."[17]

Later that day, a thirty-four-year-old miner named Jose Cuesta entered the mercantile and found the two Fraser brothers lying on the floor. Cuesta immediately jumped onto his horse and rode for the ranch owned by John Maloney, a sixty-year-old mining engineer and the local justice of the peace. According to William Oliver Parmer's account, as soon as Cuesta had described what he had seen in Ruby, Maloney, "a stalwart old Indian fighter and peace officer," grabbed his six-shooter, mounted his horse, and rode for the Ruby Mercantile. Once inside, they discovered Alexander Fraser lying beside the counter, his brother John not far away, moaning on the floor, blood still oozing from the bullet wound to his head.[18]

Maloney sent a rider to the county seat to summon Sheriff Raymond R. Earhart and his deputies, and to return with an ambulance to take John Fraser back to Nogales. "As soon as the intelligence was received in this city," the *Nogales Herald* explained, "Deputy Sheriffs Finter and White sped to the mountain camp, returning several hours later, bringing the wounded man who received first aid at the Arizona hotel, later being removed to the Military Base Hospital, where latest advices are to the effect that he has an excellent chance for recovery."[19]

Once John Fraser had been transported to Nogales, Sheriff Earhart sent a series of telegrams to Mrs. Ines Fraser in San Diego, informing her that her husband was badly wounded and that she should travel to Arizona immediately. Ines would arrive in Nogales on February 19, just two days after the robbery, only to learn that her husband had succumbed to his bullet wound that very morning. One week later, both John and Alexander Fraser were laid to rest in a Nogales cemetery. Summing up the raw emotions felt along the border in the wake of the killings, the *Bisbee Daily Review* suggested, "Unofficially it is stated that the slayers will be killed if captured."[20]

For his part, Sheriff Earhart had wasted little time in organizing a posse.

Before winning his badge in the elections of 1916, Earhart had previously served as Santa Cruz County treasurer. Though he might have lacked the long years of experience of a lawman like Harry Wheeler in Cochise County, Earhart had more than proven himself as a peace officer, and had spent much of the past three years chasing bootleggers, auto thieves, and the "slackers" who attempted to dodge the draft during World War I. On February 28, 1920, the day after the robbery, Earhart set out after Garcia and Lara with a party of officers and civilians that included Phil Clarke and deputies George J. White and Martin Finter. "Next morning we formed a posse with bloodhounds that Frank Bailey, the Chief of Police in Tucson, had brought," Phil Clarke recalled. "The bandits were so certain they were safe the first night that they found their campfire only a quarter-mile from the line. The posse followed them so closely that they found their second campfire still warm. Unfortunately, the Mexicans gave them the slip in the rough country."[21]

Earhart led his men as far as the Mexican border, though some accounts reported that the posse crossed the boundary in Sonora, something that the sheriff vehemently denied. "We followed the men just up to the international line and no further," Earhart insisted in an interview with a reporter from the Associated Press. "At one time we were within six hours of them. They had had nearly sixteen hours' start on us." With the culprits apparently safe across the border in Mexico, Earhart and his posse had no other choice but to return to Nogales. "Sheriff Earhart and his deputies declare there was no romance to riding a mule seventeen miles through a rugged and precipitous country," the *Nogales Herald* reported, "especially on a bootless quest." Throughout the next several weeks, as rewards were placed on their heads, Lara and Garcia continued to evade apprehension by area lawmen and soldiers on both sides of the border.[22]

In the meantime, while Lara and Garcia remained at large, Phil Clarke was approached by Texas native Joseph Frank Pearson, who expressed a serious interest in taking over the Ruby Mercantile and Post Office. "I was not anxious to turn the store over to anyone else, after what had happened," Clarke would later explain. "I tried to dissuade him, but he was determined to buy. His arguments made sense too. As he pointed out, my wife and I, and the Andrews [family] before us, had lived through the worst period of that part of the country. It certainly wasn't likely that lightning would strike twice."[23]

Like John and Alexander Fraser before him, Frank Pearson was in search of a new opportunity for his family. Born in Williamson County, Texas, in 1886, Frank Pearson was the eldest son of farmer Joseph H. Pearson. By the time he first arrived in Santa Cruz County, Frank had already faced his share of troubles. "My father's mother died when he was a teenager," Margaret Pearson would later recall, "and he raised the rest of the kids." A few years later, Frank developed a serious case of tuberculosis and eventually left East Texas for the more arid climate of New Mexico, where he found work as a cowboy. Once his health had improved, Frank turned his attention to Miss Myrtle Purcell, the college-educated daughter of Williamson County cotton farmer Noah Purcell and his wife Elida Jackson. "My father seems to have been in love with her for many years, and she wasn't very interested," Margaret recalled, "but finally he persuaded her from New Mexico . . . to marry him."[24]

Destined to be the couple's only child, Margaret Pearson was born on a ranch in Carrizoza, New Mexico, in 1917. The following year, Frank moved his small family to Bisbee, Arizona, where he took a job working in the mines, while Myrtle ran a boardinghouse. The Pearsons did not remain long in the "Queen of the Copper Camps," and by 1920 they were living in the town of Arivaca in Pima County, where Myrtle accepted a position teaching school. "We hadn't been there too long, I guess, when my father heard about an opening in the post office and store there together at Ruby. The Fraser brothers had been murdered there, so the place was up for new owners and a brand-new postmaster." Decades later, Margaret would still struggle to understand her father's decision to take over the mercantile. "My dad cleaned up some of the blood from those murders that was still there," she remembered, "but my father was a very religious man, and I just assume that he thought nothing bad could happen to us. I don't know, that seems like such a risk."[25]

On May 31, 1920, three months after the Fraser murders, two Chinese merchants were robbed and assaulted by a trio of outlaws at Patagonia, twenty miles northeast of Nogales. "One of the bandits is believed to be Ezequiel Lara, who with an accomplice murdered Alexander Fraser," the Tombstone *Weekly Epitaph* reported, and explained that Earhart and Deputy George White traveled to the scene of the crime, taking along a bloodhound named "Ranger" that White had recently used to track down a horse thief. "The robbers secured but $2.38 from the Chinamen," the *Epitaph* explained, adding that "Forty men from Patagonia and vicinity joined with the sheriff's men Sunday and Monday in hunting the bandits." But, once again, Earhart's posse failed to catch up with the suspects.

Then, ten days after the holdup in Patagonia, one of the injured merchants traveled to Nogales, Sonora, at the urging of Sheriff Earhart. Once across the border, the Chinese storekeeper was given the freedom of the town, and actually managed to locate and identify Jesus Amezcua and Manuel Arviza as two of the men who had robbed his business. Both suspects were taken into custody by Mexican authorities, but refused to discuss the case, "or to betray the identity of their companion, who escaped."[26]

Finally, in early October it was reported that Manuel Garcia, Lara's accomplice in the Fraser killings, had crossed the border and was believed to be laying low on a ranch west of the village of Twin Buttes. On Sunday, October 10, 1920, Pima County Sheriff Rye Miles sent deputies George McClure and George Holloway to take Garcia into custody. The two lawmen arrived at the ranch at about 8:00 a.m. and discovered Garcia in a corral. "Garcia asked to change his trousers," the *Arizona Republican* explained, "and McClure followed him into an adobe shack, where the Mexican took a gun from the bed and shot the officer."

As McClure fell to the floor with a round through his intestines, Garcia pistol-whipped him and then turned on his partner. Holloway ducked just as Garcia swung down with his weapon, and the deputy caught the blow on his shoulder. "As he struck the gun bounced out of the Mexican's hand and he grasped Holloway by both arms to prevent him from drawing," the *Tucson Citizen* explained. The two men struggled for several more minutes, before Holloway was able to grab a handful of Garcia's hair and force the fugitive to release his grip on Holloway's gun arm. As Garcia staggered back, Holloway and McClure both raised their six-guns and shot the bandit dead. Four years after the robbery in Buckeye, and eight months after the murder of the Fraser brothers, Manuel Garcia's outlaw trail ended with two lead slugs to the chest. McClure eventually recovered from his injuries.[27]

Unfortunately, the killing of Manuel Garcia was as close as the Fraser family ever got to achieving justice for the death of their loved ones. While Ezequiel Lara would be arrested in Mexico the following year, the Bisbee *Daily Review* reported on June 14, 1921, that "he [would] be held by the Mexican

The Ruby schoolhouse, where Myrtle Pearson once taught school, as it looks today.
Mike Testin

authorities for the murder of a Chinaman near Ures a few days [prior], and not delivered to the American authorities." Though Lara was eventually imprisoned for crimes committed south of the border, he was never called to answer for the murder of Alexander and John Fraser in an Arizona courtroom.[28]

By the time Ezequiel Lara was finally arrested in Mexico, the Pearson family had had plenty of time to settle into their new life in Ruby. While Frank managed the mercantile and the post office, Myrtle's college education and background as a teacher qualified her to take over Ruby's one-room schoolhouse.[29]

The living quarters built by Phil Clarke in 1915 offered the Pearsons more than adequate comfort, considering the otherwise-rustic conditions that existed in Ruby. "As I remember there were a couple of bedrooms, and we had running water," Margaret explained, "which [was] unusual in those years, in the twenties. And we had a phone, which just seems incredible." That same spring, the Pearsons made room for Frank's seventeen-year-old sister Irene and Myrtle's twenty-four-year-old sister Elizabeth Purcell, both of whom arrived in Ruby for an extended visit from Liberty Hill, Texas. In June, Myrtle took Margaret on one of their annual trips back home to Williamson

Interior view of the Ruby Mercantile and Post Office as it looks today. *Mike Testin*

County, where she told her relatives that in the event that anything happened to either Frank or herself, "they were to be buried in Andice Cemetery, side by side, and told them what she wanted to wear." As it would turn out, Frank and Myrtle Pearson had but two months before both would suffer violent deaths in Ruby.[30]

When mining engineer George A. Camphius and his wife Hilda arrived at the Ruby Mercantile on the afternoon of August 26, 1921, Frank and Myrtle Pearson had both been dead for about three hours. "We found a scene of desolation beyond description," the Scottish-born Camphius would write in a letter later published in newspapers, "not a soul to be seen or heard in any direction, as my wife and I walked through the open doors of Pearson's store to do what we could for the unfortunate bodies of Mr. and Mrs. Pearson that we found laying there in dreadful shape—poor Mrs. Pearson—shot through and through and beyond recognition; the cruelty of her murder apart from that of Mr. Pearson ought to be enough to stir somebody to action."[31]

William Oliver Parmer was in Nogales when word reached the county seat that there had been another violent robbery at the Ruby Mercantile. By that time, he and his wife Clodie had relocated their family to Nogales, where for $200.00 per month, Parmer had signed on as a county ranger, or "special deputy," in May of 1921. Because the outlaw gang had cut the telephone lines between the Ruby store and Nogales, several hours had passed before news of the latest murders reached Nogales by horseback. "A sheriff's posse immediately left for Ruby to take up the trail of the bandits," the *Nogales Herald* reported, "but probably will not reach the scene of the crime until late tonight, because the automobile road is in bad condition." The lawmen arrived at the scene a little after daybreak on August 27.[32]

"I seen the whole store had been rifled," Parmer later testified, "shoe boxes were emptied, scattered around over the floor. Hatboxes were emptied and scattered around. Show cases were broken." When asked to describe the Pearsons' bodies, Parmer explained that Frank Pearson had suffered two bullet wounds, one in the stomach and one in the face, while Myrtle "was shot in the face and in the hip." Parmer discovered a mushroomed bullet on the floor that had been fired through Myrtle Pearson's skull. The lawman would later testify that it was probably a .32-20, a lightweight round capable of being fired in six-shooters, as well as in Winchester and Marlin rifles of the same caliber.[33]

While the bodies were loaded into a vehicle to begin the long drive back to Nogales, Sheriff White organized a posse of Santa Cruz and Pima County man-hunters that set out on the trail of the killers. While White, Parmer, and their fellow lawmen rode across the desert on horseback, a US Army airplane circled overhead, one of the first ever used in an Arizona manhunt. From the cockpit, Lieutenant R. D. Knapp of the US Army's Twelfth Aero Squadron watched as White's posse and its pack of bloodhounds made its way along the border.[34]

Considering what they had just been through, the three young women who survived the raid appear to have held up particularly well throughout their ordeal, as well as during the statements, interviews, and funeral arrangements that took place in the days that followed. "Irene is certainly a nervy little girl," her father explained to the *Nogales Herald* after he arrived from Texas to see to his son's affairs. "One would think that after what she went through," Pearson added, "witnessing the shooting of the couple, and then fleeing into the hills to save her own life, that she would never want to see Ruby again, but she declared she wanted to go back and remain with me during my stay."

Finally, on September 2, 1921, nearly a week after they had died together inside the Ruby Mercantile, Frank and Myrtle Pearson's remains were loaded onto a railcar for their final trip home to Liberty Hill, Texas. Just as she had requested during her last trip to Texas with Margaret that June, Myrtle and Frank were buried side by side. According to that day's edition of the *Nogales Herald*, Myrtle had expressed the wish that if anything happened to her, her sister Elizabeth should take charge of little Margaret, and that she "must have had a presentiment that something was going to happen, and that she did not have much longer to live on this earth."[35]

Acting on the recommendation of the US postal inspectors sent to Ruby to investigate the robbery, Chief Post Office Inspector Rush D. Simmons authorized a $5,000 bounty for the capture, "dead or alive," of the bandits responsible for the slaying of Frank and Myrtle Pearson and the theft of the US mail from the Ruby Mercantile. At the same time, a petition was circulated requesting that the War Department send US troops to Ruby, "to remain there indefinitely." Adding to the increased tension along the border during those final days of summer was the news of an attempted bandit raid on the ranch owned by famed cattleman and former Cochise County Sheriff John Horton Slaughter. "Governor Thomas E. Campbell has wired Secretary of War Weeks requesting that a detachment of federal troops be dispatched to the John H. Slaughter ranch in Cochise county," the Prescott *Weekly Journal-Miner* reported, adding that Campbell had also referred to the deaths of the Pearsons in Ruby "as an instance of what may be expected anywhere along the unguarded international boundary line."[36]

Despite the hefty reward on their heads, and the fact that lawmen on either side of the boundary line were on the hunt for the Pearson slayers, it appeared as if the outlaw gang had simply vanished in the wind. Then, that September, newspapers reported the arrest of three men for disturbing the peace at the Austerlitz Mine, only a few short miles from the Ruby store. Identified as Arivaca resident Juan Lucero, Cipriano Nunez, a former Mexican soldier, and Placidio Silvas, the three men were lodged in the Nogales County Jail to serve out a ninety-day sentence.

"The three are the men brought here several days ago, suspicioned of knowing something about the killing of Postmaster and Mrs. Frank J. Pearson at Ruby, two weeks ago," the *Nogales Herald* reported. Josefa de Ortiz and two other women would testify to having seen both Placidio Silvas and Manuel Martinez ride up to the Ruby Mercantile on the day of the murders.

On October 3, 1921, with Silvas and his two codefendants still in custody for the incident at Austerlitz, Santa Cruz County Attorney Arthur H. DeRiemer announced that Sheriff White had placed all three men under arrest in connection with the murder of Frank and Myrtle Pearson. A fourth man, Salvador Sazueta, was also taken in, though charges against Sazueta were dropped a few days later when DeRiemer failed to produce any important witnesses who could testify against him. Charges were also dropped in the cases of Cipriano Nunez and Juan Lucero, though Nunez would later be called as a witness in Silvas's trial. Then, in November, newspapers reported that Mexican authorities had arrested Juan Valencia, the man Josefa de Ortiz knew as Samaniego. But, while Samaniego was later extradited to Arizona by Mexican officials at the request of Arthur DeRiemer, and was even mentioned in witness testimony, he was never actually prosecuted in connection with the Ruby murders.[37]

On November 23, 1921, Placidio Silvas was taken to the Ruby Mercantile for a preliminary hearing before Justice of the Peace John Maloney, who had been among the first on the scene when the store was robbed the year before. Testifying that afternoon, Ramon Rothenhausler described the gruesome scene inside the store on August 26, and told Deputy County Attorney James B. Robbins that he knew Placidio Silvas and had seen him in Old Oro Blanco two days before the murders, "walking up and down the hill on horseback." He also explained that he had seen Silvas two more times that same afternoon, riding near his mother's house a little over a mile from the Ruby Mercantile. The second witness called to testify was William Oliver Parmer, who pointed out where the bodies had been found, and even produced the bullet that had been fired through Myrtle Pearson's head.

The final witness, Josefa de Ortiz, told Robbins that she had seen Silvas riding near her home in Ruby at 6:00 a.m. on August 25, the day before the robbery. She also explained that she had seen him again at about 11:00 that morning, and then for a third time just before dark, when she had watched as Silvas and Manuel Martinez reined in their horses about three hundred yards from her house and sat there in the fading light. Josefa also described what she had seen on the day of the murders, and identified Silvas, Martinez, and Samaniego as having been among the members of the gang she had watched ride into Ruby. Based on the testimony of these three witnesses, and with Silvas having nothing to offer in his own defense, Maloney ordered Silvas held without bail, and filed arrest warrants against him that officially charged him for the murder of Frank and Myrtle Pearson.[38]

Silvas's trial began on December 15, 1921, with Judge W. A. O'Conner presiding and Arthur DeRiemer serving as prosecutor. Alfred A. Trippel, a thirty-five-year-old attorney and Arizona native, was retained as Silvas's attorney. Throughout the following nine days, testimony was heard from a variety of witnesses, including Josefa de Ortiz, Rosa de Rodriguez, and her daughter Luz, who all identified Silvas as being one of the men that they had seen ride into Ruby that morning. On December 17, Irene Pearson, who traveled from her family's home in Williamson County, Texas, in order to testify, once again described the ordeal that had taken place four months earlier. "Silvas became noticeably pale while Miss Pearson was testifying," the *Nogales Herald* reported. "She spoke in a clear voice and never appeared to be confused."

"Did you see who fired the first shot?" DeRiemer asked her.

"Yes, sir," Irene told him, and pointed her finger across the room at Placidio Silvas. "That fellow sitting over there."

"Are you positive this man fired the first shot?" the prosecutor asked.

"I am as positive as anyone could be," Irene insisted.[39]

Silvas took the stand in his own defense on December 20 and denied that he had been in Ruby on the day of the murders, claiming to have been at his father's house in Arivaca. Supporting Silvas's alibi were his father Trinidad and brother Ramon, as well as Albert Shepherd, though Shepherd later recanted his testimony. B. L. Cason and his wife, both residents of Ruby, also testified that Rosa de Rodriguez and her daughter couldn't possibly have seen Silvas enter the store as she had claimed, since the mercantile could not be seen from her house. On December 22, the jury was taken to Ruby to visit the scene of the crime, and also, to Silvas's home in Arivaca. Then, on Christmas Eve, the case went to the jury for deliberation. The twelve-man panel was still out that afternoon when the sensational news that Manuel Martinez had been arrested spread throughout Nogales.[40]

A considerable amount of intrigue surrounds the capture of Manuel Martinez that December. According to an article Parmer wrote in a 1936 edition of *Startling Detective*, the lawman was in the courtroom listening to testimony in the Silvas case when he received word that Martinez was believed to be hiding in the Pina Blanca Mountains. He immediately set out on horseback to apprehend him. Two days later, Parmer allegedly encountered Martinez in the desert, and after a brief pursuit, captured him. When Martinez refused to answer any of the lawman's questions, by his own admission, Parmer says he resorted to more rudimentary methods of interrogation, allegedly wrapping his lariat around the suspect's neck and tossing the other end over the limb of a tree. As Parmer later told it, the bluff worked. Believing that the former Arizona Ranger was about to hang him, Martinez immediately confessed to having murdered Myrtle Pearson for her gold fillings. With that, Parmer and his fellow deputies transported their prisoner to Nogales, arriving while the jury was in the midst of their deliberations in the case against Placidio Silvas.[41]

While the account published in *Startling Detective* is certainly dramatic, the true story of Martinez's apprehension differed considerably from the version offered by the pulp magazine. According to a motion filed by his attorney J. L. Fitts, and an appeal to the Supreme Court of the State of Arizona, Martinez had been "brought by Mexican soldiers from his home in the said Republic of Mexico by force and violence and against his will, and in total disregard of his constitutional rights as a Mexican citizen, residing in Mexico, and was by them delivered to the officials of the State of Arizona, as a result of a trade or bargain by which the Mexican soldiers received one General Reyna, whom they immediately executed without trial," and that afterwards, "he had been intimidated and by threats forced to make a so-called confession."[42]

One month before Martinez was taken into custody, General Francisco Reyna, an exiled Mexican revolutionary, was arrested in Nogales, Arizona, on November 25, 1921. "Reyna, who has been living in the mountains northwest of here," the *Nogales Herald* reported, "is said by Mexican officials to have been implicated in a revolutionary plot that was discovered in Nogales, Sonora, early this week when several alleged leaders of the movement were arrested." By that time, Reyna was already well known among southern Arizona lawmen. It had been reported that he was in command of the bandits that had fought the Utah cavalrymen and American cowboys at the "Stone House" near Ruby in 1917. In February of 1919, Reyna pled guilty to a charge of violating US neutrality laws for having shipped weapons into Mexico three years earlier.

Then, in August of 1920, Reyna and five of his followers were arrested in Arizona, and he was again charged with violating US neutrality laws in the wake of another failed uprising in Sonora.[43]

On December 26, 1921, two days after Martinez was taken into custody, the *Nogales Herald* reported that Reyna had been captured near Canosa, Sonora, while in the process of unearthing thirty rifles, thirty saddles, and four thousand rounds of ammunition. Reyna was then tried by a military court, found guilty for plotting an uprising against the government of President Alvaro Obregon, and was executed by firing squad in a Nogales cemetery. "He participated in a number of revolutions while the 'revoluting' business in Mexico was at its height," the *Bisbee Daily Review* explained. "When the Obregon government went into office he was one of the legion of generals who was not placed favorable. Naturally he was far from satisfied. He proceeded to use Arizona soil as a rendezvous for a band of men who were as dissatisfied as himself."[44]

Though newspaper accounts indicated that Reyna had been caught redhanded out in the Sonoran desert, Martinez's attorneys claimed that the general had actually been exchanged for Martinez. However, the *Nogales Herald* offered a much different story of his extradition. "Martinez was arrested at Saric, Sonora, four days ago, and deported on orders from President Obregon, and on the ground[s] that he was an undesirable alien," the newspaper reported, adding that, "Martinez's arrest was made along with that of 'the crippled man' by Mexican soldiers at Saric, and that the cripple made a full confession, in which he implicated himself, Martinez, and Silvas. This report could not be verified this afternoon." It would seem likely that "the crippled man" might have been the mysterious Samaniego, though what fate he may have endured at the hands of the Mexican soldiers is unknown.

On December 24, while a twelve-man jury was in the process of determining the fate of Placidio Silvas, Martinez was taken to the office of County Attorney DeRiemer, where he made a complete confession in front of Sheriff White, James Robbins, Irene Pearson, reporters from the *Nogales Herald*, and a court reporter. "He named as members of the gang of bandits who raided the Pearson store and post office—Placido Silvas, Antonio Alvarado, Alfredo Soto, Jesus Cruz, Jesus Maria Martinez, and a crippled man, and himself. He said he did not know the name of the cripple," the *Nogales Herald* reported.

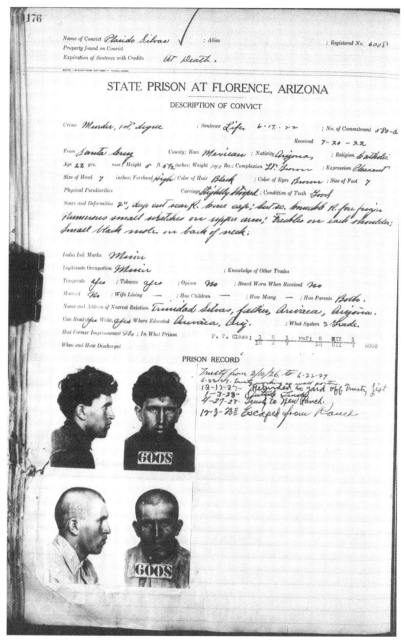

Name of Convict *Placido Silvas* ; Alias ; Registered No. *6008*
Property found on Convict
Expiration of Sentence with Credits *At Death.*

STATE PRISON AT FLORENCE, ARIZONA

DESCRIPTION OF CONVICT

Crime *Murder, 1st Degree* : Sentence *Life* *6-17-22* : No. of Commitment *580-2*

Received *7-20-22*

From *Santa Cruz* County; Race *Mexican* : Nativity *Arizona* : Religion *Catholic*
Age *22* yrs. most Height *5* ft *5½* inches; Weight *140* lbs.; Complexion *Lt. Brown* : Expression *Pleasant*
Size of Head *7* inches; Forehead *High*; Color of Hair *Black* : Color of Eyes *Brown* : Size of Foot *7*
Physical Peculiarities Carriage *Slightly Stooped* ; Condition of Teeth *Good*
Scars and Deformities *2", deep cut scar R. knee cap; Cut No. knuckle R. fore finger. Numerous small scratches on upper arm; Freckles on each shoulder; Small black mole on back of neck.*

India Ink Marks *Miner*
Legitimate Occupation *Miner* ; Knowledge of Other Trades
Temperate *Yes* ; Tobacco *Yes* : Opium *No* ; Beard Worn When Received *No*
Married *Yes* ; Wife Living — ; Has Children — ; How Many — ; Has Parents *Both.*
Name and Address of Nearest Relation *Trinidad Silvas, father, Arivaca, Arizona.*
Can Read *Yes* Write *Yes* Where Educated *Arivaca, Ariz.* ; What System *3 Grade.*
Had Former Imprisonment *No* ; In What Prison
When and How Discharged

F. P. Class; *1 R 1* ref; *0 RII 1*
16 R 7 18 UII 7 6008

PRISON RECORD

Trusty from 2/12/26 to 6-22-27
6-22-27- Trusty working at road camp
12-13-27- Returned to yard Off trusty list
1-3-28- Outside Trusty
4-27-28- Trusty to New Ranch.
10-3-28- Escaped from Ranch

Sentenced to life in prison for his role in the murders of the Pearsons in Ruby in 1921, Placido Silvas would eventually escape custody.

Arizona State Library and Archives

According to Martinez, three men—Soto, Jesus Maria Martinez, and another bandit—had gone into the store while the others remained outside, and that the gang had stolen $130.00 from the mercantile, as well as postal money orders and other merchandise, which they took across the border to Mexico, where the goods were transported to the town of Santa Ana and the money orders thrown away.[45]

Fearing that members of the jury might learn of Martinez's arrest and confession and would then find Silvas guilty based on what Martinez told Sheriff White, instead of the evidence presented at trial, Judge O'Conner dismissed the jury after seven hours of deliberation and declared a mistrial. O'Conner also ordered that Silvas was to be held without bail pending a second trial. Then, on December 30, 1921, a preliminary hearing was held in the case against Martinez, during which time the defendant and his attorney claimed that he had only made his confession because he believed that his life was in danger. According to defense attorney A. A. Trippel, on the day that he was taken into custody by White's deputies, Martinez was placed in the backseat of an automobile and was taken to "a lonely spot" on the Patagonia road by Parmer and Deputy Lou Quinn, that a rope had been placed on the car's floorboard, and then thrown over a tree to give Martinez the impression that he was about to be lynched, and that the lawmen had also stuck a gun in the man's stomach and threatened to kill him unless he confessed. He also backpedaled on his earlier claim that Silvas had ever ridden with the gang, and added that he himself had only taken part "because of threats made against him by the other members of the band if he did not participate."

When called to testify, Parmer denied that he and Quinn had used the rope or anything else to extract Martinez's confession, and stated that the only reason he and Quinn had taken him to the "lonely spot" was because there had been no private quarters at the jail where they could question him. Parmer "also denied that anyone used the statement 'If you don't admit you are guilty, we will kill you,' or the statement 'If you don't admit that Silvas was with you at Ruby, we will kill you.' " Nevertheless, Justice of the Peace M. Marsteller declared that the confession, "obtained by distasteful methods used by the officers," was inadmissible in court.[46]

In January of 1922, Manuel Martinez and Placidio Silvas were both turned over to federal authorities in Tucson to face charges for assaulting a US postmaster and theft of the US mail in Ruby. While in Tucson on March 20, 1922, Martinez made what amounted to a second confession when he told Arthur DeRiemer, Postal Inspector E. D. Chance, postmaster J. M. Ronstadt, and four others that he had indeed ridden into Ruby that morning, but that he had remained outside as a lookout while the mercantile was plundered. Martinez also claimed to have been given $20.00 as his share of the booty.[47]

Two months later, on May 16, 1922, Martinez went on trial in Nogales for the murder of Frank Pearson. Once again, W. A. O'Conner was the presiding judge, while Arthur DeRiemer served as prosecutor and attorney J. L. Fitts represented Martinez. Just as before, the same witnesses that had testified against Placidio Silvas in December were brought back to identify Martinez. Irene Pearson also returned, and was joined by Elizabeth Purcell and little Margaret Pearson. "Miss Purcell identified Martinez as one of the bandits," the *Nogales Herald* reported, "and declared that he was the one who fired a shot at her after the Pearsons had been killed."

Though the first confession Martinez had made under duress had been declared inadmissible, the second confession made in Tucson was introduced against him. Through his attorney, Martinez attempted to invoke an insanity defense, saying that his actions in Ruby were "caused by mental disease or unsoundness," and also submitted an "offer to prove" through witness testimony that Martinez had been the subject of a shady trade-off for Francisco Reyna, and that Parmer and Lou Quinn had taken him to "a lonely spot" where he had been forced to make his first confession. However, Judge O'Conner denied and overruled this potential evidence, and on May 18, 1922, the case was turned over to the jury, who, after fifteen minutes of deliberation, found Martinez guilty of murder, and recommended that he should hang. "The wife and daughter of Martinez became hysterical when they learned he is to be hanged," the *Nogales Herald* reported. "He admitted having been a member of the bandit gang, but he declared he had no hand in the shooting."[48]

The following day, Placidio Silvas went on trial for the second time for the murder of Frank Pearson. On June 4, 1922, after seventeen days of testimony, Silvas was found guilty of murder, with a jury recommendation that he receive a life sentence. A week later, on June 10, 1922, Judge O'Conner sentenced Manuel

Martinez to death and set a date of execution for August 18, 1922. Apparently, the notion that Martinez would hang while Silvas languished in prison, with a chance that he might eventually receive a pardon, wasn't something that sat well with O'Conner, who believed that Silvas was "ten times more guilty" than Martinez. "Martinez was raised in Mexico, had no opportunities for schooling, speaks no English, and does not read or write Spanish," O'Conner told the courtroom, "I have more sympathy for Martinez than Silvas."[49]

Ten days later, on June 27, Silvas faced yet another trial, this time for the murder of Myrtle Pearson. Testifying on July 3, Irene Pearson again identified Silvas as one of the three bandits who had entered the store. However, on July 12, after more than thirty hours of deliberation, the jury was unable to arrive at a unanimous verdict. Though eleven of the twelve jurors were in favor of conviction, a single holdout, D. J. Lovell, opposed, and Judge S. L. Pattee had no choice but to declare a mistrial. The following day, at 3:30 p.m. on July 13, 1922, Sheriff George White and Deputy Leonard Smith loaded Silvas into an automobile with Manuel Martinez, who had been brought to Santa Cruz County to testify in Silvas's third trial. Their destination that evening was the penitentiary in Florence, where Martinez had his scheduled date with the hangman. They never made it.[50]

The two lawmen and their prisoners got as far as the town of Tubac, twenty miles north of Nogales along the Tucson-Nogales Highway, when they experienced engine trouble and were forced to wait for a second vehicle to be brought up from the county seat. Once they were back on the road, White tried to make up for lost time. Eighteen miles south of Tucson, near the town of Continental, the sheriff's car struck a sand wash while traveling at a high rate of speed and "turned turtle." White suffered a fatal head injury in the rollover and died instantly. Leonard Smith staggered out of the wreckage with a broken collarbone and three broken ribs, as well as internal injuries. Although Martinez's legs were banged up, and Silvas sustained a slight neck injury, they were otherwise unharmed, and wasted no time in fleeing into the desert. "Deputy Smith said that five minutes after the accident had occurred, a man passed by in a car," the Bisbee Daily Review reported. The injured deputy managed to stop the driver and told him that White was dead and that their two prisoners had escaped. "The man promised to go for help and never returned," the newspaper added. "Five hours after that, help arrived."[51]

On July 14, 1922, as news of the tragic death of Sheriff White and the escape by Martinez and Silvas spread throughout Pima and Santa Cruz counties, a massive manhunt began that would ultimately involve hundreds of Arizona peace officers, professional trackers, civilian volunteers, and US Army soldiers. Among those leading the posses that fanned out across the desert were two of Arizona's most legendary lawmen, Pima County Sheriff Ben Daniels, a former US marshal, and Thomas H. Rynning, a former captain of the Arizona Rangers who now served as the superintendent of the Arizona State Penitentiary in Florence.

"New posses, from the Patagonia district, joined the search today," the *Nogales Herald* reported on July 15. "Chief of Police Jay Lowe of Nogales, with a posse, is working in the Arivaca district, while soldiers from the Twenty-fifth Infantry are stretched out along the border in the Arivaca and Ruby area." Cochise County Sheriff Joe Hood also joined the search, and with a posse of deputies mounted in automobiles, headed for Patagonia. "Practically every male resident of Patagonia and hundreds of men from Nogales are participating in the hunt," the *Bisbee Daily Review* reported, "scouring the mountains and desert between the Mexican border and the scene of the automobile accident." In the meantime, the Santa Cruz County board of supervisors appointed former sheriff Harry Saxon to serve out the remainder of White's term in office, and help lead the hunt for the fugitives.[52]

"Trails were found and lost again," the *Border Vidette* explained. "Acres of desert country were closely scrutinized until a slight lead was found and the trail was resumed again." Bloodhounds were also employed, though they proved to be of little genuine help in the search. "The bloodhounds were no good. All they were good for was to ride in a Ford car," Harry Saxon told reporters. Three days after the accident, on July 17, Deputy Leonard Smith died in a Tucson hospital after developing a severe case of pneumonia while recovering from his injuries. That same day, D. J. Lovell, the juror whose refusal to vote for a conviction had triggered Silvas's mistrial, received a letter that was purported to have been sent by the Ku Klux Klan. "If you value your life," the message read, "you had better clear hastily out of this town and country. A man of your thoughts, actions, and character is not welcome here."

That same afternoon, one of the posses on the lookout for the fugitives made a surprising discovery in the Santa Cruz Mountains, when they stumbled upon a huge still used by area bootleggers. "Operators of the still, apparently aware of the presence of scores of officers in the vicinity, had abandoned the still," the *Bisbee Daily Review* remarked, "said to be one of the largest ever unearthed in this part of the state."[53]

Just before noon on Tuesday, July 18, 1922, as Harry Saxon and his Santa Cruz posse moved through the mesquite two and a half miles from the village of Amado, Saxon's horse stumbled, "and as the officer was falling to the ground he got a glimpse of Martinez hiding in a cave between some rocks which had been cleverly covered with brush." Saxon got to his feet, immediately drew his revolver, and ordered Martinez and Silvas to come forward. Weak from hunger and exhaustion, the two men surrendered without offering any resistance. Saxon fired two signal shots from his six-gun to summon his men, and "the great manhunt was ended."

Later that day, after he and Martinez had been transported to the Santa Cruz County Jail in Nogales, Placidio Silvas provided newspaper reporters with an account of their ordeal in the desert. "We didn't know where we were going," he told them. "We had to travel slow because Martinez's legs were hurt in the accident. We traveled all Thursday night and got lost. On Friday morning we broke the chains of the handcuffs holding us together." According to Silvas, neither man had had anything to eat throughout the five-day trek, and they had traveled at night in order to rest during the day when the summer sun was at its most intense. Silvas also claimed that at one point, William Oliver Parmer and another officer had come close to capturing them on the third day of the manhunt. "They were within five feet of us. I was lying under a bush at the time."[54]

That evening, the *Nogales Herald* published a message from Thomas H. Rynning, congratulating the lawmen, soldiers, and civilian volunteers who had combed the desert in search of the two fugitives. "On behalf of the governor of Arizona," Rynning's message read, "I desire to thank the red-blooded men of Santa Cruz County who were on the five-day manhunt which just ended successfully. They were a tireless bunch of real men and deserve the commendation of the people of the state."

"Time and again the capture was doubtful, but never at any time did any member of the posse lose hope, and they stuck to the trail until the men were found," an editorial explained. "This is the Spirit of the West! It is a commendable spirit!"[55]

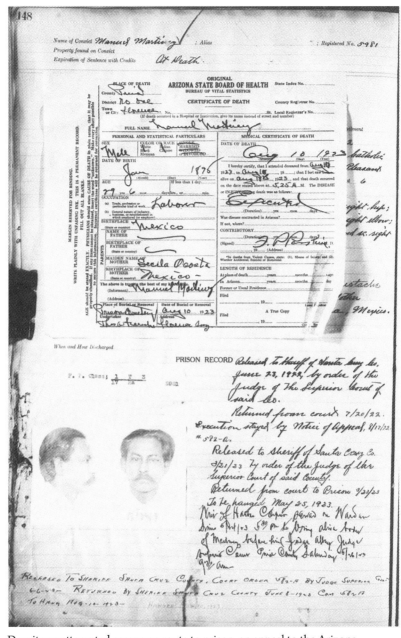

Despite an attempted escape en route to prison, an appeal to the Arizona Supreme Court, and the efforts of the Mexican government, Manuel Martinez was hanged at the Arizona State Penitentiary at Florence on August 10, 1923, nearly two years after the slayings of the Pearsons in Ruby.

Arizona State Library and Archives

At 8:00 a.m. on Thursday, July 20, 1922, Manuel Martinez and Placidio Silvas were once again loaded into an automobile for the six-hour trip from Nogales to Florence. This time, they were escorted by Saxon, Deputy R. Q. Leatherman, a driver, and Nogales Police Officer Harold Brown. The quartet of officers and their two prisoners arrived at the state prison that afternoon without incident. Almost as soon as Martinez was in his custody, however, he presented Thomas Rynning with a legal predicament. The doomed man was scheduled to appear as a witness in Silvas's fourth trial, set to begin on August 28, 1922, a full ten days after Martinez was supposed to hang. "In response to Warden Rynning's request for advice," the *Bisbee Daily Review* explained, "Attorney General W. J. Galbraith today asserted that the warden cannot do otherwise than carry out the first order unless a stay of execution is granted meanwhile."[56]

Santa Cruz County Attorney Arthur DeRiemer solved this quandary for Rynning by dropping his pursuit of a fourth trial for Silvas. "I do not believe a jury can be obtained by August 28," DeRiemer told reporters in early August, "and inasmuch as Martinez is to be hanged on August 18, and Silvas is already facing a term of life imprisonment, I do not see the need of putting the county to further expense." The board of supervisors agreed with their prosecutor, and the county attempted no further prosecution of Placidio Silvas.[57]

While his accomplice gradually adjusted to life behind the gray walls at Florence, Manuel Martinez waged a desperate battle to save his neck from the hangman, and his attorney filed an appeal for a new trial. "The eleventh-hour attempt to save Martinez from the gallows was instituted Wednesday," the *Bisbee Daily Review* reported on August 12, 1922, "by attorney Greg Garcia of Phoenix, representing the Mexican consul in the capital city."

However, this initial appeal was overruled on the grounds that Garcia, who had replaced an ailing J. L. Fitts as his lawyer, had not filed the motion within sixty days after the judgment against Martinez had been entered. Then, on August 17, the day before Martinez was set to die, Attorney General Galbraith issued an order postponing the execution pending an action by the State Supreme Court of Arizona.[58]

In his appeal to the Arizona Supreme Court, Garcia argued that among other things, Martinez, who was a citizen of the Republic of Mexico, had been forcibly taken from his home by Mexican soldiers and traded for Francisco

Reyna in violation of his constitutional rights and the laws of both countries, and that he had not been advised of his rights when making his confession. "Counsel for the defendant at the trial called W. O. Parmer and attempted to show that the witness had been intimidated and by threats forced to make a so-called confession," and that it had been prejudicial for the court to refuse to allow this evidence to be introduced. Further, Garcia argued that Fitts, "who, a short time after the trial was sent to a sanitarium in California for mental disorders, and because of his condition at the time of the trial he did not make many objections to the testimony and raise points of law, which would have been of great aid and benefit to this defendant."[59]

None of this was enough to convince the Arizona Supreme Court, who dismissed Martinez's appeal in March of 1923. The Superior Court of Santa Cruz County then set a new date of execution for May 25, 1923. But then, on May 15, Mexican President Alvaro Obregon intervened, and sent a telegram to Arizona Governor W. P. Hunt asking for executive clemency. "President Obregon does not state any legal reason for the request," one Arizona newspaper reported, "save for the exercising of the law authorizing pardons." While the Arizona State Board of Pardons and Paroles denied Obregon's request, efforts made by what the *Casa Grande Dispatch* referred to as "high minded people" to keep Martinez alive continued for several months.[60]

Finally, on August 10, 1923, just two weeks shy of the second anniversary of the Pearson slayings, Manuel Martinez was led from his cell to the gallows at Florence. As he stood on the scaffold, Martinez made a final declaration of his innocence, once again insisting that he had been forced to participate in the raid by the other members of the gang. "I am dying with a clear conscience," he told those who had gathered to witness his execution. "I am not afraid to go. But Placidio Silvas has no right to be in this prison. I once said that he was one of those who made the raid. He was not. He knew nothing about it." Manuel Martinez was hanged at 5:24 a.m., and was declared dead eleven minutes later.[61]

CHAPTER SIX

DRY AGENTS

I have been on the border for 12 years, and never before have
I seen conditions as they are today. Ten years ago there was
a great deal of Chinese smuggling, but at no time were the
runners dangerous, even though they were working under a
heavy penalty. Now it is a matter of gun play when we order
men to halt, for they are always armed and ready for a fight.

—*Unidentified US Customs Inspector,*
El Paso Herald, *February 12, 1921*

At about 9:30 a.m. on the morning of Wednesday, March 2, 1921, El
Paso farmer J. Frank Coles and Special Deputy Will Newell were moving through the brush along the edge of Coles's property line near Cordova
Island when they were "fired upon by two Mexicans, who had crossed the line
200 or 300 yards away." While Newell returned fire and drove off their attackers, Coles ran for help and called the police. A short time later, Sergeant Tom
York, a former sheriff of Bandera County, and Officer W. A. "Dad" Warnock
arrived and "searched the brush looking for a liquor cache, and when they met
with no success, reported the occurrence to prohibition officers who went to
the scene."

Among the first Federal Prohibition Agents to arrive at "the island" that
morning were thirty-five-year-old Ernest Walter Walker and thirty-six-year-
old Frank A. Hamer, a former Texas Ranger who would later achieve legendary status for his role in tracking down and killing outlaws Bonnie Parker and
Clyde Barrow in 1934. While Walker and Hamer searched the area for the
booze, the alleged smugglers were reinforced by a large party of gunmen who
crossed the boundary to retrieve their contraband. "The smugglers opened
fire on the prohibition agents as they approached. The officers returned the
fire," the *El Paso Herald* reported, "slowly advancing as they did so. The smugglers, numbering 20 or more, spread into a fan formation, firing as they lay
concealed in brush upon the officers from three directions."

In March of 1921, Federal Prohibition Agent Ernest W. Walker became the first "dry agent" to fall in the line of duty in El Paso, when he was fatally wounded in a shootout at Cordova Island. *Courtesy of Ancestry.com*

Outnumbered and clearly outgunned, Hamer and Walker managed to hold their ground until help arrived in the form of city police officers and soldiers from the US Army's provost guard, as well as other Prohibition agents. At some point during the intense gun battle that followed, "said by officers to have been one of the biggest since prohibition enforcement laws were enacted," Walker moved into a firing position well in advance of Hamer and the other lawmen. As soon as he realized that he had moved dangerously ahead of his fellow agents, Walker attempted to fall back. But, just as he rose from his position, Walker entered the crosshairs of a gunman hidden in an adobe house and was hit by a jacketed bullet that tore through his abdomen. Despite his injuries, as the battle raged on, Walker continued to fire his weapon at the bootleggers. "The smugglers withdrew after fighting had continued two hours. They scattered to adobe houses in the neighborhood. Some crossed to the Mexican side and continued firing from there," the *El Paso Herald* reported.

As the gunmen pulled back across the boundary, Walker was transported to the Hotel Dieu ("House of God"), a hospital located about a mile and a half from the scene of the shoot-out at Cordova Island. While doctors attempted to treat his injuries and make the badly wounded agent as comfortable as possible, Walker's supervising inspector, James A. Shevlin, sent a telegram to his superiors in Washington that called for an increase in the forces on hand to combat bootlegging on the border. "We feel," Shevlin told them, "that we were fortunate in that all of our men were not killed. At times they were nearly surrounded, and were being fired upon by men who could see them but whom they could not see."[1]

Gunfire once again broke out at the edge of the Island on March 3, 1921, when federal agents returned to the previous day's battleground to recover Walker's pistol. According to newspaper reports on the incident, "American officers learned today, Mexican smugglers have established trenches a short distance south of the boundary from where they can maintain a fire to protect the operations of the smugglers." Two days later, at 6:00 p.m. on Saturday night, March 5, 1921, Ernest Walker died in his hospital bed at the Hotel Dieu, leaving behind a wife and son. Walker was the tenth Federal Prohibition Agent to die from injuries sustained in the line of duty, and the first one killed in El Paso, Texas. Though three men were later taken into custody in connection with Walker's murder, a grand jury failed to return an indictment, and the suspects were released.

On March 7, 1921, the *El Paso Herald* published an interview with James A. Shevlin that appeared alongside Walker's death notice. In reporting the progress made by his men since the previous October, Shevlin described the number of arrests his agents had made, as well as the challenges they had encountered in enforcing the law on the border. "In the main," Shevlin explained, "the men we now have are young, active, willing, and efficient, and the majority are familiar with the conditions existing along the border. There is no doubt within my mind that within a year, a good control will have been gained over smuggling and moonshining throughout this section. We realize the gigantic task at hand, but we are all willing to do our level best to enforce the laws we are sworn to uphold."[2]

By the time that federal Prohibition laws went into effect in January 1920, customs officials in El Paso reported that heavy shipments of alcohol had already been taken across the international boundary into Ciudad Juarez. According to Deputy Collector of Customs W. W. Carpenter, by mid-December, 448 barrels and 7,218 cases of whiskey had been shipped to El Paso for transport to Juarez. A month later, as the January 16 deadline loomed, Carpenter reported that since the beginning of the year, 741 barrels and 5,507 cases of whiskey had been exported, "which at the present price of the contraband on the El Paso market is said to be worth $3,000,000." At the same time, the *El Paso Herald* informed its readers that federal agents, "who will work on nothing but liquor law violations, have arrived in El Paso and are in readiness to begin their work Saturday morning. Offices for this department, which will also work on narcotic cases, will be opened in the county court house in a few days."[3]

On Friday night, January 2, 1920, Captain Pablo Delgado, commander of the Mexican fiscal guards in Juarez, was on patrol near the Island when he apprehended two Americans attempting to cross the border with booze and narcotics. "Later in the evening," the *El Paso Herald* reported, "Delgado arrested a Mexican in a buggy, attempting to smuggle 210 quarts of tequila into the United States." Three days later, Delgado and his men intercepted another smuggler, three miles west of the Santa Fe Bridge, in the process of hauling 24 quarts of tequila across the river. Contraband seized by Delgado and his officers that winter suggested that at least some of the booze being exported to Mexico was already making its way back across the Rio Grande in the days just before the Volstead Act went into effect. On January 7, 1920, Delgado invited reporters to his office, where in every corner and piled high in the center of the room "were bottles and cases which he estimated contained 1,000 quarts of intoxicants, mostly whiskey. Included in the lot, however, were 13 cases of wood alcohol, which he said he believed was intended to be used in making 'bootleg' whiskey in the United States."

"The poor Mexican has not the money to buy liquors in large quantity," Delgado explained. "This lot here was purchased with American money on the Texas side and your authorities could well look into the matter closely. As far as possible the border is closed. A bottle of whiskey here and there are not getting by my men, who are cooperating to their fullest ability to stop the liquor traffic into the United States even though there is no Mexican law to prevent the exportation of liquors," Delgado told them.[4]

For a time, El Paso Police Chief Montgomery and Sheriff Seth B. Orndorff had been able to rely on the presence of the Texas Rangers of Company B, under the command of Captain Charles F. Stevens, to help stem the flow of bootleg into the city. However, a number of incidents at the end of 1919 resulted in the removal of Rangers by Governor William P. Hobby.

On Christmas night, December 25, 1919, Horace G. Lay was riding in an automobile with his brother Louis, Louis's wife, and a man named Paul Atkinson and his wife, when they were stopped by three Rangers on the valley road. "I saw a revolver stuck in my face," Louis Lay later reported, "and felt a hand at the back of my neck. The revolver was cocked. The man tried to pull me out of my seat over the door. I asked him to 'hold on' and asked him what he wanted. He said he wanted to search the car and kept pulling at me. I asked him to release me and asked him for his authority for searching my car, and if he had a warrant. He said he didn't need a warrant and struck at me with his gun."

Before their encounter with the three lawmen was over, Louis and Horace Lay and Paul Atkinson were each pistol-whipped and otherwise manhandled by the Rangers. "We threatened to report them to Mayor Davis and to have them investigated. One of them said 'to Hell with the mayor'; that he didn't have anything to do with them, and added: 'We are Rangers.' "[5]

Following a public outcry against the state force, and an investigation by Assistant Adjutant General H. C. Smith, the Rangers under Captain Stevens were recalled from El Paso in early January. However, not everyone celebrated the company's departure. "If Governor Hobby sends the Rangers somewhere and tells them to do something," the Bryan *Eagle* declared, "it is a mighty safe bet to lay odds they will do it. Business for the undertakers may pick up and the price of mourning apparel may rise, but they'll do it. And we suspect one reason their withdrawal from El Paso is asked is that they are striving, in their hardboiled, rough-shod way, to do what they were told to do."[6]

Within days of the departure of the Texas Rangers from El Paso, another force of lawmen began to gather in the border city to join the liquor battle being waged by local police officers, deputy sheriffs, and customs inspectors. On January 14, 1920, as American distilleries shipped some of their final cargoes through El Paso on their way to warehouses in Juarez, newspapers announced the arrival of J. H. Fleming, "who formerly was connected with the federal revenue office at Denver," and who would now spearhead the enforcement of federal liquor and narcotics in El Paso.[7]

As a result of the National Prohibition Act of 1919, primary enforcement of the Eighteenth Amendment fell to the Federal Prohibition Agents employed by the Bureau of Internal Revenue. "This work is essentially unrelated to taxation, which is the subject matter of this bureau," an annual report by the commissioner of Internal Revenue stated, "and both the Secretary of the Treasury and the Commissioner urged upon the committees of Congress the recommendation that this important responsibility not be upon the Treasury Department, which is already burdened with the fiscal, and revenue, problems of the Government. However, Congress, evidently considering the similarity of some phases of the work of internal-revenue agents in the field who are assigned to secure evidence and aid in the prosecution of persons who have evaded the taxes imposed by law on the manufacture and sale of alcoholic beverages with the police function of prohibition enforcement officers, decided that the Bureau of Internal Revenue should undertake, in addition to its functions as a tax gathering agency, the enforcement of the prohibition law."[8]

From 1920 until 1927, when it was reorganized and rechristened as the Bureau of Prohibition under the Treasury Department, the Prohibition Unit would function as its own branch of the Bureau of Internal Revenue. And in

Arguably one of the most famous western lawmen of the twentieth century, veteran Texas Ranger Frank Augustus Hamer served as a Federal Prohibition Agent during the early 1920s. He left the Bureau of Internal Revenue a few months after Agent Walker was killed in 1921 to accept an appointment as a captain in the Texas Rangers. He is best remembered today as being one of the leaders of the posse that killed Bonnie Parker and Clyde Barrow in Louisiana in 1934. *Courtesy of Ancestry.com*

addition to their mission of enforcing national liquor policies, the Prohibition Unit would also absorb the Bureau's Narcotic Division, whose agents were responsible for the enforcement of America's narcotics policies.[9]

By 1921, there would be more than two thousand "dry agents" and narcotics officers working under the direction of a dozen supervising Federal Prohibition Agents in twelve separate districts throughout the United States and the territories of Puerto Rico and Hawaii. While some of these officers, like Frank Hamer, had prior experience in law enforcement, many agents had never worn a badge and received little in the way of formal police training. Alfred M. Monroy had recently worked as a clerk in the El Paso post office when he joined the Prohibition Unit in April of 1920. When Roy A. Fridley signed on as a Prohibition agent in Phoenix, Arizona, in June of 1920, his previous employment experience had included a stint as a smelter worker in Douglas and the management of a pool hall in the town of Kingman. Prior to taking over as Federal Prohibition Director for the State of Arizona in 1921, Irish-born Michael E. Cassidy, a witness to the 1919 Riot in Bisbee, had worked as a claims adjuster for the Phelps-Dodge Corporation. Having previously been employed as a pharmacist, Samuel Woolston brought at least some practical experience to the job when he became one of the Bureau's narcotic inspectors in 1921.[10]

Still, there were at least a few agents stationed in the Southwest who were not complete novices when it came to police work. Before signing on as a Prohibition agent in April of 1920, S. Mackie "Mac" Jester had previously served as a deputy sheriff, a Texas Ranger, and a Deputy US Marshal. Also joining the Prohibition service that year was thirty-two-year-old Stafford E. Beckett, a former immigration inspector and Texas Ranger who had once served alongside Frank Hamer. In February of 1920, Hamer and Beckett's former commander, Captain Charles F. Stevens, resigned from the Rangers and became a Prohibition agent that April, bringing to his new federal position thirty years' worth of experience. Likewise, Arizona's Harry D. Midkiff had already handled his share of bootleggers as a Cochise County deputy sheriff when he signed on as a "dry agent" in 1921.[11]

Throughout its existence, the Prohibition Unit would be plagued by criminal behavior and corruption. Between January of 1920 and February of 1926, no fewer than 121 Prohibition agents would be sacked for extortion, bribery, or soliciting money, and another 80 officers would lose their jobs for falsifying expense accounts. During this same period, 61 agents were also fired for collusion or conspiracy, and 187 were canned for intoxication and other misconduct. Prohibition agent Roy Fridley landed in hot water in February of 1921 when he was arrested in a Phoenix hotel room on charges of transporting and selling intoxicating beverages. Released from custody under a $5,000.00 bond, Fridley decided to take his chances on the run, rather than in a courtroom. Fridley fled the state of Arizona and eventually made his way to Kellogg, Idaho, where he briefly found work in one of the mines there before being tracked down by government agents. On May 6, 1921, Fridley was found guilty of conspiracy to violate federal Prohibition laws, and was sentenced to two years at the federal penitentiary in Leavenworth, Kansas.[12]

Nationwide, Federal Prohibition Agents experienced a considerable attrition rate. The Bureau of Internal Revenue would later report that between 1920 and 1926, 45 officers had been killed in the line of duty, while another 297 had been injured. During that same period, the agents in turn had killed a total of 89 people and wounded another 72. "A too free use of firearms has been one of the criticisms directed against prohibition agents," an agency history later explained, "and alleged cases of unjustifiable use of weapons have been reported. The casualties among agents may indicate that they were dealing with criminals, although it is possible that some casualties resulted from unlawful acts."[13]

Throughout the first year of nationwide Prohibition, plenty of Southwestern dry agents and their Treasury Department counterparts in the US Customs Service went about their work of shutting down illicit stills and seizing contraband liquor without the taint of corruption or other criminal behavior. In many instances, officers went to great lengths and endured numerous hardships and dangers in order to enforce the largely unpopular federal liquor laws.

Assisted by two deputy sheriffs, Federal Prohibition Agents Clomar Martin and J. T. Brown journeyed high into the mountains above Rodeo, New Mexico, in March of 1920 in order to locate a still operated by rancher D. M. Phillips. "The officers report that they reached the still only after a hard climb approximately 3,000 feet up the mountains. The last 2,000 feet of the climb, they say, was too steep for a burro to climb and was made on foot." When they finally reached Phillips's distillery, they discovered two hundred gallons of sour mash ready for distillation, which, according to the agents, when manufactured would have made seventy-five gallons of moonshine whiskey.[14]

On June 28, Agents Stafford E. Beckett and Arch Gregg journeyed into the Manzana Mountains of New Mexico on orders from Chief Inspector Fleming to "trace the source from which the people of that state were obtaining moonshine whiskey, of which there was apparently an inexhaustible supply." Assisted by a team of deputy sheriffs, the two "prohis" headed into the high country north of Scholle, New Mexico, and eventually discovered a still capable of churning out an estimated fifty gallons of corn whiskey per day. They also found three hundred gallons of moonshine and an assortment of firearms on the premises. "The plant was in full operation when the officers came upon it. Two men were at work making whiskey," the *El Paso Herald* reported, "and the revenue men and their guides lay concealed in the bushes watching the process for several hours in the hope that others would appear. It was only when the alleged moonshiners finished their work, and were preparing to leave the still, that the officers stepped out with leveled guns. The men were captured without a fight."[15]

Many other encounters between law enforcement and Southwestern bootleggers did not end so peaceably. On Monday, March 15, 1920, El Paso police officers Charles Wood, W. P. Hoey, and W. E. Smith surprised five men crossing the international boundary carrying several sacks of tequila. After swapping lead with the city officers for a few minutes, the five smugglers scattered into the darkness, four of them retreating to a house on San Marcial Street. "On entering the house," the *Herald*'s account continued, "the police say they found Eugenio Vialobos, and his brother, Felix, Emilio Garcia, and Filomeno Sifuentes." They also discovered a woman and a child inside the home using the sacks as bed pillows. "The sacks contained, according to the police, 43 quart bottles of tequila," the *Herald* explained.[16]

On the night of Wednesday, April 21, 1920, Prohibition Agents Robert W. Nourse and Mac Jester were fired on while the officers were in the process of seizing thirty gallons of whiskey and twenty-three gallons of tequila near Val Verde. "The Mexican smugglers, when ordered to halt, dropped the sacks of tequila and separated in the darkness," the *Herald* reported. Then, as Nourse and Jester were in the midst of loading the liquid cargo in their automobile, the bootleggers opened fire from different directions, then scattered into the brush without having wounded either officer. Nourse had another close call on the morning of June 5, 1920, when he and agent S. J. Shaw were ambushed by another group of smugglers at the edge of Cordova Island. "The prohibition agents told the police they were fired on from a 'dobe house on the island and fought back at long range without crossing the line. So far as is known, no one was hit," the *Herald* stated.[17]

On Sunday, June 20, 1920, Customs Inspector Tom Armstrong and El Paso County Deputy Sheriff Charles Litchfield received word from an informant that one Rosendo Magallanes and two accomplices were planning to leave El Paso with a shipment of alcohol. Acting on this intelligence, the two officers trailed Magallanes's car out of the city to the Fort Bliss branch of the Southern Pacific railroad, where the vehicle pulled off to the side of the road. Then, the lawmen watched as Magallanes climbed out of his automobile and whistled. Moments later, a man named Augustin Valencia emerged from the brush and joined Magallanes in the road. "Seeing the car of the officers," the *El Paso Herald* later reported, "the two started toward it, and when ordered to halt Magalance [*sic*] drew his revolver and aimed it at Litchfield." Litchfield immediately jerked out his own weapon and shot Magallanes through the right arm, the bullet passing through the man's torso and lodging near his spine. "Valencia was captured by Armstrong before he succeeded in escaping to the car in which his companions made off," the *Herald* stated.

Valencia was taken to the county jail and was charged with illegal possession of forty-two quarts of tequila. Magallanes was transported to the Hotel Dieu, where he died twelve days later on July 2, 1920. The following day, Litchfield was charged with murder, though the complaint "[was] merely technical, in order that the shooting of Rosendo Magallanos [*sic*] might be cleared up." On July 7, Litchfield was acquitted of any and all charges in connection with the death of Magallanes.[18]

A much larger battle between smugglers and area lawmen took place a week after Magallanes was shot. At 2:30 a.m. on the morning of Tuesday, June 29, 1920, Ernest W. Walker and two other dry agents encountered a dozen men in an alfalfa field near the Peyton Packing Plant on the edge of Cordova Island. The strangers were apparently waiting for the arrival of an automobile so that they could transfer a large shipment of illegal liquor. As soon as they realized that Walker and his companions were "prohis," the bootleggers opened fire on them with shotguns and rifles. "Although outnumbered four to one, and at a further disadvantage because they were armed only with six-shooters while the smugglers fought with high-powered rifles and pump shotguns, using buckshot," the *El Paso Herald* explained that evening, "the officers held their ground, engaging the smugglers until the arrival of reinforcements led by Sheriff Seth B. Orndorff." With only the bootleggers' muzzle flashes to guide their own fire, the federal agents and the county officers succeeded in driving the smugglers back across the international boundary, and later recovered some forty gallons of whiskey from the battleground, with another thirty gallons destroyed during the shoot-out. Though there were no known casualties in this exchange of gunfire, during which some two hundred rounds were reportedly discharged, Prohibition Agent Ernest W. Walker would be killed near this very spot only nine months later.[19]

On Wednesday, September 8, 1920, US Customs Inspector Herff Alexander Carnes and a fellow officer were lying in the weeds near Cinecue Station, not far from the town of Ysleta, when they spotted four Mexican men heading their way from the direction of the international boundary. "One man was riding a horse and the other three were afoot," the *El Paso Herald* later reported. Carnes, who had once served as a Texas Ranger under the legendary Captain John R. Hughes, was no man to trifle with. In August of 1915, four years after he had signed on as a mounted customs "line rider," Carnes had ridden with the posse that had shot and killed famed Mexican revolutionary Pascual Orozco. Later, in 1919, Carnes had survived a brutal pistol-whipping at the hands of a Mexican fugitive he had just placed under arrest. "Quick thinking on the part of Mr. Carnes when he discharged the cartridges in his pistol probably saved the inspector's life," one newspaper account read, "for the Mexican succeeded in wrenching the revolver from Carnes's hand during the struggle and would no doubt have shot the inspector had the weapon remained loaded."

Now, Carnes and his partner watched as the four men closed in on their position, the former Ranger once again bracing himself for a fight. Sure enough, as soon as Carnes ordered the Mexicans to throw up their hands, one of the men, later identified as laborer Miguel Garcia, reached for his gun. Carnes shot Garcia through the heart and killed him instantly. Garcia's companions immediately scattered into the darkness, leaving behind five sacks of whiskey and tequila.[20]

M1911 Colt .45 automatic pistol and holster attributed to Customs Inspector Herff
Alexander Carnes, a former Texas Ranger who had once served under legendary
Captain John R. Hughes.   *Paul Goodwin*

Carnes had yet another brush with danger six weeks later when he and
fellow Ranger veteran George Spencer tangled with thirty-year-old Domingo
Chavez and four other smugglers south of Ysleta. The trouble began on Tuesday, October 19, 1920, when Carnes and Spencer spotted a man with a sack
over his shoulder crossing back into Mexico from the American side of the
Rio Grande. "Suspicions aroused," the *El Paso Herald* reported, "the officers
concealed themselves near a pathway up the bank on the American side. A few
moments later, they saw a horse approach this point, and watched as a sack
was lifted from the animal's back by its rider. The horse then returned to the
Mexican side, making five trips in all."

A little while later, Carnes and Spencer watched as Chavez and four other
men started up the riverbank, each carrying a heavily loaded sack. The two
inspectors fell in behind them and followed the suspected smugglers one hundred yards inland before calling out "Hands up!" When the officers searched
the men's bundles, they discovered fifty-three quarts of tequila and placed the

entire party under arrest. Once the line riders had taken the men into custody, they then began to march them back to Ysleta, with Carnes leading the procession and Spencer bringing up the rear. As they made their way through the brush, "the man identified as Chavez dropped to the rear, and suggested to Spencer in Spanish that 'if you'll let us go, we'll fix you up.' " Spencer ordered the man to take his place back in the line, but he had no sooner barked his instruction than Chavez lunged at him and snatched Spencer's rifle out of his hands. Chavez first tried to use the rifle as a club, then "attempted to snap the gun, which was on safety and did not fire."

In the meantime, while the bandit fumbled with his rifle, Spencer drew his revolver and opened fire, squeezing off shots until Chavez disappeared into the darkness. "While this had been going on," the *El Paso Herald* reported, "the remainder of the prisoners attempted to charge Carnes, who ordered them to stand back." When the smugglers did not heed Carnes's demands, he pulled out his own gun and shot two of the men down. "The officer saw another escaping in the darkness," the *Herald* added, "while the fourth had made his getaway at some time prior." Uncertain as to where Chavez had gone with Spencer's rifle, the two lawmen hesitated to move out into the open. Finally, they agreed to go to Ysleta to get help for the men that Carnes had wounded. But, when the officers later returned, the two smugglers that Carnes had shot had apparently dragged themselves away into the brush. After a brief search, the line riders discovered Chavez lying on the ground, dead, and retrieved Spencer's weapon. It was later reported that the men that Carnes had wounded had eventually made their way back across the border, where they received medical aid in Zaragosa, Mexico.[21]

While bootlegging would remain an acute problem for authorities all along the Rio Grande Valley throughout the 1920s, and moonshiners continued to crank out corn liquor and "white mule" from backwoods distilleries hidden in the high country of Arizona and New Mexico, at very few points along the US-Mexican border, or anywhere else in the American Southwest, was illicit liquor traffic and narcotics smuggling as epidemic as it was in El Paso. By the end of June 1920, W. H. Kennedy, the Internal Revenue Bureau's assistant field supervisor for Texas recognized that the force of dry agents under J. H. Fleming's command was simply too small to combat the traffic in illicit drugs and liquor in El Paso. During a visit to the border city on June

29, Kennedy promised to petition Washington for additional officers, and also "expressed gratification at the results obtained by Mr. Fleming with his small force of men."[22]

Later that summer, the Bureau took steps to reorganize its forces in the American Southwest, and announced that former Yale football player James A. Shevlin would be transferred from New York to El Paso to succeed Fleming, who was promoted to assistant supervising inspector for the Southwestern department, and to take command of a new "border department" consisting of the states of Arizona, New Mexico, and portions of Texas, including El Paso. "The border prohibition problem along the Mexican boundary is regarded by prohibition agents as the biggest faced by federal agents in the enforcement of the Volstead Act. Practically the entire problem lies within the border district," the *El Paso Herald* reported in late October. Earlier that month, Charles Archibald "Arch" Wood, who took charge of El Paso's Prohibition office in September, pending Shevlin's arrival, reported that within just the previous three weeks, his agents had seized some 1,000 quarts of alcohol and another 10,900 grains of narcotics, along with five automobiles used for smuggling.[23]

In reporting on a visit made to their city by James A. Shevlin in November, the *San Antonio Evening News* reported that "in spite of the fact that Texas is comparatively 'dry,' El Paso is still one of the worst liquor-smuggling localities in the United States," and suggested that the border city would pose one of the greatest challenges to Shevlin's agents. Still, Shevlin attempted to put a positive spin on the situation his men faced in the new border department. "The really wonderful thing about the enforcement of prohibition is the way in which the public has responded," Shevlin explained. "Without the cooperation of the rank and file of citizens," he continued, "it would have been practically impossible to have enforced, except in a small way, the National prohibition amendment. As it is, considering the vast numbers of people, who before a National law was passed, were classed as 'anti-prohibition,' there are comparatively few who will willingly violate the law in order to secure contraband liquor."[24]

Not all of Shevlin's federal colleagues agreed with his statements in the *San Antonio Evening News*, at least not as far as El Paso itself was concerned. "Bootlegging and smuggling gangs are more desperate than ever before," according to W. W. Carpenter, collector of customs of the El Paso border district, regarded as among the most important on the entire United States frontiers," the *El Paso Herald* reported at the end of the year. "The bootleggers will kill federal agents if by doing so they could escape with their contraband. The life of the officer is of less concern to them than their liquor, it seems," Carpenter added.[25]

On the night of March 21, 1921, three weeks after Prohibition Agent Ernest W. Walker was fatally wounded on the edge of Cordova Island, dry agents Stafford E. Beckett, Charles "Arch" Wood, W. C. Guinn, and J. F. Parker left El Paso at about 7:00 p.m. and headed for the Shearman hog ranch five miles east of the city. Riding with them that night was eighteen-year-old Pascual Ornelas. Pascual would later explain that he had known Beckett for several years and had frequently acted as his informant, infiltrating groups of smugglers attempting to cross the Rio Grande. Earlier that evening, Beckett and Wood had received intelligence that Neil T. Shearman, who operated the ranch with his father, Charles "C. P." Shearman, and his brothers, John and Allen, was expected to ship a load of bootleg liquor. The agents had then secured a search warrant and set out to intercept the contraband.[26]

Despite the fact that Neil Shearman had held a commission as a special deputy, had been a member of the El Paso Rotary Club, and could boast various other professional and civic accomplishments, the thirty-two-year-old hog farmer had been involved in at least two different gunfights and other brushes with the law. In October of 1918, Neil shot and killed thirty-five-year-old Tranquillo Serrana, "the Mexican having been found by Mr. Sherman [*sic*] in a feed shed on the Sherman hog ranch, near the five-mile point in the lower valley." Two years later, on Tuesday, July 27, 1920, while still serving as one of Orndorff's deputies, Neil got into a fight with Ben Williams, a private investigator hired by Neil's wife to keep tabs on her husband. "When Williams went to the Shearman home to report on Monday," the *El Paso Herald* noted, "Mr. Shearman was there and accosted and attempted to disarm the detective. He states that Williams was shot in the shoulder by the accidental discharge of his own revolver. Shearman says he had wrenched it from Williams and struck him on the side of the head with it, when it was discharged."

Then, just a few months later, in December of 1920, Neil was arrested when Prohibition agents raiding his home discovered twenty-six quarts of whiskey, four quarts of gin, five pints of unlabeled beer, twenty-five pints of unlabeled whiskey, and another gallon keg of whiskey, all of which Neil claimed had been in his possession since well before either the Texas dry laws or the Volstead Act had gone into effect. No doubt nursing at least a small grudge against the federal lawmen involved in his arrest, Neil Shearman was released from custody pending an April court date, and was still out on a $5,000.00 bond when Stafford Beckett and his fellow "prohis" headed for the Shearman hog ranch on the night of March 21, 1921.[27]

At about 8:00 p.m., the four dry agents and their civilian informant pulled up to a position near the Shearman ranch. "Beckett, Wood, and Pascual left Parker and I in the car," W. C. Guinn later recalled, "and went to watch for a load expected to leave the ranch. Beckett and Wood returned in about an hour. They had left Pascual in some bushes to watch. He was to signal with a flashlight if the load came out." But, as Pascual later explained, no car emerged from the ranch, "and I went back to Mr. Beckett. He sent me back a second time to keep watch. This time I heard a rattling of bottles but saw nothing. Then, I heard an automobile coming from near the Shearman ranch. From there, I went back to Mr. Beckett, and reported what I heard."[28]

Moments later, a vehicle driven by sixty-two-year-old C. P. Shearman pulled onto the county road and approached the spot where the four Prohibition agents stood in the cold darkness. "I was planning to leave El Paso for Tularosa, New Mexico, on March 22, to buy cattle, sheep, and hogs. I was on my way to El Paso when the officers stopped me, to make final arrangements for the trip," C. P. Shearman later recalled. "Mr. Beckett blew a police whistle," J. F. Parker remembered, "and Mr. Shearman said, 'All right, boys; I haven't anything.' Mr. Beckett told him he wanted to look in the car. Mr. Beckett and Mr. Wood just looked over the rear door of the car. They saw nothing, and said, 'We won't detain you any longer. We are going to the ranch with a search warrant.'" According to Guinn, C. P. Shearman then started to drive away, but then stopped and asked the officers to show him the warrant. "He was shown the document and said: 'There's nothing to it anyway, there's nothing to it. There's no whiskey there. Neil isn't there, only Allen who is sick,'" Guinn later explained in court. However, after some discussion about whether it applied to him or his son Neil, the elder Shearman agreed to return to the ranch with the lawmen. Beckett and Parker then climbed into Shearman's car for the ride back to the ranch, while Guinn, Wood, and Pascual followed in the officer's vehicle.[29]

Once the two automobiles pulled up to the ranch, little more than a small square adobe house with a garage on one side and a chicken house on the other, all six men dismounted and a "conversation between Shearman, Wood, and Beckett followed, Shearman saying his boy in the house was very sick, nervous, and that he would like to go in first and tell him about it, so as not to disturb him if we all came in suddenly," Guinn recalled. Beckett and Wood consented to C. P. Shearman's request, and even allowed him to retrieve an automatic shotgun from his car before heading toward the house.

Then, as C. P. walked away, the agents spread out across the yard, Beckett and Wood moving toward the north side of the ranch house, and Guinn and Parker making their way toward a chicken house. Suddenly, as C. P. Shearman walked up to the house, Guinn thought he spotted Neil Shearman moving in the shadows by the garage. According to the officer, C. P. Shearman then ducked behind the corner of a well house, raised his shotgun, and opened fire. "I then fired at the part of him that I could see," Guinn remembered, "there being shadows. I fired instantly, without much aiming. Almost simultaneously a fusillade of shots, 25 or 30, broke out from the north side of the house, in less time than you need to tell it."[30]

C. P. Shearman later claimed that it was the agents who fired the first shot. "As I went around the corner of the house a shot was fired from my rear. I hollered, 'Boys, they are shooting at me.' John, Neil, and Allen were there," he recalled. Inside the ranch house, John Shearman heard the first gunshots and his father's call for help, grabbed his own shotgun, and opened fire on one of the figures standing near the chicken house. As he later explained to a jury, "I was protecting my father's life. I shot three or four times." When John spotted movement between the two cars parked in the front yard, he blasted off two more shells toward the vehicles. As buckshot cracked the air and peppered the steel and glass of the two automobiles, Pascual Ornelas took cover in the backseat of C. P. Shearman's car. "While I was in the automobile," Pascual later told a prosecutor, "I saw a big tall man at the northwest corner of the house. I thought he was Mr. Beckett and called to him. The man shot at me, and then fired five more shots. I ran."[31]

Beckett and Wood were both shot to pieces before either man had a chance to return fire. At some point, one of the Shearmans also put a pistol round through Stafford Beckett's head, fired at such close range that it left powder marks on his face. It was later determined that Wood, whose body was found torn by buckshot, had been on his hands and knees when he received some of the injuries that killed him, and may have even dragged himself ten or fifteen feet across the yard before he died.[32]

By now, agents Guinn and Parker had both taken cover near the chicken house. "Then someone remarked, 'There are two more behind the chicken house,'" Parker recalled, "and then more shots were fired. It sounded like all kinds of shots. I could hear shots hit the chicken house, and the splinters were falling. We went into the chicken house and then several more shots were fired." According to John Shearman, it was only after C. P. Shearman had decided to send Allen off into the sand hills to hide that their father informed him that the men they were shooting at were Federal Prohibition Agents. "That's the first I knew who they were," he explained. "I then saw Neil and told him who they were." With the two remaining officers pinned down inside the chicken house, C. P. Shearman loaded Allen into a car and drove him a short distance from the ranch house. "My father returned shortly and said, 'For God's sake, let's get away from here, there'll be more here.' Dad and I went to the car," John Shearman later remembered, "and he said 'There's some more of 'em in the chicken house. Let's smoke 'em out.'"[33]

All three Shearmans then trained their weapons on the chicken house and opened fire. "It looked to me like there were 1,000 shots," Guinn later testified. "When the firing ceased," he added, "I could hear the crowd retreat to the house. I heard a screen door close. Then Parker and I left the chicken house, going back towards the road on the south." As the two federal agents ran for cover, the Shearmans fired a few more rounds in their direction and then climbed into C. P. Shearman's car and headed up the road, where they picked up Allen and drove off into the night.

In the meantime, Agent Parker climbed out of the ditch where he had taken cover and returned to the ranch. As he later explained in court, "I saw the body of Mr. Beckett about 75 feet west of the house lying in the sand. I saw a wound in his neck. He had on a duck coat with a sheep-lined collar." Parker found Wood's body laying ten feet from Beckett's. "He was lying on his back and his right leg was shot off," Parker explained, "doubled back and hanging by shreds. His face was up, with his eyes open. His rifle was six or eight feet away. One of his pistols and flashlight were nearby. I rolled the body over and took his keys to start the car."[34]

Within an hour a large number of area lawmen, Prohibition agents, customs and immigration officers, policemen, and sheriff's deputies descended on the Shearman ranch. One of the lawmen to arrive on the scene that night was Clifford Alan Perkins. "Vegetation in the area was limited to small greasewood bushes from a few inches to perhaps a foot in height," Perkins later recalled, "and was so sparse that the wind-rippled sand resembled a white sea against which every one of us stood out sharply in the bright moonlight." Unaware that the Shearmans had all fled the property, and unwilling to risk another officer being killed, Perkins and the other agents spread out and encircled the ranch, and then slowly closed in. "We soon reached the bodies of Beckett and Woods, but finding them past any need for attention, we continued to reduce our circle to the point where two or three officers were able to work their way up against the main house." Only then did the lawmen realize that the Shearmans had all left, "leaving nothing behind them but a bunch of empty cartridges." Interestingly, the officers found only a single bottle of alcohol on the premises.

Veteran police detective and Deputy Sheriff Jesse Stansel was put in charge of the criminal investigation, and headed the posse that set out after C. P. Shearman and his sons. The following day, Tuesday, March 22, 1921, Stansel and his team of officers tracked the Shearmans to an El Paso house owned by C. P.'s son-in-law. "Search of the house led to a small closet," the *El Paso Herald* reported, "through whose ceiling was a narrow aperture opening into an attic. Mr. Stansel, using the butt of his revolver, knocked a board from over the opening, placed his hat on the end of his gun, and lifted it through the hole, giving appearance to those in the garret of a man peeping over the edge." When nobody ventilated his Stetson with gunfire, the plucky lawman attempted to crawl through the hole into the attic, "which was too small to admit his body." Motorcycle Patrolman Bernard Holzman then stepped forward and volunteered to climb into the narrow space, and within a few minutes three of the Shearmans, C. P., Neil, and John, were in custody. When Stansel asked where Allen was hiding, the elder Shearman simply pointed toward the crowd gathered across the street, and Deputy J. B. Kilpatrick pulled the young man out of the group of onlookers and placed him under arrest. According to Stansel, C. P. Shearman denied that Neil had been at the ranch during the gunfight, and insisted that Allen was too sick in bed to have been involved in the shooting. "I've got some mighty good boys, though, and they wouldn't fail to help their daddy," Shearman told Stansel.[35]

All four Shearmans, along with a ranch hand named Tomas Mendoza, who had apparently left the hog farm hours before the shooting, were charged by Texas authorities for the murder of dry agent Charles Archibald Wood. The defendants also faced federal indictments on charges of having resisted agent Beckett with deadly weapons. "The absence of one name from each indictment is to forestall a possible plea of former jeopardy should the federal case be called to trial after the state case has been completed," the El Paso Herald explained.

The Shearmans' first trial was held in the Thirty-Fourth District Court of Texas in El Paso in May of 1921, and despite the fact that they had clearly killed both lawmen, a jury was unable to render a unanimous verdict in the case against the four hog farmers and their employee. "Defense attorneys attacked what they characterized as abuses of enforcing the federal laws, the El Paso Herald reported the day before the trial ended in a hung jury, "and as result of which, they asserted, the prohibition officers were killed. They contended that every circumstance indicated Mr. Shearman had fired in self-defense and that his sons had hurried to his assistance."

The Shearmans were later acquitted of the murder charges during a second trial held in Midland that September, and Neil Shearman even secured a court order that returned the weapons that Prohibition agents had seized from their ranch. Ultimately, the US government's case against the Shearmans proved to be no more successful than the state's, and in May of 1923, more than two years after they had shot and killed Charles Archibald Wood and Stafford E. Beckett, the Shearmans were acquitted in federal court. Just as in the case of Federal Prohibition Agent Ernest W. Walker, there would be little in the way of justice for the families of the fallen officers.[36]

CHAPTER SEVEN

LIQUOR WAR ON THE RIO GRANDE

> So gunfights came to the Rio Grande, and officers working
> along the border commenced carrying rifles as part of their
> regular equipment. So, too, there were increasing instances
> of officers' firing at each other while working the river at
> night, for there was no sure way to determine whether some-
> body approaching was a fellow officer, a Customs Service
> line rider, a Prohibition officer, or a smuggler bringing whis-
> key or aliens into the country.
>
> —*Clifford Alan Perkins*, Border Patrol[1]

On the night of April 30, 1921, Federal Prohibition Agents John Watson and Bernard W. Holzman drove out of the town of Anthony, New
Mexico, and headed for El Paso, Texas. The two lawmen were both new to
the Prohibition Unit. Watson, a thirty-year-old former army captain from
Missouri, had been with the federal service for barely a month, while Holzman, a twenty-six-year-old native of Deming, New Mexico, who had recently
participated in the arrest of the Shearmans for the murders of Agents Beckett and Wood, had only signed on with the Bureau nine days earlier. The two
dry agents were about three-quarters of a mile from Anthony, on their way
back to El Paso that evening, when their headlight beams flashed on a group
of men gathered around a pair of seven-passenger automobiles parked along
the side of the rural highway. Suspicions aroused, the officers decided to stop
and investigate. As Holzman later recalled, "A flat tire on the front car had held
up their progress. We drove past the car. Then I said to Watson, 'They look
peculiar. Let's go back and see what they are doing.' I backed our car alongside
of the rear machine on the left of the road and stopped."[2]

"Need any help, boys?" Holzman asked the men standing by the road. At
the same time, Watson opened his door and stepped over toward the rear car,
a Hudson Super-Six, and looked inside. Spotting a large quantity of liquor,

Watson immediately reached for his sidearm. "He called out to me, 'The back seat of the machine is full of booze.' Then he told the bootleggers, 'Put up your hands, men, you are under arrest,' " Holzman told the *El Paso Times*. The words were barely out of Watson's mouth when the men in the road opened fire. Watson fell to the ground with a bullet through one of his lungs. "I jumped out of the car on the right and started around toward the back of it to shoot. I emptied two clips of shells at them," Holzman recalled. Suddenly, more gunfire erupted from the brush on the side of the road. "The bootleggers were firing from behind both cars and protected by a cross-fire," Holzman explained, "which came from the bushes about 20 yards to the left of the road and behind their cars. When the automobile in front broke down, as we found later, they had begun transferring the booze from that to a hiding place in the bushes."[3]

It was later estimated that between six and eight gunmen participated in the attack on the officers. Buckshot fired from shotguns, 7mm jacketed bullets from Mauser rifles, and .45 caliber pistol rounds rained in on the two Prohibition agents and ventilated their vehicle. One bullet went through the cushion of the backseat and tore a hole about three inches wide as it exited through the steel in the rear of the automobile. Another round punctured the radiator, and one of the headlights was knocked out. "Mr. Watson was hit in the left lung. A dumdum bullet is believed to have been used. Part of the lung was torn away and a gaping hole resulted where the bullet emerged," the *El Paso Herald* reported. Holzman was hit by a similar bullet, which shattered his right wrist and fractured his arm, while another round broke both bones in his left arm as well. Despite the severity of his own injury, Watson continued to fire back at the bootleggers, even switching to his rifle when his automatic pistol jammed.[4]

As Watson and Holzman both continued to fire their weapons, the bootleggers jumped into one of the automobiles and sped away into the night. They left behind a large cache of liquor stashed in the brush beside the road, in all about one hundred quarts of whiskey. "I got Watson back behind our car. He bandaged up my arm with a pocket-handkerchief. I tried to help him," Holzman later explained, "but couldn't do much with his internal wound. We wandered around for about two miles before we got help. Deputy sheriffs from Anthony heard the shooting and came later." The local lawmen transported Watson and Holzman to a nearby doctor's house where they waited until an ambulance could arrive from El Paso to take them to the Hotel Dieu. Two days

Prior to becoming a Federal Prohibition Agent in April of 1921, World War I veteran Bernard W. Holzman had served as a Mounted Customs Inspector and as a member of the El Paso Police Department, during which time he participated in the arrest of Charles P. Shearman and his sons for the slaying of Agents Stafford E. Beckett and Charles Archibald Wood.   *Courtesy of Ancestry.com*

A native of Missouri and a former captain in the US Army, John Watson had served as a Federal Prohibition Agent for just under a month when he was fatally wounded in a gunfight with bootleggers outside of Anthony, New Mexico.

Courtesy of Ancestry.com

later, on May 2, 1921, John Watson died from his injuries. Five men were later apprehended in New Mexico in connection with Watson's murder, and four of the suspects were identified by Holzman as being among the gunmen who had opened fire on the agents. One of the alleged gunmen, Agapito Rueda, was later executed for his role in the murder of a payroll guard in 1924.[5]

Holzman would experience a long and painful recovery from the wounds he sustained in the shoot-out at Anthony. By late May, Holzman had made enough of a recovery that he was able to testify in the murder trial of the Shearmans for the shooting death of Agent Wood the previous March, though his arm remained weakened and was slow to completely heal. Later that summer, a friend's firm handshake was enough to cause another fracture of his wrist.[6]

Under the headline "Liquor War Now Ranging Along Rio Grande," the *Bisbee Daily Review* in Arizona reprinted an article on May 29, 1921, that had already appeared in a number of newspapers throughout the country in the weeks following the death of Agent John Watson. "War, grim war that costs human life," the article declared, "is being fought along the 1,500-mile front of the Rio Grande. The cause is whiskey. Whiskey phalanxed by men armed to kill in its defense, is brought to the United States from Mexico. It is carried on the backs of burros and men. Old women and young boys are employed as bootleg runners. Most of the smugglers are Mexicans, but the men who direct their activities, who give orders for the killing of United States officers, are citizens of the United States." The author then listed a grim tally of those who had been killed or wounded in firefights between smugglers and authorities in El Paso during the first few months of 1921:

Dead
E. W. Walker, prohibition officer
S. E. Beckett, prohibition officer
Arch Wood, prohibition officer
Lenaro Lopez, smuggler
Jose Avila, smuggler
Ramon Mena, auto driver

Wounded

Joe Davenport, customs officer
Joseph F. Thomas, immigration officer
Corporal Kurns
Private Keller
Private Petrowski
Gertrude Montalva, smuggler

"Many engagements between federal forces and smugglers," the article added, "in which no one is wounded or no liquor confiscated, are not reported. A number of smugglers have been wounded, but were hidden or cared for by comrades."[7]

One of the largest gun battles between federal lawmen and Mexican smugglers during the early years of Prohibition in El Paso took place on the evening of March 17, 1921. Immigration Officers Joseph H. Thomas and J. O. Bell were driving toward El Paso when they spotted three men wading across the Rio Grande near the barrio of Smeltertown, which sat in the shadow of the ASARCO smelter just upstream from the city. "The officers said they called to the Mexicans," the *El Paso Herald* reported, "who instantly dropped sacks which they carried, drew weapons, and opened fire. Thomas and Bell returned the fire and two of the Mexicans dropped, one to rise immediately, and aid the third one in carrying the more seriously hurt companion back to the other side." Bell and Thomas quickly dismounted from their vehicle and moved forward to take the men into custody. The two officers had no sooner climbed out of their car when they were met by "a fusillade opened from 15 or 20 men concealed on the Mexican side." Bell and Thomas took cover near a railroad embankment, and for nearly an hour they waged a battle against the men firing from the opposite bank of the Rio Grande.

Inspector-in-Charge Clifford Alan Perkins was off duty and on a date with his wife Gladys when he and several other officers were called out to the smelter to aid Bell and Thomas. Dropping Gladys off at home, Perkins picked up an officer who lived nearby, then stopped by their office to retrieve extra rifles and ammunition before setting off for the scene of the ongoing firefight. "During the fighting, under the dim moonlight, figures frequently appeared on the Mexican bank, calling to the then eight immigration officers then engaged to 'come and get us.' They also cursed the American officers," the *Herald* declared. "By the time we reached our men on the river," Perkins remembered later, "they were running low on ammunition, and it quickly became obvious to me we had not brought enough to hold our own barrage until we could get them out of danger."

As the battle raged on, Perkins rushed to a nearby railroad depot where he telephoned a detachment of US Army soldiers under the command of Lieutenant Charles Stevens, who was stationed nearby to guard the smelter from any lingering unrest left over from the Mexican Revolution. Stevens called for twenty volunteers to help reinforce the immigration men, though at least thirty soldiers stepped forward with their Springfield rifles, eager to join in on the nighttime skirmish. "Those extra men turned out to be especially welcome," Perkins explained, "for practically every automobile on the road from town to the Smelter District had stopped, a good-sized crowd had gathered to see what was going on, and the whole situation had become extremely ticklish."[8]

When the soldiers arrived on the scene, Perkins "arranged with the soldiers that they should lie back of the embankments formed by foothills, railroad track, and county road," the *Herald* reported, "that immigration officers would go to the river edge, showing themselves to Mexican fire. The plan was that those on the American side would open on the first flash." Just as Perkins and Stevens had planned, as soon as the next muzzle flash was spotted from the Mexican shoreline, all twenty-four troopers and eight immigration officers opened fire at once, and for the next two hours the two sides continued an almost incessant fire. At one point, streetcar service between the city and Smeltertown was halted because of the fighting, with a trolley struck by two bullets, one of which shattered a window. Immigration Inspector Joseph Thomas was the first man wounded on the American side, "when a bullet whizzed through his hat, cutting a gash from front to rear of his head, exposing his skull."[9]

At the height of the battle, a soldier named Petrowski was shot through the hip. The moment they heard Petrowski's cries for help, Perkins and an army first sergeant named Daugherty left their cover and exposed themselves to the Mexican gunfire in order to carry the wounded man to safety. With Perkins's dark-green service uniform clearly silhouetted against the lightly colored embankment on the American side of the river, the Mexicans concentrated

Contemporary view of the Rio Grande near where Smeltertown once stood. The international boundary lies just beyond the floodgates in the background.

Mike Testin

their fire on the immigration officer, "their bullets coming so close I could feel bits of gravel ricocheting against my legs."[10]

Intermittent gunfire continued all night and into the early-morning hours of May 18, when the Mexicans opened up with one final, intense salvo at daybreak. In all, three men on the American side were wounded, Thomas, Petrowski, and another soldier, M. J. Koller. According to the smugglers that chief of the river guard Raphael D. Davila's officers arrested, none of them had been wounded by the American fire other than the man wounded by the rock. What became of the smuggler that Thomas and Bell reportedly wounded while crossing the river is unknown.

As the sun rose over the battlefield outside of El Paso, Perkins's men recovered three sacks containing fifty-seven quarts of whiskey. "Mr. Perkins says the fight Thursday night indicated that the liquor runners who attempt to cross the river apparently move under the protection of armed henchmen who lie in the weeds on the Mexican side, ready to open fire if their companions are stopped by American officers. The fighting, he believes, was continued in the hope that they would be able to drive the Americans away, and thus save the liquor, and in the further hope of killing the enforcement agents, for whom the runners have developed an intense hatred. It probably was the latter motive, Mr. Perkins says, which inspired them to the bitter fight over the comparatively small quantity of liquor," the *Herald* declared.[11]

For their part, Mexican authorities were not completely idle in the war on liquor trafficking. "Mounted smugglers and Mexican river guards clashed Saturday night, 300 yards west of the eastern end of 'the island,'" the *El Paso Herald* reported on Monday, March 28, 1921, "more than 50 shots being fired, according to a report given out Monday by Raphael D. Davila, chief of the river guards." Davila's men had been patrolling the southern bank of the Rio Grande when they spotted four horsemen ride into the river about two hundred yards away. When the Mexican officers ordered the suspected smugglers to halt, the riders opened fire. "The guards dismounted, took cover, and opened fire. The smugglers escaped," the *Herald* stated.

Earlier that month, Colonel Davila had promised American authorities, including James A. Shevlin, head of the Prohibition Unit's "border department," that he and his men would do their part to help stop smuggling on the Mexican side of the boundary. Davila posted thirty-five of his river guards at the two main fords in the Rio Grande that smugglers used to cross the river onto Cordova Island. "I have given my men instructions to shoot to kill in case they spot a bootlegger," Davila told the *El Paso Herald* in mid-March. "We are going to clean up 'the island' if it is the last thing we do."[12]

As badly as Davila may have wished to assist his American counterparts, there were limits to what he could accomplish on the Mexican side of the boundary line. Davila's entire force only numbered 140 men, who had to guard the border from a point opposite Columbus, New Mexico, all the way to Presidio del Norte, opposite Presidio, Texas, a distance of over 300 miles. Making matters worse, Davila's river guards were only paid a paltry $1.50 to $2.75 per day, out of which they were expected to support themselves and their families, as well as provide their own horse and furnish their own weapons, ammunition, and forage for their mounts. On top of that, there were no laws in Mexico that expressly forbade the smuggling of liquor out of the country.

"We do not arrest persons caught trying to smuggle goods into the United States," Colonel Davila told the *Herald* later that summer. "We are not empowered to take the men into custody. However, we promptly confiscate their contraband possessions and drive them from the federal zone, a strip along the river 220 yards wide. Thus we are helping to check smuggling." In fact, when Davila's men captured five of the gunmen involved in the shoot-out with Clifford Perkins and his fellow immigration officers at the smelter in March, they were almost immediately released because they were caught twenty meters outside of the federal zone. "This being true," Davila declared, "we could not charge them with smuggling."[13]

Complicating matters for those border lawmen, whose job it was to enforce the nation's liquor laws, was the fact that at least a portion of America's nightlife had relocated across the narrow Rio Grande after Prohibition took effect in January of 1920. On Monday, April 25, 1921, just a few days before Prohibition Agent John Watson was fatally wounded while battling smugglers in New Mexico, the *El Paso Herald* announced the opening of the new Oasis Café, just across the Rio Grande in Ciudad Juarez. "With its jazzy jazz band jazzing away at one end of the big dining room, its maple dance floor in the center, raised a little above the level of the red-coated concrete floor, in the rest of the room, its softly shaded lights, prettily decorated walls and its new, comfortable furniture, it is the very last word in restaurants as restaurant last words are registered in the cities," the *Herald* declared. "With the waiters in their evening clothes gliding from table to table, the entertainers flitting about among the diners, singing, and the cigaret [sic] girls in their Spanish costumes, it is all redolent of the white way and recalls the 'all night' gathering places in the big cities before the great drouth [sic] came upon the United States."[14]

Opening its doors in the Hotel Rio Bravo on Avenida 16 de Septiembre on Saturday, April 23, 1921, the Oasis Café was owned by George Evans and Earl O. Smith, both from Kansas City, and was managed by English-born Harry Mitchell, a former US Army soldier who had previously served as the manager of the Central Café, another popular nightspot in Juarez. "We are going to conduct the place on a high order, so that families will not be afraid to visit us, and we are going to provide a high class of entertainment, and excellent music," Evans had told the *Herald* a few days before opening night. Sure enough, as El Pasoans flocked to the Oasis during its opening night, they were treated to a spacious dining hall decorated with paintings of bullfighting scenes that occupied the entire first floor of the Rio Bravo. That weekend they were entertained by band leader George Lloyd's orchestra, "one that Baron Long had been using on the coast; everybody who has ever been to a California cabaret knows that Baron Long trains 'em right. There are several good singers in the lot, and the diners do not lack for music. For dancing—'oh boy,' as the little blonde said when she caught the first strains, fully tells the story. The floor is excellent and the music is better."[15]

Opening the Oasis just weeks after the United States had repealed a wartime law that had required its citizens to carry passports when they crossed the international boundary into Mexico, Evans and his business associates were among the numerous American and Mexican entrepreneurs to take advantage of a dramatic increase in tourism in El Paso's sister city. With the coming of national Prohibition in the United States, and with northern Mexico experiencing greater stability with the end of the Mexican Revolution, Americans began to descend on Juarez in search of the liquor and other vices that had either dried up or become illegal back home. Before long, a wide array of saloons, cabarets, brothels, and—when not experiencing periodic forced shutdowns by the Mexican government—gambling halls and casinos, were established to cater to the desires of tourists who flocked to the border town. Both the railroads and the El Paso Chamber of Commerce were quick to capitalize on this sudden increase in visitors and convention attendees to the Southwestern metropolis and its neighbor across the Rio Grande, promoting the climate and its geographic setting, while also suggesting the delights which could be found by simply crossing one of the bridges that connected the two communities.

In promoting Ciudad Juarez, the Santa Fe railroad's own monthly corporate publication, declared:

> [A]cross the Rio Grande from El Paso—the only interesting foreign city that may be seen for a street car fare from the United States—is a striking example of contrast between the ancient and the modern, impressing the visitor that time has been turned backward a hundred years. On the streets of Juarez, bordered by quaint adobe buildings, affording occasional glimpses of the flower-decked patios, may be

seen the primitive ox-cart alongside a high-powered motor car; the curbstone vendors of native foods and fruits near modern restaurants and hotels; the sandal-shod, peak-hatted peon from the interior, the brightly uniformed federal soldier and the swaggering bullfighter rubbing elbows with the smartly dressed American tourist. Customs, speech, business are all peculiarly different from American standards, but easily acquired because of the innate courtesy of the Mexican people.

El Paso is the logical point through which to handle Mexican trade in great volume. It has been the principal gateway for passenger travel and trade traffic to and from the Republic of Mexico.

Let's not forget that El Paso is the only city in the United States that possesses a river, dry on one side and wet on the other.[16]

The saloons, cafes, and other nightspots that flourished in Ciudad Juarez during the early 1920s owed much of their success not only to the liquor-friendly conditions that existed in northern Mexico, but also to the large supplies of alcohol that had been shipped across the border by American distilleries in the weeks before America had gone dry in January of 1920. The rail-car shipments of whiskey and other intoxicants that had reached warehouses in Juarez at the end of 1919 paved the way for a wholesale liquor business to take root. While some of this booze soon found its way north again on the backs of smugglers' burros, along with more regional exports like tequila, much of it wound up on the tables of the Oasis Café, the Palace, and other similar establishments.

Additionally, by the early 1920s, at least some portion of America's defunct brewing and distilling industry relocated to Juarez. In the spring of 1921, the *El Paso Herald* reported the organization of the Juarez Brewing Company. "Work will begin at once on the brewing plant," the *Herald* declared, "which is to be situated near the race track. The equipment of the El Paso Brewing company has been purchased and will be used in the Juarez plant. The estimated cost for the buildings for the new plant is $60,000, and the brewery will be ready for

At the height of the liquor war along the Rio Grande, other than the river itself, monuments such as this one in El Paso were all that marked the international boundary between the United States and Mexico. *Border Heritage Center, El Paso Public Library*

operation in four months, it is believed." The El Paso Brewery's chief engineer, S. C. McVey, went with the equipment, as did Frank Brenk, a former employee of Anheuser-Busch, who would serve as the new company's chief brewmaster. "Malt and other ingredients will be bought in the United States, it is said," the *Herald* explained. " 'There is a great need for a brewery in Juarez,' said one of the promoters. 'We will operate with practically the same personnel formerly used by the El Paso Brewing company. I think that the demand in Juarez is sufficient for any quantity of beer that we may turn out.' "[17]

"The crux of the situation is our proximity to Juarez and its big store of liquor," Federal Judge W. R. Smith told the *Herald* in the spring of 1921. "The solution of the situation would be a larger force of border guards. I am told that the prohibition enforcement officers and customs men do not believe they are arresting 10 percent of the violators of the law. The force on the border is entirely inadequate. It should be greatly enlarged. If we can get a larger force to arrest law violators, the juries will soon make it so unpleasant that smuggling will gradually die out."[18]

Armed with a Colt single-action revolver, an immigration inspector mans a traffic checkpoint along the US-Mexican border, circa 1920s.   *Courtesy of the National Border Patrol Museum, El Paso, Texas*

Traffickers crossing the Rio Grande typically worked at night and might be paid five pesos, $2.50 in US currency, for their efforts. Given a jolt of tequila, or a marijuana cigarette to bolster their nerves, smugglers were handed weapons and given instructions as to where their sacks of liquor were to be delivered on the American side of the river. Often, they were guarded by a handful of marksmen who would take up positions on either side of the boundary in order to ambush American lawmen from rooftops, trees, or from the cover of levees.[19]

Gunfights between smugglers and lawmen in and around El Paso became so common that the federal officers took steps to better ensure their safety, arming themselves with shotguns in addition to rifles and pistols, and patrolling the river in groups of five or six, instead of in pairs of two that could be more easily outgunned. "Gunfights on the job never worried me," Clifford Perkins recalled. "The fact that at times I had to kill another human being was part of the duty and did not weigh on my conscience afterwards to any extent, because the only time I did shoot was to protect myself or someone else. When my life, or that of another officer, was in danger, it seemed to me the person killed was simply less fortunate than the survivors, and his bad luck should not disturb me later."[20]

Early on the morning of October 20, 1922, Immigration Inspectors Charles Gardiner, Charles T. Birchfield, and A. R. Green patrolled Upper Valley Road, not far from the smelter, where Clifford Perkins and other immigration men had waged an all-night gun battle with smugglers the year before. Green was new to the job, and, according to Perkins, this trip to the smelter was part of his initiation into service on the border.[21]

As Gardiner and his two companions sat in an automobile along the main road leading into El Paso on that crisp morning, they spotted two men in Mexican serapes and large straw hats approaching in a horse-drawn wagon. "We hailed them. They stopped, and we approached, intending to ask them questions," Birchfield would recall. Just then, farmers H. E. Ducsten and H. T. Herring pulled up to the scene in a car, having just driven into the city from New Mexico. "As we made a turn in the road, driving to El Paso," Ducsten later told the *El Paso Herald*, "we saw three men approach a wagon in which two men were sitting. I recognized Mr. Gardner [*sic*], the immigration inspector, among the three approaching the wagon." As the farmer looked on, one of the men on the wagon rose from his seat, giving the impression that he was willing to be questioned and searched. "But quick as a flash," Ducsten declared, "after the immigration officers had got within two or three feet of him, he drew a pistol and started shooting at Mr. Gardner. Then, the other man on the wagon started firing and shooting became general."

Gardiner was shot through the lungs, while Birchfield took bullets to the hip and the jaw, the second round passing through the left side of his face and exiting through the back of his neck. "The pistol which shot me in the face was not more than three feet from my head," Birchfield explained to reporters later that day. "The two smugglers then jumped from their wagon," the officer added, "and continued shooting. I got one man in the shoulder as he stood across the wagon from me, apparently taking deliberate aim at one of my partners." Then, the two gunmen made a dash for the footbridge that spanned the Rio Grande and led across the state boundary of New Mexico. From there, the smugglers made their escape across the border into Mexico. Though Birchfield would state in his account to the *Herald* that Green had fired at them with his rifle, half a century later, Perkins would suggest otherwise. "The new man was so petrified he stood near the wagon, his rifle by his side, while the Mexicans escaped, even though they were in full view and in range of his gun, except for the few minutes they were among the houses between the road and the footbridge." According to Perkins, Inspector Green left the Immigration Service soon afterwards.[22]

Gardiner and Birchfield were both transported to the Masonic Hospital in El Paso, where Gardiner died of his wounds the following day. "His life was lost over five cases of tequila—all the wagon contained—worth perhaps sixty dollars in Mexico," Perkins recalled. Throughout the next several days, law enforcement officers attempted to track down and identify Gardiner and Birchfield's assailants. In the meantime, F. W. Berkshire, a supervising inspector of the immigration service on the border, defended the casual way in which his men had attempted to question the suspects. "There may be those who say the officers were careless in approaching the two men who later fired on them," Berkshire told the *Herald*. "But persons should realize the peculiar problems on the border often compel officers to take the chance of being martyrs to law enforcement."[23]

A few days after Gardiner was killed, twenty-five-year-old Adolpho Chaves was located in the town of Rodey, New Mexico. Suffering from a bullet wound, Chaves refused to tell authorities who had shot him. "I have called all other branches of federal law enforcement in El Paso," Perkins told the *Herald*, "and so far as I have been able to find, the only battle of recent occurrence was that in which Mr. Gardner [*sic*] was shot." Chaves died on October 28, 1922, without ever explaining how and when he had been injured. However, the possibility that Chaves had been one of the men who had wounded Birchfield and Gardiner was ruled out by Dr. E. C. McKowen of Rincon, New Mexico, who explained to immigration officials that he had treated Chaves's bullet wound as early as October 15, and that it was already old by then.[24]

Though federal authorities continued to search for Gardiner's assassin for several months, the officer's killer was never positively identified or brought to justice. Just as in the case of the Prohibition agents shot down in El Paso in 1921, and other lawmen that were either killed or wounded by smugglers or *tequileros* along the border throughout the Prohibition era, the investigation into the murder of Charles Gardiner ended inconclusively.[25]

WHERE ROUGH NECKS ARE NEEDED

In the entire state of Arizona there may be one or two frontier mining camps where "rough necks" are needed. In the
Salt River Valley, municipalities will do well to rid themselves of gun men in office—the [W]est has a reputation
for firing from the waist for bad men and gun men; and the
[W]est wants to live down that reputation.

—Mesa Tribune, *autumn of 1922*[1]

On the evening of Saturday, June 3, 1922, a posse of deputies, local cowboys, and other citizens surrounded a one-room shack in the town of
Hope, New Mexico, a village of just a few hundred souls about twenty miles
west of Artesia, and sixty miles from the Eddy County seat in Carlsbad. Led
by Sheriff George Washington Batton, the lawmen were on the trail of Pedro
Galindo, aka, "Juan Lopez," a convicted killer who had escaped from a Texas
prison several months earlier. "Information was brought to Sheriff Batton by
a Mexican man living at Loving that the outlaw had taken his, the Mexican's,
wife, and gone to Hope," the *Carlsbad Current* later reported.[2]

Elected as Sheriff of Eddy County in 1920, Batton took office in January
of 1921, and appointed his son Sam Batton as one of his deputies. Throughout
his tenure as the county's principal peace officer, Batton more than proved his
worth as sheriff, tracking down the killer of a Torrance County storekeeper,
and generally making life hard on area bootleggers. Just two weeks before, Batton, his son Sam, and Deputy Sid Bearup had intercepted two automobiles
just a few miles north of the Texas border, arresting three men and one woman
and seizing thirty-three cases of whiskey.

However, while Batton was certainly an experienced man-hunter, escaped
convict Pedro Galindo had demonstrated a particular knack for dodging the
veteran officer. According to the *Current*, Batton had once come close to capturing Galindo in the town of Loving, fourteen miles south of Carlsbad, and

had even engaged the fugitive in a mounted pursuit. "The outlaw had the fastest horse. He fired back over his shoulder as he ran," the *Current* proclaimed. Throughout the spring of 1922, Galindo was spotted in Eddy County on numerous occasions, and quickly developed a reputation as a "Longhorn will-o-wisp" for his ability to evade arrest by local authorities.[3]

Acting on the tip from the distraught husband, who was certain that Galindo and his wife were in Hope, Batton and the men riding in his posse were fairly positive that they had their man cornered. "It was after dark and the shack was surrounded by cowboys and citizens of Hope," the *Current* explained, "all armed, who intended to prevent the escape of the outlaw." Apparently, Batton had been in favor of setting fire to the shack in an effort to smoke Galindo out, but his small army of cowhands and special deputies had grown impatient and had already started to surround the building, when two women suddenly emerged from the shack. The sheriff then asked the women if Galindo was inside, but "they replied that no one was in the shack, and for the officers to come in and see."

Batton ordered the women to light a lamp inside the room and then step outside. Then, he instructed Deputy Stone Wilburn to go around the shack and enter from a back door, while Batton himself would enter through the front door. But, when the officers entered the house, the bandit was nowhere to be seen. Then, Wilburn noticed that a dresser had been turned across a corner of the room and had been covered in bedding. "He pulled back the bedding and said, 'Here he is, George,' whereupon the Mexican shot Wilburn in the side, the bullet hitting a rib and glancing off, then shot Batton," the *Current* reported. Accounts vary, but according to the *El Paso Herald*, Batton got off five rounds before dropping to the floor with a .45 caliber bullet from Galindo's automatic pistol that penetrated his bowels. As the lights went out from the concussion of the gunfire in the confined space, Wilburn pumped two rounds into the outlaw. One of his bullets hit Galindo in the chest, while another struck the bandit in the neck. Then, just as suddenly as it had begun, all firing ceased. Deputy Wilburn staggered out the back door, where he was caught and carried away by members of the posse before he fell.[4]

"In the meantime the two women started to run away but were caught by cowboys, who made the younger one go in the shack and see what had happened," the *Current* declared. "She crawled in on her hands and knees and secured the gun of the outlaw, bringing it out and telling those outside that all were dead inside." The posse of deputies and civilian volunteers then entered the house, where they found Sheriff Batton's body on the floor, and Galindo's propped in a corner, with bullet wounds in his neck and heart.[5]

The two women, identified as Angelita Lujan and Secra Gonzales, were both later charged with murder, "it being alleged that they led Batton into a trap knowing that he would be killed." On Monday, June 5, 1922, the Eddy County board of supervisors appointed Batton's son Sam, who had been present for his father's death, to serve out the sheriff's term of office. George Washington Batton was buried in Carlsbad the following day, Tuesday, June 6, 1922.

In late August of 1922, a little over two months after the death of Sheriff George Batton in Eddy County, New Mexico, the Tombstone *Weekly Epitaph* reprinted an editorial that had first appeared in the *Mesa Tribune*. A somewhat harsh indictment of Western lawmen who, according to the author, were sometimes too quick to use their firearms, the article was published after an incident in the Salt River Valley in which the city marshal of Tempe, Arizona, had opened fire on an automobile driven by a speeding motorist. "That an officer of the law may fire on a fleeing automobilist who has committed no crime against society, or whose most flagrant crime is a misdemeanor, is one of the arrogant prerogatives which officers of the rough-neck type seemed to have gathered into themselves. There is no excuse by law or authority for such action, and the sooner officers learn this fact, the better off they themselves will be," the editorial stated.

"However," the author continued, "there is another side to the same question. The day is gone when Arizona cities need gun-men and bad-men for officers, and when they can well afford to place in authority gentlemen. In the entire state of Arizona there may be one or two frontier mining camps, where 'rough necks' are needed. In the Salt River Valley, municipalities will do well to rid themselves of gun men in office—the [W]est has a reputation for firing from the waist for bad men and gun men; and the [W]est wants to live down that reputation."[6]

But, while the West may have indeed wanted to distance itself from its wild and violent past, the fact still remained that the late 1910s and early 1920s had proven to be a deadly period for lawmen in Arizona, and elsewhere in the Southwestern border states. In the four years since the end of World War I,

Arizona had suffered the loss of at least eight city and county peace officers, all of whom had either died as the result of violent acts or through accidents in the line of duty. Likewise, numerous officers in New Mexico and Texas had also laid down their lives while keeping the peace and enforcing the law. The attrition rate among the federal officers who served as Customs "line riders," immigration inspectors, and Prohibition agents along the border, particularly in and around El Paso, Texas, was especially high.[7]

If anyone needed any further examples of the untamed wildness of the American Southwest, the mining town of Bisbee, Arizona, offered up plenty of evidence. Officer Tex Barton, a lawman who had once patrolled the streets of Bisbee with Joe Hardwick, was working at the city jail on the evening of Thursday, September 16, 1920, when he received a phone call from Mrs. T. J. Swope. According to Mrs. Swope, two suspicious Mexicans were loitering near the entrance of a nearby mine shaft, not far from the Calumet and Arizona Hospital. Thinking that the men might have been involved in the burglary of the H. E. Wooten Hardware Store the night before, Barton headed for the scene in an automobile driven by fifty-one-year-old Constable Alexander E. Sheppard. A third man, fireman Charles Long, joined the two peace officers on the ride to Mrs. Swope's. "Arriving at the Swope residence," the *Bisbee Daily Review* later reported, "Mrs. Swope said that the two Mexicans had left the mine tunnel and started down the railroad track carrying a sack. Her small son, Rush Swope, was following and watching from a distance."

At some point, sixteen-year-old Rush Swope had returned and climbed into the backseat of Sheppard's car. Barton climbed out of the vehicle and decided to follow the two subjects down the tracks, while Sheppard, Long, and young Swope drove down the road, planning to cut them off near an ice plant. Sure enough, a few minutes later Sheppard and his companions encountered the two suspects between the ice plant and the Copper Queen Hospital. With his hands still on the steering wheel, Sheppard leaned out the window and asked the Mexicans what they were up to. "The two men immediately drew guns, covered the occupants in the car, and ordered them to throw up their hands. Saying that they would kill them," the *Daily Review* declared. Sheppard had barely started to let go of the steering wheel when the two men suddenly opened fire, pumping four rounds into Sheppard's chest and striking Long in the left arm. Then, just as suddenly, the two gunmen fled on foot.

The badly wounded Sheppard handed Long his revolver, and, despite his own injuries, the firefighter immediately began to give chase. "The men fled toward the Copper Queen Hospital, jumped the fence, and disappeared in the shrubbery," the *Daily Review* explained. "Long pursued, firing as he ran, but when he reached the fence he began to feel the effects of his wound and fell over from it." Meanwhile, Tex Barton, who had apparently not heard the gunfire, continued down the tracks toward the scene of the shooting, "and did not know what had happened until he met George Haigler, who had helped bring Sheppard to the hospital in his own car." Sheppard died at 7:00 p.m., a half-hour after Mrs. Swope had first called the police.[8]

In the hours and days that immediately followed the murder of Constable Sheppard, posses composed of Bisbee police officers, citizens, and members of the Cochise County Sheriff's Department searched the borderlands for the two slayers. A sack left behind at the scene of the crime was found to contain numerous items stolen from the H. E. Wooten store. Within a few days, authorities had rounded up a number of suspects. In the meantime, while local officers continued to investigate those brought in for questioning, or held on vagrancy charges, Bisbee's frontier vigilante spirit once again began to surface, and there was talk of lynching one or more of the suspects held in the city jail.

In early October of 1920, the Bisbee police began to focus their investigation on a man named Pedro Mesa. According to the *Daily Review*, several days before the robbery of the Wooten store in September, Officers William Sherrill and Walter Sheppard, son of the murdered constable, raided a Bisbee hotel room used by Mesa, who they suspected was involved in a bootlegging operation. Though Mesa had already left, the officers discovered a quantity of insulated electrical wire, identical to the wire later used by the burglars to lower themselves from a skylight into the Wooten store. Mesa was eventually tracked to Naco, Sonora, a few miles south of Bisbee across the international boundary. However, he refused to willingly accompany Bisbee police chief James Kempton across the border for questioning, and efforts to extradite him to the United States appear to have been unsuccessful. Pedro Mesa was never made to answer for his crime in an Arizona courtroom.[9]

While the possibility of violent death was obviously a daily peril for the border lawman, those officers assigned to the job of guarding and caring for prisoners in city or county jails were not completely immune to the dangers

Constable Alexander E. Sheppard was fifty-one years old when he was shot and killed in Bisbee in September of 1920. *Mike Testin*

associated with the handling of desperate criminals. Late on the night of Saturday, April 2, 1921, Rumaldo Lazano, a seventeen-year-old dishwasher nearing the end of a thirty-day sentence for larceny, and sixteen-year-old Elentario Corral, recently sentenced to a reform school for his role in the robbery of an elderly citizen of Santa Rita, managed to tunnel through the wall of their cell in the Grant County Jail in Silver City, New Mexico. Once the youths had climbed over the door of an adjacent cell, they reached the jail corridor, where one of the young outlaws secured a hand axe used for cutting firewood. Lazano and Corral then proceeded to a room where they found Ventura Bencoma, a sixty-year-old father of twelve who had served as the jailer of Grant County for a dozen years, lying fast asleep. As the aging lawman slumbered, one of the youths buried the hatchet blade deep into Bencoma's skull. "The gash made by the axe reached from the center of the face almost to the top of the man's head," the *Alamogordo News* later reported. Despite his gruesome injury at the hands of Lazano and Corral, Bencoma lived until 5:00 a.m. the following morning.

Taking Bencoma's keys and revolver, the two young hoodlums attempted to liberate fellow prisoner Jesus Rocha, but failed to open his cell. Leaving

Rocha behind, Lazano and Corral bolted from the county jail and, dashing through the darkened streets of Silver City, they headed into the mountains north of Hanover. Meanwhile, back in the jail, Mrs. Ruey Bradshaw, a female prisoner who was being held for violation of the Harrison Narcotics Act, sounded the alarm. Alerted by a cook awakened by Bradshaw's calls for help, Grant County Sheriff John E. Casey climbed out of bed and was soon on the trail of Bencoma's assailants. "The first trace of the boys, which was reliable, was secured on Sunday night when a man living temporarily in the neighborhood of Hanover, reported seeing two boys," the *Alamogordo News* declared. Sheriff Casey and his party of deputies were soon joined by a number of citizens, several of whom were likely motivated to join the manhunt following the offer of a $250.00 reward that was posted for the two killers.

"This resulted in the finding of Lozano [sic], the older of the two boys, in an abandoned mine tunnel to which he had crawled on his hands and knees," the *Alamogordo News* explained. "Lozano was unarmed. He said he had separated from Corral on Sunday night when they had gone to a house in Hanover and Corral had told him to go up a hill and he would follow soon. He had not seen him again."

The following day, Monday, April 5, 1921, Deputy Sheriff John Parrott encountered Corral at another old mine shaft, and the two men briefly traded gunfire. Emptying Bencoma's pistol at Parrott, Corral then slipped into an old shack before the officer could get a better shot at the fugitive with his Winchester. Sheriff Casey and other members of the posse soon arrived on the scene and quickly surrounded the building where Corral had taken cover. A few minutes later, Casey boldly stepped up toward the shack, kicked open the door, and took Corral into custody without further incident. "Both boys talked freely after their capture. Each lays the actual killing on the other as might have been expected," the *Alamogordo News* reported.[10]

Lazano and Corral were both later sentenced to death for the murder of Ventura Bencoma, and on January 20, 1922, they were both hanged at the Grant County Jail. Implicated in the breakout and murder of Ventura Bencoma, Jesus Rocha was later pardoned. Twice deported to his native Mexico, Rocha was again arrested in the summer of 1922 for having violated federal Prohibition laws. "Unfortunately a man can't be jailed for life for selling booze," the *Deming Headlight* later reported.[11]

Just as in the horse and saddle days of the nineteenth century, innocent bystanders were occasional victims in the Western gun battles of the 1920s. On the evening of January 11, 1921, two men approached the Baber-Jones Mercantile located on the corner of Sixth Street and Mill Avenue in Tempe, just a few blocks from the modern campus of Arizona State University. One of them, later identified as Tomas Roman, walked with a noticeable limp. His companion, Victoriano Martinez, carried a Winchester rifle. While Martinez stood guard outside, Roman entered the store. Inside, thirty-seven-year-old Howard C. Baber had just closed for the day when Roman stepped through the door and asked to buy a pack of cigarettes. "When Baber was in the act of accommodating the late arrival, the Mexican suddenly presented a revolver and commanded the merchant to give him money," the *Arizona Republican* reported the next day. Baber did as he was ordered and opened the cash register, inviting the bandit to help himself. Then, without any apparent provocation from Baber, the outlaw opened fire and shot the merchant through the left arm. "Then commanding him to march to the front of the store the bandit followed that order with one to return to the rear. As Baber was at his office door, having complied with the order of the Mexican," the *Republican* declared, "the bandit shot again, this time the bullet passing through Baber's body, piercing the left lung just above the heart."[12]

Outside the mercantile, Martinez began firing his rifle. "The first shot was fired inside the store and seemed to serve as a signal for shooting to begin from the outside as bullets immediately began to fly," the *Republican* reported. Eight-year-old August Ernest Hintze and his father were just passing the mercantile when gunfire exploded all around them. August, who was known as an "unusually intelligent and loveable little boy," was struck in the chest by a stray rifle round that pierced his heart. Mrs. Gertrude E. Kinney, who had passed by the Baber-Jones store only moments before the shooting had started, rushed over to the wounded child and helped August's father carry him across the street where they vainly attempted to render aid. Little August was dead within a few minutes.[13]

Tempe Night Marshal Cyrus M. Spangler was walking along Mill Avenue with Charles Kearey when the two men heard a woman shout, "There has been a holdup and they have shot a little boy." Though neither man had yet heard any gunfire, both Spangler and Kearey raced toward the scene. A fifty-year-old native of Fall City, Nebraska, Spangler had lived in the Salt River Valley for twenty-eight years and had spent most of that time farming or working for the Pacific Creamery Company. He had only assumed the duties as night marshal two months earlier, in November of 1920, and had no particular prior experience as a lawman. According to Kearey, he and Spangler ran toward the Baber-Jones store and tried to enter the front door, which was locked. Peering through the window, Kearey spotted Roman, who was apparently still inside the mercantile. "Both himself and Spangler, he said, looked around the corner of the store and saw another Mexican standing in the light from the side door," the *Republican* reported. "This Mexican, he said, had a Winchester rifle, and as he and Spangler looked around the corner, the Mexican raised the weapon and fired. They ducked back, Kearey said, and the ball went [past] them and buried itself in the bricks of the bank across the street."[14]

With the angry buzz of Martinez's rifle round still ringing in his ears, Spangler pulled out his six-shooter and returned fire, trading shots with the bandit. "Kearey said he did not see what became of the man inside of the store, but after several shots had been fired," the *Republican* explained, "Spangler appeared to drop as though he would fall, then straightened up and said, 'They have got me.' " Chief of Police A. N. Smith had just reached the scene, when Spangler was hit by a rifle round that penetrated his abdomen. "Spangler, Smith said, sat down on the street curbing and then fell over backward, saying he had been shot. Smith said he took him to the drug store, where others took charge of the wounded man," the *Republican* stated.[15]

Though there was a considerable amount of confusion among the dozen or so witnesses as to the number of bandits involved in the robbery, and the method by which the culprits fled the scene. Roman and Martinez made their initial escape from the Baber-Jones store on foot, heading across Sixth Street for the Tempe National Bank. Fourteen-year-old Annie Kyle later told the *Republican* that she had been standing in front of the bank when Roman backed across the street and then used her as a human shield. "The Mexican, she said, got behind her and fired several shots," the newspaper declared. "He did not take hold of her, she said." After firing these final rounds, the two bandits then dashed down an alley that ran alongside the bank and right past fifty-year-old butcher David S. Teeter's meat market. Teeter later testified that he had been eating his supper when he and his family heard the gunfire outside. Stepping to the door, which opened on the alley, Teeter watched as Martinez and Roman ran past. "I said to him, 'What is the matter, man?,' and he said, 'For God's sake, get out of my way,' " the butcher recalled.[16]

While Roman and Martinez successfully eluded any would-be pursuers and somehow managed to slip out of Tempe, Cyrus M. Spangler and Howard Baber were both transported to St. Joseph's Hospital in Phoenix, where Spangler died of his injuries at 8:30 p.m. "Dr. Orville Harry Brown said he had performed an autopsy on the body of Spangler," the *Republican* reported two days later. "The bullet, he said, entered the abdomen and went through both walls of the stomach, piercing an intestine three times. The bullet was removed from the skin in the back just above the hip bone, Dr. Brown said. Death was caused, he said, by hemorrhage."

Though it was initially believed that the night marshal had been hit by a rifle round fired by Victoriano Martinez, the bullet recovered from Spangler's body was found to have been fired from Tomas Roman's .38 caliber revolver.

Cyrus M. Spangler had been serving as night marshal in Tempe, Arizona, for only two months when he was shot and killed during the robbery of the Baber-Jones Mercantile in January of 1920. *Courtesy of City of Tempe Archives*

Baber, who had taken two rounds from Roman's six-gun, one in the arm and another in the chest, would ultimately survive. On January 13, 1921, Cyrus M. Spangler was buried in Double Butte Cemetery, following one of the largest funerals ever held in Tempe. Eleven days later, on January 24, 1921, eight-year-old August Ernest Hintze, who was struck and killed by a stray bullet during the holdup, was also laid to rest at Double Butte Cemetery.[17]

As funeral arrangements were being made for the two victims of the Baber-Jones robbery, a massive search effort began for the killers. "There was a growing rumble of lynching around Tempe last night and scores of citizens, armed with shotguns, rifles, and revolvers, went man-hunting," *The Arizona Republican* reported. "Chief of Police Smith of Tempe sent out calls to Phoenix and Mesa shortly after the crimes had been committed and received immediate response. Phoenix sent officers from both the sheriff's office and the police department, and a scouring search of all the country in the vicinity of Tempe was made." Maricopa County Deputy Sheriff Earnest Smith set out across the desert before daybreak on January 13, with a party of other lawmen and Mike Burns, a noted Yavapai-Apache tracker who lived at the Fort McDowell reservation. "The most important part of this labor had been undertaken by Si Williams, rancher of Tempe," the *Republican* reported, "who had uncovered the trail of the alleged murderers at the Maricopa mountains, and who also had found it on the other side of the hills at the Fowler ranch." Williams had spent all of Wednesday, January 12, following the footprints left behind by Roman and Martinez, and had then joined Smith's posse after catching a few hours of sleep.

According to the *Republican*, the search for Roman and Martinez presented the modern reader with a type of dramatic imagery which could only be duplicated in the Southwest, "and which will soon be numbered with the things that have passed." Following the tracks of the two fugitives, Burns and Williams led Smith and his fellow deputies over the hills to the Fowler ranch. "The trail led across a canal and into a cotton field," the *Republican* declared, "the field slowing up the chase for a while. Soon, however, Burns started out again at a fast walk, and after trailing about a mile, word was sent back to saddle some horses and bring them to the trailers, who now had a track so plain that the Indian could follow it as fast as a horse could gallop."[18]

Using bloodhounds, horses, and Smith's seven-passenger automobile, which at times he was forced to drive overland through the rough country, the posse trailed the killers to the Gila River. Unable to cross the Gila in his car, Smith left the posse and drove for the town of Maricopa, where he planned to rendezvous with Burns and the other trackers who had forded the river and continued cross-country on foot and horseback. Smith managed to reach Maricopa at 2:00 p.m., and within an hour met with the posse that had followed the killers' trail across the desert. The man-hunters followed the tracks left by Martinez and Roman as far as the tracks of the Southern Pacific Railroad, where the trail was lost completely about a half-mile from the Maricopa station.

The following day, January 14, 1921, Maricopa County Sheriff John Montgomery, who had arrived in Maricopa with fresh bloodhounds from the state penitentiary in Florence, sent Mike Burns and another deputy to scour the countryside east of the railroad. At the same time, Deputies Smith and Sterling Price were directed to canvas the desert west of the Southern Pacific's steel rails. However, while Smith and Price managed to locate a rancher and his son who had both seen the two fugitives on the morning January 12, by the time the lawmen received this information, Martinez and Roman were already more than 150 miles away.[19]

At about 8:30 a.m. on the morning of January 14, 1921, while lawmen from Maricopa County continued to search the desert for the two killers,

The youngest man ever elected as sheriff of Santa Cruz County, rancher Harry Saxon, was a key player in two notable cases in Arizona in the early 1920s. In January of 1921 he participated in the apprehension of Tomas Roman for the murder of Cyrus M. Spangler and August Hintze. Following the tragic death of Santa Cruz County Sheriff George White eighteen months later, Saxon would be appointed as White's temporary successor, leading the posse that recaptured Manuel Martinez and Placidio Silvas. *Courtesy of Darlynn Lee*

Tomas Roman and Victoriano Martinez stepped off a motor stagecoach at the town of Calabasas, Arizona, just a few short miles from the Mexican border. From Maricopa, they had boarded a freight train and ridden it to Tucson, where they had arrived on January 13 and stashed Martinez's rifle before continuing on to Calabasas. Waiting for them at the station were US Immigration Inspectors Henry R. Swink and Earl A. Lemon, who had gone to Calabasas after receiving word that the fugitives might attempt to reach the international boundary. Also there at the Calabasas stage stop that Friday morning was former Santa Cruz County Sheriff Harry Saxon and thirty-eight-year-old cattleman Robert Q. Leatherman, both of whom would later play a role in bringing the Ruby Mercantile murderers to justice in 1922.[20]

Roman and Martinez had no sooner dismounted the motor stage when the driver noticed Inspector Swink standing a short distance away, talking with Saxon, and told them that the two passengers appeared to be "bad customers." Eyeing the two men, Swink ordered them to surrender and then called on Lemon to bring him a pair of handcuffs from the officer's car. Then, as Swink stepped toward the fugitives with the metal bracelets, Roman suddenly jumped back, yelled "No!," pulled out a long-barreled revolver, and demanded that the officer surrender. Without waiting for the lawman to reply, Roman opened fire on Swink from a distance of about four feet. "He fired twice at Swink but missed, and then, wheeling, fired at Saxon," the *Bisbee Daily Review* later reported. "The former sheriff, rated a crack shot, dropped the Mexican with a bullet through the chest." Swink then managed to draw his own weapon and put a second bullet through Roman's wrist. In the meantime, Martinez had pulled his own gun and had tried to shoot, but the weapon failed to discharge. "Seizing Roman's gun from the ground," the *Daily Review* declared, "Martinez straightened up to shoot, but Saxon, firing from the back of the horse he was riding, shot him through the neck."[21]

Once the smoke had cleared, both of the wounded bandits were placed upon a blanket and made as comfortable as possible. After a while, both men asked to sit up and were allowed to do so. Then, according to newspaper accounts and court documents, Harry Saxon took a seat on the ground beside the desperadoes and began to question them. "Boys, you are about to die now," Saxon told them. "We understand you are the two who did the killing at Tempe, and if you don't tell the truth before you go, some innocent

Mexicans may be hanged." Martinez and Roman responded by admitting they were responsible for the Tempe tragedy, and after being taken to the hospital in Nogales, made more detailed confessions."

Tomas Roman and the lawmen that were at the scene would later offer slightly different accounts of the bandits' confessions. According to Saxon, when the former sheriff asked them, "What have you boys done that makes you so wild?" the two bandits both hesitated for a moment. Then, Martinez glanced at Roman and said, "We might as well tell, we are up against it now," to which Roman only nodded his head. "Roman didn't talk much. He seemed to be pretty sick," Saxon later explained in court. "Martinez then said, 'We robbed a store and killed some few people in Tempe,' and I said to Roman, 'Is that right?,' and he said, 'Yes.'" Roman later denied making any admission of his guilt or innocence to the officers at Calabasas. "One of the gentlemen in the crowd says to us, 'If you are the ones that made the assault at Tempe, why do you not say it,'" Roman explained, speaking through a courtroom interpreter. "As I did not consider myself guilty, I didn't answer and kept quiet. Then Martinez answered and says, 'Yes, I am,' and they says, 'Are you?,' and I says, 'I want some water.' That was all, and I didn't speak a word ... I didn't nod my head when they asked me whether what Martinez said about the crime in Tempe was true ... I was sick, but I was with my five senses."[22]

Martinez and Roman were both transported to St. Joseph's Hospital in Nogales, where they were attended by Dr. William F. Chenoweth. Chenoweth personally held out little hope that either man would survive to face an Arizona jury. Sure enough, at 7:30 p.m. on the night of January 15, Victoriano Martinez died from the effects of the neck wound he had received from Harry Saxon. A half-hour later, Maricopa County Sheriff John Montgomery arrived in Nogales with a party of officers that included Tempe Chief of Police A. N. Smith, and identified both Roman and Martinez as the men wanted for the bloody holdup in the Salt River Valley.

By that time, newspapers had begun publishing details on the two men, who, according to federal authorities, were believed to have been members of a gang involved in a mining company strike in Mexico. Immigration records indicated that Roman and Martinez had journeyed north of the border the previous fall, and had originally gone to the Salt River Valley to pick cotton. "The condition of Roman seemed greatly improved yesterday," the *Republican* reported on January 16, "and he chatted cheerfully with the guard at his bed-side, a deputy sheriff of Santa Cruz County. A constant guard is kept over Roman at the hospital to prevent his escape." Meanwhile, officers in Tempe located Roman's wife Maria and took her into custody, though she told police that she knew nothing of the robbery.[23]

Fearing that there may be some attempt to rescue Roman from the Nogales hospital and carry him across the border, on January 20, 1921, Sheriff Montgomery loaded his prisoner into an automobile and raced north for Phoenix, reaching the state capital in seven hours and fifty minutes, and lodged Roman in the Maricopa County Jail. In addition to possible efforts to liberate Roman from custody, Montgomery was equally concerned that if the suspected murderer did not finish recuperating behind bars, he might fall prey to some act of vigilante justice on behalf of the residents of Tempe and other communities in the greater Phoenix area. "Roman was brought into Phoenix early this morning, and every effort is being made to [ensure] his recovery, so that his preliminary examination may be held as soon as the patient is able to take part in the proceedings," the *Arizona Republican* reported. "Until that time he will be kept in the jail under a strict supervision, so that neither friend nor enemies may have an opportunity to obstruct due course of law."[24]

By January 24, Roman had made enough of a recovery that with the assistance of deputies, he was able to walk from his cell to a motorcar, which carried him to the East Phoenix Precinct Justice Court for arraignment before Justice of the Peace Henry J. Sullivan. One week later, on February 1, 1921, Roman was again taken from his cell, and this time was escorted to Sheriff Montgomery's private office, where he was identified by Howard C. Baber, David S. Teeter, Annie Kyle, and sixteen-year-old Virgil Washburn, who stated that Roman had taken a shot at him while fleeing the Baber-Jones store. "All who watched Roman walk said his limp was identical with the limp of the Tempe bandit," the *Republican* reported. Despite being placed at the scene by Baber and the three other witnesses, Roman declared that they were mistaken, and insisted that he had left Tempe before the robbery had taken place, and had only met Martinez while having supper in Maricopa, "after which Martinez drew a gun and thrust it against his side and told him he was his partner from then on."[25]

Charged with the murders of both Tempe Night Marshal Cyrus M. Spangler and eight-year-old August Hintze, Tomas Roman's trial began on

Name of Convict *Tomas Roman* ; Alias

Property found on Convict *None*

Expiration of Sentence with Credits *at Death*

: Registered No. 5699

ORIGINAL
ARIZONA STATE BOARD OF HEALTH
BUREAU OF VITAL STATISTICS

State Index No.

PLACE OF DEATH

County Pinal

District

County Registrar No.

CERTIFICATE OF DEATH

Town or City Florence No. Arizona State Prison St. Local Registrar's No.

(If death occurred in a Hospital or Institution, give its name instead of street and number)

FULL NAME Tomas Roman

Commitment 5354

MEDICAL CERTIFICATE OF DEATH

PERSONAL AND STATISTICAL PARTICULARS

SEX Male   COLOR OR RACE Mexican   SINGLE MARRIED WIDOWED or DIVORCED

DATE OF DEATH January 13th.

DATE OF BIRTH

I hereby certify, that I attended deceased from

19....., to ....., 19....., that I last saw h...
alive on Jan, 13th , 19 22 , and that death
on the date stated above at 5.20 A. M. The DISEASE
or INJURY causing death was as follows:

AGE 32 yrs. ....days....mo, or ....min.

Legal Execution

OCCUPATION
(a) Trade, profession or particular kind of work Miner
(b) General nature of industry, business, or establishment in which employed or employer.

(Duration).....yrs....mos....days
Was disease contracted in Arizona?
If not, where?

BIRTHPLACE Mexico

CONTRIBUTORY

NAME OF FATHER Not known
BIRTHPLACE OF FATHER Not known
MAIDEN NAME OF MOTHER Not known
BIRTHPLACE OF MOTHER Not known

(Duration).....yrs....mos....days
(Signed) *Geo. F. Huffman*
Jan. 13 , 192...

*In death from Violent Cause state: (1). Means of Injury; and Whether (Accidental, Suicidal or Homicidal)

The above is true to the best of my knowledge.
(Informant) *Prison Records*
(Address)

LENGTH OF RESIDENCE
At place of death ....years....months
In Arizona ....years....months
Former or Usual Residence

Place of Burial or Removal Florence, Ariz.   Date of Burial or Removal Jan.13th 19 22

Filed ....19....

Undertaker None   Address

A True Copy

Local Registrar

Filed ....19....

County Registrar

When and How Discharged —

PRISON RECORD

F.P. Class ...

4-1-1921 Appeal Pending in
Supreme Court.
11-1-21 Decision of Superior court
Affirmed to be executed Jan 13th 1922
Executed at the A.S.P. on Jan. 13, 1922
at 5.30 am by being hanged by the
neck until dead.

On January 13, 1922, two years after the murders of Cyrus M. Spangler and eight-year-old August Hintze, Tomas Roman was hanged side by side with Ricardo Lauterio, in what was Arizona's first double hanging.   *Arizona State Library and Archives*

February 16, 1921, and lasted for three days. Among those testifying against the accused was little August's father, Ernest A. Hintze. "He heard a shot, Hintze said, and then another shot, and his son cried out 'Oh, papa!' and fell to the walk," the *Republican* explained. On February 19, a jury found Roman guilty and condemned him to the gallows at the state penitentiary. As the verdict was read aloud in court and translated into Spanish by interpreter Frank Orduno, Roman reportedly listened without showing any trace of emotion. Three days later, Roman was sentenced to hang on April 29, 1921.[26]

Meanwhile, Maricopa County Attorney R. E. L. Sheppard felt that something should be done on behalf of Harry Saxon, Robert Q. Leatherman, and the two immigration inspectors who had participated in the shoot-out at Calabasas, and had helped to bring Tomas Roman to justice. On February 27, 1921, the *Arizona Republican* printed a letter from Sheppard in which the prosecutor explained that he wished to pay for a newspaper subscription for the four men. "I hope that the citizens of this county will respond to this subscription," Sheppard stated, "each one with that he feels able to give, whether it be large or small. I have talked to the four men and think that they would be best pleased if each one of them were presented with a .45 Colt Automatic, with pearl handle, and the balance of the money divided equally among the four men."[27]

That spring, Tomas Roman's attorneys appealed his murder conviction, and the killer managed to avoid his scheduled appointment with the hangman at Florence. Then, in October of that year, after his conviction had been affirmed by the Supreme Court of the State of Arizona, Roman's date of execution was rescheduled for January 13, 1922, when he would join fellow convict Ricardo Lauterio on the scaffold for Arizona's first double hanging.

Lauterio had been sentenced to death in April of 1921 after he was found guilty of the murder of his sweetheart, Adelia Sosa, in November of 1920. "During a quarrel with the woman, Lauterio stated at his trial, he drove a homemade knife to the hilt in her right temple," the *Bisbee Daily Review* reported.

Finally, just before dawn on January 13, 1922, a year after the robbery of the Baber-Jones Mercantile, Roman and Lauterio climbed the scaffold steps at Florence, and within a few minutes both men had been hanged for their respective crimes. "The two prisoners went to their death stoically," the *Copper Era and Morenci Leader* declared a few days later, "but before the trap was sprung, Roman, in a brief statement, denied his guilt."[28]

A bloody holdup and shoot-out on the streets of an Arizona city, a manhunt that featured pursuit on horseback and an Apache tracker, a showdown on the Mexican border, and, finally, a double hanging; while the West may have wanted to live down the reputation of a land policed by fast-shooting frontier peace officers, the robbery of the Baber-Jones Mercantile, the unwarranted shooting of the proprietor, the murders of August Hintze and Tempe Night Marshal Cyrus M. Spangler, and the fate of those responsible were all grim reminders that the West still had some growing up to do. But, despite the level of bloodletting that still occurred throughout Arizona, New Mexico, and West Texas, there were still those living in the Southwest who insisted the old days were gone for good.

On May 12, 1922, four months after Tomas Roman and Ricardo Lauterio swung from the gallows at Florence, the *Mohave County Miner and Our Mineral Wealth* published a story about Arizona lawmen written by one Jem McKem. Under the heading "Old Time Arizona Sheriffs," McKem offered up a number of colorful stories from Arizona's wild past, while also attempting to write its epitaph:

> Arizona's frontier days have passed. The curtain on the last act was rung down when the State went dry in 1914. The wide open saloons with the gamblers and their layouts, the bedizened women of the dance halls and "bad men" have "folded up their tents like Arabs and silently stolen away." The carbine and Colt's .45 are relics laid away with old memories, and a new generation of red men peacefully tend their flocks and herds and cultivate their fields and the ways of the pale faces. Where a few years since were only the desert sage and cactus or the non-descript collection of houses typical of the frontier town, now stand modern cities. Civilization has come to Arizona.
>
> No longer on the long trail ride the old representatives of law and order with jingling spurs and wide-brimmed

Stetsons. They have been succeeded by a different breed of men who affect black store suits and polished shoes who ride in high-powered motor cars, doing nothing more exciting than chasing bootleggers and jailing hobos.[29]

Three days after McKem's article was published, at 12:40 a.m. on May 15, 1922, the Chicago, Rock Island and Pacific Train No. 3, "The Golden State Limited," was halted at a Southern Pacific flag station outside of Tucson, Arizona. "The Limited, carrying several hundred sleeping passengers bound for Los Angeles, was approaching Jaynes, a small station six miles west of Tucson, when it struck several torpedo signals. Farther ahead, between the tracks, the engine crew saw a red fuse light flaring," the *Los Angeles Times* reported. As the train came to a halt, Conductor D. M. Madigan stepped out of the vestibule of the Pullman car that was coupled to the baggage car. "As I opened the vestibule," Madigan later told a reporter, "a man fired four shots at me. I was temporarily blinded by fragments of flying glass."[30]

Suddenly, a bandit climbed into the locomotive's cab and trained a pair of revolvers on the engineer, demanding that he uncouple the engine and the baggage car from the rest of the train. With the assistance of a tramp, who was discovered sleeping between the lead Pullman and the baggage coach, the engineer did as he was ordered. "In the meantime several bandits ambushed in the brush along the tracks kept up a volley of shooting at the sleeping cars," the *Times* declared. "Women screamed, men rolled out of their bunks. One masked man sent a burst of bullets down the aisle of the first coach, firing through the front door. All vestibule doors were locked, but the entire train seemed to be surrounded by men who continued their shooting."[31]

Inside the mail car, sixty-two-year-old Railway Express Messenger Harry Steward was jolted awake by the sounds of gunfire. "I had been sleeping soundly," Steward later told the *Times*. "I was in my sock feet and was suddenly awakened by shooting outside the car. I had no idea what was going on, but I knew something was wrong." Steward quickly doused the lantern inside the mail car, then reached around in the dark for his sawed-off shotgun. The aging expressman, who had ridden the rails for the better part of forty years, then took up a position at one end of the darkened car. "I stood at the little window," Steward explained, "but it was so high I could hardly see through it. While I waited I judged that sixty shots were fired at the train."

"Come on, boys—come on! If you don't open up and climb out we'll dynamite the cars," one of the bandits shouted.

"Well—let's get busy," another commanded.

From his window, Steward watched as one of the armed holdup men emerged from the brush alongside the tracks. "The window was too high for me to get a good line on him—and I've got poor eyesight besides—but I let him have the first barrel," Steward explained. As soon as Steward's shotgun boomed, the outlaw dropped to the ground and quickly crawled back into the brush. The echo of Steward's scattergun had barely faded when he heard footsteps approaching from the direction of engine. He couldn't see anyone, but he listened as a man passed below his window. "I figured he was going to set off a charge of dynamite," Steward recalled, "so I let him have the other barrel." For the second time that night, Steward's shotgun roared from the mail car, belching out a flurry of buckshot. "I knew I hit him," Steward told the *Times*. "He fell like a dog, and, groaning, crawled into the bushes for about fifteen feet. Then he didn't groan anymore." The second blast from Steward's shotgun was enough to take the fight out of the bandits. "Don't shoot anymore, boys!" one of the robbers hollered from the brush. Steward then heard the sound of an automobile's engine start up a short distance from the tracks. "Then I saw five or six men jump into a machine. The car sped away without lights," Steward remembered.[32]

Before that day was over, details of the incident, particularly Steward's bold defense of the mail car, were reported in newspapers throughout the West and as far east as Brooklyn, New York. When the train arrived in Los Angeles, Steward was greeted by a delegation of railroad and express company employees, friends, and his wife, fifty-six-year-old Carrie Steward. "I would have felt pretty bad if Harry had killed a young man," Mrs. Steward told the *Los Angeles Times,* "but the bandit was a rough-neck and probably would have killed Harry first if he had a chance. I guess Harry did the right thing by shooting him."[33]

News of the incident reached authorities in Tucson that morning, courtesy of the crew of an eastbound freight train, which had passed the Golden State Limited at Jaynes while the holdup was still under way. Pima County

Sheriff Benjamin F. Daniels and a party of deputies soon arrived on the scene, where they located the body of the man Steward had blasted into eternity and identified him as Tom Dugat, the owner of a goat ranch located west of Tucson. "Sheriff Daniels announced that a large force of deputies has been dispatched and is hot upon the heels of the bandit gang, who left the scene of the robbery by automobile on the Casa Grande-Tucson highway," the *Oakland Tribune* reported later that day.[34]

If Winchester carbines and Colt .45 six-shooters were indeed "relics laid away with old memories," then Sheriff Ben Daniels would have been something of a museum piece himself. Rapidly approaching his seventieth birthday and the closing act of a long and eventful life, Daniels had been a buffalo hunter on the Southern Plains in the 1870s, fought Comanches, and later spent a little over three years in the Wyoming Territorial Penitentiary for the theft of US government mules. Following his release from prison in 1883, Daniels spent the next fifteen years as a lawman and gunfighter in Kansas, Oklahoma Territory, and Colorado, before volunteering with the Rough Riders during the Spanish-American War in 1898, making the acquaintance of the regiment's eventual commander, Colonel Theodore Roosevelt.[35]

When Theodore Roosevelt assumed the presidency following the assassination of President William McKinley in 1901, Daniels was Roosevelt's choice as US Marshal for the Territory of Arizona. However, after details of the new marshal's criminal past were made public, Roosevelt called on Daniels to resign. Daniels managed to survive this professional and personal disappointment, and in 1904, Governor Alexander Brodie, another former Rough Rider, appointed Daniels to the post of superintendent of the Territorial Penitentiary at Yuma. This was followed in 1905 with a reappointment of Daniels as US Marshal by President Roosevelt, a position he held until 1909, when Roosevelt left office. Eleven years later, in November of 1920, after having been defeated in the elections of 1914 and 1916, the voters of Pima County, Arizona, selected the aging pioneer as their new sheriff.[36]

Now, nearly a year and half into his two-year term as sheriff, "Uncle Ben" Daniels was about to embark on one of his last adventures as a Western lawmen.

Tracks found at the scene by Daniels and his men indicated that not one, but two automobiles had been used in the attempted robbery, and it was quickly determined that the holdup men were probably hiding in Tucson. "Beside the body of Dugan [*sic*] was found a thermos bottle filled with nitroglycerine and several pounds of putty," the *Los Angeles Times* reported, "which was to be utilized in blowing open the strongboxes in the mail and baggage cars." When Daniels journeyed to Dugat's goat farm in search of other evidence, he discovered five barrels of mash on the premises, indicating that Dugat had also been involved in the illicit liquor trade. Deputies returning to the ranch several weeks later eventually uncovered a massive distillery, said to be one of the largest ever found in Pima County.[37]

Three days after the holdup at Jaynes, on May 18, 1922, Daniels arrested Richard R. Starr, a pipefitter for the Southern Pacific Railroad, at his home in Tucson. Starr was suspected of having known Dugat prior to the robbery, and it was believed that he had harbored the fugitive holdup men after Dugat had been killed. Four days later, a second man, Frank W. Jirou, was also apprehended, and was charged with having been one of the robbers. Both the train's fireman and the hobo who had been found sleeping in one of the cars were able to identify Jirou from the sound of his voice. Jirou eventually confessed to having participated in the holdup of the Golden State Limited, and on May 29, 1922, identified his accomplices as George Winkler, a forty-two-year-old tailor; his seventeen-year-old-son, George Jr.; and Santiago Valdez, a Mexican goat herder who had once worked for Tom Dugat. "Jirou declared that three meetings were held prior to the holdup for the purpose of perfecting their plans in every detail," the *Bisbee Daily Review* reported. "These sessions were held at the Dugat ranch during the month of April."[38]

In November of 1922, six months after the robbery of the Golden State Limited, George Winkler Sr. and his son George Jr. were both found guilty by a Pima County jury for their role in the attempted robbery, and were each sentenced to serve ten years in the Arizona State Penitentiary at Florence, though the younger Winkler later had his term in prison suspended. That December, Frank W. Jirou was banished from the State of Arizona for a period of twenty-five years. However, in light of his earlier confession and promises of leniency, he also received a suspended sentence on condition that he report to a probation officer twice a month for the next twenty-five years. Santiago Valdez was believed to have slipped across the border and was never apprehended, while the case against Richard R. Starr was dropped due to lack of evidence. For

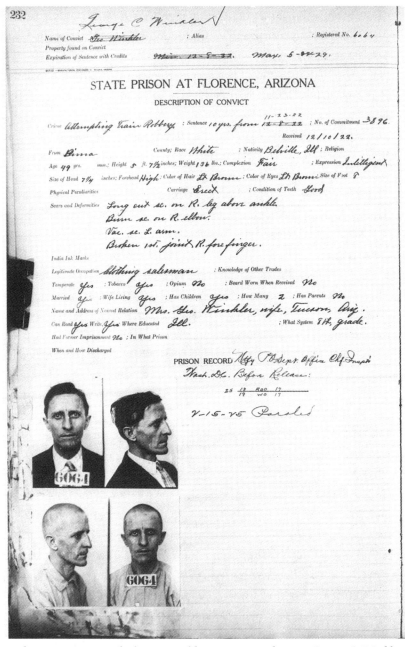

George C. Winkler

Name of Convict *Geo. Winkler* ; Alias ; Registered No. *6064*
Property found on Convict
Expiration of Sentence with Credits *Min. 12-8-22.* *May. 5-8-29.*

STATE PRISON AT FLORENCE, ARIZONA

DESCRIPTION OF CONVICT

Crime *Attempting Train Robbery* ; Sentence *10 yrs. from* *11-23-22* *12-8-22* ; No. of Commitment *3896*

Received *12/10/22.*

From *Pima* County; Race *White* ; Nativity *Belville, Ill* ; Religion
Age *49* yrs. mos.; Height *5* ft. *7½* inches; Weight *134* lbs.; Complexion *Fair* ; Expression *Intelligent*
Size of Head *7¼* inches; Forehead *High* ; Color of Hair *Lt. Brown* ; Color of Eyes *Lt. Brown* ; Size of Foot *8*
Physical Peculiarities Carriage *Erect* ; Condition of Teeth *Good*
Scars and Deformities *Long cut sc. on R. leg above ankle.*
Burn sc. on R. elbow.
Vac. sc. L. arm.
Broken 1st. joint R. fore finger.

India Ink Marks
Legitimate Occupation *Clothing salesman* ; Knowledge of Other Trades
Temperate *yes* ; Tobacco *yes* ; Opium *No* ; Beard Worn When Received *No*
Married *yes* ; Wife Living *yes* ; Has Children *yes* ; How Many *2* ; Has Parents *No*
Name and Address of Nearest Relation *Mrs. Geo. Winkler, wife, Tucson, Ariz.*
Can Read *yes* Write *yes* Where Educated *Ill.* ; What System *8th, grade.*
Had Former Imprisonment *No* ; In What Prison

When and How Discharged

PRISON RECORD *Idfy. P.O. Dept. Office Chf. Insp'r*
Wash. D.C. Before Release:

25 *13 Rao 17*
19 WO 17

7-15-25 Paroled

For his participation in the last train robbery in Arizona history, George O. Winkler was sentenced to serve ten years in the Arizona State Penitentiary at Florence. He was paroled after having served a little over two years behind bars. *Arizona State Library and Archives* having thwarted the bandits with a couple of blasts from his shotgun, Harry Steward was later presented with a check for $1,000, an engraved watch, and a letter of thanks from the president of the American Railway Express Company.[39]

The holdup of the Golden State Limited in May of 1922 was the last attempted train robbery in the history of the state of Arizona. The pursuit and rapid apprehension of those responsible had offered the aging Benjamin F. Daniels something of a last hurrah at the end of a long and adventurous life in the American West, and proved to be the closing chapter of Daniels's storied career as a frontier peace officer. Later that year, Daniels lost his bid for reelection, and in April of 1923 the former Rough Rider, gunfighter, and outlaw-turned-lawman suffered a fatal stroke while sitting in his car in front of his doctor's office.[40]

But, even though Arizona had witnessed its final train robbery by masked, gun-toting bandits, and while Ben Daniels could easily be seen as one of the last of the Copper State's old-time peace officers of "the rough-neck type," the passing of the former sheriff and US Marshal hardly signaled the end of an era. As the early 1920s gave way to the middle years of the decade, lawmen in the American Southwest would continue to face the traditional, decades-old issues stemming from livestock theft, bank robbery, and "general outlawery," while also dealing with the enormous challenges posed by apprehending bootleggers and narcotics smugglers, as well as motorized criminals who roamed far and wide across the United States, no longer limited to the geographical boundaries imposed on outlaws on horseback. In the face of these ever more modern concerns, lawmen in the border states would have to adapt to the changing times—the increased reliance on automobiles and both semi-automatic and fully automatic firearms—while also standing by to once again climb into the saddle when the job required it.

CHAPTER NINE

"HONOR FIRST"

The border patrol is a young man's organization; it appeals strongly to the lover of the big outdoors—the primeval forests, the sun-parched deserts, the mountains, the plains; the business upon which it is engaged calls for manhood, stamina, versatility, and resourcefulness in the highest degree. "Honor first" is its watchword; privations and danger but serve as a challenge which none refuses.

—*Harry E. Hull,*
Commissioner General of Immigration, June 30, 1927

Saturday, December 13, 1924, found US Border Patrol Inspectors Frank Horace Clark and Herbert Brown on duty near the end of Park Street in El Paso, a few blocks east of Stanton Street Bridge and just west of Cordova Island. A native of Cambridge, Massachusetts, Clark was closing in on his forty-sixth birthday. Prior to having joined the newly organized "land border patrol" four months earlier, Clark had lived in Albuquerque, where he had served as an investigator with the New Mexico Cattle Sanitary Board. Like all early members of the US Border Patrol, neither Clark nor Brown wore an official uniform, and rather than carry a more modern double-action revolver or semiautomatic pistol, the New England–born Clark had opted to uphold the frontier tradition and instead packed a nickel-plated .44-40 caliber Colt single-action six-shooter with pearl grips. By that late-autumn evening, nearly five years had passed since America had gone bone dry, and almost seven since wartime restrictions had shuttered the once-prominent saloons in the former "Monte Carlo of the United States." During that time, Cordova had proven to be one of the deadliest battlegrounds in the liquor war along the Rio Grande.[1]

Since the death of Ernest W. Walker, four other federal lawmen had been killed and numerous others wounded while battling bootleggers and smugglers in or near the city. In several instances these gunfights, the vast majority of which had taken place at night, had nearly turned into full-fledged battles.

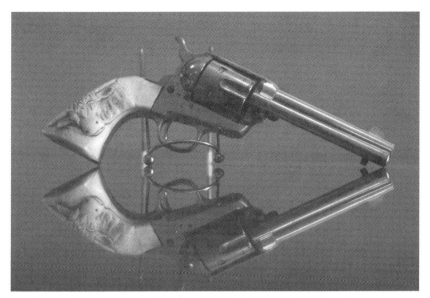

Border Patrol Inspector Frank Horace Clark's nickel-plated Colt single-action revolver. Most early members of the Border Patrol provided their own guns, and even by the mid-1920s, the Colt "Peacemaker" was still a favorite among Western lawmen.   *Courtesy of the National Border Patrol Museum, El Paso, Texas and Mike Testin*

On the night of May 21, 1922, a party of Federal Prohibition Agents, some of them armed with newly acquired M1918 Browning Automatic Rifles, swapped lead with a large force of liquor smugglers attempting to ford the river with a shipment of booze. "For a time the brush-covered space between the riverbank and the Santa Fe railway embankment at Eighth Street became a miniature 'No Man's Land,' " the *El Paso Herald* reported, "with bullets from pistols, rifles, and a Browning Automatic Rifle flying thick. Some members of the government force say they saw rocket signals used by the Mexicans during the skirmish." Despite the ferocity of the shoot-out, however, one of the first known gunfights between law enforcement and outlaws in that region to feature fully automatic weapons, there were no confirmed casualties, nor were the dry agents able to apprehend any of the smugglers.[2]

Though the burden for facing off against rumrunners in the city and elsewhere along the boundary line fell largely on the shoulders of federal officers, local law enforcement had not been immune to the bloodletting that took place in El Paso during the early 1920s. On the night of July 10, 1922, El Paso County Deputy Sheriff Tony Apodaca traded shots with a band of suspected bootleggers traveling in a pair of automobiles near the town of Fabens. Firing his rifle at both vehicles, Apodaca's marksmanship drove two men to abandon one of the cars and take off on foot. Both vehicles were later taken into custody, along with a large amount of contraband liquor. Three days later the *El Paso Herald* reported that the body of alleged liquor runner Victoriano Frausto had been found across the Rio Grande in the town of San Augustine, Chihuahua. It was generally believed that a high-powered round from Apodaca's rifle had struck Frausto in the heart.[3]

Between 1921 and 1924, members of El Paso's underworld murdered four officers of the El Paso Police Department, and a fifth would receive wounds that eventually led to his death. On the night of June 13, 1921, El Paso Police Captain Harry P. Phoenix, Sergeant Schuyler C. Houston, and Patrolman J. F. Keevil were leaving a chili parlor located at 2901 Alameda Avenue, when they noticed two shabbily dressed men loitering in the shadows across the street. Under orders to question anyone found under suspicious circumstances at night, Phoenix and Houston walked up to the men and asked them what they were doing. "Without warning," the *Herald* declared, "one of the men drew a pistol from his hip pocket and opened fire on Houston." Wounded in the stomach and chest, Houston managed to draw his weapon and fired at his assailant as he fell to the sidewalk.

At the same time, the second man pulled his own weapon and shot Captain Phoenix through the head, killing the thirty-seven-year-old lawman instantly. Then, as Houston and Keevil both fired at their darting figures, the two gunmen made their escape. Neither man was ever brought to justice. Though badly injured, Houston was soon promoted to captain. He would continue to serve the El Paso Police Department for another six years, until finally succumbing to complications stemming from his wounds in October of 1927.[4]

By 1923, South El Paso had become the scene of a flourishing drug trade and the base of operations for a number of notorious gangsters and hoodlums who went by such colorful names as Salvador "The Buffalo" Jacquez, Arnulfo "El Diablo" Valles, and Ysobel "Horseface" Murillo, a career burglar and armed robber who earned his nickname for the cryptic letters he sent his victims that featured the picture of a man with the laughing head of a horse for a face.[5]

Raids by both city detectives and federal narcotics agents in South El Paso throughout the 1920s were common, and often presented the officers with scenes of utter despair. When detectives Frank Burns and Harry Giffen raided a room at 1115 Hill Street in March of 1922, they found two hundred grains of cocaine and arrested a man named Martinez and three companions. However, when a third detective returned to the apartment later that evening, he discovered Martinez's children, five-year-old Filberto and his three-year-old brother Diego, both of whom had managed to hide when the officers arrested their father. "The children had had nothing to eat," the *Herald* reported. "One ragged quilt and a pile of straw was their only bed, while a fire in a small stove had died out. The only food in the place was the end of a loaf of bread."

Just as the nightclubs and liquor available just across the river in Ciudad Juarez brought tourists from across the United States to El Paso, so too did the availability of narcotics attract addicts to the border city.[6] In the winter of 1923, Frank Burns was one of several El Paso detectives loaned out to Will S. Wood, in charge of federal narcotic enforcement along the border. Among those detailed to work with Burns were Detectives Ira Cline, Ivy Fenley, D. W. Pitchford, C. H. Young, and police officers Juan Escontrias, R. E. McKnight, and J. E. Beck. While working with federal narcotics agents on the afternoon of Wednesday, April 11, 1923, Burns entered a confectionary stand located at 1005 South El Paso Street in "Little Chihuahua" in search of a suspected drug dealer. But, almost as soon as Burns stepped into the establishment, a pair of gunmen ambushed the twenty-nine-year-old detective.

"As I got inside the door one man started firing and then the other. They were wide apart and had me between two fires," Burns explained. "Two shots hit me, and I ran outside and fell on the sidewalk. They ran outside, and turned at the doorway in the direction opposite to that in which I had fallen. But they turned after running a few feet and cut loose on me again." Already shot twice, Burns was hit for a third time by a bullet that struck him in the neck. "I got my pistol out and fired once before they got around the corner," Burns explained. "I am sure I hit one of them." Transported to the Hotel Dieu, Burns held on until the following day, when he quietly died while holding his wife's hand. Burns's killers escaped across the border and were never apprehended.[7]

In November of 1923, Special Officer Enrique "Yaqui" Rivera was lured away from a dance hall and shot to death by Arnulfo "El Diablo" Valles, said to be one of the most dangerous gunmen in El Paso. On the morning of July 14, 1924, Sergeant John "Jack" Coleman was shot and killed by ambush as he drove away from his home. The following day, alleged dope dealer Salvador "The Buffalo" Jacquez was arrested while warming himself by a brush fire on Rosa Street in El Paso. Betrayed by a girlfriend who had told authorities that "The Buffalo" had boasted of having "killed a cop," Jacquez himself soon confessed to the crime, telling officers that he had murdered Coleman in revenge for the detective arresting him for vagrancy several months before. Valles and Jacquez would both be sentenced to death in 1925, though Governor Miriam "Ma" Ferguson would later commute their sentences to life in prison. In October of 1926, the two convicted cop killers would take part in a jailbreak at the Blue Ridge Prison Farm in Hobby, Texas. Joining them on the run would be "Horseface" Murillo, then serving a fifty-year sentence for armed robbery. Neither Arnulfo Valles, Salvador Jacquez, nor the one-armed "Horseface" Murillo would ever be recaptured.[8]

Now, at approximately 6:40 p.m. on the evening of December 13, 1924, just five months after Sergeant Jack Coleman was gunned down by Salvador Jacquez, and less than seven months since the US Border Patrol had been established by the passage of the Department of Labor Appropriations Act of May 28, 1924, Inspectors Herbert Brown and Frank H. Clark were on patrol near the Rio Grande when they spotted a man wading across the river near the Rio Grande Oil Refinery. As soon as Brown called out to the man, four gunmen lying in concealed positions suddenly opened fire from the opposite shore.[9]

Struck in the chest by a round fired in the first volley, Clark fell to the ground, mortally wounded. "Brownie, I'm shot. Run and get some help," Clark reportedly called out to Brown, before dying from his injury. According to Clifford Alan Perkins, at daybreak, the officers spotted a Mexican woman moving through the area near where the ambush had taken place, and watched as she retrieved an old single-shot .45-70 rifle. Trailing the woman back to her home, officers took the woman's son, Eulalio Aguilar, and three others into custody. Indicted for the murder of Border Patrol Inspector Frank H. Clark, Aguilar was later sentenced to serve a ten-year sentence in the Texas State Penitentiary. In May of 1931, Aguilar was released from prison after having only served six years for the death of the federal lawman.

Another suspect, identified as Manuel Vasquez, and also believed to have taken part in the shooting, managed to elude authorities for several months.

A modern view of the end of Park Street in El Paso, looking toward the Mexican border. Patrol Inspector Frank Horace Clark was killed near this spot in December of 1924, and this would be the location of numerous other shoot-outs with smugglers throughout the 1920s and early '30s.   *Mike Testin*

Finally, in October of 1925, Vasquez was arrested after being wounded in a "liquor battle" with customs officers. However, within days of his capture, Vasquez managed to escape from the Hotel Dieu and cross the Rio Grande into Mexico. He would remain on the run for another three years.[10]

Frank Horace Clark was the second member of the US Border Patrol to fall in the line of duty and the first to die as the result of a deliberate act of violence. He was also the tenth peace officer killed in El Paso since the start of nationwide Prohibition. In January of 1925—one month after Clark was shot to death near the banks of the Rio Grande, and in the wake of the murder of yet another Federal Prohibition Agent—newspapers throughout the country carried a Newspaper Enterprise Association article, which reported that since the Volstead Act had taken effect five years earlier, twenty-one men had been killed and another twenty-three wounded in the "rum-war" against smugglers in El Paso. "Life is cheap to these men, mostly Mexicans," the article reported. "They know the risk they are taking, but they go ahead with it just the same."[11]

On May 15, 1924, almost exactly seven months before Frank Horace Clark was shot to death by suspected liquor smugglers in El Paso, Texas, the US House of Representatives approved the Immigration Act of 1924 by a vote of 308 to 58. That same day, the bill cleared the Senate by 69 to 9, seventeen votes over the necessary two-thirds majority. Known as the National Origins Act—or the Johnson-Reed Act, after its two principal architects, Congressman Albert Johnson of Washington and Senator David A. Reed of Pennsylvania—the bill restricted the number of immigrants permitted to enter the United States each year by establishing a quota system that favored Western Europeans and completely barred any immigration from Asian countries not already affected by the Chinese Exclusion Act of 1882 or the Asiatic Barred Zone established by the Immigration Act of 1917. Exempted from the bill were any immigrants from the Western Hemisphere, including Mexicans, who were permitted to enter the United States without any set quota limiting their immigration.

On May 26, 1924, President Calvin Coolidge signed the National Origins Act into law. "In signing this bill which in its main features I heartily approve, I regret the impossibility of severing from it the exclusion provision which, in light of existing law, affects especially the Japanese," read a statement issued by the president. "I fully recognize that the enactment of this provision does not imply any change in our sentiment of admiration and cordial friendship for the Japanese people, a sentiment which has had and will continue to have abundant manifestation."[12]

The National Origins Act placed a strain on relations between the Empire of Japan and the United States, adding to the tensions that would eventually lead the two countries to war. "If history teaches anything," nationalist publicist Shinkichi Uyesugi told Tokyo reservists during an anti-exclusion demonstration in Tokyo, "an eventful collision between Japan and America on the Pacific is inevitable."[13]

The National Origins Act was only the latest in a series of immigration policies passed into law since the Civil War sixty years earlier, beginning with the Anti-Coolie Law of 1862, which forbade any American citizens from building, equipping, loading, or otherwise preparing any vessel "for the purpose of procuring from China, or from any port or place therein, or from any other port or place the inhabitants or subjects of China, known as 'Coolies,' to be transported to any foreign country, port, or place whatever, as servants or apprentices or to be held in service or labor." The Anti-Coolie Law had been followed thirteen years later by the Page Act of 1875, which among other things banned "the importation into the United States of women for the purposes of prostitution," and all those convicted of felonies other than political offenses. Seven years later, in the spring of 1882, Congress passed the Chinese Exclusion Act, suspending the immigration of any Chinese laborer to the United States. This was followed that August by the Immigration Act of 1882 that prohibited "any convict, lunatic, idiot, or any person unable to take care of himself or herself without becoming a public charge" from entering the country, and established a fifty-cent tax on each immigrant.[14]

During the four decades that followed the Chinese Exclusion Act and the Immigration Act of 1882, Congress outlawed the importation of all foreign contract laborers, not just those coming from China, authorized the deportation of anyone who had entered the country illegally, banned from legally immigrating any "persons suffering from a loathsome or a dangerous contagious disease," "persons who have been convicted of a felony or other famous crime or misdemeanor involving moral turpitude," polygamists and anarchists, and raised the 1882 head tax from fifty cents to four dollars in 1907. The Immigration Act of 1917 raised this tax again, to eight dollars, required all potential immigrants to pass a literacy test, and established the Asiatic Barred Zone. Finally, in 1921, Congress passed the Emergency Quota Law, a precursor to the National Origins Act, which limited the number of immigrants from any foreign country to 3 percent of the total number of residents of the same nationality living legally within the boundaries of the United States at the time of the 1910 census.[15]

But, while the United States government had been in the business of passing increasingly restrictive immigration legislation for more than half a century, it had been slow to create a single permanent constabulary solely devoted to adequately enforcing the nation's immigration policies. Just as state liquor laws and the National Prohibition Act would kick-start the rum-running business on the Mexican border, the Chinese Exclusion Act triggered a wholesale epidemic of human smuggling during the late nineteenth and early twentieth centuries. During the early years, the primary responsibility for apprehending smugglers and "aliens" fell on the shoulders of the mounted inspectors serving in the customs service's "Chinese Bureau" and their fellow "line riders" in the US Immigration Service, as well as the US Marshals of the various states and territories and their deputies. After the turn of the twentieth century, following a reorganization of the US Customs Service and the transfer of the Bureau of Immigration from the Treasury to the Department of Commerce and Labor, this task largely remained the purview of the "Chinese inspectors" and "mounted guards" of the Immigration Service, though the marshals also continued to enforce the Chinese Exclusion Act until 1913.[16]

Most of the Chinese smuggling was conducted by Mexican and Anglo outlaws, the forerunners of the modern "coyote," who in turn were in the employ of the Chinese Six Companies, a San Francisco–based organization that controlled nearly all of the city's Chinese business ventures, as well as the smuggling of opium and immigrants to the American West. "As I understood their procedure," Clifford Perkins later explained, "if a Chinese here had a relative or friend for whom he was willing to pay to have brought from China, he got in touch with the local representative of the Chinese Six Companies." Once a prospective immigrant had made contact with a company agent in a port city like Shanghai or Hong Kong, they were given basic instruction in English and arrangements were then made for them to travel to Mexico.

For a time, the immigrant would be employed in a restaurant or laundry by agents of the Six Companies, and would receive additional indoctrination in American customs and gain a better understanding of the work that they would do once they had entered the United States. Eventually, immigrants were transported to a border town like Nogales, Sonora, Naco, Agua Prieta, or Mexicali, where they were turned over to Mexican smugglers who would ferry them over the boundary line. If not intercepted by federal authorities, the immigrants would be delivered to a contact in the American interior. According to Perkins, they would then memorize a complete description of the house where they had supposedly been born, an account of who their parents and neighbors had been, their teachers and the identities of children they had once played with, "all individuals who could establish their identity in this country."[17]

In some cases, smugglers murdered their contraband rather than deliver them to their destination. One such incident reportedly took place near Nogales, Arizona, during the winter of 1911. "The wholesale murder of Chinese laborers by Mexicans in connection with smuggling contraband Celestials across the border was revealed in the story of a wounded Chinaman found in an isolated mountain located not far from this city and brought here today," the *Arizona Republican* declared. According to the wounded man, he and several companions were being smuggled into the United States by two Mexicans, when they were led into a remote canyon and attacked by their escorts, who set upon them while they were asleep. They had all recently worked on ranches in Sonora; each man carried the money they had earned for their labor, and it was assumed that the Chinese had been killed for their wages. "Word comes from Nogales, Mexico, today, that many Chinese that have passed over the border during the past month have never been heard from, and it is thought that they have been murdered and robbed," the *Republican* reported.[18]

On January 4, 1911, just a month before the *Republican* reported the murder of the Chinese immigrants near Nogales, Clifford Alan Perkins took his oath of office before the US commissioner in the Territory of Arizona and joined the Immigration Service. "As it turned out," Perkins later explained in his autobiography, "I was the last inspector appointed to enforce the Chinese Exclusion Acts." Destined to become one of the principal architects of the US Border Patrol, Perkins was born in Sharon, Wisconsin, on October 17, 1889, and first arrived in El Paso, Texas in 1908. "To a young man from a small Wisconsin farming community with a suspected case of tuberculosis, disappointed in his hopes for a college education and a career in professional baseball, it was a strange and wonderful place," Perkins recalled.[19]

Unable to find anyone else interested in employing a "nineteen-year-old semi-invalid," and having already passed a civil service examination before leaving Wisconsin, Perkins took a job as a clerk in the registered mail division of the US Post Office. It was not long, however, before Perkins tired of the monotonous routine and the job's modest fifty-dollar-per-month salary. "If I were a young man your age," an older woman working with Perkins told him, "I'd get a job with the Immigration Service." Perkins had never heard of it before. " 'It's a branch of the government,' she replied, and went on to explain that it dealt with immigration, exclusion, deportation, and expulsion of aliens," Perkins recalled. The starting salary was also more than twice what Perkins earned at the post office. That was all the encouragement he needed. As soon as an announcement was posted on the post office bulletin board for a civil service examination for Immigration Service positions on the border,

Perkins signed right up. While waiting to take his exam, he studied pamphlets on immigration laws and service regulations. Once he had taken the examination, Perkins had to wait six months just to find out that he had passed, and another eight before he received notification of his appointment. Perkins made the most of his time, enrolling in a Spanish-language course at a local business college.[20]

Finally, in late December of 1910, Perkins received his appointment with orders to proceed immediately to Tucson, Arizona Territory. At that time, the authorized force in Tucson consisted of an inspector-in-charge, nine immigration inspectors, one Chinese inspector, an interpreter, two male clerks, a female matron, and six guards. Officers were expected to provide their own uniforms and firearms within thirty days after being sworn into office. The uniforms, olive drab woolen suits for the winter months, cotton shirts and trousers for the summer, were to be worn while working in town or while inspecting passenger trains. When on scouting details, however, the men were permitted to wear casual work clothes. "My appointment as Chinese inspector was made to fill the vacancy created when another officer left the service. The title made the job sound exciting, possibly dangerous, and eventually an open sesame to the mysteries of the Orient," Perkins recalled. But, as the newly appointed officer soon learned, his duties were essentially the same as those of the other immigrant inspectors, and by 1917, Perkins's job title had been changed to immigration inspector.[21]

During the next several years, Perkins gained experience with the Immigration Service while working at various posts along the Mexican border, from Tucson to Douglas, and, eventually, to El Paso, Texas, where he became acquainted with Pancho Villa during the early years of the Mexican Revolution. Though the enforcement of the nation's immigration laws still remained the chief concern of Perkins and his fellow mounted guards, by the early 1920s immigration inspectors stationed in El Paso and elsewhere on the line increasingly found themselves dealing with bootleggers and narcotics smugglers.[22]

In October of 1920, Perkins was promoted to inspector-in-charge of the service's twelve-man Chinese Division, and by the time President Coolidge signed the National Origins Act into law in 1924, he was a seasoned veteran of thirteen years' service on the boundary line and the survivor of numerous shoot-outs with rumrunners along the Rio Grande. Thus, Clifford Perkins was in an excellent position to play a direct role in shaping the United States Border Patrol when it came into existence just a few days after President Coolidge signed the act into law.[23]

By the spring of 1924, it had become apparent that the situation along the border involving the smuggling of liquor, narcotics, and human contraband was such that an entirely new constabulary would be required to enforce the conditions of the National Origins Act, as well as the existing laws passed since 1882. Congress began the steps of creating the Border Patrol while still debating the conditions of the National Origins Act. "It is the intention of the committee to follow this legislation with a bill for the deportation after serving sentence to aliens convicted in courts of record of violations of liquor and narcotic laws," Congressman Albert Johnson had declared that April. "Also it is the intention of the committee to present a bill for the establishment of a border patrol with authority to enforce immigration, customs, health, liquor, narcotic, and all other laws."[24]

The Appropriations Act of May 28, 1924, allocated $4,500,000 to the Bureau of Immigration, "*Provided* that at least $1,000,000 of this amount shall be expended for additional land-border patrol, of which $100,000 shall be immediately available." Thus, with that modest budget, less than 10 percent of the annual amount provided to the US Coast Guard, the United States Border Patrol was born.[25]

El Paso was destined to become the patrol's initial mustering point and its birthplace. As Perkins would later explain, District Director George J. Harris was enthusiastic about the project, but given his numerous administrative duties, was unable to devote himself fully to the labor involved in organizing the new patrol. So, Harris called on Perkins to take on the task, and for the next six months the Wisconsin native went about developing a plan for the new policing agency. Perkins would use as models the Royal Canadian Mounted Police, the Michigan State Police, and the Pennsylvania Constabulary, along with a number of other organizations. The $1,000,000 allocation allowed for the hiring of 450 officers, most of whom would serve on the US-Mexican border in one of three Immigration Service Districts.

The Los Angeles District covered the Pacific Coast from San Luis Obispo, south to the international boundary, and east to a point about fifty miles from Yuma, Arizona. The El Paso District ran from Yuma to Devil's River, Texas, and included Arizona, New Mexico, and West Texas. From there the San Antonio District extended down along the Rio Grande all the way to Brownsville and the Gulf of Mexico. Transfers from the now-defunct mounted guards formed the nucleus of the early Border Patrol, and the ranks soon included a number of recruits who had worked as Texas Rangers and those who had served as peace officers in New Mexico and Arizona. Among those who signed on in 1924 were veteran border lawmen such as Jefferson Davis Milton, Texas Ranger Emmanuel A. "Dogie" Wright, son of legendary Ranger Captain William L. Wright, the ill-fated Frank Horace Clark, and Alonzo Harrington "Lon" Parker, a World War I veteran and one-time Nogales police officer who had participated in the manhunt for Manuel Martinez and Placidio Silvas in 1922.[26]

Though some 24 percent of the first 104 men to join the Border Patrol had seen duty as mounted guards in the Immigration Service, and while others had served as rangers, policemen, and deputy sheriffs, many aspirants to the service had no such experience. Employment with the Border Patrol was subject to a civil service examination, and applicants had to be at least twenty years old and either be a citizen or someone who owed their permanent allegiance to the United States. However, considering the speed with which the force was organized in the summer of 1924, the Patrol was unable to implement its own exams, and instead turned to the Civil Service Commission for lists of applicants who had taken exams for other types of government employment. Curiously, Perkins and his subordinates received a register with the names of those who had passed the examination for the Railway Mail Service. According to the 1925 report of Harry E. Hull, commissioner general of immigration, the Patrol's early recruitment methods contributed greatly to its own manpower issues, and "this was early demonstrated by the large turnover, which amounted to approximately 25 percent in the first three months."[27]

Training facilities, uniforms, and weapons were another concern. An abandoned barracks formerly used by the military police was used as a headquarters for the El Paso sector, and Clifford Perkins managed to secure three Model T Fords for patrol work and a converted Reo truck for hauling prisoners. Training consisted of a series of lectures given by veterans from the Immigration Service, as well as members of the El Paso police and sheriff's departments and the district attorney's office. Though a forest-green uniform—not unlike the one previously worn by the mounted guards, with blue cuffs and epaulets, along with silver insignia for the inspectors and gold for the senior personnel—was eventually adopted, early Patrol inspectors wore civilian clothes. "Patrol inspectors were greatly handicapped in the beginning by lack of uniforms," Hull explained to the secretary of Labor, "as there was nothing aside from their badges to distinguish them from the ordinary citizen. This gave smugglers and others an excuse for ignoring their commands, and at times the lives of the officers were endangered in the attempted performance of their duties."[28]

"No one knew what we were supposed to do or how we were supposed to do it," Patrol Inspector Wesley E. Stiles recalled in 1986. Stationed in Del Rio, the twenty-five-year-old Stiles's introduction to the service was typical of many early recruits. "Five other men reported for duty. They were a day or two ahead of me because they said they didn't have anything to do but come on. So we just walked around and looked wise. Nobody knew what to do, how to do it, or when to do it," he remembered. According to Stiles, for the first months the inspectors in Del Rio worked without badges or any transportation. "They said we could get us some guns if we wanted to. You should have seen the old relics that were pushed off on us." Many early inspectors carried their own guns. Later, officers were issued surplus US Army M1917 rifles, Colt double-action revolvers, and shotguns.

When Patrol Inspector Edwin M. Reeves showed up for his first day of work in El Paso in 1925, he was handed a ".45 single-action revolver and a web belt—and that was it." Reporting for duty wearing his best blue serge trousers, a white shirt, and tie, Reeves was taken down to the Stanton Street Bridge by Assistant Chief Willis B. "Bud" Perry and ordered to catch anybody that attempted to cross the Rio Grande. Reeves hadn't been at his post long before gunfire erupted downstream at the end of Park Street, not far from where Inspector Clark had been shot to death the previous December. Jumping into an automobile with Bud Perry, the two officers headed for the scene where their comrades had encountered a party of smugglers. "The shooting had stopped by then," Reeves recalled, "and there were piles of liquor out on the water's edge. It wasn't too deep, but it was knee-deep anyhow. I was a rookie, so I was elected to go out, wade out and get the liquor and bring it back in. My trousers and my white shirt were a mess." Later, Reeves acquired a set of

Patrol Inspector Edwin Reeves stands second from the right, beside writer Dilit Holliday, in this photo taken in the El Paso District in the 1930s. *Courtesy of the National Border Patrol Museum, El Paso, Texas*

brown duck canvas work clothes, "bugger reds," to wear while on duty. "We always had the Baden Powell hats for dress. We had a kind of cowboy hat to wear for river work," Reeves explained, "to wear with your brown ducking."[29]

The men of the Border Patrol finally began receiving their official uniforms in December of 1924, but it was not until the passage of the Act of February 27, 1925, that Patrol inspectors were legally empowered to enforce the nation's immigration laws, and "to arrest any alien who in his presence or view is entering or attempting to enter the United States in violation of any law or regulation made in pursuance of law regulating the admission of aliens," or those attempting to commit a felony. By that time, two members of the Patrol had already been killed: Frank Horace Clark in December, and James F. Mankin, who had died as the result of the accidental discharge of a rifle in Laredo, Texas, a few months earlier, on September 9, 1924.

By June of 1925, the men of the Border Patrol would travel some 2,288,000 miles by vehicle, boat, or on foot; question or investigate 1,252,379 persons; apprehend 1,185 people for violations of customs laws; arrest 2,847 "aliens" on warrants, 331 smugglers, and 4,641 human contraband. But while the Border Patrol had been specifically created to enforce the Immigration Acts of

1917, 1921, and 1924, for the first decade of their service's existence, Patrol inspectors would find themselves heavily engaged on the front lines of the liquor war, fighting alongside their counterparts in the US Customs Service and the Bureau of Prohibition, shooting it out with rumrunners and narcotics smugglers.[30]

On Friday night, April 3, 1925, Border Patrol Inspector James Cottingham was seriously wounded and one suspected smuggler was killed when officers attempted to halt a party of *tequileros* in the process of crossing the Rio Grande near the South Texas border town of Mission. Shot twice through the lungs and once in the arm, Cottingham was unconscious for several hours after the incident, but eventually recovered.

Two months later, on the evening of June 6, 1925, Patrol Inspectors Roy O. Stott and E. N. Crossett exchanged gunfire with a party of smugglers that included eighteen-year-old Alfonso Saltero. Badly wounded in the firefight, Saltero, who had reportedly been a heroin addict since the age of fifteen, died of his injuries at City-County Hospital on Sunday, June 7, 1925. "We believe the gang was attempting to smuggle dope over the border," Clifford Perkins declared. "Saltero has been arrested by our men three times recently, but each time we found no dope on him, and all we could do was turn him back across the river. Once while under arrest he became sick, and I believe this was caused by the dope he had swallowed to avoid being held as a smuggler."[31]

"The work in which patrol officers are engaged is an extremely hazardous one, and already quite a number of officers have lost their lives in the line of duty," Harry E. Hull stated in his annual report to the Secretary of Labor in June of 1926. "In some sections of the country they are not infrequently fired upon from ambush, and it is a tribute to their courage that in spite of these dangers, they carry on with unwavering zeal."[32]

Shoot-outs between smugglers and members of the Border Patrol along the Rio Grande took place throughout 1926. On April 19 of that year, the *El Paso Herald* reported that Manuel Vasquez, an alleged liquor runner, was recuperating in a Juarez hospital after having been shot by Patrol inspectors for the second time in two months. When El Paso Inspectors J. Q. Gillis and C. C. Mattox challenged a party of four smugglers who were in the process of wading across the Rio Grande on the night of May 11, 1926, the smugglers opened fire on them. Gillis and Mattox returned fire and mortally wounded twenty-year-old Ysodor Lopez. Lopez's companions immediately fled the scene, leaving behind ninety-two pints of whiskey, eighteen pints of tequila, and one pint of sotol, a beverage common in the borderlands and distilled from the "desert spoon" or *sotol* plant.

Encounters with would-be immigrants, barred from entering the country by the nation's quota laws, also occasionally led to gunplay. During the early-morning hours of June 26, 1926, Patrol Inspectors G. C. Dennis and Lester R. Dillon stopped an automobile driven by Japanese immigrant Andow Churoku and an unidentified Japanese "alien." When the two inspectors attempted to place Churoku under arrest, the man pulled a gun and started shooting. His first bullet grazed Dennis in the forehead, only slightly wounding him. "We fired back and a bullet struck him in the leg. He fell to the ground and stopped shooting. We immediately rushed him to the hospital," Dennis explained to the *Herald*.[33]

Though El Paso and the Rio Grande Valley would ultimately prove to be the deadliest battleground for the US Border Patrol during the Prohibition era, Southern Arizona would be the setting for the deaths of two members of the force in 1926. On the evening of April 23, Border Patrol inspectors working in Nogales received intelligence that a pack train loaded with contraband alcohol had left Sonora and was expected to arrive that night at the Alhambre Ranch, some forty miles southwest of Tucson. Setting out to intercept the shipment of booze in a pair of automobiles were two deputy sheriffs and six Border Patrol Inspectors, including Lon Parker and Robert Q. Leatherman, a participant in the shoot-out with Tomas Roman and Victoriano Martinez at Calabasas five years earlier. Also in the party that evening was Inspector William W. McKee, a US Army veteran and Mississippi native closing in on his fortieth birthday, who had only just joined the Border Patrol that February.

Later that night, the officers managed to stop the rum-running train and seize the liquor shipment without firing a shot, the bootleggers taking flight rather than risking capture. Packing the contraband into their vehicles, the officers started back toward Nogales and had gone just two miles when they were fired on by several assailants. Riding in the second car, McKee jumped out of the vehicle and rushed toward the gunmen with a rifle in his hands. He hadn't gone very far when he was struck in the chest by a round from a .30-30 rifle and killed instantly.[34]

The late afternoon of July 25, 1926, found Inspector Lon Parker on horseback patrolling the borderlands west of the Huachuca Mountains near the boundary of Cochise and Santa Cruz counties. By that summer afternoon, Parker, a native of this same stretch of wild countryside, had been with the Border Patrol for nearly two years. Born William Alonzo Parker on April 26, 1892, "Lon" Parker, as he is better remembered, was raised on his family's cattle ranch in Parker Canyon, just west of the Huachucas. At the age of twenty-four, Parker would see action in France while serving in Battery A of the 340th Field Artillery Battalion in the 89th Infantry Division during World War I. "While in the Argonne, he was severely gassed and spent several months in the hospital, but has completely recovered," the *Bisbee Daily Review* reported when announcing his return from Europe in the summer of 1919.[35]

After serving as a member of the Nogales Police Department, Parker joined the US Border Patrol on September 26, 1924, and was one of two newly appointed temporary Patrol inspectors for the El Paso District, with an annual salary of $1,680.00. Over the course of the next year, Parker steadily moved up through the ranks, receiving a permanent appointment in November of 1925, and by the summer of 1926, was expecting a transfer from Nogales to Tucson. Throughout that time, Parker had survived a number of encounters with armed liquor runners.

In one such incident, Parker was on horseback patrol, riding some distance ahead of Inspector Albert Gatlin, when he came across a small band of smugglers who had stopped to rest their heavily loaded pack animals. According to one early chronicler of the Border Patrol, as soon as Parker ordered the men to surrender, one of them took a shot at the officer with his rifle. The gang then took off on foot, with Parker in hot pursuit. Armed only with his pistol, Parker finally managed to get within range and brought down one of the *tequileros* with a shot to the leg; within a short time, he had subdued all three suspects. Fearing that his friend had been bushwhacked by bandits, when Gatlin galloped onto the scene, he was relieved to find his friend Parker triumphantly guarding his trio of prisoners. "You're too late for the fun!" Parker allegedly told him.[36]

On Sunday, July 25, 1926, Parker was attending a picnic when he was "tipped off" to some bootlegging activity near the small settlement of Canelo, a few miles north of the international boundary. "Late that afternoon he left camp alone to take up the trail of mounted liquor smugglers," an official report later explained. "Tracks of a man and a horse had been discovered with evidence that the man had ridden the horse where the terrain was smooth and walked over rough places, indicating that the horse was loaded with liquor or other contraband." About two and a half miles from the Wills Ranch, Parker encountered a man later, identified as Artilio Espinosa, in Brushy Canyon, leading a horse with twenty gallons of mescal strapped to its back. Investigating officers would later theorize that Espinosa was accompanied by a second smuggler, who was purposely riding some distance away in order to protect his companion and their shipment of liquor. As Parker drew his pistol to cover Espinosa, the unseen gunman shot him in the back. Somehow, Parker "retained sufficient command of himself to kill Espinosa and his horse, using one shot for each, and then rode two and a half miles to the Wills Ranch, where he collapsed."

Parker, who had last been seen alive by rancher John Merritt at 4:30 that afternoon, was later discovered by the Wills family when they returned home at about 6:00 that evening. Lon Parker died a short time later without ever regaining consciousness. Espinosa's body, with a .30-30 rifle held in the "grim clasp of death," and that of his horse were both discovered the following day by a posse of lawmen searching for Parker's assailants. "Indications point to the fact that Parker 'got his man,' although mortally wounded," the *Nogales Herald* reported. Parker's remains were transported to Nogales, where on the afternoon of July 27, 1926, he was laid to rest with full military honors. Lon Parker was the fifth member of the Border Patrol to die while serving on the US-Mexican border, and the third officer in the El Paso District to die at the hands of smugglers.[37]

"The border patrol is a young man's organization; it appeals strongly to the lover of the big outdoors—the primeval forests, the sun-parched deserts, the mountains, and the plains; the business upon which it is engaged calls for manhood, stamina, versatility, and resourcefulness in the highest degree," Harry E. Hull explained in his annual report to the secretary of Labor in the summer of 1927. " 'Honor First' is its watchword; privation and danger but serve as a

Dedicated by the US Border Patrol eighty years after his death, this monument stands just a short distance from where Patrol Inspector Lon Parker was fatally wounded in a shoot-out with Mexican liquor smugglers in 1926. *Mike Testin*

challenge which none refuses. Unfailing courtesy to all, and helpfulness to the helpless in distress, are emphasized above every other requisite. These young men are proud of their jobs—proud of their organization—with a code of ethics unsurpassed by any similar organization of this or any other day."

By the time Hull submitted this report, a fourth Patrol inspector stationed in the El Paso District had been shot and killed in the line of duty. On the evening of Thursday, April 21, 1927, Patrol Inspectors Thad Pippin and E. N. Crossett had just arrested two smugglers five hundred yards from the border, just west of the ASARCO smelter near El Paso, when they were ambushed by unidentified triggermen armed with sawed-off shotguns. Pippin immediately returned fire, getting off two shots before falling dead. Crossett, who was also wounded, managed to empty his six-shooter; he even got off two shots at the gunmen from his shotgun before they made their escape. He was later taken to El Paso's Masonic Hospital, where he eventually recovered. Inspector Pippin was thirty-seven years old and had been with the service for less than a year.

Commissioner General Hull was careful to acknowledge this loss, and included in his report the names of those officers who had been killed on the border since the death of Frank H. Clark in 1924. "Before closing this subject," Hull explained in his report, "I wish to pay tribute to those brave men of the border patrol who have made the supreme sacrifice in the line of duty. These heroes have died less gloriously, perhaps, but no less honorably than those who have given their lives on the battlefields for their country. The bureau's files are replete with stories of courage, devotion to duty, and sacrifice rivaling anything afforded by fiction."[38]

CHAPTER TEN

"YOU WERE LOOKING FOR ME LAST NIGHT"

Seven attempts have been made by underworld gangs to assassinate policeman Juan Escontrias during the four years he has been a member of the police force, according to police records.

—El Paso Herald, *April 20, 1923*

Detective Juan Franco was two weeks past his sixtieth birthday when he took Ignacio Dosamantes into custody at the Hotel Lennox in El Paso, Texas, on the morning of November 10, 1928. The El Paso that Franco now saw was a wholly different city compared to the wild frontier border town that he had seen when he first arrived in 1887. "El Paso was a bad man's town when I went to work," Franco would later recall. Between the 1890s and 1915, when he became an El Paso city detective, Franco had variously served as a deputy sheriff, deputy constable, jailer, police officer, railroad agent, and Deputy US Marshal.

While wearing his numerous badges during the later years of the nineteenth century and the first years of the twentieth century, Franco had rubbed shoulders with some of the most notable characters to call the city home during its final frontier heyday. According to one story he later told, Franco had once been called on to arrest the infamous Texas man-killer John Wesley Hardin on an assault charge in 1895. While this particular incident may or may not be true, Franco was in fact serving as a deputy constable in El Paso when Hardin was killed by Constable John Selman at the Acme Saloon in August of 1895, and it's quite possible that the two men had come into contact prior to Hardin's violent demise. Franco also knew Hardin's cousin, gunfighter Mannie Clements, who, just like Hardin, was destined to die in an El Paso saloon in 1908. Franco and Clements served together as members of the city police force, and after the ill-fated Clements had been elected constable, Franco had served as one of his deputies.[1]

Throughout his career as a border lawman, Franco would witness the end of the frontier, the reforms that gradually shuttered El Paso's red-light district, the violent decade of the Mexican Revolution, the arrival of state and national Prohibition, the purity squads, and the proliferation of narcotics in South El Paso. During that time, Franco had personally arrested hundreds of burglars, thieves, bootleggers, dope peddlers, drug addicts, drunken soldiers, and car thieves. He had ridden in posses led by legendary Texas Ranger Captain John R. Hughes, raided opium dens, and investigated more than his share of robberies, rapes, and homicides, tangling with countless members of El Paso's underworld.[2]

By 1928, Franco was a well-known officer in El Paso, and Ignacio Dosamantes wasn't some low-level rumrunner or South El Paso hoodlum. Dosamantes was a major in the Mexican Army, and the very man that the attorney general of Mexico had sent to Juarez earlier that year to investigate the activities of narcotics peddlers. He was also credited with busting up a counterfeiting ring involved in selling counterfeit American currency in Juarez.[3]

When Franco and Dosamantes pulled up to the police station and climbed out of the major's car, three officers were standing on the sidewalk near the entrance: Patrolman E. C. Stull and Detectives Tom Donnelly and Juan Escontrias. Thirty-seven years old that autumn, Escontrias was perhaps just as familiar to the readers of the city's newspapers as Juan Franco. Much like his older colleague, Escontrias had variously served as a police officer, city detective, deputy sheriff, and deputy constable, and had often had his exploits published in the local papers. However, unlike Franco, who had seldom used his six-gun during those long years as a borderlands peace officer, Escontrias had frequently used both his gun, and his fists. "Escontrias was leaning on a windowsill in front of the station when I walked up with Dosamantes," Franco would later tell reporters. "Escontrias said to Dosamantes, 'You were looking for me last night.' Dosamantes said 'No,' and then I heard the shot," the lawman added. "At first I didn't know what had happened, and then I saw Escontrias shoot again. I thought they were friends."[4]

Born in Fabens, Texas, on September 6, 1891, Juan Escontrias was the oldest child of rancher and sometime El Paso County Deputy Sheriff Silverio Escontrias and his wife Pilar. Escontrias was raised on his family's ranch at Hueco Tanks, located northeast of Socorro and a few miles south of the

El Paso, Texas, as it appeared in the early 1930s, a few short years after Juan
Escontrias shot and killed Major Ignacio Dosamantes.   *Courtesy of the National Border
Patrol Museum, El Paso, Texas*

Texas–New Mexico boundary. In October of 1908, when Juan Escontrias was
only a few weeks past his seventeenth birthday, he married seventeen-year-
old Sofia Marquez, with whom he would ultimately raise two sons and five
daughters. For the first few years the couple was married, they remained at
Hueco Tanks, where Escontrias continued to work as a cowboy on his father's
ranch. Exempted from military service during World War I, Escontrias held
a commission as an El Paso County deputy sheriff in the years prior to his
employment with the El Paso Police Department. According to a profile later
published in the *El Paso Herald*, while serving as a sheriff's deputy Escontrias
once trailed a livestock thief from New Mexico for more than two hundred
miles before arresting the outlaw and recovering several head of stolen horses
near Sierra Blanca.[5]

In 1920, the twenty-nine-year-old rancher turned lawman signed on as a
patrolman with the El Paso Police Department, and within a few short months
he had engaged in the first of many gun battles he would be involved in. During the predawn hours of Friday, March 4, 1921, Escontrias and Officer W. F.
Smith responded to a report that someone was stripping an automobile in an
alley behind the Hotel Bristol at 600 San Francisco Street. When the policemen arrived on the scene they discovered a man later identified as T. W. Crews
working beside a car that had been jacked up. As soon as Escontrias and Smith

called out to Crews, the man immediately pulled out a gun, fired off a couple of shots, and then started running. Escontrias and Smith both returned fire, and Crews suddenly halted and surrendered himself. It turned out that Crews had been on his way from the Leon Hotel to the cafe at the Bristol, which he was about to open for business. "He said he fired because the policeman threw a flashlight on him and he thought they were robbers," the *El Paso Herald* later reported. Crews, who was initially charged with vagrancy, was later arraigned for illegally carrying a concealed weapon, and was released on bond.[6]

Three months later, on the night of June 14, 1921, Escontrias and his "walking partner," Officer Tom Threepersons, were on the hunt for the men who had just slain Captain Harry Phoenix and wounded Sergeant S. C. Houston when they were fired on by three unidentified Mexicans at the corner of Eighth and Leon Streets in South El Paso. Threepersons and Escontrias both returned fire at their assailants, wounding two of them before they jumped into the Rio Grande and quickly fled across the border into Mexico.[7]

Of all the lawmen that Juan Escontrias would work with in El Paso during his first years with the city police, Tom Threepersons is perhaps the most legendary. Born in Oklahoma on July 22, 1890, Threepersons was a full-blooded Cherokee who has sometimes been confused with a well-known rodeo cowboy of the same name. Best known today for a popular style of holster he is credited with designing, the story of Threepersons's life before he arrived in El Paso and his reputation as a gunfighter have often been so overblown and inflated that it's difficult to separate fact from fiction. Even in his own lifetime, there were attempts by writers to exaggerate his career as a peace officer, and the number of notches on his gun.

In an article published in *NEA Magazine* in 1928, author Oren Arnold claimed that Threepersons had served in both the Northwest Mounted Police and the Texas Rangers, and had killed an estimated twenty men in shoot-outs. However, in January of 1929, Threepersons himself attempted to lay to rest some of the more outrageous statements that Arnold had made about him. "I've never been a Ranger and never expect to," Threepersons declared. "I have been an officer and tried to do my duty, but I don't want the public at large to think that I'm a gunman and will kill people on such slight provocation." According to Threepersons, writers such as Arnold "go a little too far when they detract from a man's character when he has spent all his life trying to keep it above reproach."[8]

That said, Threepersons was nevertheless a force to be reckoned with. A veteran of the US Army's Eighteenth Infantry Regiment and a former mechanic for the Army's Motor Transport Service at Fort Bliss, Threepersons joined the El Paso Police Department in 1920. Not long after he had been hired, on the night of July 13, 1920, Threepersons responded to a complaint that a man had been held up at his store that evening by a pair of robbers. "As the policeman walked into an alley he saw Matthew Johnson, a negro, and told him to answer some questions. With him was a white man," the *Herald* reported. As soon as Threepersons had issued his orders to the two suspects, both attempted to flee the scene. Threepersons pulled his gun and dropped Johnson with a bullet to the thigh. Johnson's companion escaped and was never apprehended. Held on a $750 bond, Johnson was charged with burglary, though he was later found not guilty and released that November.[9]

The following March, Threepersons was involved in another shooting incident near a bridge at Charles and Canal Streets in El Paso. Under the headline, "One Man Is Threepersons; Fights with Three Persons," the *El Paso Herald* reported that the officer was approaching the bridge when the trio of gunmen opened fire on him. "One of them fell when he fired," the *Herald* declared, "but his companions helped him to escape. While the officer was Threepersons, there would have been no one to assist him if he had been hurt."[10]

A week after they were fired on while searching for the killers of Captain Phoenix, Juan Escontrias and Threepersons were on foot patrol near the intersection of Seventh and South El Paso on the evening of June 21, 1921, when they were passed on the street by a nineteen-year-old blacksmith named Silverio Vasquez. As soon as Vasquez, who had allegedly been drinking that night, climbed into an automobile with his friend Joaquin Villanueva, he began cursing the two policemen. When Escontrias and Threepersons approached the vehicle to question the young men, Vasquez suddenly pulled out a gun and leveled it at Escontrias's partner. Without hesitation, Escontrias drew his own weapon and opened fire, fatally wounding Vasquez, who died later that evening. The following day, an inquest was held in the matter before Justice of the Peace R. B. Rawlins, and while the testimony was sent to the grand jury in compliance with the law, Escontrias's actions were deemed justifiable.[11]

At least some of the shooting incidents that Escontrias and Threepersons engaged in that year probably had something to do with the enmity the two officers had aroused among South El Paso's underworld. In a profile written on Escontrias in 1923, the *El Paso Herald* reported that he and his partner had arrested five members of a gang of hoodlums suspected in a series of thefts, and had received an anonymous note warning them that they would both be killed. "An offer of a safer and more congenial beat was made to Threepersons," an article published in the *Oakland Tribune* stated on July 19, 1921, "but he declined. Liquor and drug smugglers, it is said, do not care to meet him." Then, at about 1:00 a.m. on August 17, 1921, Threepersons was shot from ambush as he was standing beside his car near the South El Paso substation. "Officers who investigated were told by Threepersons that he wheeled about when he was struck and saw a man about 50 yards away fire a second time. A search of the vicinity failed to result in the arrest of the assailant," the *Herald* declared. Suffering from a flesh wound to his left arm, Threepersons was taken to the Hotel Dieu and soon made a complete recovery.[12]

In the spring of 1922, Escontrias was involved in yet another gunfight, though this time his partner in the episode was Policewoman Virginia Mendez. On Saturday, May 27, Escontrias and Mendez went to the home of Leopoldo Gomez, whose two teenage daughters, fourteen-year-old Anita and thirteen-year-old Amelia, had run away from home two weeks earlier. According to their father, the girls were believed to be keeping company with two men that Mr. Gomez had since located living in an alley in South El Paso's "Little Chihuahua." When the two officers arrived at the alley that evening, they encountered the two men in question, later identified as escaped convicts Luis Bahena and Francisco Alonis, who also went by the aliases Francisco Rodriguez and Francisco Granado. According to a statement later made by Captain Claude Smith, Bahena was believed to have escaped from a prison farm near Austin the year before. Before going on the run in El Paso, Alonis had been sent to the Texas State Penitentiary on a conviction of burglary. As Escontrias and Mendez approached, both men reportedly drew weapons and opened fire, one of them putting a round through Mendez's hat. "Bullets from the fugitive's guns wounded two bystanders. Escontrias dropped one of the men," a newspaper report published in the *Bisbee Daily Review* declared, "but he struggled to his feet and escaped, the police being forced to hold their fire

South El Paso, Texas, circa 1930s.   *Courtesy of the National Border Patrol Museum, El Paso, Texas*

by a crowd of women at the other end of the alley." Though Bahena and Rodriguez both managed to flee the scene, the two Gomez girls were eventually located and arrested in early June on charges of delinquency and seduction, and turned over to County Probation Officer Emma Webster.[13]

Escontrias continued in his duties as a policeman and, as it would turn out, had not seen the last of Luis Bahena and Francisco Alonis. At about 10:00 a.m. on the morning of Thursday, June 22, 1922, Leopoldo Gomez once again spotted the two men in South El Paso. Afraid to approach them on his own, Gomez went to the police substation and reported the sighting to Escontrias, who in the weeks since he and Virginia Mendez had traded shots with the men, had obtained a warrant for their arrest. Escontrias would later state that at least four attempts had been made on his life since the initial exchange of fire on May 27. "Wednesday night a shot was fired by someone in concealment at Fourth and South El Paso Street, the bullet passing through the windshield of Escontrias's car," the *Herald* reported, adding that two weeks earlier, "someone in hiding fired a shot which passed over the policeman's head."[14]

A short time later, Escontrias found the two men sitting near a coal car in the Santa Fe rail yard just west of Santa Fe Street. Eyewitness accounts of what happened next would vary, but in any event, within a matter of a few moments, Luis Bahena was lying on the ground, mortally wounded. "When I placed the men under arrest," Escontrias testified during an inquiry the next day, "Bahena lifted one hand and with the other, pulled a handkerchief from his belt. The handkerchief covered a pistol, and I shot when I saw the barrel leveled at me."

Gomez, who was standing nearby at the time, backed up the officer's testimony. "Escontrias tried to arrest two fellows and one of them pulled a gun," Gomez explained. "He put up his right hand and pulled his gun with his left hand. I was about 25 feet away and could see it all."[15]

Later, however, other witnesses stated that they saw something entirely different unfold in the rail yard that morning. "The officer searched me and then he searched the deceased," Alonis testified. "When he found the gun on [the] deceased, he shot and killed [the] deceased. The deceased had his hands up when the officer shot him. At the time of the shooting the officer had Bahena's gun in his left hand and his own gun in his right hand." Romana Lujan, who witnessed the killing from a nearby laundry, corroborated Alonis's testimony during the inquiry. "Escontrias drew his pistol and told them to put up their hands," she explained. "He searched them and took a pistol from one of them. The officer had a pistol in each hand when he fired. The man he shot dropped his hands at the report and fell to the ground." Albert Brown, who worked at the laundry with Ms. Lujan, remembered seeing Escontrias standing in front of Bahena and Alonis with a pistol in each hand, and that both men had their hands raised when the officer opened fire. "Neither made any attempt to escape," Brown declared. "All of a sudden the officer fired and one of the men dropped his hands and crumpled up on the ground."[16]

Within minutes of the shooting, police and employees of the Santa Fe Railroad had descended on the scene. As Bahena lay bleeding beside the tracks with a bullet through his abdomen, Sergeant Tom York made a futile attempt to get a statement from the fugitive before he expired. Charged with Bahena's murder, Escontrias was released on his own recognizance under a $7,500 bond, and allowed to remain on the job. Citing that the conflicting testimony brought out during the inquest that Friday did not justify condemning Escontrias, Chief Edwards chose not to suspend him from duty. "I shall report the occurrence to the civil service commission," Edwards explained, "but if I make any recommendations at all, it will be that he not be suspended." The next day, El Paso's civil service commission declined to suspend Escontrias, and instead chose to await the action of a grand jury in the fall. In the meantime, Escontrias continued to perform his duties as a fully functioning member of the city's police force.[17]

The summer of 1922 continued to be an eventful one for Juan Escontrias. On Saturday, August 19, Joseph Stout, a recently discharged US Army soldier who claimed to have been the lightweight champion of the American forces in the Far East, knocked down two members of the El Paso Police Department during a fight at Union Depot. According to newspaper accounts, it took five men to load the belligerent scrapper into a patrol wagon and another five to get him into the jail, where the struggle then continued.

A month later, on September 19, 1922, Escontrias and other officers were called to the scene of a disturbance at an apartment building on Madera Street. Once police arrived, they found a mob of angry citizens manhandling sixteen-year-old Martin de la O, who had allegedly assaulted a five-year-old girl. "Policeman Escontrias said the little girl pointed to de la O and said: 'He hurt me,' " the *Herald* explained. Escontrias and the other lawmen managed to take de la O into custody before he could be taken apart by his justifiably enraged neighbors, and transported him to jail. De la O was later sentenced to an "indefinite period" at a state reform school.[18]

On Thursday, December 14, 1922, Escontrias was indicted for the murder of Luis Bahena nearly six months earlier, though he continued to remain on the police department's payroll while awaiting trial. Three days later, Escontrias was attending a dance in the town of Socorro with Detective Ira Cline when he allegedly assaulted one Eugenio Olguin, inflicting three deep cuts on the back and left side of Olguin's head. Charged with aggravated assault, both Escontrias and Cline denied that any such altercation took place, and Escontrias was eventually cleared of any wrongdoing.[19]

Escontrias's murder trial began on March 1, 1923, and lasted for three days. "I heard loud talking among three men," testified a witness, who had been standing near the laundry where Romana Lujan and Albert Brown worked on the day of the shooting. "One had a gun in each hand. Another had his hands in the air, and the third had his hands halfway up. I turned away a minute and that was when the shot was fired. Then I saw one man fall and the officer make the other one kneel. The man who was shot had been stepping backward." Despite the testimony of several eyewitnesses who claimed that Bahena had been shot down while his hands were raised, it took the all-white jury just five minutes to exonerate Escontrias on March 3, 1923.[20]

By the time he was acquitted, Juan Escontrias had been assigned to a task force under the direction of Federal Narcotics Agent Will S. Wood. The consumption of illicit drugs and the smuggling of narcotics between Ciudad Juarez and El Paso both remained severe problems in the border city. In 1918, it had been estimated that a quarter-ounce of cocaine, the drug which by then had become the most popular in El Paso, brought the middleman about $21.00 and netted the wholesaler an estimated $94.00, plus 0.25 in delivery charges for each bindle, or package, of dope.[21]

Nationwide, narcotics use and addiction rates had been on the rise since the years prior to America's entry into World War I. In some cases, the increase in addiction was attributed to state Prohibition laws; it was thought that some drinkers had turned to narcotics in the absence of readily available alcohol.[22] Drug addicts came to El Paso for the same reason that thirsty tourists in search of a stiff drink were drawn to the city. Narcotics were readily available across the Rio Grande in Juarez, and the underworld element of both communities was there to ensure that the needs of "snowbirds" were met in the same way that *tequileros* and bootleggers provided for the demands of their own customers. "The twin cities on the banks of the Rio Grande cannot escape the fate of Sodom and Gomorrah, while Juarez continues to be the reservoir of booze, the haven of bootleggers, the refuge of criminals and dope fiends, and the nest of gamblers and prostitutes," Reverend S. D. Athans declared in March of 1921.[23]

Throughout the early 1920s, authorities on both sides of the river waged war on narcotics. In the summer of 1921, while city police and federal agents continued their campaign against bootleggers and drug smugglers north of the Rio Grande, Valentine Onate, chief of police in Juarez, announced a drive on the estimated three hundred "dope fiends" then residing within El Paso's older sister city. Another, more aggressive campaign against the narcotics trade began in the winter of 1923 and came in the immediate aftermath of the fatal overdose of seventeen-year-old Marjorie Dell Greene, a native of Knoxville, Tennessee, who worked as a stenographer for ASARCO in El Paso, and was the niece of Santa Cruz County Sheriff George White, who had died on an Arizona highway the previous summer while transporting Manuel Martinez and Placidio Silvas to prison. "My sister first went to Juarez to dance only a few months ago," her brother John Greene later explained. "At first she did not drink. Then she fell in with the wrong crowd. She took a few drinks and after a while, according to information I have, she may have started using drugs. I don't know whether the part about the drugs is true, but I guess it is."[24]

Known to frequent the dance floor at the Modern Café in El Paso and the nightclubs across the river in Juarez, Greene had recently traveled to Los Angeles with the intention of living there, but as Justice of the Peace Arthur M. Horn explained to reporters, she had found the price of narcotics too high in that city, and had returned to El Paso. "Never get started using the stuff," Greene had allegedly told a friend in the days leading up to her death. On the night of February 18, 1923, she joined a party of between six and ten others, and crossed the river to take in the nightlife of Juarez. According to her death certificate, Greene died the following morning at 1:30 a.m. from acute alcoholism and cocaine poisoning.[25]

Though drug use and the personal suffering of those who became addicted wasn't anything particularly new in El Paso, the death of a young socialite, an Anglo teenager, was front-page news. On February 20, 1923, as Marjorie Dell Greene was laid to rest at Evergreen Cemetery, the authorities on both sides of the Rio Grande initiated a renewed "War on Dope" in Juarez and El Paso. "The suppression of drug traffic, in my opinion," El Paso Police Chief Benjamin F. Jenkins declared, "rests more with parents than with officers. They can do more to keep children from starting the use of liquor and drugs than every law ever enacted." All the same, Jenkins, who had succeeded Peyton Edwards as El Paso's top policeman in December of 1922, assigned several city detectives and police officers, including Juan Escontrias, to work with federal narcotics agents under the direction of Will S. Wood, whose brother Charles Archibald Wood had been killed in the shoot-out at the Shearman hog ranch in 1921.[26]

During the first week of "warfare" in El Paso, Wood's team of five federal agents and seven members of the El Paso Police Department made twenty-five arrests for violations of the narcotics act. In the meantime, their counterparts in Juarez brought some two hundred addicts and low-level dealers in for arraignment in municipal court. This number included twenty-four Americans and ten Chinese immigrants arrested for opium possession. "The drug evil is just as threatening to the people of Juarez as it is to the people of El Paso," Judge Felipe Rodriguez declared. However, regardless of the number of arrests and interrogations Mexican authorities conducted in Juarez, no large-scale traffickers were brought to justice.

Nevertheless, on Thursday, March 22, 1923, an estimated $300,000 worth of narcotics, including what was believed to be enough cocaine, heroin, and morphine to supply legitimate demand for the two drugs for fifty years, and enough marijuana to roll some two million ten-cent cigarettes, was destroyed in a massive bonfire on the orders of Governor Ignacio Enriquez. Watching the contraband literally go up in smoke, Will S. Wood was encouraged by the renewed sense of cooperation between the two countries. "Governor Enriquez and Judge Rodriguez are sincerely interested in aiding United States officers in the dope problem. We have known for some time that they want to help us. But the destruction, aside from forever eliminating the narcotics, does more; it shows their hearts are in the work," Wood declared. "All the dope smuggled into El Paso comes from Juarez. If we can be sure that Mexican officials will do all they can to stop it before it crosses the river, half the battle is won."[27]

The war on drugs turned bloody three weeks later when Detective Frank Burns was fatally wounded by unidentified gunmen at a South El Paso con-fectionary stand on the afternoon of April 11, 1923. Not long afterward, Juan Escontrias was lured into a trap that nearly cost him his own life. Escontrias went to Juarez, where he reportedly made contact with one of the two trigger-men who had been on the scene when Burns was shot. "I didn't shoot Burns. It was my partner who shot him," the suspect told Escontrias. "We'll get you both, sooner or later," Escontrias replied. "If I could get my partner across the river so that you could arrest him, do you think they would let me alone?" the suspect asked. The officer told him that he wasn't sure, but said that he would try to find out.

In the meantime, Escontrias also met with an informant in Mexico, who explained that both suspects were known to cross the river on a regular basis to see their girlfriends in El Paso. "I'll tip you off the next time they are to cross so you can get them," the informant told Escontrias. Within a few days Escon-trias was notified that the two gunmen were expected to cross the Rio Grande on the night of April 20. That evening, Escontrias drove out to a stretch of the riverbank known as "Long Beach," parked his car, and walked a short distance toward the river, where he was met by the man who had given him the tip. "They won't come over tonight," the informant told Escontrias. "I walked back toward the police car, parked a little distance away," Escontrias later recalled. "As I got near the car, someone started shooting." As a bullet passed over his head and crashed through the windshield, Escontrias spun around, pulled out his revolver, and fired three shots into the darkness. "I don't think I hit anyone," Escontrias explained, "because they had dropped from sight." According to the *El Paso Herald*, it was the eighth attempt by local hoodlums to assassinate Escontrias since he had joined the police department less than three years earlier.[28]

Two weeks later, on the evening of Friday, May 4, 1923, Escontrias was a key player in another violent episode that occurred when he and three other officers attempted to arrest Gabriel Ramirez, a South El Paso gangster who was wanted for crimes on both sides of the Rio Grande. Escontrias received a tip that Ramirez was hiding out in the ground-floor apartment of a two-story tenement house located at First and St. Vrain Streets. During the early-morning hours of May 5, Escontrias, along with Detectives Ira Cline, Ed Stevenson, and Ivy Fenley, set out to take the suspected killer into custody.[29]

When they arrived at the tenement house, the quartet of officers split up, with Cline and Escontrias covering one of the apartment's two entrances, and Fenley and Stevenson the other. "We started knocking on the door," Escontrias later recalled. "We heard a man move at our door, and heard him moving as if to shift a weight against the door. Then we heard him run to the opposite side of his rooms." Fenley and Stevenson both heard the man they believed to be Ramirez come to the door they were guarding and then immediately turn around and start back toward the other officers. "I opened the screen and started kicking on the door," Fenley later told reporters, "then I put a skeleton key in the lock in an effort to get inside."

Suddenly, the door opened a few inches and the barrel of a gun poked out of the darkness and exploded at nearly point-blank distance. From somewhere inside the apartment, a woman began screaming hysterically as Fenley was struck in the face by a bullet that entered just below his right eye, ranged downward, and exited through his neck. "It knocked me down and the blood blinded me. The man inside then rushed out, after I had fallen, and shot me a second time." Though temporarily blinded by the bright flash of the shots fired at close range, Stevenson nevertheless pulled out his pistol and popped off a few rounds at the fleeing gunman as he raced by and darted from the scene.

"Cline and I, on the other side of the building, heard the shooting, and ran to the end of the tenement," Escontrias later stated. "We saw a man running from the opposite side, and opened fire on him, but he escaped."[30]

Fenley, seriously wounded in the head and chest, was transported to the Hotel Dieu. Despite the severity of his wounds, Fenley eventually made a full recovery and was back on duty by the summer of 1923. Searching the suspect's apartment later that morning, Chief Jenkins and a reporter from the *Herald* discovered a quarter-ounce of morphine and a marijuana cigarette, though there was no sign of the mysterious woman that officers had heard scream-ing during the shoot-out. A few hours later, when detectives located Ramirez's wife Delfina at an apartment at Seventh Street and South Mesa Avenue, she claimed that she hadn't seen her husband for a month. "We separated after he was charged with stabbing Garcia," she stated. "I don't know what woman could have been with him when the policeman was shot."[31]

On May 8, the *El Paso Herald* reported that the police department had received a threatening letter allegedly sent by Gabriel Ramirez. "I'll keep after Juan Escontrias until I drink a cupful of his blood," the fugitive declared. "Ramirez's warning is a further confirmation that he is receiving the protec-tion of the underworld," Chief Jenkins told reporters, "and that policeman Escontrias is a particular object of underworld hatred." A few days later, as officers in El Paso and Juarez continued the hunt for Gabriel Ramirez, Escon-trias went to Chief Jenkins and said, "Give me badge number 13." According to newspapers, badge number 13 had more than lived up to superstition and had been worn by several officers who had experienced bad luck or who had been injured in the line of duty, including Ivy Fenley. Apparently, Escontrias got what he asked for and boldly started wearing the unlucky shield on May 11, 1923.[32]

As Escontrias prepared for an expected showdown with the South El Paso gangster, Ramirez fled El Paso, ultimately making his way to Los Angeles. Finally captured there in early 1925, Ramirez was returned to El Paso. Unfor-tunately, the county attorney's office failed in its efforts to prosecute him for the murder of Jose Garcia and the wounding of Detective Fenley. In truth, other than Garcia's dying statement and the belief that Ramirez was the man who had shot Fenley, there was little more than circumstantial evidence to tie him to either offense. In September of 1925, Gabriel Ramirez, "terror of the

Modern view of South El Paso as seen from the corner of Sixth Avenue and South El Paso Street, a short distance from the El Paso Port of Entry and the Santa Fe Street Bridge. *Mike Testin*

South El Paso underworld," was released on probation, under the condition that he leave El Paso for good. He soon faded into obscurity.[33]

By the time Ramirez departed the city, Juan Escontrias had long since turned in badge number 13. In 1924, Escontrias tendered his resignation with the police department and went to work as a deputy for El Paso County Constable William A. Simpson. But, while Escontrias had traded job titles and now worked on a fee system instead of a regular salary, the deputy constable's job proved to be no less eventful than his time with the police department.[34]

Though Escontrias personally engaged in fewer gunfights while serving as a deputy constable, his six-shooter nevertheless came in handy on the night of June 23, 1927, when he tangled with an African-American prizefighter known as "Schoolboy." According to Escontrias, the trouble between him and School-boy began when he attempted to arrest two young women he found living in Schoolboy's house on charges of vagrancy. "And unlike many of his battles in the squared circle," the *El Paso Herald* reported, "Schoolboy came out second best in his encounter with the officer." Claiming that one of the women was his wife, Schoolboy allegedly pulled a gun on Escontrias and tried to prevent him from taking her into custody. Escontrias promptly pulled out his own weapon and bashed Schoolboy over the head with it and then hauled the trio off to jail.[35]

Two months later, on Tuesday, August 16, 1927, the *El Paso Evening Post* reported that a new saloon had been discovered at the end of Eucalyptus Street, just across the international boundary on Cordova Island. Known as the "Hole-in-the-Wall," the informal beer garden was owned and operated by Esteban Torres and quickly became a favorite nightspot, especially after the international bridges leading to and from Juarez shut down at 9:00 p.m. In order to visit Torres's establishment, all that thirsty El Pasoans had to do was park their cars on the American side of the line, walk fifty feet down a street that ran parallel to the border, and then another fifteen feet into Mexico. "The liquor is served at oil-cloth-covered tables under a shed roof that is made of corrugated iron," the *Evening Post* explained, adding that the booze was kept on ice in a room adjacent to the open-air barroom. "Children play about the yard. Dogs and chickens walk about at will," the newspaper added.[36]

As soon as he heard about the new saloon, Constable Simpson drove down to the edge of Cordova Island and watched as Americans came and went from the Hole-in-the-Wall and drank beer at Torres's crude establishment. "It is headquarters for smugglers," Assistant Customs Collector W. W. Carpenter declared. "That is a dangerous part of the border for Americans. Officers frequently have battles with smugglers down there."[37]

Three days later, the *Evening Post* announced that Border Patrol Inspectors had arrested Torres when he tried to cross the border and that Juarez Chief of Police Valentine Onate had shut down his business. "I was swamped with business and it looked as if I might grow rich until the officers swooped down upon me. The news articles that brought me prosperity also ruined me," Torres explained. The following week, Manuel Mungia, a former liquor wholesaler and alleged bootlegger, filed an application for a saloon permit with Juarez officials and immediately began construction on a new "Hole-in-the-Wall" near Torres's former beer garden.[38]

Officers in El Paso, including Constable Simpson's deputies, soon learned that the area just across the boundary line from the Hole-in-the-Wall was an excellent location to catch lawbreakers. On the evening of Sunday, October 9,

1927, Juan Escontrias started out after a carload of drunken revelers who had just returned from a visit to the Cordova Island nightspot. "They began throwing bottles out. They threw out several. One was thrown through the windshield," Escontrias reported. "I stopped them and one man started to jump out at me. I shoved him back and another leaped out and hit at me. I knocked him cold and arrested all of them. . . . Hundreds of folks go to the saloon after they come back from Juarez at 9:00 p.m. They get partly drunk in Juarez and finish up at the 'Hole-in-the-Wall,'" Escontrias declared. "Many young boys and girls go there," he added. "The place is an awful dump. There is going to be a killing down there some night."[39]

In response to the statements that Escontrias had made about the Hole-in-the-Wall, Manuel Mungia accused Escontrias of having recently caused a scene in his establishment. "Escontrias came in a few nights ago and got into an argument with an American," Mungia declared. "The American hit him. Escontrias drew his gun. A Mexican customs officer took the gun away from Escontrias. I kept Escontrias from being arrested." According to the Mexican customs officer, Escontrias had visited the saloon that night accompanied by two women, and had flown into a rage after he gave the bartender a $1.00 bill and demanded change for $5.00. "I was informed today that Escontrias stood on the American side of the border Monday night and fired his gun into the air in an attempt to create a scandal," Chief Onate reported. "The only trouble at the saloon recently was that started by Escontrias."[40]

Escontrias faced further accusations that November, when a man named Roberto Fuentes accused him of assault. "I caught him in the act of taking a motometer off a car in South El Paso and, when I asked him what he was doing, he cursed me and I slapped him," Escontrias explained. By January of 1928, it appears that Escontrias had had enough, and it was reported that he had tendered his resignation with Constable Simpson and planned to return to his father's ranch at Hueco Tanks. "I quit because I am tired of arresting drunks and stopping fights," Escontrias declared.[41]

If Juan Escontrias and his family had departed El Paso and had the veteran lawman indeed returned to Hueco Tanks as planned in early 1928, it's likely that many of the unfortunate events that would culminate in gunfire at the El Paso Police Department's headquarters later that year might have been averted. Escontrias had used his gun and his fists frequently enough. And if the shooting death of Luis Bahena is any indicator, then Escontrias may have used them both to excess. However, when comparing Escontrias to many of his contemporaries, his use of force is hardly unusual or remarkable. So, perhaps if Escontrias had quit then as he himself indicated he would, the darkest chapter of his life might never have unfolded as it did. However, four days after the *El Paso Herald* reported his resignation as deputy constable, on January 11, 1928, it was announced that Juan Escontrias had been hired as a detective with the El Paso Police Department.[42]

On the night of April 25, 1928, Escontrias and Detectives Emmett Dawson and Frank Rooney raided a house located at 1116 South Stanton Street, where they arrested Catalina de Cruz and twenty-eight-year-old Celso Hinojosa for possession of one hundred grains of heroin. During the altercation that followed, Escontrias knocked Hinojosa down after the suspect threw several bindles of heroin into a woodstove. Escontrias then boldly reached into the flames to retrieve the packets, and despite suffering a severe burn to his left hand, managed to recover most of the evidence. During Hinojosa's trial in federal court the following month, his attorney would claim that the officers had used threats to send Hinojosa's wife to prison in order to obtain a confession from Hinojosa, in which he admitted to importing the narcotics. Hinojosa's attorney also alleged that Escontrias had struck Hinojosa while the suspected dope dealer had been holding a baby, and that he had also slapped Hinojosa's wife. These accusations ultimately did little to tarnish Escontrias's reputation, however, and even less to save Hinojosa from a conviction. On May 30, 1928, Hinojosa was sentenced to a fifteen-month term in federal prison.[43]

Things began to unravel for Juan Escontrias a few weeks later. On the night of Thursday, July 12, 1928, Escontrias crashed his Nash sedan into the rear of a Cadillac parked on South Eucalyptus Street, just a short distance from the international boundary at Cordova Island and the Hole-in-the-Wall saloon. It was reported that Escontrias, who was off duty at the time, then slapped the Cadillac's driver. Later that evening, Escontrias was relieved of his badge and gun by Captain Tom York and sent home. The following day, Chief of Police Lawrence T. Robey placed Escontrias on indefinite suspension for conduct unbecoming an officer. Then, less than a week after the incident at the Hole-in-the-Wall, tragedy struck the Escontrias family, when on the evening of July 16,

1928, the detective's twenty-six-year-old brother, Pedro Escontrias, was killed by the accidental discharge of a pistol he was cleaning.

On July 20, two days after his brother Pedro was laid to rest at Evergreen Cemetery, Escontrias took the first steps in trying to save his job and filed an application for a hearing before the civil service commission. Perhaps in light of the recent tragedy, and in consideration of Escontrias's long service to the city and county, the commission decided to cut his suspension to ten days, and by that August he was back on duty.[44]

At about 1:15 a.m. on the morning of August 25, 1928, gunfire erupted in the lobby of the Hotel Rio Bravo in Ciudad Juarez. The participants in this fracas were Enrique Fernandez, a partner in Harry Mitchell's Mint Café and Bar, and a central figure in the Juarez underworld, and Major Ignacio Dosamantes, a forty-two-year-old officer in the Mexican Army who was then on assignment with the Mexican Secret Service. Under orders from Mexico's attorney general to investigate narcotics and counterfeiting operations in the border town, Dosamantes had arrived in Juarez two months earlier. Just a few weeks after launching his investigation, Dosamantes managed to uncover an international drug-smuggling operation that involved Fernandez and seized an estimated $150,000 worth of dope. The seizure came as a result of surveillance conducted by Dosamantes and his subordinates on Julio J. Cesarman and Leontin Hechtman, Romanians who were reportedly involved in smuggling narcotics to northern Mexico by way of Paris, France, via the Mexican port city of Vera Cruz. As soon as the two men realized that they were being monitored by the federal authorities, on July 9, 1928, Cesarman and Hechtman boarded a train and left Juarez for Chihuahua City.

Accompanied by a Juarez detective, Dosamantes boarded the same train as the two smugglers and followed them to Chihuahua City. "Fernandez was in their company on this train," Dosamantes later reported. After tailing Hechtman and Cesarman in Chihuahua City for two more days, the major took both men into custody and discovered over ten kilograms of cocaine and morphine hidden in packages they had waiting for them at the local post office. "We found papers which show extensive narcotic operations have been conducted [through] Mexico to Los Angeles, San Francisco, Dallas, New York, San Antonio, and other large cities in the United States," Dosamantes declared.[45]

Dosamantes and Enrique Fernandez collided in a violent encounter at the Hotel Rio Bravo six weeks later. "I have heard that Fernandez has been boasting that I could not catch him, and also rumors that he was looking for me," Dosamantes later explained. "I doubted these rumors, though, and took no precautions to keep away from him." Fernandez and Dosamantes would each offer their own wildly conflicting accounts of what had led to the early-morning showdown. According to Fernandez, Dosamantes and his men had previously arrested his brother, Antonio Fernandez, and had accused him of selling narcotics. "When he flatly denied it, they took him out in the country, put a gun in his stomach, and told him if he would sign a complaint against me, they would let him go," Fernandez stated. "In order to save his own life, which he thought was in danger if he didn't sign the paper, he signed a declaration that I was involved." Fernandez claimed that Dosamantes had then come to him at the Mint Café. "Enrique, you are in bad shape; I have a statement against you made by your brother," the major allegedly told him. "Later, a man came to me and said he could fix things for me. I replied that the major could go ahead and file charges, if he had anything on me."[46]

Fernandez told reporters that he had just locked up the Mint for the night and was on his way home when he encountered Dosamantes and two other men in front of the Hotel Rio Bravo. As soon as he saw them, Fernandez said he ducked into the hotel lobby and drew his weapon. "The major came to the door and fired first. When I fell, I shot back. I emptied my gun and reloaded and fired again. I had 50 cartridges in a belt," Fernandez recalled. "I exchanged shots with the three men for about ten minutes." For his part, Dosamantes denied that any force had been used to get a statement from Fernandez's brother, and on the morning of the shooting claimed to have been alone. Dosamantes first spotted Fernandez when he was about to climb into his car, which was parked in front of the hotel. "I paid but little attention to him, but when he saw me he pulled his pistol and shot at me six or seven times," Dosamantes explained. "I shot him in the leg, walked in, and disarmed him," Dosamantes declared. "His statement that I fired first, that my two friends shot at him and that he thought I was trying to shake him down for money is without foundation." Suffering from a bullet wound just below his right knee, Fernandez was transported to Liberty Hospital and held under guard. "I am investigating whether Maj. Dosamantes is guilty of abusing his authority," Juarez district attorney Alberto Terrazas Valdez told reporters, "or whether Fernandez was to blame for the shooting."[47]

Two days later, on August 27, 1928, Fernandez was released from Liberty Hospital and returned home without ever being charged in connection with the shoot-out at the Rio Bravo. Later referred to as the "Al Capone of Mexico" by El Paso newsmen, by the late 1920s Enrique Fernandez had risen from something of a two-bit bootlegger and dope smuggler in the early years of Prohibition, to the leader of the first truly organized criminal syndicate involved in the Juarez narcotics trade, a precursor to the modern cartel. Fernandez would rule the Juarez underworld until 1934, when his reign was finally toppled by a rival organization. Perhaps taking a few of his cues from his big-city counterparts in the United States, throughout his rise to power, Fernandez made the most of the political chaos and dysfunction that had followed in the wake of the Mexican Revolution, amassing a considerable amount of influence among regional politicians. Having friends in high places had helped Fernandez to avoid a prison sentence for drug trafficking in 1927, and it's possible that his ongoing manipulation of Juarez's elected officials had something to do with his avoiding any serious trouble following his shoot-out with Dosamantes.[48]

Whether or not Fernandez used this same influence to cause problems for Dosamantes with the civil authorities in Juarez is uncertain. But, in any event, Major Dosamantes soon had legal troubles of his own. Within a matter of a few weeks the federal agent would face charges for the exchange of gunfire at the Hotel Rio Bravo, accusations of accepting "hush money," and more seriously, allegations that he and his subordinates were responsible for the disappearances and deaths of several alleged underworld figures.

On Monday, September 3, 1928, Dosamantes was taken into custody and jailed in connection with the August 25 shoot-out, but after spending some thirty minutes behind bars, the major posted a $500 bond and was released. A few days later, three of Dosamantes's men were arrested and jailed on charges of assault, robbery, and exceeding their authority after casino operators Samuel Cheng and Fernando Lee claimed that Dosamantes and his agents had raided their establishment and demanded 230 pesos. Rather than surrender to the authorities in Juarez, Dosamantes instead chose to seek refuge in El Paso. "The charge is a frame-up," he declared. "A Chinese, Fue Wo, complained to me that operators of a lottery game at the casino had refused to pay him the amount he had won. He gave me lottery tickets as evidence."

According to Dosamantes, when he and his agents arrived at the casino, the proprietors explained that they had been paying "certain high officials," specifically members of the Juarez police and the Mexican military, $150.00 a month to "keep their mouths shut," and offered to pay Dosamantes the same amount to look the other way. "I refused to accept the bribe," Dosamantes explained. "Dosamantes charged Juarez police and military officials with accepting bribes to leave the Chinese lotteries alone, just as a blind to his own activities. He was trying to discredit the forces which are really acting to curb vice in this city," District Attorney Alberto Terrazas Valdes declared a few days after Dosamantes made his statements to the press. "He waited till he got out of Mexican jurisdiction before he made his charges," Juarez Police Chief Albino Frias added. "He was afraid to say anything here."[49]

A few days after he and his wife Adelaida took up residence in El Paso, Dosamantes received orders by the Mexican attorney general to report to Mexico City in person in order to provide the details of his activities in Juarez. While Dosamantes and his wife were preparing to leave the St. Regis Apartments on September 12, 1928, Detective Juan Escontrias stepped into the unfolding drama. In a letter written to American Consul John W. Dye two months later, E. B. Elfers, an El Paso attorney working for the Mexican consulate, explained what happened next. "About the middle of September, at a time when Dosamantes had made his plans to leave for Mexico City by way of Laredo, and was in fact already in his car ready to go, Escontrias stopped him, claiming that Mexican officials from Juarez had requested his arrest, and that he would be compelled to hold Dosamantes unless proper financial arrangements could be made." According to Cecilio Gonzales, one of Dosamantes's agents who was with him at the time, Escontrias told the major that he would not execute the arrest order if he was paid $100.00. "Major Dosamantes said that he had no money but that he would reward him when he returned to El Paso," Gonzales later explained in court. "Escontrias then said he would not execute the order of arrest if he were paid $50. Major Dosamantes got a $50 bill from his wife, had it changed, and gave Escontrias $25 and an order on Salvador Ateca for another $25."[50]

It was a complete shakedown. Even if Escontrias hadn't extorted a bribe from the embattled Mexican lawman, neither he nor any other El Paso officer were under any orders whatsoever to take Dosamantes into custody. The following day, the *El Paso Evening Post* reported that officials in Juarez had indeed requested the assistance of Chief Robey in apprehending Dosamantes, only to have Robey inform them that their warrant was invalid north of the Rio Grande. According to Cecilio Gonzales and E. B. Elfers, when Dosamantes discovered that Escontrias had duped him, he sent the detective several letters demanding that Escontrias return the $50.00 bribe, and threatened to report the incident to his superiors with the El Paso Police Department if he failed to do so. As Gonzales later testified before a jury that December, Escontrias eventually agreed to return the money on Saturday, November 10.[51]

In the weeks that followed Dosamantes's departure to Mexico City, the decomposing body of thirty-five-year-old Policarpio Rodriguez was discovered buried in a shallow grave in the hills of "La Piedrera," three miles south of Juarez. "He was a confirmed criminal," one federal officer declared. A known associate of Enrique Fernandez who was said to be involved in the gangster's counterfeiting and narcotics operations, Rodriguez had first been reported missing in August, about the time that Dosamantes and Fernandez had traded shots in Juarez. At the time, his family believed that he had been "taken for a ride" and assassinated. An autopsy conducted on October 3 revealed that in addition to having been beaten with rocks, Rodriguez had been shot twice with a .38 caliber pistol. By October 6, three men, including Dosamantes's assistant, Cecilio Gonzales, had been arrested in connection with the slaying.[52]

Two other Juarez gangsters, twenty-three-year-old Manuel Martinez and Joaquin "Carnitas" Garcia, had also supposedly been taken for rides that summer, from which they had never returned. Marks found on Martinez's body suggested that he had been beaten with a heavy iron rod, while Garcia was found with his hands tied behind his back and his own belt wrapped around his neck. It was later suggested that Dosamantes and his deputies were responsible for these murders as well, something that the major vehemently denied. When "Horseface" Murillo, noted South El Paso holdup man and accomplished jail-breaker, suddenly turned up missing, it was thought that he too might have been "taken for a ride" along with other Juarez criminals.[53]

Dosamantes returned to El Paso in early November with new instructions to "clean Juarez of dope sellers and smugglers." Dosamantes explained that on his way to El Paso he had traveled north from Mexico City to Monterrey with President Plutarco Calles and Mexico's procurator general of justice, and that both had expressed their confidence in the major. "I will clean up Juarez," Dosamantes declared.[54]

In the meantime, it appears that Escontrias was preparing to take steps to ensure that Dosamantes would never report the $50.00 he had extorted from him in September. "I will be compelled to notify your chief and the federal authorities," one of the major's letters to Escontrias had warned. "I paid the money only to quiet the nerves of my wife and Gonzales." In testimony before a jury that December, US Secret Service Agent F. V. Sorrels recalled a conversation he had had with Escontrias prior to Dosamantes's return to El Paso. "Escontrias told me he had received a letter from Dosamantes," Sorrels explained, "and that he was going to kill him if he came back here."[55]

In the days that followed Dosamantes's return to El Paso, he and Escontrias had a number of run-ins that were later described in testimony by several witnesses. On Wednesday, November 7, 1928, Escontrias stopped to talk with former policewoman Virginia Mendez. While Escontrias was visiting with Mendez and her brother at the corner of Seventh and Stanton Streets, Dosamantes pulled up in a car and, according to Mendez, began taunting the detective. "He said to Juan, 'Where are those Mexican officers who are looking for me?' Juan said he knew of no Mexican officers who were looking for him," Mendez recalled. "Then Dosamantes said, 'You had better hurry and get me, or I'll get you.'" Escontrias and Dosamantes had another encounter that Thursday night at a Seventh Street restaurant, during which, according to both Escontrias and eyewitness S. S. Beech, the major threatened to kill him. "I can kill you right here. I am a better man and officer than you are," Dosamantes allegedly barked. "I asked him why he didn't go ahead," Escontrias recalled. "Later Beech and I went out of the place. All during the time we were in the place Dosamantes was cursing me," Escontrias explained.[56]

The following evening, Dosamantes and Cecilio Gonzalez stopped Rojelio Sanchez and his girlfriend near the corner of San Antonio and Oregon Streets and searched their car. "I had just started my car after going to a moving picture show, when Dosamantes came up behind me, in front of the Union Clothing Store, and searched me, and then ordered the girl out of the car and talked ugly to her," Sanchez later recalled. Dosamantes warned Sanchez that unless he returned to Juarez that night and reported back to him the following day with intelligence regarding narcotics smuggling, he "would get his." "I'll get you like I got the others," Dosamantes supposedly declared, and then confiscated the man's wallet, which contained $24.00 and two notebooks. Rather than return to Juarez and make contact with members of that city's underworld, as ordered, Sanchez instead drove to the Santa Fe Street Bridge and notified his brother, a Mexican customs officer, of his exchange with the two government agents. Sanchez's brother then told him to return to El Paso and report the incident to the El Paso Police Department.[57]

For whatever reason, Sanchez did not report to the El Paso Police Department until the following morning, when he informed Captain Jon Stowe of what had transpired the night before and swore out a complaint against Dosamantes for the theft of his wallet. It was then that Stowe ordered Detective Juan Franco to go to the Hotel Lennox to arrest the Mexican major. "I told Dosamantes he was under arrest," Franco recalled that afternoon. "I then asked him about the robbery, and pointed to two pocketbooks, which had been described by Sanchez as the ones taken from him, on the dresser." Franco later said that Dosamantes admitted that the pocketbooks, money, and other papers the detective saw on the dresser were indeed Sanchez's, and then calmly surrendered to the aging lawman. Taking the evidence and Dosamantes into custody, Franco then departed for police headquarters with his prisoner, leaving the major's pistol behind in his hotel room.[58]

When Franco and Dosamantes pulled up to the police station at about 8:45 a.m., Juan Escontrias, Detective Tom Donnelly, and Patrolman E. C. Stull were standing out front on the sidewalk. Perhaps due to professional courtesy, Franco had neglected to handcuff the major. "I saw Juan Franco and Dosamantes get out of the car and walk toward the station entrance," Escontrias would later recall. "I did not know that Dosamantes was in custody or that an order for his arrest had been issued."

"I heard you were looking for me," Escontrias said as Dosamantes marched toward him. "He called me a name in Mexican language," Escontrias explained. "I saw him throw his hand to his hip pocket. I shot twice from the hip." Escontrias fired his first round without even pulling his gun from its holster, then drew his revolver and fired a second time. Franco and the other bystanders immediately grabbed Escontrias and placed him under arrest. On hearing the gunfire, Captain Stowe and Detective Sergeant Charles Matthews ran out of the station where they found Dosamantes lying on the sidewalk, shot once through the lungs and a second time through both hips. They also discovered a set of keys and what looked like a policeman's whistle, which were later identified as the only items that the otherwise-unarmed major could have been reaching for when Escontrias opened fire. "I'm not going to have him after me all the time," Escontrias declared, before several colleagues told him to be quiet. Matthews then took Escontrias into the station and held him in an inner office.[59]

Though Dosamantes remained conscious throughout the ordeal, he reportedly said nothing of the affair or his dispute with Escontrias. Instead, he repeatedly cried out for his wife as he was loaded into an ambulance and transported from the police station to a hospital, dying while en route. "My husband had never done anything to Juan Escontrias," Adelaida Dosamantes tearfully declared when informed that her husband had been shot down by the city detective. "What am I going to do? He was all I had in the world." As soon as he learned of the shooting, Mayor R. Ewing Thomason ordered Chief Robey to relieve Escontrias of his detective's commission, as well as his badge and gun, and place him on suspension. "I'm sorry it happened but I had to shoot him," Escontrias stated that afternoon. "He had made threats against me and had been after me for a long time."[60]

When Consul Dye submitted his confidential report on the incident to the secretary of state, he suggested that Dosamantes's death appeared to be part of a plan by the Juarez underworld to get rid of the federal agent, and also hinted that Mexican authorities might somehow be involved. "Juan Escontrias, the El Paso city detective known as a bad man who had already killed several persons and escaped punishment, has been very friendly with the police in Juarez," Dye explained. Eight hours after he killed Dosamantes and three hours after a murder charge was filed against him, Escontrias was taken to the county jail. Even then, Escontrias was given his own private hospital room and was supplied with candy and cigarettes, and "all the conveniences one would find in a hotel." "Why hasn't Escontrias been locked up," a reporter asked Deputy Constable Ira Cline. "I am guarding him," Escontrias's old friend replied. "That's just the same as being in jail." Cline, who himself would soon face charges for extortion, refused to answer any further questions.[61]

Though it's tempting to believe that Ignacio Dosamantes was murdered as part of a conspiracy between Enrique Fernandez and the Juarez police, as

Consul Dye suggested, and while Escontrias himself admitted that he had close ties to his counterparts across the river, little evidence supports the notion that Escontrias was in any way a triggerman for the Mexican Mob, and was instead trying to cover up the matter of the $50.00 he had taken from the major. "Inasmuch as it was known that Major Dosamantes had been active in efforts to suppress the narcotic traffic and counterfeiting in Juarez and El Paso," E. B. Elfers wrote Consul Dye a week after the killing, "it was generally assumed that his murder was in some way the result of such activities. I find upon investigation, however, that it was a personal matter between Escontrias and Major Dosamantes." According to Elfers, it was clear that when Escontrias saw Dosamantes arrive at the police station on the morning of November 10, "he concluded that Dosamantes intended to report the facts to the Chief of Police, and that he shot him down with the purpose of preventing such disclosure."

The trial of Juan Escontrias for the murder of Major Ignacio Dosamantes began on December 17, 1928, and lasted for seven days. Among those who testified against him were Cecilio Gonzales and Dosamantes's widow, who both recalled Escontrias taking the $50.00 bribe. On December 20, Escontrias took the stand in his own defense. He claimed that when he went to Juarez in September in connection with a murder case he was investigating, that he was approached by Alberto Terrazas Valdez, who told him that Dosamantes was wanted in Juarez, and that later he was approached by two Juarez policemen who requested his assistance in arresting the major. Escontrias admitted to talking to Dosamantes, but denied taking any money from him and his wife, and also denied telling Agent F. V. Sorrels that he intended to kill him. As to the shooting itself, Escontrias maintained that he had acted in self-defense. "Dosamantes walked straight toward me," Escontrias explained. "He was staring at me. I asked if he was looking for me and he said 'Here I am, you ———,' and he reached for his hip."

The jury was unconvinced, however, and on December 22, 1928, Escontrias was found guilty of murder. According to the *El Paso Evening Post*, Escontrias, openly wept when the verdict was read. On December 28, Escontrias was sentenced to five years in prison, and the following day he was transported to the state penitentiary at Huntsville by Highway Patrolman Norman Chamberlain.[62]

CHAPTER ELEVEN
CONTRABANDISTAS

It is impossible to convey to the mind of the laymen the confusion and pandemonium which reigns in a situation of this
kind, and from the writer's experience the stress far exceeds
that of a soldier in a planned battle.

—*Chief Patrol Inspector Herbert C. Horsley, July 26, 1929*

It was about 3:35 a.m. on the morning of July 20, 1929, when US Border
Patrol Inspectors Tom P. Isbell, Donald C. Kemp, and Ivan E. Scotten first
heard the sound of horses wading through the Rio Grande near the town of
San Elizario, about twenty-five miles southeast of El Paso, Texas. The three-
man team of officers were half of a six-man detail that also included Inspectors
Robert N. Goldie, Girard M. Metcalf, and Richard Coscia, sent to stand guard
over the Los Pompos river crossings, which had long been popular with liquor
runners, and had been the scene of numerous encounters between federal
lawmen and bandits. The crossings were paralleled by drainage and irrigation
ditches that fed water to several nearby cotton fields, and were surrounded by
dense brush that lined the shoreline of the Rio Grande. "Inspectors Goldie,
Metcalf, and Coscia were to patrol what is known as the lower Los Pompos
crossing, Inspectors Kemp, Scotten, and myself the upper Los Pompos crossing; these two crossings are about one-fourth mile apart by river and something like a mile by way of road," Isbell later recalled. The inspectors had first
taken up their positions at 8:00 p.m. the previous evening, and had remained
there throughout the night, during which a steady rain had fallen.[1]

Suddenly, a rider appeared in the mist just a few yards from Isbell, Kemp,
and Scotten's position. "I called upon him to halt, but instead of doing so he
whipped out a pistol and emptied it at us," Isbell declared. The three lawmen
immediately returned fire and blasted both man and horse. The unidentified
gunman fell from the saddle and disappeared in the dense brush along the
riverbank, while his horse galloped into one of the nearby cotton fields. "The
others apparently re-crossed the river, as we never saw but the one man and
horse," Kemp recalled. After waiting a few minutes, the trio of officers moved

forward to search the brush for the man they'd shot, but were unable to locate the suspected smuggler. However, when the officers managed to retrieve the wounded horse, they recovered four half-gallon cans strapped to the animal's back. Climbing into their automobile, the inspectors then raced to the other crossing to notify their colleagues.[2]

Once the two groups of inspectors had reunited and returned to where they had found the horse and liquor, Inspector Coscia was detailed to stay behind while the others went in search of the man Isbell, Kemp, and Scotten had traded shots with. Moments later, as the officers drove up to a point about 250 feet from where the gunmen had been shot off of his horse, they were suddenly fired on by a party of gunmen concealed in the brush on either side of the road and to their front. "I immediately turned the car to the right side of the road and we all fell out of the car, Inspectors Isbell, Metcalf, and Kemp getting out on the right-hand side, Inspector Scotten and myself on the left-hand side of the car," Goldie explained.[3]

As the officers raced to take cover behind their vehicle, Scotten was struck by a high-powered rifle round that passed through his right hip, shattered his hip bone, severed an artery, and exited near his rectum before lodging itself in his left thigh. As he collapsed into the mud beside the automobile, Scotten called out "I'm hit!" and then fell silent. Unable to reach their wounded comrade, the other officers remained pinned down behind the right side of the car and were soon forced to fall back into the nearby brush. "Upon taking up this secured position I called to Scotten but he failed to answer, and I am of the opinion that he had been shot by the Mexicans in the brush joining the left front of the car and at a very close distance," Goldie later recalled.[4]

With the muzzles of rifles flashing all around them, the surviving inspectors found themselves in a full-fledged battle with a gang of smugglers. "The fire was coming from the left, right, and front, and I moved over about forty yards to the right to try to quiet a fire that was coming from that direction," Isbell reported. "[T]he fire was so heavy that I had to move back to within twenty yards of the car where the other men were, at which time I crawled to the car, called out to Inspector Scotten several times, but he did not answer and appeared to be dead." According to Goldie, the Mexicans soon began crawling across the road, where they took up positions near the car where Scotten lay. "The firing continued and about fifteen Mexicans were advancing on us with heavy rifle fire from three sides, and after an exchange of one hundred or more shots we were forced to crawl back into a cotton field where we fought the Mexicans twenty or thirty minutes more until the Mexicans retreated to the brush and ditches along the river at this point; shortly thereafter the firing ceased."[5]

Having used up most of the ammunition they carried, Goldie used the lull in the battle to call for reinforcements for the outnumbered team of officers. "Inspector Goldie by crawling through the brush went to a telephone and called Border Patrol Headquarters for help, and within thirty or forty minutes, Chief Patrol Inspector Herbert C. Horsley* with Senior Patrol Inspector Pyeatt, Patrol Inspectors Scales, Torres, Steinborn, and Bush arrived," Isbell explained.

As soon as Horsley arrived on the scene, he immediately took command and led the party of officers through the brush toward the abandoned automobile where they found Scotten's body. After he had been wounded, the young officer had crawled under the car. But, when the smugglers had reached the vehicle, they had dragged Scotten out and shot him through the head at close range. The killers had then taken his wristwatch and both of his pistols. Once the officers were certain that the gunmen had completely withdrawn from the battleground, Scotten's body was loaded into a car and transported to the Peak-Hagedon Mortuary in El Paso. The liquor that was recovered from the wounded horse was turned over to Chief Mounted Customs Inspector Grover C. Webb in El Paso, while the animal's saddle was taken to Border Patrol headquarters, where it was held, "awaiting claimant."[6]

"All officers and investigators visiting the scene of action, including such investigators as Harry Moore and Frank Bailey of the Sheriff's office, have expressed the most utter surprise that all of our officers were not immediately killed and that such was only prevented by determined resistance and well-directed fire by the patrol inspectors involved," Chief Horsley explained in his report to the district director of immigration. "There can be no question but that all of the officers involved displayed rare judgment and valor under the tremendous stress of such a surprise attack by overwhelming numbers."

---

* A veteran of the United States Army, Herbert C. Horsley had previously served with the Border Patrol in Arizona before taking over as chief patrol inspector in El Paso in 1928.

Border Patrol Inspectors and members of the El Paso County sheriff's department managed to identify several potential suspects in Scotten's slaying, including an alleged gang member named Demecio Gandara. However, justice would be slow in coming for Scotten's family, as those responsible evaded capture in Mexico.

In late August, Mexican customs officials in Juarez did arrest one man, Gregorio Ortega, after he was found in possession of Scotten's .30-30 Winchester and .45 Colt automatic pistol. Ortega claimed that he had bought the guns from another man to use in his duties as a special police officer in the Mexican village of San Isidro. Though many lawmen on

Border Patrol Inspector Ivan E. Scotten was twenty-six years old when he was shot and killed by smugglers on July 20, 1929.
Special Collections, University of Texas at El Paso

both sides of the border strongly suspected that Ortega had been involved in Scotten's death, he was eventually released.[7]

Patrol Inspector Ivan E. Scotten was buried at Concordia Cemetery on July 22, 1929, following a well-attended and very emotional funeral. "Cutthroats such as those who murdered Inspector Ivan Scotten respect bullets. They have no regard for law. They yield to nothing but superior force," an editorial in the *El Paso Herald* declared on July 23, 1929. "To kill a large number of them would reduce smuggling as nothing else can. It seems barbaric and cold-blooded to say so, but such is the fact." Scotten was the fourteenth federal officer killed on the border within the decade.[8]

The death of Ivan E. Scotten came in the midst of an especially violent period along the international boundary with Mexico. On the night of December 30, 1926, Mounted Customs Inspector John W. Parrott, who as a Grant County deputy sheriff had once traded shots with one of the slayers of Ventura Bencoma in 1921, and his partner Leon Gemoets were both badly wounded after they stopped a suspicious-looking truck driven by Victor Arriola, said to have once served under Pancho Villa during the Mexican Revolution. While the two lawmen were inspecting Arriola's vehicle, two shots suddenly rang out and Gemoets fell to the ground with a bullet that entered his back just two inches from his spine. While Parrott took off after Arriola, Gemoets kept a pair of pistols trained on his two passengers, later identified as Alejandro Anaya and Francisco Rodriguez. When Anaya made a threatening move in the front seat, Gemoets shot him through the head, killing him instantly. He then turned his weapons on Rodriguez. "The Mexican in the back of the truck moved, and I shot him," Gemoets declared.

Having traded shots with Arriola, Parrott staggered back toward the truck a few minutes later, clutching his lower abdomen. "He said he was shot in the stomach," Gemoets recalled. "He handcuffed the Mexican in the back of the truck to the car. The other Mexican was dead. Then he lay down beside me and we waited until aid came." At first it appeared as though Gemoets was the more seriously wounded of the two officers, but Parrott's condition rapidly deteriorated, and on January 7, 1927, the father of four died at the Masonic Hospital. Arriola managed to reach a shack in Smeltertown, where he was later found hiding under a pile of blankets by a team of Border Patrol Inspectors. With Gemoets as the key witness at his trial, Arriola was later sentenced to life in prison.[9]

On April 21, 1927, Border Patrol Inspector Thad Pippin was killed in a battle with smugglers just across the Rio Grande from Smeltertown in the hills of New Mexico. Then, in February of 1928, Mounted Customs Inspector Steve Dawson was fatally wounded in another shoot-out with bootleggers in the Smelter District. Ten months after Dawson's death, on Sunday, December 23, 1928, Customs Inspector Thomas S. Morris and his partner Wilton R. Rogers stopped a car on the Tres Jacales Road on San Elizario Island, a short distance from the town of Fabens, Texas. After discovering ten cases of whiskey and an additional twelve gallon-and-a-half jugs of hooch stashed in the vehicle, the two lawmen took the driver, J. H. Pringle, and his passenger, John Q. Hancock Jr., into custody.

Just as Morris and Rogers were about to handcuff the two suspects, Hancock asked permission to roll a cigarette before his wrists were bound, and the officers allowed him to do so. However, instead of pulling a tobacco pouch out of his pocket, Hancock instead jerked out an automatic pistol. "Just as Morris started to handcuff Pringle, the other man, who had asked permission to smoke, began firing," Rogers recalled the next day. Morris was struck three times while Rogers was grazed in the shoulder. "We reached for our guns and began shooting. The man escaped across the line into Mexico," Rogers declared. "Pringle ran around behind the car and kept begging us not to shoot him." Morris was transported to Masonic Hospital in El Paso, where he died at 4:30 p.m. that same afternoon.[10]

While Pringle was held under a $2,500 bond for violation of federal liquor laws, a search was begun for Morris's assailant. A little over a month later, on the night of January 28, 1929, Hancock was arrested in Claremore, Oklahoma, by Hugh Larimer, an agent with the US Department of Justice working out of Oklahoma City. That evening, while Larimer was in the process of booking Hancock in the Claremore city jail, he reportedly attempted to attack the federal officer. Larimer pulled out his gun and shot Hancock through the chest. Hancock eventually recovered from his injuries, and in February of 1929 he was taken to El Paso, where he was charged with murder. Later that year, with Pringle as the state's star witness against him, Hancock was sentenced to twenty years in prison. Pringle was later sentenced to twenty-five years at Huntsville for another murder in Fort Worth.[11]

On the night of May 30, 1929, Border Patrol Inspectors Donald C. Kemp and Benjamin Thomas Hill were on duty along the international boundary near Cordova Island in El Paso when they spotted a suspected narcotics smuggler crossing the boundary. After the two officers ordered the man to halt, he darted down an alley near the intersection of Findley and Latta Streets, pulled a gun, and opened fire, striking the twenty-eight-year-old Hill in the chest and killing him. Hill, who had been with the Border Patrol for only two weeks, and was the tenth member of the service to die at the hands of outlaw gunmen, was later buried in Wheeler County in North Texas. His killer was never apprehended.[12]

Contrabandistas and their illicit cargo are apprehended along the Rio Grande in this photo taken in El Paso in the 1920s. *Courtesy of the National Border Patrol Museum, El Paso, Texas*

The ongoing liquor war along the Rio Grande and throughout the borderlands in the late 1920s and early 1930s was by no means a one-sided affair. On the afternoon of December 21, 1927, Border Patrol Inspectors E. N. Crossett, M. R. Rogers, and H. C. Pugh encountered four men attempting to cross the boundary at the foot of Hammett Street in El Paso with sacks of bootleg. During the exchange of shots that followed, smuggler Senobio Velos was hit in the leg and arm and later died at City-County Hospital. One of Velos's companions, Antonio Garcia, suffered a severe scalp wound when one of the officers pistol-whipped him while he was being disarmed. The other two men arrested at the scene were identified as Velos's brother Valentin and Cresencio Castaneda.

A week later, on December 28, alleged smuggler Pedro Luera was shot through the abdomen by Customs Inspectors while crossing the Rio Grande with a sack of liquor near the grounds of Old Fort Bliss. The following night, on December 29, three Border Patrol inspectors encountered a team of smugglers crossing the river near the end of Park Street, not far from where Frank H. Clark had been killed three years earlier. As they reached the American shoreline, the inspectors rose from their positions and ordered them to surrender. Suddenly, a volley of rifle shots exploded from the brush along the Mexican side of the river, and the Border Patrol officers returned fire. The smugglers dropped their sacks of liquor and turned back toward Juarez, abandoning twelve four-and-a-half-gallon cans of alcohol. During the exchange, twenty-three-year-old Mariano Moreno was struck by three rifle rounds that shattered his right leg. Collapsing in the shallow water, Moreno would have drowned in a bed of quicksand if not for the efforts of two Mexicans living near the scene of the shoot-out who answered his calls for help. Moreno's leg was later amputated at Liberty Hospital in Juarez. The body of another man, identified as twenty-three-year-old David Colunga, was later fished out of the Rio Grande by members of the Juarez police.[13]

The frequency with which American lawmen and suspected smugglers exchanged gunfire soon led to friction with Mexican authorities, who accused the Border Patrol and other agencies of heavy-handedness. "The killing of David Colunga in the Rio Grande by American border patrolmen, Thursday, was nothing less than an assassination," Juarez District Attorney Alberto Terrazas Valdez declared on Saturday, December 31, 1927. Valdez added, "I have been told the men could have been arrested without shooting Thursday. The smugglers, one of them told me, did not fire." The Border Patrol countered Valdez's statements with accusations of corruption among their counterparts across the river. An unidentified inspector told the *Evening Post*, "For years it has been common knowledge among the officers of this service that Mexican fiscal guards have assisted smugglers of contraband. This assistance has taken the form of directing such smugglers to points of crossing, 'spotting' on the American officers, and in protecting smugglers with rifle fire from the Mexican side of the Rio Grande," Chief Patrol Inspector Nick D. Collaer reported in early January of 1928. "Upon one occasion (perhaps more), fiscal guards have themselves been arrested with contraband—one was sent to the federal penitentiary at Leavenworth."[14]

Several weeks later, on the evening of Saturday, January 28, 1928, Mounted Customs Inspector Wilton R. Rogers and two fellow officers encountered a party of eight smugglers attempting to ford the river with two horses and a shipment of booze six miles east of El Paso. As soon as the trio of lawmen ordered the rumrunners to surrender, they allegedly opened fire with rifles and six-shooters. Rogers and his companions returned fire, killing one man, later identified as repeat liquor violator Jose Marcos Garcia, with a shot that tore away part of his skull, and wounding a second man, later identified as Ignacio Soliz, who managed to reach the Mexican shoreline and eventually made his way to Liberty Hospital in Juarez.[15]

Three days after the shoot-out, the *Evening Post* reported that a wounded Soliz had provided Mexican authorities with a statement in which he claimed that he and Garcia had already surrendered and had had their hands raised when the American officers opened fire, that they were unarmed at the time, and that they were the only two men in the party, as opposed to the eight smugglers the customs officers reportedly encountered. "I have invited the American officials so that they may learn from the man's lips that his companion was needlessly slaughtered and he himself was shot down cowardly," District Attorney Valdez declared. Assistant Customs Collector W. W. Carpenter later issued his own statement denying the accusations made by Soliz and Valdez. "Nine sacks of liquor were brought to this office and two more were reported lost in the river," Carpenter explained. "Two horses were reported with the party. I don't believe that two unarmed men would try to handle such a load of liquor."[16]

Violent encounters between federal lawmen and smugglers in El Paso and elsewhere along the Rio Grande in the late 1920s and early 1930s became almost weekly occurrences. In early March of 1928, Border Patrol officers G. N. Bogel and Henry W. Bush encountered a pair of *tequileros* fording the Rio Grande below San Elizario with a team of horses laden with booze. When the inspectors ordered the men to surrender, they instead opened fire. Though the smugglers managed to escape, seven cases of liquor were confiscated.[17]

On the afternoon of July 2, 1928, a forty-five-year-old Juarez customs guard named Carlos Alvarez was wounded during an exchange of fire between US Border Patrol Inspectors and smugglers near the Santa Fe Street Bridge. The incident occurred after two off-duty Border Patrol officers spotted two men coming across the Rio Grande with twenty-five gallons of bootleg. When the two officers gave chase, the smugglers immediately abandoned their shipment and started back across the river. "When they got on the other side of the river, about five or six men concealed on the Mexican side opened fire on us," one of the inspectors declared. "About this time we were joined by another patrolman who was armed and returned their fire." By taking turns with the third officer's rifle, the trio of inspectors managed to fight off the Mexican gunmen. While it's unclear if Alvarez was one of the participants, or was merely struck by a stray round, the Mexican officer was hit in the left side and taken to Liberty Hospital.

A few weeks later, Manuel Vasquez, who was believed to have been involved in the shoot-out that claimed the life of Border Patrol Inspector Frank H. Clark in 1924, and who had been on the run since his escape from the Hotel Dieu in October of 1925, was finally rearrested in South El Paso after a struggle with federal officers, and charged with the importation of five gallons of alcohol and thirteen and a half gallons of Mexican sotol. He eventually received an eighteen-month sentence in Leavenworth.[18]

Just before midnight on Wednesday, October 3, 1928, a team of five Border Patrol Inspectors waged a battle with a party of Mexican smugglers near San Elizario during which twenty-eight-year-old Aniceto Regalado was killed and some fifty gallons of liquor were seized. The following morning, two more smugglers were shot near the edge of Cordova Island in El Paso after their group refused to surrender and exchanged fire with US Customs Inspectors. Though the suspects all managed to escape, it was later reported that one man had taken a bullet in the spinal column and the other had been hit in the lungs, and that both men were dying in Liberty Hospital in Juarez. Two days later, on the morning of Saturday, October 6, 1928, another shoot-out took place at Cordova Island. Though nobody was hit during what was the fourth such incident in the area during the past four days, American officers managed to seize two sacks of gin, a sack of Three-Star Hennessy cognac, two sacks of American whiskey, and two jugs of wine.[19]

After District Attorney Valdez referred to American lawmen as "barbarians" for their treatment of Mexicans in the ongoing liquor war, R. M. Mathews, assistant director of immigration in El Paso, laughed it off. "Border patrolmen are instructed to challenge first, and never fire unless fired upon," Mathews declared in February of 1929. "An innocent person, illegally entering the United States, or Mexico, has three things to watch out for: Mexican officers, American river guards, and smugglers. Smugglers shoot first and figure it out later."

Just a few short weeks after Mathews's comments were published in the *El Paso Evening Post*, on the morning of February 28, Mounted Customs

Inspectors Rollin C. Nichols and R. W. Wadsworth intercepted four men who had just crossed the Rio Grande and were in the process of loading a shipment of booze into a waiting automobile. Nichols had just dismounted and was running ahead of Wadsworth to make the arrest, when the smugglers jumped into their car, stepped on the gas, and knocked Nichols to the ground. Then, the bootleggers opened fire on the two lawmen. Lying on the ground, Nichols emptied his own gun at their car. Three of the smugglers quickly abandoned the vehicle and made their escape on foot, while the fourth man was taken into custody, and the car—along with sixty-five pints of whiskey, cognac and beer, and another twenty-five gallons of liquor—was seized.[20]

Two days after Ivan E. Scotten was killed at San Elizario, on the evening of July 22, 1929, a team of four Border Patrol Inspectors engaged a large gang of bootleggers in a massive firefight on the west side of Cordova Island, during which they killed two of the suspected smugglers. "As a result of the battle, a truck with the sign of a local company on its side, three automobiles, and 150 gallons of liquor in barrels and 24 pints in a sack were seized. Three Negroes were arrested. They gave the names of Lee Warren, Hugh Parker, and Victor Phodberg," the El Paso Herald reported. According to an editorial published in the Herald on July 24, the deaths of the two smugglers evened the score. "These are at least a partial offset for the killing of Inspector Ivan Scotten, of the border patrol, US immigration service," the Herald proclaimed. "The more thugs and bandits killed, the more effective will be the suppression of their murderous bands. They respect nothing but bullets."

The following day, the newspaper published another editorial, fixing the blame for Scotten's death on the citizens of El Paso, who maintained the market for bootleg. "So long as our people stand with money in their hands to trade for liquor," the article declared, "bandits will kill Ivan Scottens to get it to them."[21]

In spite of any evening of the score, the violence would continue into the 1930s.

During the early-morning hours of February 24, 1930, twenty-six-year-old Pedro Rodriguez, believed to be a member of the Jose Pinedo Gang, a

Juarez-based operation in the business of smuggling both liquor and human beings, was shot and killed in El Paso by Border Patrol officer Irvin H. Cone. Then, on the morning of Thursday, March 6, just two days after a Customs Inspector was wounded in a large-scale firefight with rumrunners that featured a World War I–style "over the top charge," Border Patrol Inspectors were fired on by a smuggler armed with a Luger semiautomatic pistol near the corner of Central and South Piedras Streets. Returning the man's fire, the officers shot the smuggler through the jaw and shoulder, killing him.

Less than three weeks later, on the night of March 26, twenty-six-year-old Francisco Beltran and a companion were loading a shipment of liquor into a car near the smelter when they encountered a pair of Customs Inspectors. "I put up my hands," Beltran's friend recalled, "but Beltran fired and started to run and the officer shot him." Struck in the head by a load of buckshot, Beltran was killed on the spot.

In some cases, especially when firefights occurred in or near the El Paso city limits, the lives of innocent people were put at risk. During one hour-long struggle between the Border Patrol and a gang of smugglers in February of 1930, in which some 250 rounds were fired, stray bullets nearly struck a guest at the Paso del Norte Hotel several blocks away, while another round crashed through a window and lodged itself in the mattress where a woman was sleeping with her three-month-old baby.[22]

That spring, the *El Paso Evening Post* reported that *contrabandistas* were now attempting to avoid El Paso as much as possible. "The officers caught so many loads of liquor in El Paso that the smugglers are getting their loads out in New Mexico and Arizona," Customs Agent J. B. Morgan declared. "Last week Arizona officers caught two big truckloads of liquor that came across the border in Arizona." However, just six weeks after Morgan made these comments, at about 9:00 p.m. on the night of June 18, 1930, Mounted Customs Inspectors challenged two Mexicans crossing the Rio Grande on horseback with a load of liquor near San Elizario, just a short distance from where Ivan Scotten had been killed the year before. As soon as the customs men ordered the pair to halt, both men reportedly opened fire. The American lawmen returned fire, pouring a volley into the river that killed one of the smugglers and the horse he was riding, also shattering the wooden stock of the man's Winchester. The second rider managed to escape back to Mexico, though it was thought that he too was probably wounded.

Only a little more than nine hours later, at 6:30 a.m. on June 19, a trio of Border Patrol Inspectors stationed along the river just west of the Santa Fe Street Bridge spotted three smugglers wading across the Rio Grande toward an automobile that had just pulled up to take on a shipment of booze. When the officers emerged from cover to take the men into custody, they immediately came under the fire of gunmen stationed along the Mexican shoreline. Caught in the crossfire, the three smugglers turned and started back across the river. One of them, a repeat offender named Pedro Perchardo, who had previously spent time in Leavenworth for smuggling, was struck by a round that passed through his leg. He was later taken to City-County Hospital. The officers involved in this shooting believed that a second man on the Mexican side of the river was also probably wounded or killed.[23]

Three weeks later, during the early-morning hours of July 8, 1930, sixty-seven-year-old Dionicio Garcia, an "asserted Juarez rumrunner," was shot through the head and killed on Cordova Island by a gang of hijackers intent on stealing a shipment of whiskey, cognac, and tequila he was hauling in a wagon. The following night, less than an hour after US Border Patrol Inspectors waged a brief and bloodless battle with smugglers near the edge of Cordova Island, twenty-three-year-old Felix Garcia (no relation to Dionicio) was also mortally wounded by another band of Cordova hijackers. In light of the ongoing violence, as he prepared to retire from the US Customs Service after forty years on the border that same summer, seventy-five-year-old Joseph Dwyer seemed relieved to be closing out his career. "In the old days the marauders were not smart," Dwyer told a reporter with the *El Paso Evening Post*. "They were dangerous and didn't mind shooting, but the rustler, Mexican smuggler, and other bad men were not clever. Now it's more dangerous than ever to be an officer, and the game is faster all around."[24]

By the end of that year, the *Evening Post* reported that Juarez-based bootleggers were arming their poorly paid "cargadores" and ordering them to open fire on any American lawmen who attempted to halt them while crossing the Rio Grande. When an eighteen-year-old *contrabandista* was brought before the US commissioner in El Paso on charges of smuggling that fall, he explained that he had been instructed to "shoot if any officers bother you," and that he and another man had each been promised $2.00 a piece to carry cans of sotol across the border. These so-called "shoot to kill" orders by Juarez gang leaders were later reported to be the reason why two more *contrabandistas* were lying in the Peak-Hagedon Mortuary after an intense firefight between smugglers and US Border Patrol Inspectors in El Paso on the night of December 2, 1930. The unidentified Mexicans, one armed with an old double-barrel shotgun and the other with a six-shooter, were both killed when three officers returned the fire of an estimated nine gunmen near Cordova Island.[25]

While shoot-outs between smugglers and federal lawmen occurred with regularity at numerous points along the Rio Grande—from Brownsville, McAllen, and Laredo in South Texas, to Del Rio, Presidio, and the wild country of the "big bend," to San Elizario and El Paso's Smelter District, and the deserts of Southern New Mexico—El Paso's Cordova Island, or "bootlegger's island," as it had come to be known by the early 1930s, remained one of the deadliest battlegrounds anywhere along the international boundary with Mexico. In the summer of 1931, H. C. Marshall, a staff writer with the Associated Press, published a six-part series of articles on Cordova Island that highlighted the routine sacrifices made by members of the US Border Patrol in the frequent firefights there.[26]

By the time Marshall arrived in El Paso, the Border Patrol had evolved throughout its first seven years of existence. While visiting the Border Patrol headquarters in El Paso, Marshall came into contact with several individual inspectors and was struck by their youthful appearance, their diverse backgrounds, and the fact that many were college graduates. He also took note of the fact that most of the officers packed six-shooters and automatic pistols on their hips and carried them in holsters worn on wide cartridge belts. "After you've been in some of those island fights, been shot

A very young *contrabandista* poses with members of the Border Patrol in El Paso in 1929. *Courtesy of the National Border Patrol Museum, El Paso, Texas*

at from around corners of buildings and from behind trees and saved your life simply because you were faster on the draw, you'll wear a gun too," Assistant Chief G. W. Linnenkohl told Marshall, adding that many of his men wouldn't go to church without a pistol hidden under their coats, or consider sitting down in a public place without their backs against the wall. "They're not afraid," Linnenkohl explained. "They know the men they're dealing with. The average smuggler has many friends, on both sides of the river, and if one of them kills a 'Federal' or inspector, he's a hero."[27]

CHAPTER TWELVE
BRAVE MEN

Since January 16, 1920, according to Border Patrol records, fifty smugglers have been killed in the El Paso vicinity, and nineteen immigration and customs officers have met death at the hands of the smugglers. Besides these figures of actual deaths, a number of persons have been wounded on both sides of the river.

—William P. Blocker, American Consul,
Ciudad Juarez, January 6, 1934

At 9:15 p.m. on the night of Friday, November 24, 1933, US Mounted Customs Inspectors Rollin C. Nichols, John H. Shaffer, and Leslie S. Porter were scouting the international boundary near the end of Glenwood Drive, just east of the El Paso city limits, when they spotted a suspicious-looking automobile sending signals across the Rio Grande with its headlights. Believing that the car was probably driven by bootleggers making a scheduled rendezvous with smugglers, Nichols and his companions decided to investigate. According to a statement Nichols made the following day, by the time he and his fellow officers had turned their own vehicle around and driven up to the scene, the mysterious automobile had vanished, perhaps having already had time to take on a load of liquor. However, while the bootleggers' car had disappeared, the lawmen were not alone, and counted at least seven men still lingering in the darkness nearby. "Seeing a man about 25 feet from our car south towards the border, two other men about 30 yards south of him, and four other men about 75 yards to the southwest of the two," Nichols recalled, "I got out of the car to cover the first man, followed by inspectors Porter and Shaffer to take care of the other six."

Nichols had no sooner opened his door and stepped out onto the road when the men scattered along the riverbank and others concealed on the other side of the Rio Grande suddenly opened fire with Mauser rifles, shotguns, and even a machine gun. Nichols was hit almost instantly, struck in the left side of the head by a blast of buckshot fired at close range. The lead pellets tore his left ear and scalp, broke several teeth, and penetrated his skull. The badly wounded officer, who had survived being struck by a bootlegger's automobile during a firefight in February of 1929, fell to the ground unconscious, the right side of his body completely paralyzed. As Shaffer and Porter both dove for cover, the car they had just been riding in was riddled with bullets, with some sixty rounds striking the automobile and several passing all the way through. The two officers attempted to return fire, though it appeared that none of their shots had any effect on their attackers.

As bullets whined overhead, Nichols lay on the ground, unable to fight and slowly strangling on his own blood. Braving the heavy gunfire, Shaffer crawled forward and managed to drag Nichols into a better position, which saved him from choking to death. Then, in an equally courageous move, Porter jumped into their badly damaged vehicle, turned it around, and with Shaffer's assistance, loaded Nichols into the backseat. Within moments they were racing back toward El Paso. It was later reported that Nichols and his comrades had been deliberately led into a trap, ambushed in revenge for the seizure of $1,000 worth of hooch in San Elizario a few days earlier, during which time former San Ysidro municipal guard Raul Galvan was taken into custody. Following his arrest, Galvan, a veteran of the Mexican Revolution, was charged in connection with the slaying of Ivan E. Scotten in 1929, after the pistol he was carrying was identified as one of the guns taken from the murdered Border Patrol Inspector. "There is no possible way, as we now see it, whereby the assailants can be identified," Shaffer explained to the Commissioner of Customs after Nichols was shot, "and there must have been several of them in addition to the seven men seen by our inspectors in the moonlight."[1]

Nichols was transported to Masonic Hospital, where X-rays revealed that three buckshot pellets were lodged in his brain. The following day, Nichols was able to provide authorities with a verbal account of the incident, and on Monday, November 27, the El Paso Herald-Post reported he was still able to recognize members of his family and his fellow officers, though it was clear that in order to survive, he would have to undergo surgery to remove the buckshot from his brain. An infection soon set in, and at 9:05 a.m. on Tuesday, November 28, four days after he was wounded, the thirty-nine-year-old Customs Inspector died from his injuries.[2]

Rollin C. Nichols was the sixteenth federal officer killed in or around El Paso, Texas, since April of 1919. He was also the last US government agent shot to death by armed bootleggers in the American Southwest, or anywhere else in the United States, before the repeal of the Eighteenth Amendment and the end of nationwide Prohibition on December 5, 1933. "The fact that brave men must die in that line of duty is one of the tragedies of the Mexican-American border," the *Herald-Post* declared.[3]

While El Paso and the borderlands had experienced a slight decrease in violence and overall criminal activity with the worsening of the Great Depression during the early 1930s, the final years of national Prohibition were nevertheless a deadly period for law enforcement in the Southwest, and particularly along the brush-covered banks of the Rio Grande. During a meeting between the representatives of both nations in July of 1933, Mexican authorities, including the commander of the Mexican Army's Juarez garrison, had pledged to better assist their American counterparts in suppressing smuggling. Specifically, this included an agreement to clear at least some of the dense brush along their side of the river, which offered excellent concealment for the gunmen who guarded liquor shipments, and provided that members of the Border Patrol cease using shotguns in their operations against smugglers.

American officials had agreed to these conditions; however, due to one of the periodic changeovers of those in command of military forces in Juarez, little was done to clear the brush. And though Rollin C. Nichols would have the dubious distinction of being one of the last federal lawmen killed during America's thirteen-year experiment with nationwide sobriety, as it would turn out, his was not the last death associated with liquor smuggling on the border. Arizona, which had been the first of the Southwestern states to ban the sale and introduction of liquor for anything other than "personal use" in 1915, would repeal its state dry laws in 1932. Arizona's older sister, New Mexico, where state Prohibition had been in effect since October of 1918, would follow in 1933. Texas, on the other hand, which would permit the sale of 3.2 percent beer after ratification of the Twenty-First Amendment in late 1933, otherwise remained a dry state until 1935, with the result that a few more lives would be lost in shootouts with *contrabandistas* after the national policy was ended.[4]

The eighteen months that had preceded the death of Rollin C. Nichols in November of 1933 had been especially bloody ones in the liquor war on the Rio Grande, and for the officers who also faced off against thieves, killers, and other bandits.

Shortly after nightfall, on the evening of June 20, 1932, Senior Border Patrol Inspector Irvin H. Cone, along with Patrol Inspectors Tom Isbell and Charles Williams, and a party of Texas Rangers and Mounted Customs Inspectors, took up a position in the brush overlooking a dirt road that led toward the Rio Grande, about one and a half miles south of San Elizario. Cone and the other federal officers had been directed to work with the Rangers after authorities received a tip that a gang of outlaws based in the Mexican village of San Ysidro was expected to cross the river that night, "for the purpose of perpetrating another of the frequent crimes of theft, robbery, and murder, which have recently occurred in the vicinity of Clint and San Elizario, Texas."[5]

At 8:45 p.m., the lawmen heard the sound of hoofbeats crossing a wooden bridge between their position and the Rio Grande. "Shortly thereafter a man afoot approached the officers from the direction of the boundary," Herbert C. Horsley explained, "but believing him to be a lookout and advance man, the officers allowed him to proceed up the road." Moments later, a second man riding a horse came into view, and as he drew near Ranger Fred Griffin ordered him to halt. Instead of heeding the Ranger's command, however, the man whipped out a revolver and fired a wild shot at Griffin. The seven lawmen immediately returned fire, shooting the horse out from under its rider and riddling the gunman with a reported twenty-three bullets. In the meantime, the advance man had turned back and also started shooting at the combined force of state and federal officers. The lawmen fired several rounds in his direction, and as bullets cracked the air all around him, the "lookout" made a run for it, disappearing into the brush unscathed.

Once the dust had settled and after no other bandits appeared in the road leading up from the river, a coroner based in Clint, Texas, and the El Paso County sheriff's office were both notified of the shoot-out at San Elizario. On searching the body of the dead man and his horse, the officers recovered a .44-40 caliber Colt revolver and a handful of marijuana cigarettes. It turned out that the deceased was none other than "bad man" Gregorio Ortega, long believed to be among the gunmen responsible for the death of Ivan E. Scotten, and who had once been arrested for possession of the murdered Patrol inspector's firearms. Since Scotten's murder in 1929, Ortega had also been implicated in the slaying of Deputy Sheriff Robert A. Trice in Clint, Texas, in November of 1931, and in the killing of a San Elizario hotel clerk named Tomas Montes in January of 1932.[6]

It had taken nearly three years, but an alleged member of the gang of smugglers that killed Ivan E. Scotten had finally answered for the death of the twenty-six-year-old Border Patrol Inspector. Gregorio Ortega was buried at Concordia Cemetery on June 23, 1932.[7]

Six months later, on the night of December 1, 1932, former Texas Ranger and veteran Mounted Customs Inspector Herff Alexander Carnes was badly wounded during a shoot-out with a gunman operating as an advance guard for a gang of rumrunners. Acting on a tip that a shipment of liquor was going to be transported across the Rio Grande near the town of Ysleta, earlier that evening Carnes and three other officers had taken up positions in the brush overlooking the crossing where the smugglers were expected to ford the river. When Carnes emerged from cover and ordered the lookout and his companion to surrender, he was struck by a bullet that ricocheted off his pistol, split into two fragments, and entered his abdomen. Carnes and his companions returned fire and later reported that despite the fact that the smugglers had all escaped, they believed they had wounded at least one of the men. Carnes, who was fifty-three years old and had survived numerous shooting scrapes along the border during his long career as a peace officer, was taken to El Paso, where he died on December 4. He was the fourth Mounted Customs Inspector to die in the line of duty in 1932.[8]

On August 26, 1933, Texas voters went to the polls to cast ballots for convention delegates either for or against the ratification of the Twenty-First Amendment to the Constitution of the United States, the repeal of nationwide Prohibition. Despite a passionate eight-hour filibuster by Senator Morris Sheppard of Texas, "so-called father of prohibition," on February 14, 1933, the amendment to end America's thirteen-year experiment with legislated sobriety had cleared the US Senate by 63 to 23; two days later, it passed in the House of Representatives by 289 to 121 votes, in favor of repeal. During a meeting of the United Prohibition Forces at the First Baptist Church in El Paso a few weeks before Congress voted on the amendment, Dr. Henry Van Valkenburgh delivered a passionate prohibitionist speech entitled "The Wets Are Counting Their Chickens Before They Hatch." Valkenburgh followed this up on January 15 with "Our State: Dry or Die" at El Paso's Immanuel Baptist Church. In response to Valkenburgh's speeches, El Paso resident Henry S. des Landes wrote a letter to the *Herald-Post* summing up how so many others in El Paso, and throughout the nation, then felt about the ongoing efforts of dry forces in America. "Why cannot the clergy confine itself to the proper vocation in life, which is the expounding of the gospel of Jesus Christ, and leave politics alone?" des Landes asked. "They have no place in political life other than a vote individually and not as a church organization, but they band their churches and forces together to defeat the wishes of the great majority of the people—organize their forces politically to impose their will upon the people." The day was coming, des Landes explained, when the American clergy would be relegated to its "proper position and duties," and that those same duties would not include "the right to impose on the wishes of the people."

On April 10, 1933, Michigan became the first state to ratify the Twenty-First Amendment, and by the time Texas elected its convention delegates in August, eighteen other states had followed. Three months later, on November 24, 1933, the very day that Customs Inspector Rollin C. Nichols would be mortally wounded by rumrunners in El Paso, Texas ratified the Twenty-First Amendment. Less than two weeks later, on the afternoon of December 5, 1933, Utah became the thirty-sixth and final state to ratify the amendment. National Prohibition was finally over.[9]

Still, there remained the problems posed by the Dean Law and Texas's dry-state status, which resulted in further bloodshed along the Rio Grande after the repeal of the Eighteenth Amendment. After receiving a report from a railroad worker that a large party of "destitute Mexicans" had been seen near the end of Park Street in El Paso on the night of December 6, 1933, District Director of Immigration G. C. Wilmouth dispatched a team of six US Border Patrol inspectors to the scene to investigate. They included Bert G. Walthall, J. T. Love, Pedro Torres, Lester Coppenbarger, Robert Clance, and thirty-one-year-old US Marine Corps Reservist Doyne C. Melton. At about 3:30 a.m. the following morning, the officers spotted a force of thirteen smugglers fording the Rio Grande near a cotton compress located at the bottom of Park Street. "We saw the men coming across the river carrying loads," Inspector Love recalled. "They stopped when they reached the American side. One man, carrying a rifle, came up over the levee and disappeared in the shadows of the compress building. Two other men, neither of them carrying loads, followed him." Armed with rifles and shotguns, the Border Patrol officers waited until the smugglers had all crossed the boundary and then charged forward. "A shot was fired from the direction of the compress," Love explained. "We called to the men to halt, saying we were federal officers."

Then all hell broke loose. After the first shot was fired, the smugglers dropped their load of contraband and turned back toward Mexico, firing as they fell back across the Rio Grande. The Patrol inspectors returned fire, fatally wounding both twenty-five-year-old Francisco Gonzalez and his twenty-one-year-old cousin Higinio Perez as they waded through the river. American gunfire also wounded a third man, later identified as Francisco Mosqueda.

As soon as the smoke had cleared, and the last of the smugglers had disappeared across the boundary line, the officers realized that Inspector Melton was missing. A few minutes later, Inspector Clance found Melton's body. He'd been shot through the chest by a single rifle round and killed instantly. "One of the smugglers, Heriberto Alaniz, was captured by us in the battle," Love explained. "Inspector Torres found a .32 caliber automatic pistol, containing several cartridges, at the water's edge. The gun apparently was dropped by a smuggler in his retreat across the river." The inspectors also recovered a single .30-30 rifle casing on the ground near the cotton compress, forty yards from where Melton's body was found. "We had to abandon the fight and bring Melton in," Love explained. "It all was pretty tough and it was a mighty hot battle while it lasted."[10]

"Melton was a fine fellow and we all liked him," Assistant Chief G. W. Linnenkohl explained. "It is the first slaying in our department since 1929, when Patrolman Hill was killed down there near Hammett Street." The following afternoon, a funeral was held for Melton at the Peak-Hagedon Chapel, after which his remains were transported to his hometown of Marshall, Arkansas, for burial.[11]

Nearly a week after the shoot-out, on December 13, 1933, Maria Luisa Hernandez de Salmeron, whose seventeen-year-old daughter was married to

Francisco Gonzalez, gave a statement to Border Patrol Superintendent Nick D. Collaer and Patrol Inspector Taylor C. Carpenter that shed some light on the smuggling operation. "Juan Salmeron, my son, told me some time back that he was crossing liquor to the United States. Francisco smuggled some liquor the night before the fight, and Juan was also with them," she explained. According to the thirty-nine-year-old widow, her son and son-in-law and the other *contrabandistas* were all working for a man named Leon Antonio "El Pelon" Alarcon, whose smuggling operation also included Francisco's brothers, Demecio and Leonso Gonzalez. "I tried to get them to stop that business," Mrs. de Salmeron explained to Collaer. "Juan had crossed liquor several times before Francisco was killed, but that was Francisco's second trip. The day before Francisco was killed I tried to get him to not go when he told me he was going to work again. He said that while he knew it was dangerous, he had to take a chance. He was brought back dead."[12]

Adding a layer of intrigue to the story, in his own statement to Collaer on the day of the shoot-out, Heriberto Alaniz claimed that a pair of Mexican customs officers had collected a "customary smuggling fee" from the *contrabandistas* and had then "bid good-bye" to the party of rumrunners before they set out across the river, an accusation that both officials in Juarez and Francisco Mosqueda vehemently denied. Before American authorities could act on Alaniz's claims, however, the captured smuggler hanged himself in the El Paso County Jail on the morning of December 9, 1933. "I'm doing this because I don't want to be a prisoner anymore," Alaniz's suicide note read. "I don't want to be bothered anymore and don't want to bother you . . . tell my woman 'Good-bye, Blackie.' " According to Sheriff Chris P. Fox, Alaniz's actions were probably motivated "by fear of vengeance by border liquor runners."[13]

In January of 1934, Leon Antonio "El Pelon" Alarcon, alleged ringleader of the rum-running gang involved in Melton's death, was arrested during a raid in South El Paso by members of the El Paso Sheriff's Department and Constable's Office, and charged with the murder of the fallen Border Patrol Inspector. However, when Alarcon's case was presented to the grand jury on February 9, authorities failed to secure an indictment and he was released from custody.[14]

Three weeks after Melton was killed, on the night of December 27, 1933, Border Patrol Inspectors Bert G. Walthall, Louis A. Smith, and Curtis D. Mosley spotted a suspicious-looking automobile in East El Paso and decided to give chase. The trio of officers finally forced the vehicle to the curb near the intersection of Findlay Avenue and Raynor Street, and then started to climb out of their own car to question the three occupants, later identified as thirty-three-year-old Jose Estrada, an ex-convict who had previously served time on liquor charges, Ramon Rico, and Fidel Ortega. "I could see their figures silhouetted against a fence beyond their automobile that showed clearly in the moonlight," Mosley later recalled. "I saw them swing rifles toward us . . . I yelled a warning to my companions . . . It was too late . . ." According to Mosley, the three gunmen opened fire as soon as Walthall had stepped out onto the road. "He didn't have a chance—he couldn't even reach for his gun," Mosley remembered. "Mr. Walthall fell forward on his face in the dust . . . Patrolman Louis A. Smith fell back into our vehicle, struck in the head." Mosley managed to return fire, pumping seventeen rounds into the smuggler's car as it sped down the street. "I fired first into the front seat and then into the rear seat until the rifle was empty," he explained. "Then I tried to care for my companions." Walthall, who had been struck in the head during the first volley, was transported to Masonic Hospital, where time of death was fixed at 9:15 p.m. Smith, who had been just slightly wounded, would make a full recovery.[15]

The smuggler's booze-laden vehicle was later found smashed

Shot through the head during an altercation with suspected smugglers on the night of December 27, 1933, Border Patrol Inspector Bert Walthall was the nineteenth lawman killed by rumrunners in and around El Paso, and died nearly three weeks after the Twenty-First Amendment repealed national Prohibition. *Courtesy of the National Border Patrol Museum, El Paso, Texas*

against another car several blocks away, with Estrada dead behind the steering wheel. Later that evening, Chief Horsley and Nick Collaer received a tip that Estrada's companions were believed to be hiding at the dead *contrabandista*'s house, located at 3210 Manzana Street in East El Paso. A short time later, a posse of some forty Border Patrol Inspectors, sheriff's deputies, and El Paso police officers descended on the residence. The officers fired tear gas into the house and then stormed inside, where, according to one account, they found Estrada's terrified wife and two small children huddled around their Christmas tree. Though neither of the two men they sought was hiding at the Estrada home, the posse discovered over a hundred gallons of alcohol stashed in the house and a trail of blood near the back door. About two hours after Walthall was murdered, the combined force of local and federal lawmen arrested Rico and Ortega at their own residence, located at 157 Madison Street. Ortega had been shot through the right eye, while Rico had received a wound in his right hand. Also taken into custody were Estrada's father-in-law, Juan Lopez, and Rico's brother Ruben, though both men were released the following day.[16]

Bert G. Walthall was the nineteenth peace officer killed in the line of duty while battling rumrunners in and around El Paso, Texas. Charged with Walthall's murder on December 28, 1933, Ramon Rico and Fidel Ortega were both sentenced to life in prison in the winter of 1934. Ten years later, in September of 1944, Rico received a conditional parole from Governor Coke Stevenson, specifying that he should be deported from the United States. However, Rico allegedly returned to Texas on numerous occasions after his release, and in the spring of 1954 he was arrested by members of the US Border Patrol while crossing the boundary at Cordova Island, and returned to the Texas State Penitentiary at Huntsville.[17]

On May 14, 1934, Raul Galvan went on trial for the murder of Border Patrol Inspector Ivan E. Scotten five years earlier. On May 19, while Scotten's brother Frank Scotten sat in the courtroom, Galvan was found guilty and sentenced to death in the electric chair. A few minutes after the verdict was read, Assistant District Attorney John W. Penn returned to his office where he found a note written on a scrap of paper torn from the notebook of court stenographer B. F. Stuart that read: "This is to warn you, Mr. Scotten's baby is in danger—Galvan's friends." As soon as Judge W. D. Howe learned of the threatening message, he immediately ordered police officers and sheriff's deputies to guard Frank Scotten's four-year-old daughter Shirley Anne at their home at 1300 Cincinnati Street. Armed lawmen cordoned off the Scotten residence, and the child was placed inside a locked room that could only be reached by running a gauntlet of officers. "We've got things fixed so that anyone meaning to harm the child not only won't get in the house—they won't even get near the house," Detective Bennett Wilson declared that afternoon.[18]

Though Deputy Sheriff James C. Warren reported seeing a stranger make his way through the courthouse that morning, and while numerous staff members were questioned, officers were unable to make any arrests in connection with the threat to the Scotten child. "I had no knowledge of the note. I have no feeling against Mr. Scotten or his family—I would not harm a hair on his daughter's head," Galvan declared. On the day of the verdict, Galvan's attorney Carroll Smith said: "She is an innocent child and should not be harmed for any reason. Mr. Scotten's daughter has no place in this trial. I am seeking justice for Galvan—not vengeance against Mr. Scotten or his family. Galvan's friends should feel the same way. Their actions will hamper my efforts to obtain justice for Galvan on an appeal from the death penalty."[19]

While Smith filed an appeal on his behalf, Galvan remained in the El Paso County Jail, where he lingered for several months, smoking cigarettes, reading Mexican newspapers, and staring through a tiny window at the mountains across the Rio Grande. "It's so lonesome here—the rats are my only visitors," Galvan told a reporter that June. "So I caught a little fellow to keep me company."[20]

In March of 1935, the Court of Criminal Appeals in Austin upheld Galvan's sentence, though Carroll Smith immediately filed a second appeal for his client, who by now had grown increasingly weary of the ordeal. "Death is better than this—I had rather die than stay cooped up in this little cell," Galvan declared. "It is so lonesome. Death would be a relief." That October, Galvan lost his second appeal, though that hardly seemed to phase the onetime Mexican lawman, who claimed that several of the witnesses against him held grudges because he had occasionally arrested their relatives. "If I go to the electric chair—I guess I must—I will die innocent," Galvan proclaimed. "But what can I do alone. I expected nothing else."[21]

Despite his client's apparent resignation to his fate, Smith continued to wage a campaign for Galvan throughout the rest of 1935. Others soon joined the fight as well. In addition to the efforts of the El Paso Raul Galvan Committee, Mayor Richardo Espinoza Ramircz of Juarez sent telegrams to the American ambassador in Mexico City and to Texas Governor James V. Allred, asking for their assistance and for clemency for the convicted killer. That December, Allred granted Galvan a reprieve in order to review his case, and Galvan's pending execution was postponed until February 14, 1936. Then, the day before the execution was to take place at Huntsville, Allred commuted Galvan's sentence to life in prison. Though the governor felt that Galvan was indeed guilty, he felt that the evidence presented at Galvan's trial was "not entirely satisfactory in certain respects, and frankly, the most damaging evidence, in my judgment, is circumstantial." Eleven years later, in May of 1947, Raul Galvan was pardoned by Governor Beauford H. Jester, and shortly thereafter returned to Mexico. Thus ended a saga that began on a foggy morning along the Rio Grande eighteen years earlier, when twenty-six-year-old Ivan E. Scotten was killed in the line of duty.[22]

On the morning of April 27, 1934, Border Patrol Inspectors halted five men hauling forty gallons of liquor through the sand hills ten miles west of El Paso in New Mexico. When the officers moved forward to take the men into custody, two of the *contrabandistas* pulled out weapons and started shooting. The Border Patrol officers returned fire, wounding two of the smugglers and killing a third. Dressed "like a Juarez customs officer" and armed with a .38 caliber revolver and 114 rounds of ammunition carried in what was described as a "beautifully carved" cartridge belt, the dead man was taken to Las Cruces, New Mexico, where he was identified as Dionicio Gonzales.[23]

Minor incidents continued throughout that summer and into the fall, though none of these encounters resulted in any real bloodshed. Then, in late October, thirty-seven-year-old Feliciano Collaso was shot in the knees by a blast of buckshot while resisting arrest a few minutes after Border Patrol Inspectors stopped him and six other men with a load of booze at the end of Park Street. Collaso's injuries resulted in the amputation of his right leg. A few days later, on the morning of October 31, 1934, Border Patrol Inspectors James M. Motts, O. A. Toole, Lester Coppenbarger, and Murray E. Hutt encountered a gang of smugglers fording the Rio Grande three hundred yards west of the Santa Fe Street Bridge. As the inspectors challenged the men, the *contrabandistas* opened fire. Two more gunmen, reportedly armed with automatic rifles, also began shooting at the officers from concealed positions across the river. The team of officers returned fire, scattering the party of smugglers and killing two men, identified as thirty-two-year-old Manuel Patino and thirty-five-year-old Tomas Lopez.[24]

That El Pasoans had grown weary of bloodshed after sixteen years of mayhem along the Rio Grande was evident in the reactions of many residents to an article entitled "Hot Spot" that appeared in the June 1935 edition of *The American*, in which author Courtney Ryley Cooper described El Paso as a city of some "50,000 white persons and a Mexican district of 60,000," peaceful by day, yet by night, "when the lights sparkle on the mesa, and the Rio Grande runs silvery in the moonlight, men hunt men, rifles blaze—and humans die." Though some took offense to Cooper's article, at least a few saw some truth in his characterization of the city. "I believe that it gives a true picture of conditions," former deputy sheriff turned probation officer J. S. Guinn explained. "We live among these happenings and they seem ordinary to us. We can't see the woods for the trees." "How many times, pray, has your paper greeted us with headlines as follows: 'River Battle,' 'Battle Between Guards and Smugglers,' 'River Warfare Results in—Dead and—Wounded'?" one resident asked, in a letter to the *Herald-Post*. "A few years ago a border patrolman quit the service," he added, "explaining his reasons thusly: 'I love a fight once in a while, but every day is too much for me.'"[25]

Finally, on August 24, 1935, Texans went to the polls and voted 297,597 to 250,948 to repeal the Dean Law, thus ending statewide Prohibition. While many of the counties which had voted to go dry in 1919 would remain so, and although some liquor smuggling would continue after repeal, the twenty-year battle between lawmen and rumrunners in the American Southwest that had first begun when Arizona had gone dry in 1915, intensifying along the Rio Grande as a result of wartime restrictions and national Prohibition in January of 1920, was finally over.[26]

AUTHOR'S NOTE

Nothing has changed.

—*Groundskeeper, Concordia Cemetery, June 2015*

In June of 2015, while I was nearing the completion of this manuscript, I traveled to El Paso, Texas, with my good friend and colleague Mike Testin, who had generously agreed to join me on a road trip through the Southwestern borderlands in order to take several of the photographs featured in this book. While visiting that famous and historic city, Mike and I paid a visit to the National Border Patrol Museum, where the staff very graciously allowed us to photograph Inspector Frank Clark's Colt single-action revolver. Earlier that same day, we had journeyed to the end of Park Street in South El Paso, to shoot photos of the approximate location where Clark had been killed and where so many other shooting scrapes had occurred throughout the long liquor war on the Rio Grande. After touring the museum, which offers a fantastic display of firearms and other artifacts pertaining to that now-legendary law enforcement agency, Mike and I paid a visit to Concordia Cemetery.

While walking through this well-known burial ground, El Paso's equivalent to Tombstone, Arizona's, Boot Hill, I encountered a groundskeeper taking a break from the searing heat in the shade of a small tree. We passed the time for a few minutes, and before long the reason for my visit came up. I told the man about the stories of bandits, smugglers, and fast-shooting lawmen I intended to highlight, and explained that at least half of the book would cover El Paso, with an emphasis on bootlegging and smuggling. Though the groundskeeper was not an El Paso native, he had nevertheless lived there for most of his life, and was familiar with the city's violent experience during Prohibition—the gun battles with rumrunners, and the origins of the drug war on the border. Shaking his head and smiling, he looked at me and said, "Nothing has changed."

Of course, I knew just by wandering through the city that some things had changed. Smeltertown—once a sizable barrio, and home to the employees of the ASARCO smelter—is no longer standing, nor are the massive smokestacks of the smelter itself, which once loomed over the area. Long since vacated and torn down, little remains of Smeltertown except for a few historical markers and a cemetery that lies on a hill overlooking the smelter site, the final resting place of several hundred of Smeltertown's mostly Hispanic residents. Nowhere is there a monument to mark the location where Clifford Alan Perkins and a team of immigration inspectors and US soldiers fought an all-night battle with rumrunners in 1922, or the spot where Customs Inspector John W. Parrott was fatally wounded in December of 1926, or to any one of the dozens of smugglers who died along this stretch of the Rio Grande or in the rocky hills of New Mexico, just west of the river.

Some things have changed in South El Paso as well, though enough older buildings in this part of the city remain that, driving through this portion of the city today, the visitor can still get an idea as to what it would have looked like when Patrolmen Juan Escontrias and Tom Threepersons walked its streets in 1921. As a result of the Chamizal Treaty of 1964, nearly two hundred acres of nearby Cordova Island—once a hotbed of smuggling and illegal border crossings, and the scene of numerous violent clashes between smugglers and members of the Border Patrol—was ceded to the United States, and is currently the location of Bowie High School and the Chamizal National Memorial, commemorating the peaceful settlement of a century-long dispute over this portion of the boundary line. Just northeast of "the Island," the intersection of Findley and Latta Streets, where Border Patrol Inspector Benjamin Thomas Hill was shot to death three hundred feet from the border by a suspected smuggler in June of 1929, is now a relatively isolated pocket of residences and the St. Francis Xavier Church, wedged between US Interstate 110 as it approaches the Bridge of the Americas Port of Entry, Paisano Drive, and the Patriot Freeway.

Nonetheless, although I had seen for myself how much El Paso had changed since Texas repealed its dry laws eighty years ago, I fully understood what the groundskeeper meant when he said that nothing had changed. While writing this book, the ongoing and well-publicized drug war across the Rio Grande in Juarez continued to make headlines, just as it has for years. Two months before my visit, in April of 2015, the El Paso Times reported the arrest of Jesus Salas Aguayo in Chihuahua. Aguayo, whose aliases include "Zorra 5" and "El Chuyin," was suspected of having participated in a number of gangland homicides, including a 2009 assassination in El Paso, numerous kidnappings, and a 2010 car bombing. At the time of his arrest he was reputed to be the leader of the Juarez cartel, having taken over after the arrest of cartel boss Vicente Carrillo Fuentes in October of 2014.

Following Salas's apprehension, leadership of the Juarez cartel fell to Salas's second in command, Rafael Chavira Renteria, also known as "El Borrego" (The Lamb). Four months later, in August of 2015, Renteria was reported killed in a shoot-out with rival gangsters. Thus, the cycle of violence among the leaders of organized crime in Juarez, which traces its criminal heritage back to Enrique Fernandez and other Mexican gangsters of the 1920s, continues, though its hard to compare the hyper-violence of the borderlands of the 1990s, 2000s, or 2010s with the violence of the 1920s or 1930s.[1]

Two hundred and fifty miles west of El Paso, the former mining town of Bisbee, Arizona, "Queen of the Copper Camps," lies less than a half-hour's drive from the popular tourist destination of Tombstone, and remains little changed since the days when Joe Hardwick patrolled its narrow, winding streets as a member of the police force. While the Silver Leaf Club and the other nightspots that stood in Upper Brewery Gulch the night local lawmen clashed with members of the Tenth Cavalry are long gone, the Copper Queen Hotel and many of the city's other historic buildings remain intact. The Bisbee Historical Society and Museum, one of the finest institutions of its kind in Arizona, now occupies the former offices of the Copper Queen Mine, and includes a marvelous display of photographs and other artifacts from the Bisbee Deportation in 1917. Though the copper mines ceased production many years ago, modern Bisbee remains a very vibrant and progressive community, where numerous hotels, restaurants, and shops cater to the tourist trade. Just below Bisbee, in nearby Lowell, lies Evergreen Cemetery, final resting place of Sheriff Harry Wheeler, as well as Special Deputy Orson McRae and miner Jim Brew, both of whom died while on opposite sides of the Bisbee Deportation. Not far from these gravesites is that of Constable Alexander E. Sheppard, shot to death in Bisbee in September of 1920.

Some forty-five miles farther west of Bisbee on the far side of the Huachuca Mountains stands a monument erected by the US Border Patrol in honor of Patrol Inspector William Alonzo "Lon" Parker, who was killed by Mexican smugglers in July of 1926. Located in a fairly remote canyon south of

Final resting place of Harry Wheeler, captain of the Arizona Rangers and sheriff of Cochise County, Evergreen Cemetery, Lowell, Arizona.   Mike Testin

Elgin, Arizona, just a short distance from where Parker was fatally wounded, the marker is well off the beaten path for the average tourist. However, standing there at the lonely spot on a hot summer afternoon, listening to the wind blow through the juniper trees, a visitor can very easily imagine what it must have been like for a solitary lawman to patrol that country on horseback. Today, several of Parker's relatives still live in the area, and each year his family, along with members of the US Border Patrol, gather for an annual ceremony honoring fallen officers.

Still farther to the west lies the former mining camp of Ruby. Scene of a series of brutal murders in 1920 and 1921, Ruby is now a privately owned ghost town, open year-round to visitors. Well worth the fifty-mile drive from Tucson, many of the camp's structures remain intact, including the schoolhouse where Myrtle Pearson once taught the camp's children, although the mercantile where she and her husband were both shot to death on a hot summer afternoon in August of 1921 is little more than an adobe ruin. The living quarters first built by Phil Clarke in 1915, which both the Pearsons and the ill-fated Fraser brothers before them called home, have long since deteriorated, as have the post office where Frank Pearson was killed and the screened-in porch where four-year-old Margaret Pearson ran for her life as bandits gunned down her mother. Still, standing in the now-empty store and gazing out at the nearby hills through the doorway, where Deputy Parmer would have entered the morning after the Pearsons were slain, it's easy to imagine what it was like for the Clarkes, the Frasers, and the Pearsons to live and work in that rough little community a few short miles from the border. Whether or not you believe in such things, ghost towns have a haunted feeling about them, and Ruby is no exception.

Nearly three hundred miles to the north, the communities of the Verde Valley are among the most popular tourist destinations in the state of Arizona, thanks in large part to the iconic red rock scenery of Sedona. Like Bisbee, the former mining town of Jerome, where abandoned tunnels once hid elaborate distilling operations, is now an art community, and remains a favorite haunt for both valley locals and outsiders alike. Clarkdale, where aging frontier lawman Jim Roberts faced off against holdup men Earl Nelson and Willard Forrester, still looks very much as it did on the morning of June 21, 1928. The bank robbed by Nelson and Forrester is well preserved, and is now home to a wine-tasting room, where Lee Snyder's bullet-dented pocket watch is on display. Each year, Roberts's final Arizona shoot-out is the subject of a reenactment performed by local actors, and "Uncle Jim" remains a well-known figure in the town's history.

Nearby, the city of Cottonwood, that "wide open" and "vicious" community where Yavapai County lawmen spent so much time busting up stills and arresting bootleggers, has undergone a bit of a transformation in recent years. Wine-tasting rooms and the addition off several new restaurants have helped revitalize the area known as "Old Town," which by the late 1990s had fallen into serious decline. Though many Arizona communities are quick to embrace their rough and rowdy heritage, most visitors to Cottonwood (and perhaps quite a few longtime residents, as well) are unaware of the town's turbulent past. Nearby, the town of Verde, later known as Clemenceau, where former Yavapai County Sheriff Jim Lowry was killed in a wild shoot-out in 1918, is no longer a separate community, and is now a part of the city of Cottonwood.

Once known as "The Toughest Town on the Santa Fe," Williams, Arizona, is a popular stop along Interstate 40, where attractions include the Grand Canyon Railway and a very impressive outdoor wildlife park. While the Wild West is certainly showcased in Williams, the murder of Constable Victor H. Melick by Simplicio Torres on May 31, 1919, and the resulting afternoon of violence that swept much of the community, have all but been forgotten. Lying near his brother, Dr. Prince Albert Melick, Constable Melick's grave rests in the shade of towering pines just a stone's throw from Route 66 in nearby Mountain View Cemetery.

I first became interested in the stories of early-twentieth-century Western lawmen while growing up in the Verde Valley of Arizona, not far from where some of the events depicted in this book took place. As a boy, my father often took me to dinner at a cafe that stood directly across from the Bank of Arizona in Clarkdale, so at a very early age I was aware of Jim Roberts's final shoot-out there in 1928, a clash between the gunfighters of two disparate historical eras. Later, as I was starting out in my career in documentary television, I was given a copy of *I'm Frank Hamer: The Life of a Texas Peace Officer,* a 1968 biography of the famed Texas Ranger written by John H. Jenkins and Gordon Frost. After reading it, I quickly grew enamored of the stories of other Southwestern lawmen whose careers spanned the Roaring Twenties and the early 1930s. As the years went by, the topic became a bit of obsession of mine, though it was a long time before I ever considered the idea of writing a book on the subject.

It wasn't until after my experience working on a program for National Geographic about modern law enforcement in the Southwest that I first became inspired to write about the "transitional" peace officers of the 1920s that so fascinated me. Between 2010 and 2012, I had the unique pleasure of working closely with the fine men and women of the Navajo Nation Police Department on *Navajo Cops,* a documentary series for National Geographic that highlighted public safety on the largest Native American reservation in North America. During that time, my splendid crew and I spent an ample amount of time in the field on "ride-alongs" with the Navajo Nation police and their colleagues in other Navajo Nation law enforcement organizations as they patrolled vast portions of northern Arizona, New Mexico, and southern Utah. Joining the officers as they set out from their various district headquarters, we covered everything from routine traffic violations, auto accidents, and burglaries to gang-suppression operations, violent assaults, and the aftermath of attempted suicides.

While many of these situations were to be expected in a modern setting, most surprising to us were the cases involving livestock theft and land disputes that sometimes involved gunplay and bootlegging. Alcohol is prohibited on the Navajo Nation, and though there are no liquor stores within its boundaries, there are bootleggers willing to transport booze from the so-called "border towns" outside the reservation. While most of these contemporary rumrunners don't compare with the bootleggers who operated in the Southwest at the height of the 1920s, and there is none of the incredible violence that took place along the Rio Grande between Mexican smugglers and members of the Border Patrol, it's not uncommon for shipments of contraband liquor to be seized on the rural highways of the Navajo Nation and later destroyed in scenes reminiscent of the archival footage of Prohibition agents smashing barrels of whiskey with sledgehammers and axes.

While the time I spent with the Navajo police left me with any number of vivid memories and a greater appreciation for the men and women who serve our communities as peace officers, more than anything this experience caused me to question the accepted notion of when the rough and rowdy

Concordia Cemetery, El Paso.   Mike Testin

days of the frontier ended and our theoretically more modern, civilized era began. Though some historians might point to the end of the American Indian Wars, the arrival of the automobile, statehood for New Mexico and Arizona in 1912, or, if they're being more generous, the end of the Mexican Revolution as among the obvious conclusions to the Wild West of our collective imaginations, I would argue that the West was still very wild when Prohibition began in 1920, and remained so when it ended thirteen years later, just as it does today. If the adventures I had with the Navajo Police in Arizona and New Mexico, or the ongoing battles along the Mexican border, are any indication, then perhaps the groundskeeper at Concordia Cemetery is right: Nothing has changed.

ACKNOWLEDGMENTS

This book was made possible thanks in large part to the generous assistance of numerous institutions throughout the United States, among them the National Archives and Records Administration in Washington, DC, and the National Personnel Records Center in St. Louis, Missouri; the Archives and Records Management Department at the Arizona State Library; the Arizona State Historical Society; the Bisbee Mining and Historical Museum; the Williams Public Library; the Special Collections Department at the University of Texas at El Paso; the Border Heritage Center at the El Paso Public Library; the National Border Patrol Museum, El Paso, Texas; the Imperial County Historical Society; the City of Tempe Archives; the Ruby Mines Restoration Foundation; the Texas State Library and Archives; the Cline Library at Northern Arizona University; the *Prescott Daily Courier*; the *Verde Independent*; the Yavapai County Sheriff's Department; and Ancestry.com.

Among the many individuals who I would like to thank for having provided their invaluable time and assistance are Libby Coyner and Wendi Goen, with the Archives and Records Management Department at the Arizona State Library; researcher Rita Ackerman of Phoenix, Arizona; Ms. Jennifer Downing, Cristina Nigro, Dr. Jonathan Moreno, and Margaret Hangan with the Williams Public Library; Annie Larkin with the Bisbee Mining and Historical Museum; Dr. Nicole Mottier; Claudia Rivers, head of Special Collections at the University of Texas at El Paso; Verde Valley historian Glenda Farley; Colleen Holt at the Jerome Historical Society; Laura Hoff, archivist, librarian, and records officer at the Arizona Historical Society; Mr. David Flam, Alan Seacord, and the family of Clifford Alan Perkins, for having graciously allowed me to reprint several excerpts from Mr. Perkins's autobiography; Barbara Jordan, who shared her childhood memories of her grandfather with me; William Oliver Parmer; Darlynn Lee, for having provided me with an image of her uncle Harry Saxon; Gil Escontrias; Paul M. Goodwin; Little John's Auction Service Inc.; Wanda Pearce, Marshall County court clerk, Madill, Oklahoma; Brendan Fillingim, agency historian, Yavapai County Sheriff's Office; and Constable Ron Williams of Prescott, Arizona.

My thanks also go out to my friend, author and historian John Boessenecker, who graciously provided his support, wisdom, and invaluable advice while I wrote this book; to my friend, Ryan T. Hurst, for having proofread much of this manuscript; to my stepmother, Susan Kliewer of Sedona, Arizona, and to both my father, Jeff Dolan, and my good friend, Mike Testin, who joined me on long research trips through the Southwest, and also provided several of the photographs included in this manuscript; to historians Martin K. A. Morgan, Patrick K. O'Donnell, and Kevin Hymel, all of whom lent their expert advice and moral support throughout this project; to my friends Steffen Schlachtenhauffen and Tim Evans, for all of their years of encouragement; and to Erin Turner at TwoDot Books, for having believed in this concept. Lastly, I would like to thank my wonderful wife Suzie and our son Jack, for their support, inspiration, patience, and love.

ENDNOTES

Introduction: Six-Guns and Automobiles

1 United States of America, Bureau of the Census. *Fifteenth Census of the United States, 1930*. Washington, DC: National Archives and Records Administration, 1930. T626, 2,667 rolls, Census Place: *Clarkdale, Yavapai, Arizona*; Roll: *63*; Page: *23B*; Enumeration District: *0006*; Image: *552.0*; FHL microfilm: *2339798*. For an excellent account of Roberts's early life, see Marshall Trimble, *Arizona Outlaws and Lawmen: Gunslingers, Bandits, Heroes and Peacekeepers* (The History Press, 2015), pages 21–30. See also, Don Dedera, *A Little War of Our Own: The Pleasant Valley Feud Revisited* (Don Dedera, 1988), page 122. Author cites one of Roberts's sons in a detailed description of a gun battle between warring factions at the Middleton Cabin. See also, *Weekly Journal-Miner*, Prescott, Arizona, December 7, 1887.

2 Trimble, *Arizona Outlaws and Lawmen*, page 31. *Weekly Journal-Miner*, February 18, 1891, September 5, 1891, and January 18, 1893; *Arizona Republican*, June 26, 1891; *St. Johns Herald*, St. Johns, Arizona, December 17, 1891. *Arizona, Select Marriages, 1888–1908* [online database]. Provo, UT, USA: Ancestry.com Operations, Inc., 2014, FHL File Number: 2027417. For James R. Lowry as sheriff of Yavapai County in 1893, see *Weekly Journal-Miner*, January 4, 1893. For the incident involving Roberts's use of a wagon in lieu of a jail and his injuries from a knife attack that fall, see *Weekly Journal-Miner*, July 25, 1894, and October 3, 1894.

3 Earle R. Forrest, *Arizona's Dark and Bloody Ground* (Caxton Printers, 1936), page 277, and Trimble, *Arizona Outlaws and Lawmen*, pages 32–34. *Bisbee Daily Review*, Bisbee, Arizona, October 22, 1908. *Thirteenth Census of the United States, 1910* (NARA microfilm publication T624, 1,178 rolls). Records of the Bureau of the Census, Record Group 29. National Archives, Washington, DC. Census Place: *Pirtleville, Cochise, Arizona*; Roll: *T624_38*; Page: *35B*; Enumeration District: *0020*; FHL microfilm: *137405*.

4 Will C. Barnes, *Arizona Place Names* (University of Arizona Press, 1988), page 98. Oral History, Herbert V. Young, conducted in 1974 by Virginia Rice, University of Arizona. For Prohibition in Arizona, see Thomas K. Marshall, *The First Six Months of Prohibition in Arizona and Its Effect upon Industry, Savings and Municipal Government* (Thomas K. Marshall, 1915).

5 *Verde Copper News*, Wednesday, July 17, 1918. For the "Work or Fight Order," see, Anne Cipriano Venzon, *The United States in the First World War: An*

Encyclopedia (Garland Publishing, 1999), page 182. See also, Steven J. Diner, *A Very Different Age: Americans in the Progressive Era* (Hill and Wang, 1998), page 249.

6   *Verde Copper News,* June 22, 1928.

7   Ibid. See also, *Prescott Evening Courier,* June 21 and 22, 1928.

8   *Verde Copper News,* October 2, 1928

9   Ibid., June 22, 1928. See also, Testimony of James F. Roberts, Deputy Sheriff, before Coroner H. V. Young, Herbert V. Young Collection, Jerome Historical Society. *Prescott Evening Courier,* June 22, 1928. *Yavapai County Superior Court, Case #2596, The State of Arizona vs. Earl Nelson.* RG 92, History and Archives Division, Arizona State Library, Archives and Public Records. For Nelson's trial and sentence, see the *Prescott Evening Courier,* October 2 and 4, 1928.

10 *Verde Independent,* May 24, 2010. For Jim Roberts's obituary, see *Prescott Evening Courier,* January 10, 1934.

11 *El Paso Herald,* November 7 and 8, 1925; *San Bernardino County Sun,* November 8, 1925; *Morning Sun* (Yuma, Arizona), November 8, 1925. For biographical information on Grover F. Sexton, see the *Oshkosh Daily Northwestern,* November 1, 1907; the *Thirteenth Census of the United States, 1910* (NARA microfilm publication T624, 1,178 rolls). Records of the Bureau of the Census, Record Group 29. National Archives, Washington, DC, and *Chicago Daily Tribune,* May 23 and August 8, 1911. For details on Sexton's military service, see *Roster of the Illinois National Guard on the Mexican Border, 1916–1917, U.S., Adjutant General Military Records, 1631–1976,* page 442; *Houston Post,* October 5, 10, 12, 29, November 7, 19, 1917, and February 18, 1918; and *Chicago Daily Tribune,* December 20, 1917. For Sexton's postwar career, see *Brooklyn Daily Eagle,* September 27, 1920; *Washington Post,* March 13, 1921; *Indiana Gazette,* February 13, 1924; and *Scranton Republican,* March 18, 1924. Major Grover F. Sexton, *The Arizona Sheriff* (Studebaker Corporation of America, 1925), pages 3, 5–7, 17, 19–20, and 40–41.

12 Sexton, *The Arizona Sheriff,* pages 40–41.

13 Ibid., pages 8–11.

14 For a detailed account of George C. Ruffner's tenure as the sheriff of Yavapai County during the 1890s, see Trimble, *Arizona Outlaws and Lawmen,* pages 73–84. See also, *Weekly Journal-Miner,* May 12, 1897, and June 8, 1898; *Arizona Sentinel,* May 29, 1897; and *Graham Guardian,* June 4, 1897. *Prescott Evening Courier,* July 3, 1922, and November 8, 1922. For the death of Sheriff Warren G. Davis, see *Weekly Journal-Miner,* September 6, 1922; and *Mojave County Miner and Our Mineral Wealth,* September 8, 1922. *Prescott Evening Courier,* November 12, 1925, May 3, 1926, September 8, 1926, and November 3, 1926.

15   For an excellent history of the Mexican Revolution, see Friedrich Katz, *The Life and Times of Pancho Villa* (Stanford University Press, 1998). John S. D. Eisenhower, *Intervention!: The United States and the Mexican Revolution, 1913–1917* (W. W. Norton and Company, 1993), page 192; Katz, *Pancho Villa*, pages 110, 562–71. Charles Houston Harris and Louis R. Sadler, *The Texas Rangers and the Mexican Revolution: The Bloodiest Decade, 1910–1920* (UNM Press, 2004), pages 210–16. See also, *Houston Daily Post*, February 21, 1915, and *Liberty Vindicator*, Liberty, Texas, February 26, 1915.

16   For the Arizona Temperance Federation, see *Coconino Sun*, Flagstaff, Arizona, April 3, 1914, and *Graham Guardian*, Safford, Arizona, June 5, 1914. See also, Marshall, *The First Six Months of Prohibition in Arizona*. Women's suffrage began in Arizona in 1912. See Federal Writers' Project, *Arizona: A State Guide* (Hastings House, 1940), page 54. For the local Prohibition policies in Graham, Navajo, and Apache Counties, see Marshall, *The First Six Months of Prohibition in Arizona*, pages 8–9. For local option Prohibition in Maricopa County, see Tombstone *Weekly Epitaph*, June 1, 1913; *Arizona Sentinel and Yuma Weekly Examiner*, June 12, 1913; and *Coconino Sun*, June 6, 1913.

17   *Las Cruces Sun-News*, Las Cruces, New Mexico, September 28, 1917. James A. Burran, *Prohibition in New Mexico, 1917* (New Mexico Historical Review XLVIII: 2, 1973), page 146. Burran explains that 70 percent of the state's voters supported the liquor amendment, a tremendous increase from the 25 percent of the population that were in favor of Prohibition in 1915.

18   Burran, *Prohibition in New Mexico*. See also, *Columbus Weekly Courier*, Columbus, New Mexico, November 9, 1917.

19   *El Paso Herald*, January 15, 1917. Sheppard is often referred to as the "father of National Prohibition"; see George Brown Tindall, *The Emergence of the New South, 1913–1945* (Louisiana State University Press, 1967), pages 19 and 221; David E. Kyvig, *Unintended Consequences of Constitutional Amendment* (University of Georgia Press, 2000), page 182; and Garrett Peck, *Prohibition in Washington, D.C.: How Dry We Weren't* (The History Press, 2011), page 33.

20   Jeanne Bozzell McCarty, *The Struggle for Sobriety, Protestants and Prohibition in Texas: 1919–1935*, Southwestern Studies, Monograph No. 62 (Texas Western Press, University of Texas, 1980), pages 5–7.

21   Ibid. See also, *Southwestern Reporter*, Vol. 228, pages 230–32, and *Paris News*, Paris, Texas, November 27, 1935.

22   Lawrence F. Schmeckebier, *The Bureau of Prohibition: Its History, Activities and Organization*, Service Monographs of the US Government, No. 57 (The Brookings Institute, Washington, 1929), pages 1–9.

23   The term *transitional* has frequently been used by historian Bob Alexander in describing early-twentieth-century Western lawmen. See Bob Alexander,

Fearless Dave Allison: A Transitional Lawman on a Transitional Frontier (High Lonesome Books, 2003); and Bob Alexander, *Bad Company and Burnt Powder: Justice and Injustice in the Old Southwest* (University of North Texas Press, 2014), page xv.

Chapter One: The Wail of the Bootlegger

1 Bill O'Neal, *Captain Harry Wheeler—Arizona Lawman* (Eakin Press, 2003), pages 87–110. O'Neal has written the most complete biography on Harry Wheeler to date, and provides a detailed account of his law enforcement career. See also, *Weekly Epitaph*, May 9, 1909; *Bisbee Daily Review*, September 3, 1909, and March 7 and 8, 1917; and *Arizona Republican*, December 27, 1909.

2 O'Neal, *Captain Harry Wheeler*, page 110. O'Neal identifies the three men Wheeler killed before 1917 as Joe Bostwick, J. A. Tracy, and George Arnett, all of whom Wheeler shot during gunfights while a member of the Arizona Rangers. For details on Wheeler's shoot-out with J. A. Tracy, see *Bisbee Daily Review*, March 1, 1907, and March 7 and 8, 1917. For George Arnett, see *Bisbee Daily Review*, May 7, 1908.

3 *Weekly Epitaph*, January 7, 1917; *Bisbee Daily Review*, January 9, 1917, and February 8, 1917; and *Weekly Epitaph*, February 11 and March 4, 1917.

4 *Bisbee Daily Review*, March 7 and 8, 1917; *Weekly Epitaph*, March 11 and 18, 1917; O'Neal, *Captain Harry Wheeler*, pages 109–10.

5 Ibid.

6 Ibid. For Santiago Garcia, see *Weekly Epitaph*, April 29, 1917. See also, *Superior Court of Cochise County, Case #1802, State of Arizona vs. Santiago Garcia*, RG 92, History and Archives Division, Arizona State Library, Archives and Public Records.

7 For the arrest of Elmer Scott, see *Coconino Sun*, January 29, 1915. *Arizona Champion*, Peach Springs, Arizona, August 8, 1885, carries a brief mention of Heinrich Schuerman's "valuable ranch on Oak Creek," and reports that he was raising a large quantity of grapes. For details pertaining to Shuerman's eventual pardon by Governor Campbell, see *Coconino Sun*, December 21, 1917; and Lisa Schnebly Heidinger, Janeen Trevillyan, and the Sedona Historical Society, *Sedona* (Arcadia Publishing, 2007), pages 37 and 45. For more on the Schuerman story and area winemaking, see Steve Ayres, "The Schuerman Vines: The Effort to Resurrect a 100-Year-Old Arizona Vine," *Arizona Vines & Wines*, Summer 2009. For Schuerman's efforts on behalf of Governor Campbell's 1918 election bid, see *Weekly Journal-Miner*, November 10, 1920.

8 Marshall, *The First Six Months of Prohibition in Arizona*, pages 4, 7, 10, 65–66. *Bisbee Daily Review*, January 21, 1915.

9 *Copper Era and Morenci Leader*, Clifton, Arizona, January 8, 1915.

10 For the arrest and conviction of J. T. Sanders and Jay Foy, see *Arizona Republican*, January 9 and 12, 1915.

11 *Casa Grande Dispatch*, Casa Grande, Arizona, January 15, 1915. For the arrest of Mike Schmalzel, see *Bisbee Daily Review*, January 19, 1915. *Copper Era and Morenci Leader*, January 22, 1915.

12 *Arizona Republican*, March 1 and 2, 1915.

13 *Tombstone Prospector*, Tombstone, Arizona, November 21, 1914. Marshall, *The First Six Months of Prohibition in Arizona*, page 30.

14 For details on Allyn Wheeler's death, see O'Neal, *Captain Harry Wheeler*, pages 103–04. For Wheeler on "two per cent," see *Weekly Epitaph*, January 10, 1915.

15 *Bisbee Daily Review*, March 3, 1915; and *Arizona Sentinel and Yuma Weekly Examiner*, March 4, 1915.

16 For details on the Rodgers arrest, see *Bisbee Daily Review*, March 16, 1915; *Weekly Epitaph*, March 21, 1915; and *Arizona Sentinel and Yuma Weekly Examiner*, May 6, 1915.

17 For examples of Percy Bowden's arrests and pursuit of bootleggers in Cochise County, see *Weekly Epitaph*, October 24, 1915; and *Bisbee Daily Review*, October 23, 1915, April 23, 1916, January 12, 1917, July 12, 1917, October 6, 1917, December 27, 1917, January 26, 1918, October 9 and 27, 1918. Ned White's poem, "The Wail of the Bootlegger," appeared in *Bisbee Daily Review*, February 10, 1918. For a complete biography of Percy Bowden, see Ervin Bond, *Percy Bowden: Born to be a Frontier Lawman* (Ervin Bond, 1976).

18 *Bisbee Daily Review*, January 5, 1916.

19 *Copper Era and Morenci Leader*, March 19, 1915; *Weekly Epitaph*, April 25, 1915; and *Bisbee Daily Review*, May 4, 1915. For "Bootlegger's Boulevard," see *Bisbee Daily Review*, April 29, 1916, and *Weekly Journal-Miner*, May 9, 1917.

20 *Arizona Republican*, August 10, 1915. For more on "Tiswin," see Jeremy Agnew, *Alcohol and Opium in the Old West: Use, Abuse and Influence* (McFarland & Company, 2014), pages 47–48; and Robert M. Utley, *Geronimo* (Yale University Press, 2012), page 11. See also, Dan Thrapp, *The Conquest of Apacheria* (University of Oklahoma Press, 1967), pages 156, 164, 166, and 313.

21 *Arizona Republican*, November 6, 7, 10, and 11, 1915. See also, *Border Vidette*, Nogales, Arizona, November 20, 1915.

22 For details of the murder of Walter Brooks, see *Bisbee Daily Review*, June 29, 1915, September 14, 1915, and July 27, 1916. See also, *Cochise County Superior Court, Case #1368, State of Arizona vs. Leandro Maldonado*, RG 92, History and Archives Division, Arizona State Library, Archives and Public Records. For Walter Brooks's prior service as a member of the Bisbee Police Department, see *Bisbee Daily Review*, October 3, 1911, February 7, 1912, and August 22, 1912.

23 *Bisbee Daily Review*, July 20, 1915.

24   Ibid., March 27, 1917; see also, *Weekly Epitaph*, April 1, 1917. For the wounding of Leo Bailard, see *Copper Era and Morenci Leader*, March 16, 1917, and *Bisbee Daily Review*, March 20, 1917. For Bob Roe's shoot-out in Chloride, see, *Mohave County Miner*, Mineral Park, Arizona, September 15, 1917; *Coconino Sun*, September 21, 1917; and *Weekly Epitaph*, September 30, 1917.

25   For the killing of I. E. Brown by Haze Burch, see *Weekly Epitaph*, April 7 and 14, 1918; *Bisbee Daily Review*, June 14, 1918; *Weekly Epitaph*, June 16, 1918; and *Coconino Sun*, January 10, 1919. See also, *Weekly Journal-Miner*, March 19, 1919.

Chapter Two: Cold in Death

1   Report of O. L. Tinklepaugh, July 1–5, 1919, In re: Riot between Soldiers, Tenth Cavalry & Civil Officers, Bisbee, Arizona, on July 3, 1919. *Correspondence of the Military Intelligence Division Relating to "Negro Subversion," 1917–1941*, Vol. 348, IO-SD to MID. Security Classified Correspondence and Reports, compiled 1917–1941, documenting the period 1906–1941, Record Group 165, National Archives and Records Administration, Washington, DC.

2   *Bisbee Daily Review*, May 11, 1918.

3   Ibid., May 11, 12, and 23, 1918, and June 2, 1918. *Prison Record for Joel Smith, Inmate #5184*, Arizona Department of Corrections, RG 31, History and Archives Division, Arizona State Library, Archives and Public Records. According to the February 16, 1921, edition of *Arizona Republican*, Smith was eventually paroled, but later returned to prison after he shot and badly wounded his wife and attempted to take his own life in the town of Florence, Arizona.

4   Some accounts indicate that Joseph B. Hardwick was born in February of 1879; however, according to his WWI Draft Registration Card, and other records, Hardwick was born in 1881; see, *WWI Draft Registration Cards, 1917–1918*, National Archives and Records Administration, Washington, DC. For more on Joseph B. Hardwick's birth, his application for enrollment in the Five Civilized Tribes (which states that he is "Chickasaw by Blood," and lists his Census Card Number as 1021), as well as his marriage to Alma Bell Lindsey and the birth of the couple's first daughter, Montie Hardwick, see, *Applications for Enrollment of the Commission to the Five Civilized Tribes, 1898–1914*. Microfilm M1301, 468 rolls. NAI: 617283 Records of the Bureau of Indian Affairs, Record Group 75, National Archives and Records Administration, Washington, DC. For additional information on Hardwick's Chickasaw ancestry and the death of Montie Hardwick, see *Final Rolls of Citizens and Freedmen of the Five Civilized Tribes in Indian Territory* (as approved by the Secretary of the Interior on or before March 4, 1907, with supplements dated September 25, 1918), Microfilm Publication T529, 3 rolls. ARC ID: 608958. Records of the Office of the Secretary

of the Interior, Record Group 48, National Archives, Washington, DC, and *Oklahoma and Indian Territory, Land Allotment Jackets for Five Civilized Tribes, 1884–1934*, Department of the Interior, Office of Indian Affairs, Five Civilized Tribes Agency. Applications for Allotment, compiled 1889–1907. Textual records. Records of the Bureau of Indian Affairs, Record Group 75, National Archives at Fort Worth, Texas.

5 *Thirteenth Census of the United States, 1910* (NARA microfilm publication T624, 1,178 rolls). Records of the Bureau of the Census, Record Group 29. National Archives, Washington, DC, Census Place: *Hoquiam Ward 5, Chehalis, Washington*; Roll: *T624_1654*; Page: *10B*; Enumeration District: *0031*; FHL microfilm: *1375667*. For the birth of Roland Hardwick in Washington, see the *Aberdeen Herald,* June 16, 1910. For Hardwick's employment with the Hoquiam police and for the death of Herman Hardwick, see the *Aberdeen Herald,* May 15 and July 3, 1911.

6 For the birth of Owanda Hardwick in September of 1912, see State of California, *California Death Index, 1940–1997*, Sacramento, California: State of California Department of Health Services, Center for Health Statistics. For Hardwick's arrest and conviction for manslaughter, District Court of Marshall County, Oklahoma, *State of Oklahoma vs. Joe B. Hardwick, Case #249*, Marshall County Court, Madill, Oklahoma. For Hardwick's escape and return to prison in 1913, see the *Perry Enterprise-Times,* Perry, Oklahoma, May 1, 1913, and *Coffeyville Daily Journal*, Coffeyville, Kansas, April 26, 1913.

7 *New Era*, Davenport, Oklahoma, February 26, 1914. For Hardwick as a special officer with the S.P.R.R., see *California Railroad Employment Records, 1862–1950*. California State Railroad Museum Library, Sacramento, California.

8 *Arizona Republican*, February 27, 1917, and *Bisbee Daily Review*, February 27, 1917.

9 The exact date of Hardwick's employment with the Bisbee Police Department is unknown, though one of the first references to Hardwick as a Bisbee policeman appears in *Bisbee Daily Review,* September 27, 1917. For an excellent history of Bisbee and its mining industry, see Lynn R. Bailey, *Bisbee: Queen of the Copper Camps* (Westernlore Press, 2002). See also, Barnes, *Arizona Place Names,* page 48.

10 Ibid. Bailey, *Queen of the Copper Camps,* pages 9–40.

11 *Bisbee Daily Review,* June 26, 1903, and July 9, 1916; and *El Paso Herald,* May 17, 1902. See also, Samuel Truett, *Fugitive Landscapes: The Forgotten History of the U.S.-Mexico Borderlands* (Yale University Press, 2006), pages 111–12.

12 William S. Beeman, *The Bisbee Deportation* (Unknown binding, 1917); and O'Neal, *Captain Harry Wheeler,* page 115.

13   Arizona Historical Society Library, Tefft Bio File. In 1982, Miriam Tefft recorded an account of her memories of the Bisbee Deportation. This bio file is available from the Arizona Historical Society Library in Tucson, but is not included in the Society's oral history collection. *Bisbee Daily Review*, June 30, 1917.

14   O'Neal, *Captain Harry Wheeler*, page 117. For Wheeler's statement, see *Bisbee Daily Review*, July 12, 1917. For details on the strike, see Bailey, *Bisbee*, pages 234–41 and Truett, *Fugitive Landscapes*, pages 173–74.

15   O'Neal, *Captain Harry Wheeler*, pages 118–20; and Tefft Bio File, pages 5–8. *Bisbee Daily Review*, July 13, 1917.

16   *Bisbee Daily Review*, July 13, 1917. O'Neal, *Captain Harry Wheeler*, pages 137–38, and 151. See also, *Weekly Epitaph*, April 4, 1920. Wheeler was initially indicted by a federal grand jury while still in France, though these charges were dropped in December of 1918. Wheeler later faced state charges after he and more than two hundred other citizens were charged with kidnapping in a blanket warrant sworn out by deportee Fred W. Brown. However, these charges against Wheeler were also dropped, though he would testify in the trial of merchant H. E. Wooten, who was eventually found not guilty. For the *Plan de San Diego* and the Bisbee strike, see *Bisbee Daily Review*, March 9, 1920.

17   *Bisbee Daily Review*, January 13, 1918.

18   Ibid., February 12 and 13, and March 5, 1918.

19   Ibid., March 30, 1918.

20   Ibid., June 5, 1918. For Wheeler's departure from office, see O'Neal, *Captain Harry Wheeler*, pages 135–38. *WWI Draft Registration Cards, 1917–1918,* National Archives and Records Administration, Washington, DC. For James F. McDonald, see *Bisbee Daily Review*, August 21, 1918, and December 31, 1918; and *Weekly Epitaph*, December 15, 1918. For Hardwick's appointment as Cochise County deputy sheriff, see *Bisbee Daily Review*, January 9, 1919. For Bowden's employment with the City of Douglas, see *Weekly Epitaph*, February 16, 1919. For the Medigovitch Raid, see *Coconino Sun*, January 31, 1919.

21   *Weekly Epitaph*, February 16, 1919.

22   *Bisbee Daily Review*, March 21, 1919; *Weekly Epitaph*, March 23, 1919; and *Coconino Sun*, March 28, 1919.

23   For the details of the "Bisbee Riot" of 1919, see *Correspondence of the Military Intelligence Division Relating to "Negro Subversion," 1917–1941, Re: Trouble between soldiers and civil officers, Bisbee, Arizona*, page 16. This series of documents includes the reports of both officers from the Military Intelligence Division, and special agents of the Bureau of Investigation. It remains the most detailed official account of the events leading up to and including the evening of July 3, 1919, in Bisbee, Arizona.

24 For a history of the Tenth Cavalry, with dates of service and a record of its combat service in the Indian Wars, Cuba, the Philippines, and Mexico, see Major E. L. N. Glass, *The History of the Tenth Cavalry, 1866–1921* (Old Army Press, 1972).

25 Glass, *The History of the Tenth Cavalry,* pages 82–85.

26 *Bisbee Daily Review,* May 8, 1919. See also, *Bisbee Daily Review,* May 10, 11, and 13, 1919. For "black boys," see *Bisbee Daily Review,* August 9, 1919.

27 *Correspondence of the Military Intelligence Division,* pages 2 and 19. For Foster's background, see Bill O'Neal, *Arizona Rangers* (Eakin Press, 1987), pages 38, 44, and 143.

28 *Correspondence of the Military Intelligence Division,* page 19.

29 Ibid., page 4.

30 Ibid., page 10.

31 Ibid., pages 2 and 10. The identity of the informant cited in the report is redacted.

32 Ibid., pages 9 and 14. *Bisbee Daily Review* identified the injured soldier as George Sullivan; however, the government report indicates that it was actually Ridgeley who was hurt.

33 Ibid., page 5. See also, *Bisbee Daily Review,* July 4, 1919.

34 *Correspondence of the Military Intelligence Division,* pages 5 and 14.

35 Ibid., page 9; see also, *Bisbee Daily Review,* July 4, 1919.

36 *Correspondence of the Military Intelligence Division,* pages 7–8.

37 Ibid., page 8.

38 Ibid., pages 8 and 15.

39 Ibid., pages 8 and 10. See also, *Bisbee Daily Review,* July 4, 1919.

40 *Daily Review,* July 4, 1919.

41 *Correspondence of the Military Intelligence Division,* page 16.

42 Ibid. For Hardwick's appearance in court on assault charges, see *Bisbee Daily Review,* July 18, 1919.

43 *Bisbee Daily Review,* September 10, 1919; *Weekly Epitaph,* September 14, 1919; *Bisbee Daily Review,* September 17, 1919. For Sheriff Henry Hall's background, see *Bisbee Daily Review,* July 10, 1910, and *Casa Grande Dispatch,* May 9, 1914.

44 For the death of Alma Hardwick, see Arizona State Board of Health, Bureau of Vital Statistics, Original Certificate of Death. For the details on Hardwick's shoot-out with Jose Sierra, see *Bisbee Daily Review,* September 10, 1919, and March 16, 1920; *Coconino Sun,* March 19, 1920; and *Weekly Epitaph,* March 21, 1920. See also, Arizona State Board of Health, Bureau of Vital Statistics, Original Certificate of Death, Jose Sierra, March 6, 1920.

45 *Bisbee Daily Review,* September 10, 1921, and February 11, 1922.

46   For Hardwick in Calexico, see Steve Bogdan, "Ballad of a Well-Known Gun," *The Valley Grower*, September/October 2000, pages 25–32, Imperial County Historical Society, Imperial, California. For the killing of R. D. Feathers in 1925, see *Los Angeles Daily News*, January 6, 1925; *Los Angeles Sunday Times*, February 1, 1925; and *Huntington Press*, January 5, 1925.

47   Bogdan, "Ballad of a Well-Known Gun," pages 27, 29, and 32. See also, *Bakersfield Californian*, April 26, 1927; and the *Santa Ana Register*, May 7, 1921.

48   *Bakersfield Californian*, May 10, 1927, and November 1, 1927; *Los Angeles Times*, November 1, 1927. United States of America, Bureau of the Census. *Fifteenth Census of the United States, 1930*. Washington, DC: National Archives and Records Administration, 1930. T626, 2,667 rolls. Census Place: *Calexico, Imperial, California*; Roll: *119*; Page: *13B*; Enumeration District: *0014*; Image: *80.0*; FHL microfilm: *2339854*. See also, Bogdan, "Ballad of a Well-Known Gun," page 32.

Chapter Three: The Toughest Town on the Santa Fe

1   *Williams News*, Williams, Arizona, September 6, 1918. For Victor H. Melick's birth and family, see, Joseph Thompson Dodge, *Genealogy of the Dodge Family of Essex County, Mass., 1629–1894* (Democrat Printing Co., 1894), page 394. *Williams News*, April 1, 1905. Oral history interview with Durmont W. Melick, April 29, 1984, Cline Library, Special Collections and Archives, Northern Arizona University. *Williams News*, April 1, 1905.

2   Barnes, *Arizona Place Names*, page 448; James R. Fuchs, *A History of Williams, Arizona, 1876–1951* (University of Arizona Press, 1953), pages 24–35.

3   *Williams News*, January 13, 1916. For the killing of John Burton, see *Weekly Arizona Miner*, Prescott, Arizona, June 24, 1881.

4   *Williams News*, February 22, 1902.

5   Ibid., March 2, 1902.

6   *Acts, Resolutions and Memorials of the Fifteenth Legislative Assembly of the Territory of Arizona, 1889*, page 26. For Ralph H. Cameron as sheriff, see *Arizona Champion*, Peach Springs, Arizona, March 7, 1891; and *Coconino Sun*, November 14, 1895, and September 10, 1896. For the construction of the Williams Jail, see *Coconino Sun*, October 8, 1891.

7   For the role of the constable in Southwestern law enforcement, see Larry D. Ball, *Desert Lawmen: The High Sheriffs of New Mexico and Arizona, 1846–1912* (University of New Mexico Press, 1992), pages 42–43.

8   *Coconino Sun*, October 13, 1892, November 24, 1892, and May 23, 1895; *Arizona Sentinel*, January 13, 1894; and *Weekly Journal-Miner*, July 17, 1895 and February 10, 1897. For the shoot-out between Morrell and Constable Ed

Hardesty, see *Coconino Sun,* December 24, 1898 and *Weekly Journal-Miner,* December 21, 1898.

9   Fuchs, *A History of Williams, Arizona, 1876–1951,* pages 84–86. For James Kennedy as town marshal of Williams, see *Coconino Sun,* May 4, 1901. For Charles S. Patterson's election as town marshal of Williams, see *Williams News,* March 28 and June 13, 1908.

10   *Arizona Sentinel,* Yuma, Arizona, July 22, 1908; *Williams News,* July 25, 1908; and *Coconino Sun,* July 24 and September 25, 1908, and April 23, 1909.

11   *Williams News,* May 28, 1914. For Wade's commission as a deputy under Coconino County sheriff William G. Dickinson, see *Coconino Sun,* January 22, 1915. For Wade's resignation and Burns's appointment as marshal, see *Williams News,* June 10, 1915. For Robert Burns as "sleuth," see *Coconino Sun,* January 12, 1917, and March 2, 1917. For Burns's various encounters with outlaws and bootleggers as both night marshal and town marshal, see *Williams News,* May 21 and June 18, 1914, June 24, 1915, July 15, 1915, April 20, 1916, January 4, 1917, and May 17, 1917. Marshall, *The First Six Months of Prohibition in Arizona,* page 28.

12   For George Herbert Smalley's article for *Sunset Magazine,* see *Williams News,* January 13, 1916. For the first liquor violation in Williams, see *Coconino Sun,* January 29, 1915. "Shorty" Dunbar's arrest was reported in *Williams News* on July 15, 1915, under the heading " 'Shorty' Dunbar, Hop Jointist, Arrested." For Louis Montoya and Albicinio Rel, see *Williams News,* July 27, 1916; and *Coconino Sun,* August 4, 1916.

13   For Burns's encounter with Augustine Balderamos, see *Williams News,* September 28, 1916.

14   *Arizona Republican,* November 15, 1918; and *Williams News,* January 24, 1919.

15   *Williams News,* October 7, 1905, April 7, 1906, June 6, 1908, September 26, 1908. For Melick's role in a Williams performance of *Charley's Aunt,* see June 13, 1908. For Melick's employment with the electric and telephone companies in Williams, see *Williams News,* August 14, 1909; and *El Paso Herald,* June 2, 1919. For Melick's marriage to Saffronbelle Campbell, see *Williams News,* March 25, 1911.

16   *Williams News,* September 6, 1918.

17   *Coconino Sun,* November 22, 1918; and *Williams News,* January 10, 1919.

18   For Torres's prison records and release from custody in 1918, see *Prison Record for Simplicio Torres, Inmate #5115,* Arizona Department of Corrections, RG 31, History and Archives Division, Arizona State Library, Archives and Public Records; and *Coconino Sun,* April 25, 1919. For Torres's birth and family, see United States of America, Bureau of the Census. *Twelfth Census of the United States, 1900.* Washington, DC: National Archives and Records Administration,

1900. Census Place: *Williams, Coconino, Arizona Territory*; Roll: *45*; Page: *11A*; Enumeration District: *0012*.

19   *Williams News,* September 28 and October 5, 1916.

20   *Coconino County Superior Court, Case #542, The State of Arizona* v. *Simplicio Torrez,* RG 92, History and Archives Division, Arizona State Library, Archives and Public Records. See also, *Williams News,* December 21, 1916.

21   *Coconino Sun,* March 2, 1917. See also, *Williams News,* March 2, 1917; and *Coconino County Superior Court, Case #701, The State of Arizona v. Simplicio Torrez,* RG 92, History and Archives Division, Arizona State Library, Archives and Public Records.

22   *Case #701, State of Arizona* v. *Simplicio Torrez.* See also, *Williams News,* January 31, 1918.

23   *Prison Record for Simplicio Torres, Inmate #5115,* Arizona Department of Corrections, RG 31, History and Archives Division, Arizona State Library, Archives and Public Records; and *Coconino Sun,* April 25, 1919. *Williams News,* May 2, 1919. See also, *Coconino Sun,* May 9, 1919 and June 13, 1919.

24   *Williams News,* June 6, 1919; and *Coconino Sun,* June 6, 1919. Details on the Means family come from a phone interview between the author and Ambrose Means's daughter, Harriet Lockwood, on October 25, 2014, and correspondence between the author and Means's granddaughter, Shirley Smith, on August 21, 2014.

25   *Williams News,* June 6, 1919; and *Coconino Sun,* June 6, 1919.

26   Ibid. See also, *Williams News,* July 4, 1919; and *Coconino Sun,* July 18, 1919.

27   *Williams News,* June 6, 1919; and *Coconino Sun,* June 6, 1919.

28   Ibid. For Harrington's age and place of birth, see United States Census records for 1900 and 1910.

29   *Williams News,* June 6, 1919. For details on the charges and arraignment against Simplicio Torres, see *Coconino County Superior Court, Case #811, State of Arizona* v. *Simplicio Torres,* RG 92, History and Archives Division, Arizona State Library, Archives and Public Records.

30   *Williams News,* June 6, 1919. For details on the charges and arraignment against Simplicio Torres, see *Case #811, State of Arizona* v. *Simplicio Torres.*

31   *Case #811, State of Arizona* v. *Simplicio Torres.* See also, *Coconino Sun,* July 18, 1919; and *Williams News,* July 18, 1919.

32   *Coconino Sun,* July 25, 1919; *Case # 811, State of Arizona* v. *Simplicio Torrez.*

33   *Coconino Sun,* April 23, 1920.

34   Lockwood interview, October 25, 2014. For Shaffer and McDougal, see, *Williams News,* June 6, 1919 and July 4, 1919; and *Coconino Sun,* June 20, 1919 and September 26, 1919.

Chapter Four: The Purity Squad

1   *El Paso Herald*, December 19, 1919.

2   Ibid., January 3, 1920. Dated June 5, 1917, Henry Renfro's WWI Draft Registration Card places his date of birth as March 29, 1889. For Renfro's earlier arrest, see *El Paso Herald*, October 17 and 21, 1919. For "Snowbirds," see *El Paso Herald*, October 9, 1919. For Claude Smith's promotion, see *El Paso Herald*, December 25, 1919. For Varela's injuries and his shooting of the burglary suspect, see *El Paso Herald*, July 19, 1919, and September 24, 1919. For Elmer Reynolds's background, see C. H. Griffith, *El Paso Police Department, 1918*, an annual yearbook that was published as a souvenir for the El Paso Police Department in 1918, and includes numerous biographical sketches of members of the force who served during the 1910s.

3   For Constable Sam Stepp, see *El Paso Herald*, January 2 and 3, 1920. Stepp's death certificate lists his injuries and places his cause of death as "Hemorrhage and Shock"; see Texas State Board of Health, Bureau of Vital Statistics, Standard Certificate of Death for Samuel J. Stepp, January 5, 1920.

4   Federal Writers' Project, *Texas: A Guide to the Lone Star State* (Texas Highway Commission, 1940), page 244, "Cordova Island, an elongated tract containing about 382 acres and adjoining the Chamizal Zone on the east, lies on the northerly side of the Rio Grande by reason of an artificial cut made in 1899 across a bend of the river; this tract has remained a Mexican territory. It extends as far north as Findley Street, its twisting boundary offering difficulties to the border patrol."

5   *El Paso Herald*, January 3, 1920. For the details of Henry Renfro's fatal injuries, see Texas State Board of Health, Bureau of Vital Statistics, Standard Certificate of Death for Henry Renfro, January 12, 1920.

6   For Charles Pollock and the December meeting of the city council, see, *El Paso Herald*, December 25, 26, and 27, 1917. For El Paso as a "strategic location," see *El Paso Herald*, May 14, 1917. For El Paso as "the Monte Carlo of the United States," see *El Paso Herald*, July 9, 1909. For "El Paso, the Vile," see *El Paso Herald*, June 2, 1917. For additional details on El Paso's WWI–era cleanup efforts, see Shawn Lay, *War, Revolution and the Ku Klux Klan: A Study of Intolerance in a Border City* (Texas Western Press, University of Texas at El Paso, 1985), pages 33–48.

7   Oscar J. Martinez, *Border Boom Town: Ciudad Juarez Since 1848* (University of Texas Press, 1975), pages 50–51. Interview with Chester Chope by Wilma Cleveland, 1968, Interview No. 27, Institute of Oral History, University of Texas at El Paso. For "The Wickedest City," see *El Paso Herald*, November 22, 1915.

8   C. L. Sonnichsen, *Pass of the North: Four Centuries on the Rio Grande* (Texas Western Press, 1968), pages 336–44. Leon Metz, *John Wesley Hardin* (University of Oklahoma Press, 1996), page 279. Chope, Interview No. 27.

9   Lay, *War, Revolution and the Ku Klux Klan*, pages 37–38; *El Paso Herald,* May 23, 1917.

10   *El Paso Herald,* May 30, June 4, June 7, and June 21, 1917. *The Survey, A Journal of Social Exploration*, Volume XXXVIII, April 1917–September 1917, page 273.

11   John Howard Morrow, *The Great War: An Imperial History* (Routledge, 2004), page 274. Edward M. Coffman, *The War to End All Wars: The American Military Experience in World War I* (Oxford University Press, 1968), page 80. Allan M. Brandt, *No Magic Bullet: A Social History of Venereal Disease in the United States* (Oxford University Press, 1985), page 71. *El Paso Herald*, June 4, 1917.

12   *El Paso Herald*, June 12 and 27, 1917.

13   Biographical information on Charles E. Pollock is drawn from *El Paso Police Department, 1918*, an annual souvenir yearbook written by C. H. Griffith. For a description of Pollock and "Pollockisms," see Chope, Interview No. 27. For the "Pollockism" involving the ten-year-old boy, see *El Paso Morning Times,* July 31, 1917.

14   Martinez, *Border Boom Town*, pages 31–34. For the Wigwam Theater, see Metz, *John Wesley Hardin: Dark Angel of Texas*, pages 240, 260–62. For the showing of *Romance of the Redwoods* at the Wigwam, see *El Paso Herald*, May 11, 1917. For "Wolf Lowry," see *El Paso Herald*, June 4, 1917. For population statistics and ethnic diversity of El Paso, see Mario T. Garcia, *Desert Immigrants: The Mexicans of El Paso, 1880–1920* (Yale University, 1981), page 31; Arnoldo De Leon, *War along the Border: The Mexican Revolution and Tejano Communities* (University of Houston, Center for Mexican American Studies, 2012), page 151; and US Bureau of the Census, *Fourteenth Census of the United States, 1920.* Many historians of El Paso and the borderlands point out that El Paso's actual population in 1920 was actually much higher, but owing to challenges in obtaining an accurate count of Hispanic residents, an exact figure is not known. It's been estimated that the combined population of sister cities Ciudad Juarez and El Paso might have been about 100,000 in 1920.

15   Lay, *War, Revolution and the Ku Klux Klan*, pages 16–31. Friedrich Katz, *The Life and Times of Pancho Villa* (Stanford University Press, 1998). Interview with S. L. A. Marshall by Richard Estrada, 1975, Interview No. 181, Institute of Oral History, University of Texas at El Paso.

16   *El Paso Herald,* December 26 and 27, 1917, and January 5, 1918.

17   Ibid., December 25, 1919; see also, Griffith, *El Paso Police Department, 1918,* Texas Adjutant General Service Records 1836–1935, Texas State Library and Archives Commission. United States of America, Bureau of the Census. *Twelfth*

Census of the United States, 1900. Washington, DC: National Archives and Records Administration, 1900. T623, 1,854 rolls.

18   For Ross's company in Amarillo and Ysleta, see Brownsville *Herald,* August 14 1909; *El Paso Herald,* October 30 and November 17, 1909. For Captain John R. Hughes and the transfer of Company D to Amarillo, see Chuck Parsons, *Captain John R. Hughes, Lone Star Ranger* (University of North Texas Press, 2011), pages 214–18.

19   *El Paso Herald,* November 17, 1909, and February 23 and March 22, 1910.

20   Ibid., December 11, 1913, and March 3, April 27, and May 6, 1915. For Smith's return to the El Paso Police Department, see Griffith, *El Paso Police Department, 1918;* and *El Paso Herald,* December 15, 1919.

21   *El Paso Police Department, 1918.* For Chester Chope's description of S. H. Veater, see Chope, Interview No. 27. For Veater's 1915 gunfight in El Paso, see *El Paso Herald,* April 13, 1915. The man Veater killed was named Justo Acosta; see Texas Department of State Health Services, Texas Death Certificates, 1903–1982.

22   *El Paso Police Department, 1918.*

23   For purity squads in other cities, see *Logan Republican,* Logan, Utah, February 16, 1918, for an article that describes a raid by the Salt Lake Police Department's purity squad. See also, *Oakland Tribune,* Oakland, California, February 25, 1917; *Morning Tulsa Daily World,* Tulsa, Oklahoma, March 31, 1917; and St. Joseph *Observer,* St. Joseph, Missouri, March 24, 1917. For the purity squad raid on the home of Captain Wylie White, US Army, see *El Paso Herald,* December 29, 1917, and January 1, 2, and 4, 1918.

24   For Deputy Litchfield's arrest of the Mexican family for bootlegging in the Smelter District, see *El Paso Herald,* January 14, 1918. For the arrest and prosecution of Pearl Rogers, see, *El Paso Herald,* January 9, 11, 15, 16, and 17, 1918, and March 13 and 15, 1918, and April 20, 1918.

25   For the allegations made by Major Bascom Johnson and the comments made by Sheriff Seth Orndorff at the March 3, 1918, meeting of the Chamber of Commerce, see the *El Paso Herald,* March 4, 1918. See also, Edward Lonnie Langston, *The Impact of Prohibition on the Mexican-United States Border: The El Paso-Ciudad Juarez Case* (unpublished PhD Dissertation, Texas Tech University, May 1974), page 38. Langston's dissertation offers one of the most detailed accounts of the politics behind El Paso's wartime cleanup efforts. For the raids in March of 1918, see, *El Paso Herald,* March 9, 1918, March 16, 1918, and March 28, 1918.

26   Judge Dan Jackson quoted in the *El Paso Herald,* January 17, 1918. For El Paso's local option election, see Lay, *War, Revolution and the Ku Klux Klan,* pages 41–45.

27 Lay, *War, Revolution and the Ku Klux Klan,* pages 45–46; and Jeanne Boz-
    zell McCarty, *The Struggle for Sobriety—Protestants and Prohibition in Texas:
    1919–1935,* Southwestern Studies, Monograph No. 62 (Texas Western Press,
    University of Texas at El Paso, 1980), pages 6–8.

28 *El Paso Police Department, 1918; El Paso Herald,* July 6 and 12, 1918.

29 *El Paso Herald,* August 14 and 29, 1918, and September 7 and 11, 1918.

30 Gretchen Dickey, "Downtown Opium Dens Attracted Many" (article first pub-
    lished in Vol. 21, 2002), *El Paso International Daily Times,* September 25, 1890.
    Steven W. Bender, *Run for the Border: Vice and Virtue in U.S.-Mexico Border
    Crossings* (New York University Press, 2012), page 96. For the Opium Exclu-
    sion Act of 1909 and issues pertaining to smuggling, see, Congressional Serial
    Set, 1912, pages 18–21, "The Opium Evil." "The Attorney General had held that
    under our Opium Exclusion Act of February 9, 1909, prepared opium may be
    imported into the United States for immediate transshipment by sea. Mexico
    has no law on the subject. The result is that the great mass of Macanise opium
    is brought to San Francisco and immediately transshipped by sea to western
    Mexican ports, from whence it, added to the direct Mexican import, is mostly
    smuggled into the United States across the Mexican border." *El Paso Herald,*
    January 2, 1913.

31 *El Paso Morning Times,* July 24, 1913. Stanley Good Sr. is quoted in the *El Paso
    Herald,* June 4, 1915. Good was a longtime El Paso County deputy sheriff. His
    son, Stanley Good Jr., also served as both a deputy sheriff and city police officer
    in El Paso. For El Paso's anti-marijuana ordinance, see, *El Paso Herald,* June 3
    and 4, 1915; and *El Paso Morning Times,* June 4, 1915. For the violent deaths
    of officer Octaviano Perea and deputy tax collector Juan Garcia, see *El Paso
    Herald,* February 2, 1918 and February 4, 1918; and *El Paso Morning Times,*
    February 3, 1918. For the murder of Ike Alderete, see *El Paso Herald,* June 25
    and 26, 1918.

32 *El Paso Herald,* December 4, 1911. Thomas M. Santella and D. J. Triggle, *Opium*
    (Infobase Publishing, 2007), page 99. Interview with E. W. Rheinheimer by
    Robert H. Novak, 1974, Interview No. 124, Institute of Oral History, Univer-
    sity of Texas at El Paso.

33 *El Paso Herald,* February 21, 1919. For the arrest and prosecution of Jose Oro-
    zco and the testimony of John Force and Sonny Hooks, see, *El Paso Herald,* May
    6, 1919, October 15 and 16, 1919.

34 For the death of US Customs Inspector Clarence Childress, see *El Paso Herald,*
    April 14, 15, and 16, 1919; and Texas Department of State Health Services,
    Texas Death Certificates, 1903–1982. For the shooting involving Corporal F. J.
    Wagenbrenner, see *El Paso Herald,* April 28, 1919; and Texas Department of
    State Health Services, Texas Death Certificates, 1903–1982.

35 For the shoot-out between deputy sheriffs Jesse Stansel, Juan Parra, and smugglers on November 1, 1919, and the arrest of Mike Salazar, see *El Paso Herald*, November 3, 5, and 6, 1919, and December 1, 1919. For the gunfight between Lt. W. H. Little's provost guard detachment, see *El Paso Herald*, December 11, 1919.

36 *El Paso Herald*, December 18, 19, and 31, 1919. For the death records of Lopez and Esquivel, see Texas Department of State Health Services, Texas Death Certificates, 1903–1982.

37 *El Paso Herald*, December 20, 1919. For the death records of Pvt. Embler and "Ramirez," see Texas Department of State Health Services, Texas Death Certificates, 1903–1982.

38 *El Paso Herald*, May 20, 1919. For Captain White's claim against the City of El Paso, see *El Paso Herald*, April 10, 1919. For Davis's comments on "open town," see *El Paso Herald*, March 22, 1919. For John Montgomery's appointment as chief of police, see *El Paso Herald*, June 30, 1919. For Veater's resignation from the El Paso Police Department, see *El Paso Herald*, August 26, 1919. See also, *El Paso Herald*, December 13, 1919.

39 For the fatal accident involving Captain James Walter Reese, see *El Paso Herald*, November 7, 8, and 10, 1919, and December 12, 1919. For Smith's promotion to captain of detectives, see *El Paso Herald*, November 10, 1919, and December 25, 1919.

40 *El Paso Herald*, January 3, 1920; and Texas State Board of Health, Bureau of Vital Statistics, Standard Certificate of Death for Henry Renfro, January 12, 1920. For John Wesley Hardin and Concordia Cemetery, see Metz, *John Wesley Hardin: Dark Angel of Texas*, pages 284–86.

Chapter Five: Manhunt

1 Josefa de Ortiz's account of the events in Ruby, Arizona, on August 26, 1921, is taken from her testimony in a preliminary hearing held in Ruby on November 23, 1921; see, *Santa Cruz County Superior Court, Case #548, State of Arizona vs. Placidio Silvas*, RG 92, History and Archives Division, Arizona State Library, Archives and Public Records. The US Census for 1920 lists her age as eighteen, and identifies her husband as Jose Ortiz—*Fourteenth Census of the United States, 1920*. (NARA microfilm publication T625, 2,076 rolls.) Records of the Bureau of the Census, Record Group 29. National Archives, Washington, DC, Census Place: *Montana Camp, Santa Cruz, Arizona*; Roll: *T625_51*; Page: *7A*; Enumeration District: *123*. For Juan Valencia, aka, "Samaniego," see *Weekly Epitaph*, November 13, 1921. *Nogales Herald*, August 27, 1921.

2 Margaret Pearson Anderson, Oral History Interview with Betty Lane, August 25, 1994, Arizona Historical Society, Tucson. Margaret's 1994 interview states

her father's name as Joseph Frank Pearson; however, most accounts of the events in Ruby refer to him as "Frank" or "J. Frank" Pearson. I have opted to use "Frank Pearson" throughout this chapter. *Nogales Herald*, September 1, 1921. Irene Pearson's statement to Mexican consul Joaquin Terrazas and prosecutor Jesus T. Ruiz was made on August 29, 1921, and is included in the official court records for Placidio Silvas's second trial in 1922—see *Santa Cruz County Superior Court Case #580A, State of Arizona vs. Placidio Silvas*, RG 92, History and Archives Division, Arizona State Library, Archives and Public Records. For a detailed history of Ruby, Arizona, and the murders that took place at the post office and mercantile, see Bob Ring, Al Ring, and Talia P. Cahoon, *Ruby, Arizona: Mining Mayhem and Murder* (Bob Ring, Al Ring, and Talia Pfrimmer Cahoon, Tucson, Arizona, 2005), pages 69–114. *Arizona Republican,* August 28, 1921. For Irene Pearson's testimony, see *Nogales Herald*, December 17, 1921.

3   Margaret Pearson Anderson Interview. *Nogales Herald*, August 27, 1921.

4   Margaret Pearson Anderson Interview. *Case #548, State of Arizona vs. Placidio Silvas*. George A. Camphius account comes from a letter that he wrote to Dr. A. H. Noon, published in *Border Vidette*, Nogales, Arizona, on September 3, 1921. Parmer's account of the events in Ruby, Arizona, was detailed in a March 1936 article published in *Startling Detective Magazine*, entitled "How We Trapped the Deadly Border Bandits" by William Oliver Parmer, as told to Kathleen O'Donnell. This same article has been cited in other accounts of the Ruby Mercantile murders, including the history of Ruby, Arizona, written by Bob Ring, Al Ring, and Talia P. Cahoon, *Ruby, Arizona: Mining Mayhem and Murder,* and more recently, in the biography of Pima County sheriff Ben Daniels, written by Robert K. DeArment and Jack DeMattos, *A Rough Ride to Redemption* (University of Oklahoma Press, 2010); see pages 183–85. Although there are many correct details in the *Startling Detective* article, there are also numerous inaccuracies and inventions, which may have been added by magazine publishers to enhance the drama for the publication. I have been careful when referencing this account, relying on it only when the statements can either be verified using court documents and newspapers, or when I feel Parmer himself is describing the general conditions of the murders and the investigations that followed. While Parmer indicates that he and Sheriff White arrived in Ruby the same day that the murders occurred, August 26, 1921, according to Parmer's testimony in a preliminary hearing held in Ruby on November 23, 1921, he and White, along with deputy Charlie Jones, did not arrive until the following morning, August 27, 1921 (see *Case #548, State of Arizona vs. Placidio Silvas*). The delay in Sheriff White's arrival in Ruby is also described in an article published in the *Bisbee Daily Review* on August 27, 1921.

5   United States, Selective Service System, *World War I Selective Service System Draft Registration Cards, 1917–1918*. Washington, DC: National Archives and Records Administration. M1509, 4,582 rolls; William Oliver Parmer's WWI draft registration lists his birth date as December 19, 1880. See also, *Thirteenth Census of the United States, 1910* (NARA microfilm publication T624, 1,178 rolls). Records of the Bureau of the Census, Record Group 29. National Archives, Washington, DC, Census Place: *Douglas Ward 2, Cochise, Arizona*; Roll: *T624_38*; Page: *22A*; Enumeration District: *0018*; FHL microfilm: *1374051*. For Parmer's early background and law enforcement career, see Tucson *Daily Citizen*, January 16, 1960 and May 5, 1961. For Dud Barker's career as a lawman, see *The Eagle*, Bryan, Texas, November 8, 1898; and Waco *News-Tribune*, November 4, 1926. For Parmer's brother James M. Parmer's law enforcement career, see, *El Paso Herald*, October 13, 1906, and June 25 and 27, 1907. For John A. Parmer as an Arizona lawman, see *Weekly Epitaph*, April 6, 1919, and *Coconino Sun*, February 20, 1920. The census for 1920 lists John A. Parmer as living in Hayden, Gila County, Arizona, and serving as constable. For Arthur E. Parmer's brief career as a Cochise County deputy sheriff, see *Weekly Epitaph*, June 15, 1919, and January 25, 1920, and *Bisbee Daily Review*, January 15 and July 23, 1919.

6   Tucson *Daily Citizen*, January 16, 1960. The *El Paso Herald* for December 25, 1907, reports a property transfer between Parmer and O. R. Dan, and states that Parmer and his wife are now living in Douglas, Arizona. For Douglas as a "Mecca of 'bad men' . . .," see *El Paso Herald*, October 21, 1904.

7   *El Paso Herald*, October 21, 1904. For the badges worn by the Arizona Rangers, see O'Neal, *The Arizona Rangers*, pages 43–46. For Parmer's enlistment, see pages 153 and 182. For Ranger weapons, see Joe Pearce and Richard Summers, *Line Rider: The Autobiography of Arizona Ranger Joseph Pearce, 1875–1958*, page 102.

8   O'Neal, *The Arizona Rangers*, pages 153–54. For Van Vaeler's criminal career and escapes from custody, see *Bisbee Daily Review*, January 22, 1908 (referred to as "Van Lean"). For Parmer's gunfight with Van Vaeler and the outlaw's escape, see *Arizona Republican*, November 20, 1908; *Weekly Epitaph*, November 22, 1908; *Daily Arizona Silver Belt*, November 22, 1908; and *Coconino Sun*, November 27, 1908. Many years later, Parmer would later claim to have killed Van Vaeler, though that does not appear to have been the case; see, Tucson *Daily Citizen*, January 16, 1960.

9   O'Neal, *The Arizona Rangers*, pages 164–71. For the act that created Arizona's "Ranger Deputies," see *Acts, Resolutions and Memorials of the Twenty-Fifth Legislative Assembly of the Territory of Arizona* (McNeil Company, 1909), pages

15–16. The Ranger Deputy Act became law on March 11, 1909. See also, *Arizona Republican*, February 7, 1909; and *Coconino Sun*, April 23, 1909.

10   For Parmer's post-Ranger career as a cowboy and ranch manager, see the *Bisbee Daily Review*, August 5 and 31, 1909, and November 5, 1909; *The Oasis*, Arizola, Arizona, July 10, 1909; and *Arizona Republican*, October 17, 1914.

11   *Fourteenth Census of the United States, 1920.* (NARA Microfilm Publication T625, 2,076 rolls.) Records of the Bureau of the Census, Record Group 29. National Archives, Washington, DC, Census Place: *Tucson Ward 1, Pima, Arizona*; Roll: *T625_50*; Page: *3B*; Enumeration District: *99*. For Parmer's employment as a police officer, and the Parmer family's residence in Tucson, see City Directory, Tucson, Arizona, 1920, page 197. For Parmer's arrest of the army deserters, see *Weekly Epitaph*, March 21, 1920.

12   Bob Ring et al., *Ruby, Arizona: Mining Mayhem and Murder*, pages 18–25, 49–56. Though officially known as Ruby from 1912 onward, "Montana Camp" was still sometimes used for several more years.

13   Phil Clarke, "Recollections of Life in Arivaca and Ruby, 1906–1926," Manuscript MS990, Arizona Historical Society, Tucson, Arizona. and Bob Ring et al., *Ruby, Arizona: Mining Mayhem and Murder*, page 71.

14   Clarke, "Recollections of Life in Arivaca and Ruby, 1906–1926." For the fight between the cowboys and the Mexican rustlers on January 14, 1917, see *El Paso Herald*, January 17, 1917. For the skirmish at the "Stone House," see, *El Paso Herald*, January 27, 1917; and *Bisbee Daily Review*, January 27, 1917.

15   Clarke, "Recollections of Life in Arivaca and Ruby, 1906–1926." For details on the Fraser brothers, their years in the Oro Blanco, and their experiences in Ruby, see Bob Ring et al., *Ruby, Arizona: Mining Mayhem and Murder*, pages 75–81.

16   Clarke, "Recollections of Life in Arivaca and Ruby, 1906–1926." *Bisbee Daily Review*, February 29, 1920; *Arizona Republican*, March 1, 1920; and *San Bernardino County Sun*, March 1, 1920.

17   Clarke, "Recollections of Life in Arivaca and Ruby, 1906–1926." For Manuel Garcia and the 1916 bank robbery in Buckeye, Arizona, see *Bisbee Daily Review*, December 6, 1921. At about 3:00 p.m., December 5, 1916, the Buckeye Valley Bank was robbed of a reported $2,000.00. Charles Miner was killed when he and others rushed to the scene of the holdup. See also, *Arizona Republican*, October 11 and 22, 1920. For the most detailed newspaper account of the robbery, see *Nogales Herald*, February 28, 1920.

18   Clarke, "Recollections of Life in Arivaca and Ruby, 1906–1926," and William Oliver Parmer, "How We Trapped the Deadly Border Bandits," as told to Kathleen O'Donnell. According to the United States Census for the year 1920, John Maloney was born in Washington, DC, in 1859, and was the son

of Irish immigrants—see, *Fourteenth Census of the United States, 1920.* (NARA microfilm publication T625, 2,076 rolls.) Records of the Bureau of the Census, Record Group 29. National Archives, Washington, DC, Census Place: *Montana Camp, Santa Cruz, Arizona*; Roll: *T625_51*; Page: *7B*; Enumeration District: *123.*

19   Clarke, "Recollections of Life in Arivaca and Ruby, 1906–1926," and Parmer, "How We Trapped the Deadly Border Bandits." *Bisbee Daily Review,* March 2, 1920; and *Nogales Herald,* February 28, 1920.

20   Bob Ring et al., *Ruby, Arizona: Mining Mayhem and Murder,* pages 85–86. Parmer, "How We Trapped the Deadly Border Bandits." *Bisbee Daily Review,* February 29, 1920.

21   *Arizona Blue Book, State and County Officials of Arizona,* compiled by Sidney P. Osborn, 1917, page 34. For episodes from Raymond R. Earhart's tenure as sheriff of Santa Cruz County, Arizona, see, *Bisbee Daily Review,* February 27 and November 13, 1917; *Border Vidette,* July 14, 1917, and November 3 and 11, 1917, and August 31 and October 26, 1918.

22   *Bisbee Daily Review,* February 29 and March 2, 1920. *Nogales Herald,* March 1, 1920. Clarke, "Recollections of Life in Arivaca and Ruby, 1906–1926." Parmer, "How We Trapped the Deadly Border Bandits."

23   Clarke, "Recollections of Life in Arivaca and Ruby, 1906–1926."

24   Margaret Pearson Anderson Interview. United States of America, Bureau of the Census. *Twelfth Census of the United States, 1900.* Washington, DC: National Archives and Records Administration, 1900. Census Place: *Justice Precinct 3, Williamson, Texas*; Roll: *1679.*

25   Margaret Pearson Anderson Interview. For the Pearsons in Bisbee, see also *Bisbee Daily Review,* February 10, 1918, May 5, 1918, and August 30, 1919. For the Pearsons in Arivaca, see *Nogales Herald,* February 27, 1921; and the *Fourteenth Census of the United States, 1920.* (NARA microfilm publication T625, 2,076 rolls.) Records of the Bureau of the Census, Record Group 29. National Archives, Washington, DC, Census Place: *Arivaca, Pima, Arizona*; Roll: *T625_50*; Page: *3A*; Enumeration District: *79.*

26   *Weekly Epitaph,* June 2, 6, 13, and 20, 1920. For more on "Ranger" White's bloodhound, see *Weekly Epitaph,* April 11, 1920.

27   For the wounding of Pima County deputy sheriff George McClure and the death of Manuel Garcia, see *Arizona Republican,* October 11 and 12, 1920; and *Tucson Citizen,* October 11, 1920.

28   Bob Ring et al., *Ruby, Arizona: Mining Mayhem and Murder,* pages 88–89. *Bisbee Daily Review,* June 14, 1921.

29   Margaret Pearson Anderson Interview.

30   Ibid.

31   Camphius's letter was published in the *Border Vidette*, September 3, 1921. For
      Camphius's age and Scottish origins, see *Fourteenth Census of the United States,*
      1920. (NARA microfilm publication T625, 2,076 rolls.) Records of the Bureau
      of the Census, Record Group 29. National Archives, Washington, DC, Census
      Place: *Los Angeles Assembly District 63, Los Angeles, California*; Roll: *T625_107*;
      Page: *10B*; Enumeration District: *180*; Image: *300.* At the time of the Pearson
      murders, Camphius was working at the Austerlitz Mine in the Oro Blanco
      District.

32   *Bisbee Daily Review*, August 27, 1921; *Nogales Herald*, August 27, 1921; and
      Border Vidette, August 27, 1921. For Parmer's testimony, see transcript of
      preliminary hearing for Placidio Silvas, *Case #548, State of Arizona vs. Placidio*
      Silvas. For Parmer's employment with the Santa Cruz sheriff's office, see *Border*
      Vidette, July 23, 1921, November 12 and 19, 1921, and December 10, 1921. In
      his November testimony, Parmer would state that he was a county Ranger, as
      "Ranger deputies" were often known in the years after the disbandment of the
      Arizona Rangers in 1909. However, newspaper accounts typically refer to him
      as a deputy sheriff, or special deputy.

33   *Case #548, State of Arizona vs. Placidio Silvas.* The bullet that Parmer recovered
      at the scene was "rediscovered" by Arizona State Library, Archives and Public
      Records Archivist Libby Coyner while making these records available for this
      manuscript.

34   *Nogales Herald,* August 27, 1921. Parmer, "How We Trapped the Deadly Border
      Bandits." *Bisbee Daily Review,* August 27 and 28, 1921. It remains unclear as to
      when Josefa de Ortiz first stepped forward and identified Silvas and Martinez,
      though she had apparently done so before Silvas's preliminary hearing that
      November. During Silvas's second trial for murder in May of 1922, Mrs. Rodri-
      guez testified that she had not identified Silvas as a suspect until after the man
      was arrested in September of 1921. See, *Arizona Supreme Court Criminal Case*
      550, Transcript of Santa Cruz County Superior Court Case 580, State of Arizona
      vs. Placidio Silvas, RG 92, History and Archives Division, Arizona State Library,
      Archives and Public Records.

35   *Nogales Herald,* September 1 and 2, 1921. See also, Bob Ring et al., *Ruby, Ari-*
      zona: Mining Mayhem and Murder, pages 96–97.

36   For the investigation by postal inspectors and the reward offered by Chief Sim-
      mons, see *Weekly Epitaph,* September 4, 1921, and *Bisbee Daily Review,* Septem-
      ber 13, 1921. For additional details on the $5,000.00 reward and for the raid
      on the Slaughter Ranch and Governor Thomas E. Campbell's correspondence
      with Secretary Weeks, see Prescott *Weekly Journal-Miner,* September 14, 1921.
      The "raid" was believed to have been in retribution for the convictions of Jose

Perez and Manuel Garcia, for the murder of foreman Jess Fisher, who was killed at the Slaughter Ranch in May of 1921.

37 The arrest of Placidio Silvas as reported by the *Nogales Herald* is quoted in *Arizona Republican*, September 15, 1921. For the charges against Salvador Sazueta, see *Arizona Republican*, October 6 and 9, 1921. *Case #548, State of Arizona vs. Placidio Silvas*. For Juan Valencia, aka, Samaniego, see *Weekly Epitaph*, November 13, 1921.

38 *Case #548, State of Arizona vs. Placidio Silvas*, transcript of preliminary hearing held in Ruby on November 23, 1921. Maloney filed separate arrest warrants against Silvas, one for Frank Pearson and another for Myrtle Pearson; see, *Santa Cruz County Superior Court Case #549A, State of Arizona vs. Placidio Silvas*, RG 92, History and Archives Division, Arizona State Library, Archives and Public Records.

39 *Case #548, State of Arizona vs. Placidio Silvas*. Irene Pearson's testimony was published in *Nogales Herald*, December 17, 1921; and in *Bisbee Daily Review*, December 18, 1921.

40 *Nogales Herald*, December 20, 22, 23, and 24, 1921. See also, *Bisbee Daily Review*, December 20 and 23, 1921.

41 *Bisbee Daily Review*, December 20 and 23, 1921. Parmer, "How We Trapped the Deadly Border Bandits."

42 *Santa Cruz County Superior Court, Case #558A, State of Arizona vs. Manuel Martinez*, RG 92, History and Archives Division, Arizona State Library, Archives and Public Records. See also, *Supreme Court of Arizona, Manuel Martinez vs. State of Arizona, Case #544*, University of Arizona Law Library, Tucson, Arizona.

43 For the November 1921 arrest of Francisco Reyna, see *Nogales Herald*, November 25, 1921; and *San Bernardino County Sun*, November 26, 1921. For Reyna's various arrests and participation in revolutionary intrigue along the Arizona border, see *El Paso Herald*, January 27, 1917, and September 1, 1920; *Coconino Sun*, February 21, 1919; and *Bisbee Daily Review*, September 3, 1920.

44 *Bisbee Daily Review*, December 27 and 28, 1921; and *Coconino Sun*, January 6, 1921.

45 *Nogales Herald*, December 24, 1921.

46 Ibid., December 24, 30, and 31, 1921. See also, *Bisbee Daily Review*, December 31, 1921. For Martinez's claim that Lou Quinn and Parmer forced his confession, see *Santa Cruz County Superior Court, Case #582A, State of Arizona vs. Manuel Martinez*, RG 92, History and Archives Division, Arizona State Library, Archives and Public Records.

47 For information on the federal charges against Martinez and Silva, see *Weekly Epitaph*, January 22 and February 5, 1922. For Martinez's confession while in

custody in Tucson, see *Santa Cruz County Superior Court Case #579A, State of Arizona vs. Manuel Martinez,* RG 92, History and Archives Division, Arizona State Library, Archives and Public Records; testimony of S. F. Noon, acting as a volunteer attorney on behalf of the prosecution, who stated that he interrogated Martinez in Spanish.

48   For details on Martinez's trial for murder in May of 1922, see *Nogales Herald,* May 17 and 18, 1922; and *Bisbee Daily Review,* May 18 and 19, 1922. For Martinez's insanity defense and attempts to show through witnesses that he had been exchanged for Francisco Reyna and beaten by Parmer and Quinn, see *Santa Cruz County Superior Court, Case #582A, State of Arizona vs. Manuel Martinez.*

49   Bob Ring et al., *Ruby, Arizona: Mining Mayhem and Murder,* pages 101–04. See also, *Nogales Herald,* June 2, 5, 10, and 17, 1922; and *Bisbee Daily Review,* May 19 and 25, 1922.

50   For Silvas's third trial, see *Nogales Herald,* June 28 and July 13, 1922; and Bob Ring et al., *Ruby, Arizona: Mining Mayhem and Murder,* pages 103–04; *Nogales Herald,* July 14, 1922.

51   The death of sheriff George J. White and the escape of Silvas and Martinez were widely reported by Arizona newspapers, including *Nogales Daily Herald,* July 14, 15, 17, and 18, 1922; *Bisbee Daily Review,* July 15, 16, 18, and 19, 1922; and *Border Vidette,* July 15, 1922. Early newspaper reports suggested that the prisoners might have struck Sheriff White over the head, although Leonard Smith denied this, and explained that he was watching the prisoners when the accident occurred.

52   *Bisbee Daily Review,* July 15, 16, and 18, 1922. For Saxon's appointment as sheriff, see *Weekly Epitaph,* July 16, 1922.

53   *Border Vidette,* July 22, 1922; and *Bisbee Daily Review,* July 18, 1922.

54   For the capture of Silvas and Martinez, see *Nogales Herald,* July 18, 1922; *Border Vidette,* July 22, 1922; and *Bisbee Daily Review,* July 19, 1922.

55   Ibid.

56   *Border Vidette,* July 22, 1922; and *Bisbee Daily Review,* July 25, 1922.

57   *Weekly Journal-Miner,* August 9, 1922.

58   *Bisbee Daily Review,* August 12 and 18, 1922. For more on the lengthy battle to save Martinez from the gallows, see Bob Ring et al., *Ruby, Arizona: Mining Mayhem and Murder,* pages 110–12.

59   *Supreme Court of Arizona, Case #544, Manuel Martinez vs. State of Arizona,* University of Arizona Law Library, Tucson, Arizona. J. L. Fitts later died in Los Angeles on January 8, 1923; see Bob Ring et al., *Ruby, Arizona: Mining Mayhem and Murder,* page 110.

60   *Morning Sun,* March 23, 1923, April 1, 1923, May 26, 1923, and June 3, 1923. *Casa Grande Dispatch,* April 7, 1923, and August 9, 1923. For Obregon's

intervention, see *Morning Sun*, May 16, 1923. Parmer, "How We Trapped the Deadly Border Bandits." *Prison Record for Manuel Martinez, Inmate #5981,* Arizona Department of Corrections, RG 31, History and Archives Division, Arizona State Library, Archives and Public Records.

61 Parmer, "How We Trapped the Deadly Border Bandits." For newspaper accounts of Martinez's hanging, see *The Eagle*, August 10, 1923; *Arizona Republican*, August 11, 1923; and *Tucson Citizen*, August 10, 1923. *Prison Record for Manuel Martinez, Inmate #5981.*

Chapter Six: Dry Agents

1 *El Paso Herald*, March 2, 3, and, 7, 1921. For additional details on Prohibition agent Ernest W. Walker, see *Enforcement of the Prohibition Laws: Official Records of the National Commission on Law Observance and Enforcement Pertaining to its Investigation of the Facts as to the Enforcement, the Benefits and the Abuses under the Prohibition Laws, both before and since the Adoption of the Eighteenth Amendment to the Constitution,* Vol. 1 (US Government Printing Office, 1931), page 154. According to his government identification card, Walker became a federal Prohibition agent on February 11, 1920; see, Department of the Treasury, Bureau of Internal Revenue, Prohibition Unit (1920–04/01/1927). Identification Card Files of Prohibition Agents, 1920–1925. Records of the Internal Revenue Service, 1791–2006, Record Group 58. The National Archives and Records Administration, Washington, DC. See also, Official Personnel Records for Ernest Walter Walker, US Department of the Treasury, Internal Revenue Service, Prohibition Unit, National Archives & Records Administration, St. Louis, Missouri. Frank Hamer is among the best-known Texas lawmen of the first decades of the twentieth century, and had a long association with the Texas Rangers, serving at various times between the early 1900s and the 1930s. Just prior to becoming a federal Prohibition agent, Hamer had served as a Ranger in Company B, under the command of Captain Charles Stevens; see, Texas Adjutant General Service Records 1836–1935, Call Number 401-56, Texas State Library and Archives Commission, Austin, Texas. For Hamer's service as a federal Prohibition agent; see, Identification Card Files of Prohibition Agents, 1920–1925. Records of the Internal Revenue Service, 1791–2006, Record Group 58. The National Archives and Records Administration, Washington, DC. Though not mentioned in contemporary newspaper articles covering the shoot-out on March 2, 1921, according to Hamer biographers John H. Jenkins and H. Gordon Frost, Hamer was indeed on the scene at the Coles's farm when Walker was shot; see, John H. Jenkins and H. Gordon Frost, *I'm Frank Hamer: The Life of a Texas Peace Officer* (Pemberton Press, 1968), page 92. For a profile

on El Paso Police sergeant Tom York, see, Griffith, *El Paso Police Department, 1918*, page 18.

2 *San Bernardino County Sun*, March 4, 1921. *El Paso Herald*, March 7, 1921. See also, *Enforcement of the Prohibition Laws*, page 154.

3 *El Paso Herald*, December 15, 1919, and January 14 and 16, 1920. See also, Langston, *The Impact of Prohibition*, pages 223–24.

4 *El Paso Herald*, January 3 and 6, 1920. *The Eagle*, Bryan Texas, January 7, 1920.

5 *El Paso Herald*, January 6, 1920. For the incident involving the Rangers on the valley road on December 25, 1919, see *El Paso Herald*, December 26, 1919.

6 *El Paso Herald*, January 3 and 5, 1920. *The Eagle*, January 7, 1920.

7 Ibid., January 12 and 14, 1920.

8 Schmeckebier, *The Bureau of Prohibition*, pages 1–9. Annual Report of the Commissioner of Internal Revenue for the Fiscal Year Ended June 30, 1919, page 62. For H. M. Gaylord's remarks to agents and inspectors of the Bureau of Internal Revenue, see *Cincinnati Enquirer*, January 14, 1920.

9 Schmeckebier, *The Bureau of Prohibition*, pages 1–8 and 13. According to his personnel file, Prohibition agent Ernest W. Walker was appointed as an Inspector of Customs, "without additional compensation," on February 25, 1921. See, Official Personnel Records for Ernest Walter Walker, US Department of the Treasury, Internal Revenue Service, Prohibition Unit, National Archives & Records Administration, St. Louis, Missouri.

10 Annual Report of the Secretary of the Treasury on the State of the Finances for the Fiscal Year Ended June 30, 1920 (Government Printing Office, 1921), pages 1505 and 1508. Department of the Treasury, Bureau of Internal Revenue, Prohibition Unit (1920–04/01/1927). Identification Card Files of Prohibition Agents, 1920–1925. For Alfred Monroy's employment as postal clerk, see *Fourteenth Census of the United States, 1920*. (NARA microfilm publication T625, 2,076 rolls.) Records of the Bureau of the Census, Record Group 29. National Archives, Washington, DC, Census Place: *El Paso Precinct 22, El Paso, Texas*; Roll: *T625_1799*; Page: *12A*; Enumeration District: *68*. For Roy A. Fridley's employment prior to joining the Prohibition Unit, see *Mohave County Miner*, November 10, 1917, and July 13, 1918. For Michael E. Cassidy's appointment as state Prohibition director, see *Bisbee Daily Review*, September 2, 1921. For Samuel Woolston, see Roswell, New Mexico, City Directory, 1920.

11 For S. Mackie Jester, see Department of the Treasury, Bureau of Internal Revenue, Prohibition Unit (1920–04/01/1927). Identification Card Files of Prohibition Agents, 1920–1925. Records of the Internal Revenue Service, 1791–2006, Record Group 58. The National Archives and Records Administration, Washington, DC. For Jester's service as a Texas Ranger, see *El Paso Herald*, June 9, 1915. For Jester's service as a Deputy US Marshal, see *El Paso Herald*,

December 2, 1918. For Stafford E. Beckett, see Texas Adjutant General Service Records 1836–1935, Call Number 401-52, Texas State Archives and Library Commission, Austin, Texas. See also, *El Paso Herald*, December 10, 1918, and April 5, 1920. For Charles F. Stevens, see *El Paso Herald*, February 7, 1920; and Records of the Internal Revenue Service, 1791–2006, Record Group 58. Stevens served as a Prohibition agent throughout the 1920s, and would be killed in the line of duty during an ambush in San Antonio, Texas, in 1929; see, Clifford R. Caldwell and Ron DeLord, *Texas Lawmen, 1900–1940: More of the Good & the Bad* (The History Press, 2012), pages 478–79, and *Enforcement of the Prohibition Laws*, pages 166–67. For Harry D. Midkiff, see *Bisbee Daily Review*, August 19, 1919, October 25, 1919, and October 29, 1922; *Weekly Epitaph*, August 31, 1919; and *Mohave County Miner and Our Mineral Wealth*, November 17, 1922.

12 J. Anne Funderburg, *Bootleggers and Beer Barons of the Prohibition Era* (McFarland & Company, 2014), pages 340–41. Schmeckebier, *The Bureau of Prohibition*, pages 51–52. For Fridley's arrests and conviction, see *Bisbee Daily Review*, February 10, 1921, May 5, 1921, and May 7, 1921; and *Mohave County Miner and Our Mineral Wealth*, April 15, 1921.

13 Schmeckebier, *The Bureau of Prohibition*, page 53. *Enforcement of the Prohibition Laws*, page 219. *El Paso Herald*, March 16, 1920.

14 *El Paso Herald*, April 3, 1920.

15 Ibid., June 28, 1920.

16 Ibid., April 22 and June 5, 1920.

17 Ibid.

18 Ibid., June 21 and 23, July 3 and 7, 1920. See also, Texas Department of State Health Services. Texas Death Certificates, 1903–1982.

19 *El Paso Herald*, June 29, 1920.

20 Ibid., September 15, 1919, and September 9, 1920. For Carnes's service as a Texas Ranger, see Texas Adjutant General Service Records 1836–1935, roll 401-53, Texas State Library and Archives Commission, Austin, Texas. For Carnes's role in the death of Pascual Orozco, see Harris and Sadler, *Texas Rangers and the Mexican Revolution*, pages 298–99. For Miguel Garcia's death record, see Texas Department of State Health Services. Texas Death Certificates, 1903–1982.

21 *El Paso Herald*, October 20 and 21, 1920. For Spencer's prior service in the Texas Rangers, see Harris and Sadler, *Texas Rangers and the Mexican Revolution*, page 182.

22 *El Paso Herald*, June 30, 1920.

23 *El Paso Herald*, September 15, October 4, and October 26, 1920.

24 *San Antonio Evening News*, November 22, 1920.

25   *El Paso Herald*, December 24, 1920.

26   Ibid., March 22 and May 30, 1921.

27   C. P. Shearman was questioned about the murder of his uncle during a trial held in May of 1921; see *El Paso Herald*, May 30, 1921. For background on Neil T. Shearman, see *El Paso Herald*, April 3, 1919, and November 13, 1919. For Neil and Charles P. Shearman as deputies, see *El Paso Herald*, July 21, 1920. For Neil Sherman's fight with Ben Williams, see *El Paso Herald*, July 27, 1920. For the death of Tranquillo Serrana on the Shearman hog ranch, see *El Paso Herald*, October 11, 1918. Neil Shearman's arrest for liquor violations was published in *El Paso Herald*, December 30, 1920. For Neil Shearman's court battles, see *El Paso Herald*, January 13 and 24, 1921.

28   Ibid., May 27 and 30, 1921.

29   Ibid. See also, *El Paso Herald*, September 20, 1921.

30   *El Paso Herald*, September 20, 1921.

31   Ibid., May 30, 1921, and September 21, 1921.

32   Ibid., May 28 and 30, 1921. For more on the deaths of agents Beckett and Wood, see *Enforcement of the Prohibition Laws*, pages 152–53 and 167. See also, Texas Department of State Health Services. Texas Death Certificates, 1903–1982, Stafford E. Beckett, El Paso County, filed March 24, 1921, and Charles Arch Wood, El Paso County, filed March 24, 1921.

33   *El Paso Herald*, September 20 and 21, 1921.

34   Ibid., September 20, 1921.

35   Clifford Alan Perkins, *Border Patrol: With the U.S. Immigration Service on the Mexican Boundary, 1910–1954* (Texas Western Press, The University of Texas at El Paso, 1978), pages 87–88. *El Paso Herald*, March 22 and 23, 1921.

36   *El Paso Herald*, May 21, 1921, and July 2 and July 3, 1921. For details on the Shearmans' second trial in Midland, see *El Paso Herald*, September 20, 21, 22, and 23, 1921. For the Shearmans' final acquittal, see *Waco News-Tribune*, May 27, 1923.

Chapter Seven: Liquor War on the Rio Grande

1   Perkins, *Border Patrol*, pages 83–84.

2   The incident outside of Anthony, New Mexico, involving Watson and Holzman was reported in *El Paso Times*, May 5, 1921.

3   Ibid.

4   *El Paso Times*, May 5, 1921, and *El Paso Herald,* May 2, 1921.

5   Ibid. For the death of John Watson, see *El Paso Herald,* May 2 and 4, 1921. Texas State Board of Health, Bureau of Vital Statistics, Standard Certificate of Death, El Paso County, John Watson, May 2, 1921. For the arrest of the suspects involved in Watson's killing, see *Deming Graphic,* July 12, 1921, *Deming*

Headlight, July 15, 1921, and *El Paso Herald,* July 13, 1921. For the execution of Agapito Rueda for the murder of William Meers in 1924, see *El Paso Herald,* October 21, 1925, and *Santa Ana Register,* January 9, 1926.

6   *El Paso Herald,* May 9, 10, 28, 1921, and September 7, 1921.

7   This article was published in *Bisbee Daily Review* on May 29, 1921 under the headline "Liquor War Now Raging along Rio Grande." This same article also appeared under various headlines in *Ogden Standard-Examiner,* Ogden, Utah, May 27, 1921, *Salisbury Evening Post,* Salisbury, North Carolina, May 23, 1921, and *Abilene Daily Chronicle,* Abilene, Kansas, and *Topeka Daily Capital,* Topeka, Kansas, May 23, 1921.

8   Ibid.See also, *El Paso Herald,* March 18, 1921. Perkins, *Border Patrol,* pages 57–58.

9   Ibid.

10   Ibid. Perkins, *Border Patrol,* page 59.

11   Ibid. Perkins, *Border Patrol,* pages 57–63.

12   The fight between Mexican authorities and smugglers on March 26, 1921, was reported in *El Paso Herald,* March 28, 1921. For Davila and his efforts to combat smuggling along the Rio Grande, see *El Paso Herald,* March 7, 12, and 26, 1921.

13   *El Paso Herald,* March 9 and 28, 1921, and August 20, 1921.

14   *El Paso Herald,* April 25, 1921.

15   Langston, *The Impact of Prohibition,* pages 106–08. *El Paso Herald,* October 2, 1920, April 21 and 25, 1921.

16   Langston, *The Impact of Prohibition,* pages 64–68. Cleofas Calleros (Chief Line Clerk, El Paso, Texas), "El Paso—Gateway to Mexico and the Great Southwest," *The Santa Fe Magazine,* Vol. XV, No. 11, October 1921, pages 34–35.

17   *El Paso Herald,* February 17, 1921. See also, Langston, *The Impact of Prohibition,* pages 225–27.

18   Lee A. Riggs, *A Short History of the Customs District of El Paso,* C. L. Sonnichsen Papers, University of Texas at El Paso, page 7. Judge W. R. Smith's comments were published in *El Paso Herald,* on March 21, 1921.

19   Langston, *The Impact of Prohibition,* pages 245–46, 252–53. Perkins, *Border Patrol,* pages 83–84.

20   Perkins, *Border Patrol,* pages 85–86.

21   Ibid., pages 65–66. Caldwell and DeLord, *Texas Lawmen,* page 445. *El Paso Herald,* October 20, 1922.

22   Perkins, *Border Patrol,* pages 66–67. *El Paso Herald,* October 20, 21, and 23, 1922.

23 Texas Department of State Health Services. Texas Death Certificates, 1903–1982, Orem, Utah, Charles Gardiner, El Paso County, filed October 24, 1922. Perkins, *Border Patrol*, page 67. *El Paso Herald*, October 21, 1921.

24 *El Paso Herald*, October 24 and 28, 1922.

25 Perkins, *Border Patrol*, pages 70–71.

Chapter Eight: Where Rough Necks Are Needed

1 This excerpt from a *Mesa Tribune* editorial, called "Pistols and Officers," was reprinted in *Weekly Epitaph* on August 20, 1922.

2 *Carlsbad Current*, June 9, 1922; *El Paso Herald*, June 5, 1922; and Don Bullis, *New Mexico's Finest: Peace Officers Killed in the Line of Duty, 1847–2010* (Rio Grande Books, 2010), page 15.

3 *Carlsbad Current*, June 9, 1922.

4 Ibid. See also, *El Paso Herald*, June 5, 1922.

5 *Carlsbad Current*, June 9, 1922.

6 *El Paso Herald*, July 10, 1922; *Carlsbad Current*, June 9, 1922; *Weekly Epitaph*, August 20, 1922.

7 Tempe night watchman Albert Nettle was the first Arizona peace officer killed in the months that followed the end of World War I; see *Bisbee Daily Review*, May 18, 1919. Nettle's death was followed by that of constable Victor H. Melick in Williams, Arizona, on May 31, 1919; see *Coconino Sun*, June 6, 1919. Constable Alexander E. Sheppard of Bisbee was killed in September of 1920; see, *Bisbee Daily Review*, September 17, 1920. Tempe night marshal Cyrus Spangler was fatally wounded during the robbery of the Baber-Jones Mercantile in January of 1921; see, *Arizona Republican*, January 12 and 13, 1921. On July 1, 1921, Yavapai County undersheriff Edward F. Bowers was shot and killed in Prescott, Arizona, by one Frank George; see, *Weekly Journal-Miner*, July 6, 1921. Maricopa County deputy sheriff Almon W. Dana was fatally injured when he crashed his motorcycle while in pursuit of a speeding automobile; see, *Weekly Epitaph*, April 16, 1922. Santa Cruz County sheriff George White and deputy Leonard Smith were both killed as a result of an automobile accident while the two officers were in the process of transporting Manuel Martinez and Placidio Silvas to the Arizona State Penitentiary at Florence; see, *Bisbee Daily Review*, July 19, 1922. For the death of Charles Sherman Patterson, see, *Arizona Republican*, August 30, 1921, and *Weekly Journal-Miner*, August 31, 1921. For a listing of officers killed in New Mexico for the same period, see Bullis, *New Mexico's Finest*, page 338. For officers killed in Texas between 1918 and 1922, including members of federal agencies, see Caldwell and DeLord, *Texas Lawmen*.

8   *Bisbee Daily Review*, September 17, 1920. Arizona Department of Health Services, Arizona State Board of Health, Original Certificate of Death, Alexander E. Sheppard, filed November 8, 1920.

9   *Bisbee Daily Review*, October 5 and 13, 1920.

10 *Alamogordo News*, April 14, 1921; *Deming Headlight*, April 8, 1921; and *El Paso Herald*, June 28, 1921. See also, Bullis, *New Mexico's Finest*, pages 21–22.

11 *El Paso Herald*, January 18, 1922, and *Alamogordo News*, January 26, 1922. For Jesus Rocha, see *La Revista de Taos*, January 6, 1922, and *Deming Headlight*, August 11, 1922.

12 *Arizona Republican*, January 12, 1921, and February 2, 1921. For Baber's age and place of birth, see United States of America, Bureau of the Census. *Fifteenth Census of the United States, 1930*. Washington, DC: National Archives and Records Administration, 1930. T626, 2,667 rolls, Census Place: *Tempe, Maricopa, Arizona*; Roll: *60*; Page: *4A*; Enumeration District: *0124*; Image: *382.0*; FHL microfilm: *2339795*.

13 *Arizona Republican*, January 12 and 25, 1921. According to his death record, August Ernest Hintze was born in Mexico on April 25, 1912; see Arizona Department of Health Services, Arizona State Board of Health, Bureau of Vital Statistics, Original Certificate of Death for August Ernest Hintze, filed on February 11, 1921.

14 *Arizona Republican*, January 13 and 14, 1921. It's a little unclear as to where Martinez positioned himself, with some newspaper accounts placing him across Sixth Street from the Baber-Jones Mercantile near the Tempe National Bank, and others, much closer to the store itself. In truth, Martinez probably moved between various positions during the holdup and shootings.

15 Ibid.

16 *Arizona Republican*, January 12 and 13, 1921, and February 2, 1921. Case #5353 *&* 5354, *State of Arizona vs. Tomas Roman*, RG 92, History and Archives Division, Arizona State Library, Archives and Public Records. For David S. Teeter's age and occupation, see *Fourteenth Census of the United States, 1920*. (NARA microfilm publication T625, 2,076 rolls.) Records of the Bureau of the Census, Record Group 29. National Archives, Washington, DC, Census Place: *Tempe, Maricopa, Arizona*; Roll: *T625_48*; Page: *15A*; Enumeration District: *31*.

17 *Arizona Republican*, January 12, 14, and 25, 1921.

18 Ibid., January 14 and 18, 1921. Mike Burns, whose Yavapai name was *Hoomothya*, led a remarkable life. Born in about 1864, as a boy, Burns survived the Skeleton Cave Massacre in Salt River Canyon in 1872, and was later raised by a US Army captain. In his later years, Burns would serve as a court interpreter, and prior to his death in 1934, wrote an autobiography. For more on Burns, see, Mike Burns, *The Only One Living to Tell: The Autobiography of*

a Yavapai Indian, edited by Gregory McNamee (University of Arizona Press, 2012).

19 *Arizona Republican,* January 18, 1921.

20 Ibid., January 15, 1921. For Robert Q. Leatherman's age and background, see *Fourteenth Census of the United States, 1920.* (NARA microfilm publication T625, 2,076 rolls.) Records of the Bureau of the Census, Record Group 29. National Archives, Washington, DC, Census Place: *Nogales, Santa Cruz, Arizona;* Roll: *T625_51;* Page: *7A;* Enumeration District: *118.*

21 *Case #5353 & 5354, State of Arizona vs. Tomas Roman. Bisbee Daily Review,* January 15, 1921; *Arizona Republican,* January 15 and 21, 1921.

22 *Case #5353 & 5354, State of Arizona vs. Tomas Roman;* and *Arizona Republican,* January 15, 1921.

23 *Coconino Sun,* January 21, 1921; and *Arizona Republican,* January 16, 1921. See also, Arizona Department of Health Services, Arizona State Board of Health, Bureau of Vital Statistics, Original Certificate of Death for Victoriano Martinez, filed February 10, 1921.

24 *Arizona Republican,* January 21, 1921.

25 Ibid., February 2, 1921.

26 *Case #5353 & 5354, State of Arizona vs. Tomas Roman;* and *Arizona Republican,* February 16, 17, 18, 19, 20, 22, and 24, 1921.

27 *Arizona Republican,* February 27, 1921.

28 *Case #5353 & 5354, State of Arizona vs. Tomas Roman.* Among the various grounds for Roman's appeal were questions regarding the confession he and Martinez had made to Harry Saxon at Calabasas on January 14, 1921. Saxon, while he had previously served as sheriff of Santa Cruz County, was in fact a civilian when he questioned the two suspects. However, the Supreme Court of the State of Arizona ultimately ruled that the confession made to Saxon was admissible, largely because it was offered as a result of an appeal to the consciences of the two suspects on the grounds that by admitting to the crime, other innocent persons would not be accused or suffer as a result, and that the confession had been made without any threat on behalf of Saxon and the other officers, or in the face of any promises of leniency in exchange for their statement. For more on the appeals and details on the execution of Tomas Roman and Ricardo Lauterio, see *Arizona Republican,* April 2, 1921, October 12, 1921, and November 1, 1921; *Holbrook News,* April 8, 1921; *Bisbee Daily Review,* January 7, 1922; *Weekly Epitaph,* January 15, 1922; and *Copper Era and Morenci Leader,* January 20, 1922.

29 McKem's article first appeared in *Mohave County Miner and Our Mineral Wealth* on May 12, 1922. It was reprinted in *Coconino Sun* on May 19, 1922, with an

editor's note that pointed out a number of historical inaccuracies in regard to several of the stories McKem related from the Territorial era.

30 *Los Angeles Times,* May 15 and 16, 1922; Barnes, *Arizona Place Names,* page 224.

31 *Los Angeles Times,* May 16, 1922.

32 Ibid. See also, *Bisbee Daily Review,* May 16, 1922.

33 *San Francisco Chronicle, El Paso Herald, Ogden Standard-Examiner, Oshkosh Daily Northwestern,* and *Brooklyn Daily Eagle,* May 15, 1922. *Los Angeles Times,* May 16, 1922.

34 *Los Angeles Times* and *Oakland Tribune,* May 15, 1922.

35 DeArment and DeMattos, *A Rough Ride to Redemption,* pages 3–6, 16–21, and 22–87. See also, Theodore Roosevelt, *The Rough Riders* (P. F. Collier & Son, 1899), page 28.

36 Roosevelt, *The Rough Riders,* pages 90–101, 102–04, 107–23, 124–29, 134–38, 158–60, and 178–80.

37 *Los Angeles Times,* May 16, 1922. *Bisbee Daily Review,* May 18 and 31, 1922.

38 *Bisbee Daily Review,* May 19, 23, 28, 30, 1922, and June 3, 1922; *Coconino Sun,* May 26, 1922; and *Weekly Epitaph,* May 21 and 28, 1922.

39 *Bisbee Daily Review,* November 24, 1922, and December 12, 1922; *Weekly Epitaph,* July 16, 1922, November 26, 1922, and December 10, 1922; and *St. John's Herald,* June 29, 1922.

40 Richard D. Moore, *Too Tough to Tame* (Authorhouse, 2009), page 61. DeArment and DeMattos, *A Rough Ride to Redemption,* pages 185–92. *Morning Sun,* April 21, 1923.

Chapter Nine: "Honor First"

1 Commissioner Hull's statement is drawn from *Annual Report of the Commissioner General of Immigration to the Secretary of Labor,* June 30, 1927 (Government Printing Office, 1927), page 17. Official Personnel File, Frank H. Clark, US Immigration Service, US Department of Labor, US Border Patrol, National Archives & Records Administration, St. Louis, Missouri. See also, *Fourteenth Census of the United States,* 1920. (NARA microfilm publication T625, 2,076 rolls.) Records of the Bureau of the Census, Record Group 29. National Archives, Washington, DC, Census Place: Albuquerque Ward 3, Bernalillo, New Mexico; Roll: T625_1074; Page: 3B; Enumeration District: 17. Caldwell & DeLord, *Texas Lawmen,* page 446. *Decatur Herald Sun,* December 14, 1924.

2 For the firefight between Prohibition agents and smugglers on May 21, 1922, see *El Paso Herald,* May 22, 1922.

3 Ibid., July 11 and 13, 1922.

4 Ibid., June 14, 15, and 16, 1921, and October 5, 1927. See also, Caldwell and DeLord, *Texas Lawmen,* pages 128–29.

5 For Salvador "The Buffalo" Jacquez, see *El Paso Herald,* July 18, 1925. For Valles's nickname as "El Diablo," see *El Paso Herald-Post,* September 13, 1927. For Ysobel "Horseface" Murillo, see *El Paso Herald,* January 5 and 18, 1921, and March 12, 1921.

6 *El Paso Herald,* March 3, 1922, and April 24, 1923.

7 Ibid., March 1, 1923, April 12, 13, and 14, 1923. See also, Caldwell and DeLord, *Texas Lawmen,* page 128.

8 *El Paso Herald,* June 3, 1925, July 23, 24, and 31, 1925, and October 12, 1926. For Salvador Jacquez and the murder of John "Jack" Coleman, see *El Paso Herald,* May 18 and 21, 1925, July 18, 22, 23, 24, 28, 1925, October 15 and 17, 1925, and October 12, 1926, November 22 and 26, 1926, and December 1, 1926. For Horseface Murillo, see *El Paso Herald,* August 22, 25, and 26, 1925.

9 Official Personnel File, Frank H. Clark. *El Paso Times,* December 15, 1924. Courtesy, National Border Patrol Museum, El Paso, Texas.

10 Ibid. See also, Caldwell and DeLord, *Texas Lawmen,* page 446. Perkins, *Border Patrol,* pages 70–71. *Decatur Herald Sun,* December 14, 1924. *El Paso Herald,* October 26, 1925, August 19, 1926, and August 3, 1928; and *El Paso Herald-Post,* August 6, 1931.

11 *Hutchison News,* Hutchison, Kansas, January 2, 1925; *Waco News Tribune,* January 4, 1925; and *Albany Daily News,* Albany, Oregon, January 18, 1925.

12 *Immigration Act of 1924,* Public Law 68-139 (43 Stat. 153, Enacted May 26, 1924), 68th Congress of the United States. See also *Dunkirk Evening Observer,* Dunkirk, New York, May 15, 1924; *Republican* (Springfield, Missouri), May 16, 1924; and *Oakland Tribune,* May 26, 1924. For more on this piece of legislation and its origins, see Kelly Lytle Hernández, *Migra! A History of the US Border Patrol* (University of California Press, 2010), pages 26–32.

13 *Olean Evening Herald,* May 26, 1924.

14 *1862 Anti-Coolie Law, "An act to prohibit the 'coolie trade' by American citizens in American vessels"* (12 Stat. 340), 37th Congress; February 19, 1862. *1875 Page Law, "An act supplementary to the acts in relation to immigration"* (18 Stat. 477), 43rd Congress; March 3, 1875. *1882 Chinese Exclusion Act, "An act to inaugurate certain treaty stipulations relating to Chinese"* (22 Stat. 58), 47th Congress; approved May 6, 1882. *1882 Immigration Act, "An act to regulate immigration"* (22 Stat. 214), 47th Congress; August 3, 1882. See also, Hernandez, *Migra!,* page 26. Perkins, *Border Patrol,* page 7.

15 *1885 Contract Labor Law, "An act to prohibit the importation and migration of foreigners and aliens under contract or agreement to perform labor in the United States, its territories, and the District of Columbia"* (23 Stat. 332), 48th Congress;

February 26, 1885. *1891 Immigration Act, "An act in amendment to the various acts relative to immigration and the importation of aliens under contract or agreement to perform labor"*(26 Stat. 1084), 51st Congress; March 3, 1891. *1917 Immigration Act, "An act to regulate the immigration of aliens to, and the residence of aliens in, the United States,"* Public Law 59-96 (39 Stat. 874) 64th Congress; February 5, 1917. *1921 Emergency Quota Law, "An act to limit the immigration of aliens into the United States,"* Public Law 67 5 (42 Stat. 5), 67th Congress; May 19, 1921.

16 Perkins, *Border Patrol,* pages 8–9; John Myers, *The Border Wardens* (Prentice-Hall, 1971), pages 14–15. See also, John Boessnecker, *When Law Was in the Holster: The Frontier Life of Bob Paul* (University of Oklahoma Press, 2012), pages 380–83. Bill Broyles and Mark Haynes, *Desert Duty: On the Line with the US Border Patrol* (University of Texas Press, 2010), pages 4–5. *El Paso Herald,* August 27, 1903.

17 Perkins, *Border Patrol,* pages 11–13. See also, William Deverell and David Igler, *A Companion to California History* (John Wiley & Sons, 2014), page 235; and Jeremy Agnew, *Alcohol and Opium in the Old West* (McFarland & Co, 2014), pages 90–91.

18 *Arizona Republican,* February 3, 1911.

19 Perkins, *Border Patrol,* pages 1–3 and 7.

20 Ibid., pages 3–4.

21 Ibid., pages 4–7, 15–16, and 49.

22 Ibid., pages 24–36, 47, and 49.

23 Ibid., page 73. See also, Hernandez, *Migra!,* page 37.

24 Hernandez, *Migra!,* page 32. See also, *Muskogee County Democrat,* May 22, 1924; *Capital Journal,* Salem, Oregon, April 5, 1924.

25 Hernandez, *Migra!,* pages 32–33. See also, *Department of Labor Appropriation Act of May 28, 1924,* Public Law 68-53, 68th Congress (43 Stat. 205). Perkins, *Border Patrol,* page 89.

26 Perkins, *Border Patrol,* pages, 89–91. Hernandez, *Migra!,* pages 36–39. *Annual Report of the Commissioner General of Immigration to the Secretary of Labor,* June 30, 1925 (Government Printing Office, page 14). For Sibray's comments, see *New Castle News,* June 3, 1924.

27 Hernandez, *Migra!,* pages 38–39; Perkins, *Border Patrol,* page 92; and *Annual Report of the Commissioner General of Immigration to the Secretary of Labor,* June 30, 1925, page 15.

28 Ibid.

29 Interview with Wesley E. Stiles by Wesley C. Shaw, 1986, Interview No. 756, Institute of Oral History, University of Texas at El Paso. Interview with Edwin

M. Reeves by Robert H. Novak, 1974, Interview No. 135, Institute of Oral History, University of Texas at El Paso.

30   For the Border Patrol's police powers, see Perkins, *Border Patrol,* pages 89–90, and *Act of February 27, 1925,* Public Law 68-502, 68th Congress (43 Stat. 1049-1050). Myers, *The Border Wardens,* pages 34 and 36. *Annual Report of the Commissioner General of Immigration to the Secretary of Labor,* June 30, 1925, page 16. *Morning Sun,* February 26, 1925.

31   *Taylor Daily Press,* April 5, 1925; *Waco News Tribune,* April 6, 1925; and *El Paso Herald,* June 8 and 19, 1925.

32   *Galveston Daily News,* August 4, 1925; and *Taylor Daily Press,* August 5, 1925. *Annual Report of the Commissioner General of Immigration to the Secretary of Labor,* June 30, 1926 (Government Printing Office, 1926), page 18.

33   *El Paso Herald,* April 19, May 12, and June 26, 1926.

34   *Nogales Herald,* April 26, 1926. Official Personnel File, William A. McKee, US Immigration Service, US Department of Labor, US Border Patrol, National Archives & Records Administration, St. Louis, Missouri. For Leatherman's role in the shoot-out with Victoriano Martinez and Tomas Roman, see *Border Vidette,* January 15, 1921. Parker and Leatherman are both named as members of Harry Saxon's posse in *Border Vidette,* July 22, 1922. See also, Mary Kidder Rak, *Border Patrol* (Houghton Mifflin, 1938), pages 190–92.

35   *Nogales Herald,* July 26, 1926. Official Personnel File, Lon Parker, US Immigration Service, US Department of Labor, US Border Patrol, National Archives & Records Administration, St. Louis, Missouri. *Bisbee Daily Review,* June 25, 1919, and December 16, 1921. *Arizona Republican,* January 8, 1921. Rak, *Border Patrol,* page 229.

36   Official Personnel File, Lon Parker. Rak, *Border Patrol,* 230–31.

37   Official Personnel File, Lon Parker. *Nogales Herald,* July 26, 27, and 28, 1926. There are numerous accounts as to the ultimate fate of Parker's killer, with several potential suspects wounded or killed by other lawmen at various times in the years that followed Parker's murder. Rak, *Border Patrol,* pages 233–34; and Commander Alvin Edward Moore, *Border Patrol* (Sunstone Press, 1988), pages 5–19.

38   *Annual Report of the Commissioner General of Immigration to the Secretary of Labor,* June 30, 1927 (Government Printing Office, 1927), pages 17–19. *Bryan Daily Eagle,* April 26 and 27, 1927.

Chapter Ten: "You Were Looking for Me Last Night"

1   *El Paso Evening Post,* November 10, 1928. For a profile of Juan Franco, see *El Paso Herald,* April 23, 1923. See also, *El Paso Herald-Post,* May 5, 1933; *El Paso Times,* October 2, 1889. For Clements's career in El Paso law enforcement, see,

C. L. Sonnichsen, *Pass of the North: Four Centuries on the Rio Grande* (Texas Western Press, 1968), pages 336–43. See also, Caldwell and DeLord, *Texas Lawmen*, pages 119–20.

2 *El Paso Herald*, April 23, 1923. For Franco's experience riding in a posse with Captain John R. Hughes, see *El Paso Herald*, October 31, 1900. For the death of one of Franco's children, see *El Paso Herald*, June 27, 1904. For a sample of some of Franco's experiences as an El Paso lawman, see *El Paso Herald*, May 1, 1897, March 6, 1899, May 21, 1901, May 23, 1903, October 18, 1904, November 1, 1906, December 10, 1919, and October 11, 1922.

3 *El Paso Evening Post*, November 10, 1928.

4 Ibid. For a profile on Juan Escontrias, see *El Paso Herald*, April 20, 1923.

5 *El Paso Daily Times*, October 14, 1908. The August 9, 1917, edition of *El Paso Herald* reported that Escontrias was one of several residents of El Paso County summoned for examination by the draft board who claimed dependents, and, according to his draft registration form, by the summer of 1917 he and Sofia had four children. See, US Selective Service System. World War I Selective Service System Draft Registration Cards, 1917–1918. Washington, DC: National Archives and Records Administration. M1509, 4,582 rolls. Registration State: Texas; Registration County: El Paso; Roll: 1953281; Draft Board 1. For Escontrias's service as a deputy sheriff, see *El Paso Herald*, July 21, 1920, and April 20, 1923.

6 *El Paso Herald*, March 4, 5, and 12, 1921.

7 Ibid., June 15, 1921.

8 Official Personnel File, Tom Threepersons, Department of the Treasury, Official Personnel Folders, National Personnel Records Center, National Archives and Records Administration, St. Louis, Missouri. *El Paso Evening Post*, January 11 and 29, 1929.

9 Official Personnel File, Threepersons. *El Paso Herald*, July 14 and 30, 1920, September 6, 1920, and November 16, 1920.

10 For "One Man is Threepersons . . . ," see *El Paso Herald*, March 9, 1921.

11 Ibid., June 22 and 23, 1921. For Silverio's age and occupation, see, Texas State Board of Health, Bureau of Vital Statistics, Standard Certificate of Death, Silverio Vasquez, filed June 24, 1921, *Texas Department of State Health Services. Texas Death Certificates, 1903–1982*, iArchives, Orem, Utah.

12 *El Paso Herald*, April 20, 1923; *Oakland Tribune*, July 19, 1921. For the theft of Escontrias's and Threepersons's cars, see, *El Paso Herald*, July 20 and 25, 1921. For the ambush in front of the South El Paso substation in which Threepersons was wounded, see *El Paso Herald*, August 17 and 18, 1921. For the incident in November of 1921, see *El Paso Herald*, November 14, 1921.

13 *Bisbee Daily Review,* May 28, 1922; *El Paso Herald,* May 29, 1922, and June 5 and 22, 1922. For Francisco Alonis, see *El Paso Herald,* August 31, 1922.

14 *El Paso Herald,* June 22, 1922, and March 3, 1923.

15 Ibid., June 23, 1922.

16 Ibid.

17 Ibid., June 22, 23, and 24, 1922.

18 Ibid., August 19, September 20, and October 13, 1922.

19 Ibid., December 15, 1922, and January 5, 1923.

20 Ibid., March 1, 2, 3, and 15, 1923.

21 Ibid., March 1, 1925. Langston, *The Impact of Prohibition,* pages 266–68. *El Paso Morning Times,* June 16, 1918.

22 US Treasury Department, *Traffic in Narcotic Drugs: Report of Special Committee of Investigation Appointed March 25, 1918, By the Secretary of the Treasury* (Government Printing Office, 1919), pages 9–10, 14–15, and 22.

23 *El Paso Herald,* March 12, 1921, and November 26, 1921. Langston, *The Impact of Prohibition,* page 270.

24 *El Paso Herald,* June 29, 1921, July 13 and 14, 1921, and February 19 and 20, 1923.

25 Ibid., February 19 and 20, 1923. Texas State Board of Health, Bureau of Vital Statistics, Standard Certificate of Death, El Paso, Texas, Marjorie Dell Greene, Filed on February 19, 1923, *Texas Department of State Health Services. Texas Death Certificates, 1903–1982,* iArchives, Orem, Utah.

26 *El Paso Herald,* February 20, 1923, and March 1, 1923. For Jenkins as chief of police, see *El Paso Herald,* December 6, 1922. For Will S. Wood, see *El Paso Herald,* March 22, 1921.

27 Ibid., February 20 and 26, 1923, and March 23, 1923. See also, Langston, *The Impact of Prohibition,* pages 269–70.

28 *El Paso Herald,* April 21, 1923.

29 Ibid., February 8, 1922, and May 5, 1923.

30 Ibid., May 5, 1923.

31 Ibid., May 5 and 7, 1923; *San Francisco Chronicle,* July 29, 1923.

32 *El Paso Herald,* May 8 and 11, 1923.

33 Ibid., September 10, 1925. For the capture of Gabriel Ramirez in Los Angeles, see *Capital Journal,* Salem, Oregon, April 21, 1925.

34 Ibid., August 20, 1925, and September 11, 1925.

35 Ibid., June 24, 1927.

36 *El Paso Evening Post,* August 16, 1927.

37 Ibid.

38 Ibid., August 19 and 24, 1927. For Manuel Mungia's earlier arrests for liquor violations, see *El Paso Herald,* October 21 and 28, 1920, and November 4 and 5, 1921.

39 Ibid., October 10, 1927. See also, *El Paso Herald,* October 11, 1927.

40 *El Paso Evening Post,* October 11, 1927.

41 *El Paso Herald,* November 17, 1927. For Escontrias's resignation as a deputy constable, see *El Paso Evening Post,* January 7, 1928. See also, *El Paso Evening Post,* March 14, 1928.

42 *El Paso Evening Post,* January 11, 1928.

43 Ibid., April 26 and May 31, 1928.

44 For the incident at the "Hole-in-the-Wall" and Escontrias's suspension from duty, see the *El Paso Herald,* July 18, 1928, and *El Paso Evening Post,* July 18, 20–21 and 24, 1928. For the death of Pedro Escontrias, see Texas State Board of Health, Bureau of Vital Statistics, Standard Certificate of Death, El Paso, Texas, Pedro Escontrias, Filed on July 17, 1928. *Texas Department of State Health Services. Texas Death Certificates, 1903–1982,* iArchives, Orem, Utah. See also, *El Paso Evening Post,* July 16–18, 1928.

45 *El Paso Herald,* August 25, 1928, and *El Paso Evening Post,* July 16, 1928. Langston, *The Impact of Prohibition,* page 271.

46 *El Paso Herald* and *El Paso Evening Post,* August 25, 1928.

47 Ibid.

48 *El Paso Evening Post,* August 27, 1928. Nicole Mottier, *Drug Gangs and Politics in Ciudad Juarez, 1928–1936, Mexican Studies / Estudios Mexicanos,* Vol. 25, No. 1 (Winter 2009), pages 19–46. For Fernandez as the "so-called Al Capone of Mexico" and La Nacha, see *El Paso Herald Post,* January 15, 1934, August 21, 1935, and May 2, 1952.

49 *El Paso Evening Post,* September 4, 11, and 18, 1928, and November 10, 1928.

50 Dye to Secsta, "Death of Major Ignacio Dosamontes," November 11, 1928. CD, Part III, No. 800 DOSAMONTES (1928), USSDR, RG 84, National Archives and Records Administration, College Park, MD.

51 Ibid. See also, *El Paso Evening Post,* September 13, 1928.

52 *El Paso Evening Post,* October 2, 3, and 6, 1928. See also, *El Paso Herald,* October 3, 1928.

53 *El Paso Evening Post,* July 30, 1928, and November 10, 1928. For the disappearance of "Horseface" Murillo, see *El Paso Herald,* October 3, 1928.

54 *El Paso Evening Post,* November 6, 1928.

55 Dye to Secsta, "Death of Major Ignacio Dosamontes."

56 Ibid.

57 Ibid. See also, *El Paso Evening Post* and *El Paso Herald,* November 10, 1928.

58 Ibid.

59   Ibid. See also, *El Paso Herald,* November 12, 1928.

60   Ibid. See also, *El Paso Evening Post* and *El Paso Herald,* November 10, 1928. Texas State Board of Health, Bureau of Vital Statistics, Standard Certificate of Death, Reg. Dist. No. 47611, Registered No. 3308, El Paso, Texas, Ignacio Dosamantes, Filed on November 13, 1928. *Texas Department of State Health Services. Texas Death Certificates, 1903–1982,* iArchives, Orem, Utah.

61   Dye to Secsta, "Death of Major Ignacio Dosamontes." *El Paso Herald* and *El Paso Evening Post,* November 12, 1928. For Cline's extortion charges, see *El Paso Evening Post,* December 13, 1928.

62   Dye to Secsta, "Death of Major Ignacio Dosamontes." For details on Escontrias's trial and conviction, including testimony, see *El Paso Evening Post,* December 17–22 and 25–29, 1928. Numerous attempts by the author to retrieve a copy of the original court records in *State of Texas v. Juan Escontrias, Case #11855,* were unsuccessful. While the Special Collections Department at the University of Texas, El Paso, maintains many historical court records for El Paso County and the 34th District Court of Texas, this case does not appear to be included in their holdings. For a story about Escontrias as a "butter-and-egg man" while serving as a prison trusty, see *El Paso Evening Post,* February 25, 1929.

Chapter Eleven: Contrabandistas

1   Chief Patrol Inspector, El Paso, Texas, to District Director US Immigration Service, July 26, 1929, *File Regarding Exploits and Shooting Affrays, 1920s–1930s, District Director, El Paso,* Subject and Policy Files, 1893–1957, Record Group 85, Records of the Immigration and Naturalization Service, 1787–2004, National Archives Building, Washington, DC. See also, Statement of Patrol Inspector Tom P. Isbell, as made before Chief Patrol Inspector H. C. Horsley, in the office of the Chief Patrol Inspector, El Paso, Texas, on July 21, 1929, *File Regarding Exploits and Shooting Affrays, 1920s–1930s, District Director, El Paso,* Subject and Policy Files, 1893–1957, Record Group 85, Records of the Immigration and Naturalization Service, 1787–2004, National Archives Building, Washington, DC.

2   Statement of Patrol Inspector Tom P. Isbell. See also, Statement of Patrol Inspector Donald C. Kemp, as made before Chief Patrol Inspector H. C. Horsley, in the office of the Chief Patrol Inspector, El Paso, Texas, on July 21, 1929, *File Regarding Exploits and Shooting Affrays, 1920s–1930s, District Director, El Paso,* Subject and Policy Files, 1893–1957, Record Group 85, Records of the Immigration and Naturalization Service, 1787–2004, National Archives Building, Washington, DC.

3   Statement of Patrol Inspector Robert N. Goldie, as made before Chief
     Patrol Inspector H. C. Horsley, in the office of the Chief Patrol Inspector, El
     Paso, Texas, on July 21, 1929, *File Regarding Exploits and Shooting Affrays,
     1920s–1930s, District Director, El Paso,* Subject and Policy Files, 1893–1957,
     Record Group 85, Records of the Immigration and Naturalization Service,
     1787–2004, National Archives Building, Washington, DC.

4   Statement of Patrol Inspector Robert N. Goldie. See also, Chief Patrol Inspec-
     tor, El Paso, Texas to District Director US Immigration Service, July 26, 1929.
     El Paso Herald, July 20, 1929.

5   Statements of Patrol Inspectors Robert N. Goldie and Tom P. Isbell.

6   Ibid. See also, Chief Patrol Inspector, El Paso, Texas to District Director US
     Immigration Service, July 26, 1929. *El Paso Herald-Post,* March 27, 1935.

7   Ibid. For the arrest of Gregorio Ortega, see *El Paso Evening Post,* August 28 and
     29, 1929, and September 6, 1929.

8   *El Paso Evening Post,* July 22 and 26, 1929. *El Paso Herald,* July 23, 1929.

9   Caldwell and DeLord, *Texas Lawmen,* pages 466–67. *El Paso Herald,* December
     31, 1926, January 1, 7, 8, and 26, 1927, February 22, 23, 24, and 26, 1927, and
     December 14, 1927. *El Paso Evening Post,* December 15, 1927. For Arriola's ser-
     vice in the Mexican Revolution, see *Big Spring Daily Herald,* Big Spring, Texas,
     February 26, 1932.

10   For the death of Steve Dawson, see *El Paso Evening Post* and *El Paso Herald,*
     February 28, 1928, and Chief Patrol Inspector to District Director, US Immi-
     gration Service, El Paso, Texas, March 3, 1928, *File Regarding Exploits and
     Shooting Affrays, 1920s–1930s, District Director, El Paso,* Subject and Policy
     Files, 1893–1957, Record Group 85, Records of the Immigration and Natu-
     ralization Service, 1787–2004, National Archives Building, Washington, DC.
     Caldwell and DeLord, *Texas Lawmen,* pages 447 and 467–69. *El Paso Evening
     Post,* December 24 and 25, 1928. Texas State Board of Health, Bureau of Vital
     Statistics, Standard Certificate of Death, El Paso, Texas, Thomas S. Morris filed
     December 26, 1928, *Texas Department of State Health Services. Texas Death Cer-
     tificates, 1903–1982,* iArchives, Orem, Utah.

11   *El Paso Evening Post,* January 24, 25, 1929, February 18, 19, and 21, 1929, and
     October 26, 1929. *El Paso Herald,* January 30, 1929, February 6, 12, 18, 19, 21,
     and 23, 1929, and March 7, 1929. *Miami Daily News-Record,* January 29 and 31,
     1929. *El Paso Herald-Post,* June 26, 1931.

12   *El Paso Herald,* June 1, 1929; and *Waco News Tribune,* June 1 and 2, 1929. Texas
     State Board of Health, Bureau of Vital Statistics, Standard Certificate of Death,
     El Paso, Texas, Benjamin Thomas Hill, filed May 31, 1928, *Texas Department
     of State Health Services. Texas Death Certificates, 1903–1982,* iArchives, Orem,

Utah. *Annual Report of the Commissioner General of Immigration to the Secretary of Labor,* June 30, 1929 (Government Printing Office, 1929), page 26.

13 *El Paso Evening Post,* December 21, 1927. Texas State Board of Health, Bureau of Vital Statistics, Standard Certificate of Death, El Paso, Texas, Senobio Belas, filed December 22, 1927, *Texas Department of State Health Services. Texas Death Certificates, 1903–1982,* iArchives, Orem, Utah. *El Paso Evening Post,* December 30, 1927.

14 *El Paso Evening Post,* December 31, 1927; and *El Paso Herald,* January 5, 1928.

15 *El Paso Herald,* January 30, 1928; and *El Paso Evening Post,* January 30 and 31, 1928. Texas State Board of Health, Bureau of Vital Statistics, Standard Certificate of Death, Reg. Dist. No. 1576, Registered No. 108, El Paso, Texas, Jose Marco Garcia, filed January 31, 1928, *Texas Department of State Health Services. Texas Death Certificates, 1903–1982,* iArchives, Orem, Utah.

16 *El Paso Evening Post,* February 1 and 2, 1928.

17 *El Paso Herald,* March 8, 1928, and April 26 and 27, 1928.

18 *El Paso Evening Post,* July 2, 3, and 7, 1928. For the apprehension of Manuel Vasquez, see *El Paso Herald,* July 30, 1928, August 3, 1928, October 16 and 24, 1928; and *El Paso Evening Post,* July 31, 1928, August 2 and 6, 1928, and October 19 and 25, 1928.

19 *El Paso Herald,* October 4, 5, and 6, 1928; and *El Paso Evening Post,* October 4, 6, and 8, 1928.

20 *El Paso Herald,* February 7, 15, and 28, 1929. *El Paso Evening Post,* January 19, 1929, and February 7 and 23, 1929. For the fight between Nichols and the four smugglers, see *El Paso Evening Post,* February 28, 1929.

21 *El Paso Herald,* July 23, 24, and 25, 1929.

22 *El Paso Evening Post,* February 11 and 24, 1930, and March 4, 6, and 27, 1930.

23 Ibid., May 7, 1930, and June 19, 1930.

24 Ibid., July 8, 9, 10, and 12, 1930, and August 29, 1930.

25 Ibid., December 2 and 3, 1930. See also, *Vernon Daily Record,* December 3, 1930.

26 *Bryan Daily Eagle,* June 25, 1931.

27 Ibid.

Chapter Twelve: Brave Men

1 American Consul William P. Blocker to Secretary of State, January 6, 1934, *File Regarding Exploits and Shooting Affrays, 1920s–1930s, District Director, El Paso,* Subject and Policy Files, 1893–1957, Record Group 85, Records of the Immigration and Naturalization Service, 1787–2004, National Archives Building, Washington, DC. *Official Personnel File, Rollin C. Nichols,* Department of the Treasury, Official Personnel Folders, National Personnel Records Center,

National Archives and Records Administration, St. Louis, Missouri. Nichols's personnel file includes G. B. Slater's report to the Commissioner of Customs, dated November 25, 1933, as well as Nichols's own statement from November 25, 1933. See also, *El Paso Herald-Post,* November 25, 1933; and Caldwell and DeLord, *Texas Lawmen,* page 472. For the arrest of Raul Galvan for the murder of Ivan E. Scotten, see *El Paso Herald-Post,* January 2, 1934, and December 9, 1935.

2   Ibid. See also, *El Paso Herald-Post,* November 27, 1933.

3   *El Paso Herald-Post,* November 29, 1933.

4   Langston, *Impact of Prohibition,* pages 282–83, 289, and 294–96. Blocker to Secsta, January 6, 1934, *File Regarding Exploits and Shooting Affrays, 1920s–1930s.* McCarthy, *The Struggle for Sobriety,* pages 45–49. For the repeal of Arizona's liquor laws, see *State of Arizona Initiative and Referendum Publicity Pamphlet, 1932,* Arizona State Library, Archives and Public Records, Law and Research Library, Phoenix, Arizona. See also, *Salt Lake Tribune,* November 10, 1932; and *Vidette-Messenger,* Valparaiso, Indiana, November 11, 1932. For repeal in New Mexico, see Chuck Smith, *The New Mexico State Constitution* (Oxford University Press, 2011), page 207.

5   Office of Chief Patrol Inspector, El Paso, Texas to Director of Border Patrol, El Paso, June 24, 1932, *File Regarding Exploits and Shooting Affrays, 1920s–1930s, District Director, El Paso,* Subject and Policy Files, 1893–1957, Record Group 85, Records of the Immigration and Naturalization Service, 1787–2004, National Archives Building, Washington, DC. See also, Colonel Charles Askins, *Unrepentant Sinner: The Autobiography of Colonel Charles Askins* (Paladin Press, 1991), page 54.

6   Office of Chief Patrol Inspector, El Paso, Texas to Director of Border Patrol, El Paso, June 24, 1932. See also, *El Paso Times,* June 21, 1932.

7   Ibid. See also, Texas State Board of Health, Bureau of Vital Statistics, Standard Certificate of Death, Gregorio Ortega, filed June 24, 1932, El Paso, Texas, *Texas Department of State Health Services. Texas Death Certificates, 1903–1982,* iArchives, Orem, Utah.

8   Caldwell and DeLord, *Texas Lawmen,* pages 471–72. *Waco News-Tribune,* December 3, 1932; and *Brownsville Herald,* December 5, 1932. See also, Texas State Board of Health, Bureau of Vital Statistics, Standard Certificate of Death, Herff Alexander Carnes, filed December 5, 1932, El Paso, Texas, *Texas Department of State Health Services. Texas Death Certificates, 1903–1982,* iArchives, Orem, Utah.

9   McCarthy, *The Struggle for Sobriety,* pages 42–44. Daniel Okrent, *Last Call: The Rise and Fall of Prohibition* (Scribner, 2011), pages 351–54. *El Paso Herald-Post,* January 9, 14, and 16, 1933, and August 26 and 28, 1933.

10 District Director of Immigration and Naturalization, El Paso District to Commissioner of Immigration and Naturalization, Washington, DC, December 12, 1933, *File Regarding Exploits and Shooting Affrays, 1920s–1930s, District Director, El Paso,* Subject and Policy Files, 1893–1957, Record Group 85, Records of the Immigration and Naturalization Service, 1787–2004, National Archives Building, Washington, DC. *World News,* December 7, 1933. *El Paso Herald-Post,* December 7 and 8, 1933.

11 *World News,* December 7 and 8, 1933; and *El Paso Herald-Post,* December 7 and 8, 1933. See also, Texas State Board of Health, Bureau of Vital Statistics, Standard Certificate of Death, Doyne C. Melton, filed December 8, 1933, El Paso, Texas, *Texas Department of State Health Services. Texas Death Certificates, 1903–1982,* iArchives, Orem, Utah.

12 Statement of the Alien Maria Luisa Hernandez de Salmeron, made in the County Jail, El Paso, Texas, December 13, 1933, *File Regarding Exploits and Shooting Affrays, 1920s–1930s, District Director, El Paso,* Subject and Policy Files, 1893–1957, Record Group 85, Records of the Immigration and Naturalization Service, 1787–2004, National Archives Building, Washington, DC.

13 District Director of Immigration and Naturalization, El Paso District to Commissioner of Immigration and Naturalization, Washington, DC, December 12, 1933, *File Regarding Exploits and Shooting Affrays, 1920s–1930s.* See also, *El Paso Herald-Post,* December 8, 9, and 11, 1933; and *Hope Star,* December 8, 1933. See also, Texas State Board of Health, Bureau of Vital Statistics, Standard Certificate of Death, Heriberto Alaniz, filed December 11, 1933, El Paso, Texas, *Texas Department of State Health Services. Texas Death Certificates, 1903–1982,* iArchives, Orem, Utah.

14 *El Paso Herald-Post,* January 24, 1934, and February 2 and 9, 1934.

15 American Consul William P. Blocker to Secretary of State, January 6, 1934, *File Regarding Exploits and Shooting Affrays, 1920s–1930s, District Director, El Paso,* Subject and Policy Files, 1893–1957, Record Group 85, Records of the Immigration and Naturalization Service, 1787–2004, National Archives Building, Washington, DC. *El Paso Herald-Post,* December 28, 1933, and February 28, 1934. Texas State Board of Health, Bureau of Vital Statistics, Standard Certificate of Death, Bert G. Walthall, filed December 29, 1933, El Paso, Texas, *Texas Department of State Health Services. Texas Death Certificates, 1903–1982,* iArchives, Orem, Utah. See also, Caldwell and DeLord, *Texas Lawmen,* page 451.

16 *El Paso Herald-Post* and *El Paso Times,* December 28, 1933.

17 *El Paso Herald-Post,* December 28, 1933; January 2, 3, 6, 31, 1934; February 9, 12, 14, 24, 27, 28, 1934; March 2, 1934; and June 9, 1954.

18 *El Paso Herald-Post,* May 19, 1934.

19 Ibid.

20   *El Paso Herald-Post,* June 23, 1934, August 17, 22, and 24, 1934.

21   *Waco News-Tribune,* March 28, 1935. *El Paso Herald Post,* March 27 and 29, 1935, and October 16, 1935.

22   *El Paso Herald-Post,* December 7, 9, 16, and 30, 1935; and *Corsicana Daily Sun,* February 11 and 13, 1936. For Galvan's pardon, see *Waco News-Tribune,* May 28 and 30, 1947; and *El Paso Herald-Post,* May 29, 1947, and June 2, 1947.

23   *El Paso Herald-Post,* April 27, 1934; and *Albuquerque Journal,* April 28, 1934.

24   *El Paso Herald-Post,* October 27, 29, and 31, 1934.

25   Courtney Ryley Cooper, *Hot Spot,* originally published in *The American,* June 1935. *El Paso Herald-Post,* May 14, 15, and 22, 1935.

26   McCarthy, *The Struggle for Sobriety,* pages 48–50. *El Paso Herald-Post,* August 28, 1935.

Author's Note

1   *El Paso Times,* April 19, 2015, and August 18, 2015.

INDEX

Starr, Richard R., 177
Startling Detective, 106–7
Stepp, Sam, 59
Stevens, Charles F., 122–23, 125, 145
Stevenson, Coke, 252
Stevenson, Ed, 213
Steward, Carrie, 175
Steward, Harry, 174–75, 178
Stiles, Wesley E., 193
Stott, Roy O., 195
Stout, Joseph, 208
Stowe, John, 225
Stuart, B. F., 252
Studebaker Corporation, xii–xiii
Stull, E. C., 202, 225
Sullivan, George, 33
Sullivan, Henry J., 170
Swink, Henry R., 168
Swope, Rush, 159
Swope, T. J., 159–60

T
T.F. Miller store, xi
Taylor, William A., 39
Teeter, David S., 164–65, 170
Tefft, Miriam, 22, 24–25
Tempe National Bank, 164
Tempe, Arizona, 158, 163, 166, 169, 170, 173
Tenth US Cavalry Regiment, 30–37
Terrazas, Joaquin, 88
Territorial Penitentiary, 176
Testin, Mike, 256
Tewksbury, Edwin, ix
Tewksbury, James, ix

Tewksbury, John, ix
Texas Rangers, 58, 68–69, 122–23, *124*, 204, 246
Texas State Penitentiary, 184
Texas, Prohibition in, xix, xxi, 75
Thirty-Fourth District Court of Texas, 138
Thomas, Joseph F., 143
Thomas, Joseph H., 144–46
Thomason, R. Ewing, 226
Thompson, J. D., *60*
Threepersons, Tom, 204–6, 257
Times (El Paso), 64
Tinklepaugh, Otto L., 17, 33–34
tiswin, 13
Tombstone, Arizona, 1–3
Tombstone Prospector, 8
Tonto Basin, ix
Toole, O. A., 254
Torres, Clarita, 50, 56
Torres, Esteban, 216
Torres, Pedro, 248–49
Torres, Simplicio, 40, 47–48, *49*, 50–57, 261
train robbery, 174–79
Trice, Robert A., 247
Trippel, Alfred A., 106, 110
Tucson Citizen, 100
Tucson Daily Citizen, 90, 92
Tucson, Arizona, 10, 111, 174, 177, 190
Tucson Police Department, 94
Twelfth Aero Squadron, 103
Twenty-First Amendment, 245, 247–48
Twitty, F. O., 47
Twitty, Omar, xi

ABOUT THE AUTHOR

Samuel K. Dolan is a documentary writer, director, and Emmy Award–winning producer. Growing up in northern Arizona, he got his start in film and television at the age of thirteen, riding horses in feature films and TV shows. Since 2004, he has produced dozens of programs for History Channel, Military Channel, National Geographic, and other networks. He lives in Los Angeles with his wife and son.